FÉLIX GUATTARI'S
SCHIZOANALYTIC ECOLOGY

For my daughter, Keyla
and my wife, Nadine

FÉLIX GUATTARI'S SCHIZOANALYTIC ECOLOGY

Hanjo Berressem

EDINBURGH
University Press

Edinburgh University Press is one of the leading university presses in the UK. We publish academic books and journals in our selected subject areas across the humanities and social sciences, combining cutting-edge scholarship with high editorial and production values to produce academic works of lasting importance. For more information visit our website: edinburghuniversitypress.com

© Hanjo Berressem, 2020, 2021

Edinburgh University Press Ltd
The Tun – Holyrood Road, 12(2f) Jackson's Entry, Edinburgh EH8 8PJ

First published in hardback by Edinburgh University Press 2020

Typeset in Warnock
by Biblichor Ltd, Edinburgh

A CIP record for this book is available from the British Library

ISBN 978 1 4744 5075 1 (hardback)
ISBN 978 1 4744 5076 8 (paperback)
ISBN 978 1 4744 5078 2 (webready PDF)
ISBN 978 1 4744 5077 5 (epub)

The right of Hanjo Berressem to be identified as the author of this work has been asserted in accordance with the Copyright, Designs and Patents Act 1988, and the Copyright and Related Rights Regulations 2003 (SI No. 2498).

Contents

Overture	vii
Acknowledgements	ix
Abbreviations	xiii
INTRODUCTION: GUATTARI AND ECOLOGY	1
1. ECOGENESIS	23
2. SCHIZOECOLOGIC CARTOGRAPHIES	51
3. ECOSOPHIC TIMES AND SPACES	125
4. SCHIZOANALYTIC ECOLOGY	183
CONCLUSION: RIGHT HERE, RIGHT NOW	233
Bibliography	239
Index	248

Overture

Letizia Alvarez de Toledo has observed that the vast library is useless. Strictly speaking, *one single volume* should suffice: a single volume of ordinary format, printed in nine or ten type body, and consisting of an infinite number of infinitely thin pages. (At the beginning of the seventeenth century, Cavalieri said that any solid body is the superimposition of an infinite number of planes.) This silky vade mecum would scarcely be handy: each apparent leaf of the book would divide into other analogous leaves. The inconceivable central leaf would have no reverse.

Jorge Luis Borges, *Ficciones* (88)

IN 1984 THE German avant-garde rock band *Die Tödliche Doris* (*The Deadly Doris*) released their fourth album, which was titled, somewhat ironically, *Our Debut*. When the follow-up album, released in 1986, was called *Six*, this didn't make things any easier. In 1987, the band published a note that explained the 'missing' fifth album. *Our Debut* and *Six*, the note read, 'are constructed so that they correspond to one another in music, text and arrangement and comprise a unity if one plays them at the same time from the first piece on, on two record players with their respective A- or B-sides. The parallel pieces are the same length to the minute, from one track to the next, and offer a variety of textual, musical and semantic interactions. By playing both LPs together the invisible fifth LP, an immaterial LP emerges in the mind of the listener' (Tödliche Doris 2019). I have tried to achieve a similar effect with *Félix Guattari's Schizoanalytic Ecology* and *Gilles Deleuze's Luminous Philosophy*. Although each book can be read as an individual text, the two correspond to one another in such a way that when they are read together, an immaterial book emerges in the mind of the reader. Within the overall field of structural and thematic resonances between the two books, I will mark specific conceptual overlaps and cross-references by: square brackets, arrow, Deleuze, page number. Where I discuss co-written texts, I will reference them as Guattari and Deleuze in *Félix Guattari's*

Schizoanalytic Ecology and Deleuze and Guattari in *Gilles Deleuze's Luminous Philosophy*.

While Gary Genosko noted in 2002 that when Deleuze and Guattari is 'reversed as Guattari and Deleuze, it is a political reordering, an act of resistance, a dangerous heterodoxy' (42), in light of the growing interest in Guattari, especially after the ecological turn, this is, fortunately, no longer necessarily the case today. As Franco Berardi notes, 'there is a Deleuze without Guattari, and a Guattari without Deleuze, and then there is the rhizomatic machine put in motion by the encounter between the two' (2008: 43). If I reverse the conventional order of names in *Félix Guattari's Schizoanalytic Ecology*, therefore, I do so purely for reasons of symmetry.

Acknowledgements

SOME WORDS ABOUT influences and references. It is impossible to note all of the influences that have shaped my image of Félix Guattari's thought, although there is not as much scholarship on Guattari as there is on Gilles Deleuze, and some scholars, most prominantly perhaps Slavoj Žižek in *Organs Without Bodies*, still deal with Guattari as nothing but a somewhat detrimental influence on Deleuze. I consider the emergence of my text from within the steadily growing field of Guattari scholarship as a given. While writing, as happens so often, readings that converged with mine have tended to be both consoling and depressing, while diverging readings tended to be both scary and exhilarating. Which of these were more productive, and which to reference?

That said, there are a number of indispensible, landmark texts on Guattari, such as the work of Gary Genosko, Janell Watson and Franco Berardi. Genosko dedicates chapter 5 of his *Aberrant Introduction* to the diagrammaticism of *Schizoanalytic Cartographies*, part of chapter 3 of his *Critical Introduction* to Guattari's ecosophy, and he has written extensively on Guattari and architecture. Watson's *Guattari's Diagrammatic Thought: Writing Between Lacan and Deleuze* provides many important insights into *Schizoanalytic Cartographies*, and she relates Guattari to ecology in her article 'Culture as Existential Territory: Ecosophic Homelands for the Twenty-first Century'. As do John Tinnell in 'Transversalising the Ecological Turn: Four Components of Felix Guattari's Ecosophical Perspective' and Verena Andermatt Conley in her *Ecopolitics: The Environment in Poststructuralist Thought* and in her contribution to the collection *Deleuze/Guattari & Ecology* which is, like *An [Un]Likely Alliance: Thinking Environment[s] with Deleuze|Guattari*, edited by Bernd Herzogenrath. Michael Goddard's work focuses on Guattari's post-mediatic ecosophy. Anne Querrien, who worked with Guattari, provides, among many other things, a very helpful, telegrammatic profile of *Schizoanalytic Cartographies* in her contribution to *The Guattari Effect*, a collection edited by Eric Alliez and Andrew Goffey that brings together, like the volumes edited by Herzogenrath, many important Guattarians. There is the work of Anne Sauvagnargue, of Simon O'Sullivan, and of Paul Elliott. O'Sullivan's *On the Production of Subjectivity: Five Diagrams of the Finite–Infinite Relation* was an especially important resource and inspiration for my project. There is also the work done in Deleuze Studies, which often implies work on Guattari. Finally, although he does not really reference Guattari, there is the indispensible Manuel DeLanda. In fact, in some more confident moments I imagined my project as a perhaps more philosophy- than science-driven version of a DeLanda text.

While much of the following text was written with actual music playing in the background, such as Conor Oberst, The National, Mazzy Star and Sigur Ros, the work of the community of scholars writing on Guattari has formed the virtual, conceptual music that played in the background while I wrote. In fact, the real music did more than play in the background. Coming from within the computer, the music seemed to literally pervade the text, as if the writing itself were musicalized. With the conceptual background music, it felt very similar, which is to say that the work of all of these scholars is everywhere present in my text and has shaped it, sometimes by way of an elaborate conceptualization, an insight, at other times by way of a seemingly throw-away sentence or a reference to a specific passage in Guattari. Had I engaged in detailed discussions of all of these influences, my text would have become even more ponderous than it already is. I have noted it, therefore, only in the case of a useful, productive link, mostly in reference to work that deals with *Schizoanalytic Cartographies* or with the developing fields of a general Guattarian ecosophy and of a more specific post-mediatic ecosophy. In terms of today's more general ecology of ecologies, I have also noted, if only in passing, points of resonance but also of dissent with more deconstructive and object-oriented versions of ecology.

Concerning the sciences that I will deal with, there were early introductions to what was then called chaos theory, such as James Gleick's *Chaos: Making a New Science*, accounts by scientists that were geared towards a popular audience such as Edward N. Lorenz's *The Essence of Chaos*, Humberto Maturana and Francisco Varela's *The Tree of Knowledge*, Stuart Kauffman's *The Origins of Order: Self-Organization and Selection in Evolution* and *Investigations*, as well as the work of Lynn Margulis, Isabelle Stengers and James Lovelock, all of whose work I enjoyed to an equal degree because of their clarity of thought and their clarity of expression. As a caveat, however, I should note that I am neither a scientist nor a historian of science. Having come to the hard sciences through literary studies, I cannot fully judge the scientific viability and impact of the theories I deal with. On this level, my text cannot be critical. Also, everything I am going to say about the single sciences has been said in these sciences in more detail and in more depth.

Although it might sometimes seem to, the following text does not claim that Guattari's work can explain the world and the ways in which it functions. More humbly, it aims to show that Guattari's work forms a coherent figure of thought that might help in the overall project to make this world more ecological. Against that backdrop, I take the conceptual spine of that work, which is operative in it at all times and on all levels, to be what I call Guattari's schizoanalytic ecology. To delineate different aspects of that ecology, I will use the following terms: When highlighting its parallels to schizoanalysis, I will abbreviate schizoanalytic ecology to schizoecology. When highlighting its parallels to philosophy, I will use Guattari's term ecosophy. I will also use ecosophy in reference to the values promoted by the deep ecologist Arne Naess, from whom Guattari took the term in the first place. In relation to the larger ecological field, I will talk of Guattari's ecology or a Guattarian ecology.

Schizoanalytic Cartographies is a truly daunting text, and I am still not sure whether I could say with confidence that I feel that I have understood it fully. In particular, at certain points, it is still not totally clear to me why Guattari would talk of continuity when I would expect him to talk of discontinuity. I hope, however, that I have understood enough to make a convincing argument for its central position within Guattari's oeuvre, and to entice others to seriously engage with it, both as an important text by Guattari, as well as a crucial text for further debates about Guattari's ecosophy.

Apart from the ecology of scholarly influences that have shaped this text, there is an ecology of people who have helped it along, and who are directly present in it in various ways. Constantin Boundas was seminal in publishing my first article on Guattari in *Schizoanalysis and Ecosophy: Reading Deleuze and Guattari*, the first collection that is almost entirely devoted to aspects of Guattari's ecosophy. Jonas Neldner and Marlene Mück have helped formating the text, Jasmin Herrmann has provided valuable feedback. Wolfram Nitsch helped with some of the French translations. The two anonymous readers provided extremely helpful input and ideas, while my copy editor Tim Clark was not only a joy to work with but also caught many potentially embarrassing mistakes.

The publishing history of the two books started a long time ago in a far-away country. It was in a courtyard of Istanbul University that I first told Carol Macdonald, who has become a good friend between then and now, about the project. Her encouragement, advice and continuing support of the project, as well as her good spirit, have carried me through the writing of the text. Carol and the extended team at Edinburgh University Press, in particular James Dale, Naomi Farmer and Rebecca Mackenzie, have made the process of publishing it a truly joyful one. Joyful for me, I should add, if not for the three people who have in many ways suffered through the writing of the two books. My children Keyla and Dahlia have, too often, encountered a Dad who was lost in thought and sadly incommunicado. Sorry, kiddos! Then there is my wife, Nadine, who has not only provided countless ideas and inspirations for the project, and who has helped with many questions I had, but who has also, with infinite grace and patience, invited Guattari to live with us in our home for far too long. If each of the books is dedicated to one of my kids, the whole project is dedicated to her. It is her presence that suffuses the project, as well as my life, like the warm rays of golden-hour sunlight.

Abbreviations

Abbreviations used throughout the text correspond with the key below.

Works by Félix Guattari
- B: *Molecular Revolution in Brazil*
- C: *Chaosmosis*
- MR: *Molecular Revolution*
- MU: *The Machinic Unconscious*
- SC: *Schizoanalytic Cartographies*
- SS: *Soft Subversions*
- TE: *The Three Ecologies*

Works by Félix Guattari and Gilles Deleuze
- AO: *Anti-Oedipus*
- TP: *A Thousand Plateaus*
- WP: *What is Philosophy?*

Works by Michel Serres
- BP: *The Birth of Physics*
- G: *Genesis*

All translations from German and French sources are mine.

INTRODUCTION: GUATTARI AND ECOLOGY

> A graph, ... quadrilateral, depicting a new definition of the Unconscious by transforming four basic entities: the Flows, the Machinic Phylum, the Existential Territories, the Intangible Universe.
> Félix Guattari, *Soft Subversions* (187)

> We thus decided not to consider situations other than through the angle of crossroads of assemblages (*carrefours d'agencements*), which secrete, up to a certain point, their own coordinates of metamodelization.
> Félix Guattari, *Soft Subversions* (215)

> Subjectivity is manufactured just as energy, electricity, and aluminium are.
> Félix Guattari and Suely Rolnik, *Molecular Revolution in Brazil* (47)

> We have the unconscious we deserve!
> Félix Guattari, *The Machinic Unconscious* (9)

On the Origins of Guattari's Ecosophy

THE LIFE AND the work of Pierre-Félix Guattari – who was born on 30 April 1930 in Colombes and died on 29 August 1992 in his room at La Borde, the experimental psychiatric clinic near Cour-Cheverny in the Loire Valley that formed his life's professional and institutional spine from 1955 to his death – might be said to fall into three interrelated phases. The early Guattari is predominantly a psychoanalyst, although he never separated psychoanalysis from political theory and political practice. In his first collaborations with Gilles Deleuze, whom he met at the University of Vincennes in 1969, these psychopolitics are Guattari's main contribution. While the question of psychoanalysis pertains in particular to *Anti-Oedipus* (1972), Guattari's presence in *Kafka: Toward a Minor Literature* (1975) concerns predominantly politics and political theory. The latter also define his early collections *Molecular Revolutions* (1977) and *The Machinic Unconscious* (1979), and find their most sustained expression in *A Thousand Plateaus* (1980), his third collaboration with Deleuze.

Guattari's middle years, which span roughly the period from the early to the late 1980s, are dedicated to practising psychoanalysis at La Borde, to cultural criticism, and to political activism. Often refered to as the winter years that followed the interminable spring of the 1960s – *Les Années d'hiver: 1980–1985* is the title of a collection of magazine and newspaper articles, interviews and conference papers published in 1986 – these years were overshadowed by Guattari's struggle with the depression that Franco Berardi chronicles in the chapter 'La depressione Félix' of *Félix Guattari: Thought, Friendship, and Visionary Cartography* (2008), and that Gary Genosko writes about in 'Happy Depression: Franco Berardi and the Unpaid Bills of Desire' (2015). It was as if the cultural and political milieu, as much as his personal circumstances, had quite literally brought Guattari down. To get a feel of these moments of darkness, which started well before the 1980s, one only needs to read some of the entries from Guattari's journal that were published in *The Anti-Oedipus Papers*. The entry for 6 October 1972 is particularly bleak: 'I'm strapped to this journal. Grunt. Heave. Impression that the ship is going down. "The furniture" slides, the table legs wobble . . . Writing so that I won't die. Or so that I die otherwise. Sentences breaking up. Panting like for what. Fanny won't type this anymore. Marie-Josée. Happy, cheery. Another connection. Arlette is in Germany. Anxiety. Her libidinal space being organized elsewhere. Rip. Writing. Pitch-black night. Blue black ink. M. Cantoni pen merchant. Blue blood' (2006: 399). However, while much has been made of that depression, the winter years are also the time of the conceptualization and the composition of *Schizoanalytic Cartographies*, which was published in 1989 but is already an explicit reference in Guattari's seminar held on 9 December 1980 and published in *Soft Subversions* as 'The Schizoanalyses'. At that point, Guattari describes it as a 'crossroads of assemblages (*carrefours d'agencements*) which secrete, up to a certain point, their own coordinates of metamodelization' (215). In this light, *les années d'hiver* might also be read, more positively, perhaps, as *les années divers*. The diverse years, or the years of diversity. Below the both political and personal cold spells of that period runs the creation of Guattari's conceptual monument to diversity: of what I consider to be his *magnum opus*.

The late Guattari of *The Three Ecologies* (1989) and *Chaosmosis* (1992) is an ecologist, although *What is Philosophy?* (1991), his final collaboration with Deleuze, shows that this ecology is eminently and deeply philosophical. Throughout these phases, of which the first two are treated exhaustively and with great acumen by Janell Watson,

Guattari was a political activist who wrote prolifically on literature, painting, film and architecture.

Of the many Guattaris – the psychoanalyst, the philosopher, the scholar of the arts, the cultural critic and the activist – I believe that the most lasting one will be the ecologist. This is not to say that the other Guattaris are in any way less important, but rather that, although they operate in different conceptual theatres and even though the explicitly ecological enters Guattari's work only towards the end of his career, they are in actual fact different versions of the ecologist. If in retrospect, the political struggles of the 1960s will always already have been ecological – not only because the ecological played an important part in these struggles but even more so because they were, implicitly, struggles about an overall political ecology – something similar can be said about the ecological in Guattari's work. Although it is only from *The Three Ecologies* onward that the ecological comes to provide the explicit frame of his thought, in retrospect, all of his thought can be said to always already have been implicitly ecological. It is somewhat as if the ecological had waited in the conceptual wings to finally meet up with Guattari face to face in 1989 with the publication of *The Three Ecologies*. That year is also the year of the publication of *Schizoanalytic Cartographies*. In one year, a short book on ecological practice and a long one on theory: *explicit ecosophy; implicit ecosophy*.

This book proceeds somewhat similarly. Not only does it maintain that Guattari's pre-ecological work, in particular *Schizoanalytic Cartographies*, is implicitly ecological, it also argues that the latter is crucial in laying out the conceptual plane on which the explicitly ecological work will be situated. This is why Guattari's explicitly ecological texts *The Three Ecologies* and *Chaosmosis* will only meet up face to face with this book towards the end. Although this might be taken as a kind of retrospective reasoning – in the sense that after deconstruction, everything will have been logocentric in the same way that after psychoanalysis everything will have been oedipal – there is, I think, a case to be made for the claim that Guattari's overall oeuvre is best understood as ecological, which I define, very generally, as the attempt to be adequate to the world and to develop not only adequate images and figures of the world, but also adequate figures of thought from within which to conceptualize this world and this adequation; a project that might be considered as a conceptually updated and ecologized version of Thomas Aquinas's notion of an *adaequatio rei et intellectus*.

If I first turn to Guattari and Deleuze's reading of Lucretius' *De Rerum Natura* in *A Thousand Plateaus*, it is because Lucretius' muse, Venus Anadyomene, is one of these adequate figures of the world: *The Birth of Venus* considered as *The Birth of Ecology*. After this introductory chapter, the second chapter provides a detailed unfolding of the diagram, which I will also refer to as the fourfold, that Guattari develops in *Schizoanalytic Cartographies*. Still from within that frame, the third chapter contours Guattari's conceptualizations of ecosophic time and space. It is only after these preparations that I address Guattari's explicitly ecological texts. The fact that his two ecological books had little impact on the overall ecological field might be indicative of the fact that such a preparation is indeed necessary to fully understand and appreciate them. If they were not taken up by the discourse of and on ecology, this can be attributed to a large degree to the difficulties of reading them on their own, which means without the conceptual grounding provided by *Schizoanalytic Cartographies*. This is especially unfortunate in that until today, much of the ecological field still operates according to pre-Guattarian registers.

The general aim of this book is to open up Guattari's work to that field, and to show its potential to enrich today's ecologies. As Deleuze notes in 'For Félix', 'Félix's work is waiting to be discovered and rediscovered. That is one of the best ways to keep Félix alive' (2007: 382). Guattari's books, which cover 'three domains' – the 'psychiatric domain' (382), the 'wonderful four-headed system in his *Cartographies*' (382), and his 'artistic analyses' (383) – hold 'inexhaustible riches' (382), Deleuze writes. While I was writing this book, I felt, again and again, that these domains are, invariably, superposed. They form the overall ecology of thought from within which what I call Guattari's schizoanalytic ecology emerges.

In *The Three Ecologies*, Guattari uses Arne Naess's term 'ecosophy' (28) to designate his concept of a 'generalized ecology' (52) that aims to combine the fields of 'social ecology, mental ecology and environmental ecology' (41). A related term, 'chaosophy', serves as the title of a collection of Guattari's texts and interviews from 1972 to 1977. It is perhaps because Guattari modulates a number of the conceptual and practical coordinates of Naess's deep ecology that he does not explicitly reference him. Or, perhaps, he omits the reference because that is how he considers thought to operate in the overall ecology of discourses. As he notes in *Soft Subversions*, 'I claim the term falsifier for myself, being an idea thief and shuffler of second hand concepts' (23).

While this remark might easily be discarded as an instance of mild self-deprecation, it contains a crucial ecological lesson. Perhaps rather than considering such terminological takeovers as cases of borrowing, stealing or hijacking, it would be more adequate to think of them as cases of a mutual enrichment, in the sense that a chemical solution is enriched when something is added to it. In *Chaosmosis*, Guattari uses a similar vocabulary when he compares an enrichment of the world to the notion of 'enriched uranium' (90), or when he talks of 'virtual entities infinitely rich in possibles, infinitely enrichable through creative processes' (112). The perhaps most pervasive and consequential of such conceptual enrichments for Guattari was provided by Deleuze, with whom he shared a life-long, both personal and professional elective affinity. At the same time, Guattari enriched Deleuze's thought. When Deleuze remembers, in the short text 'Letter to Uno: How Félix and I Worked Together', that 'the best moments' (2007: 239) of *A Thousand Plateaus* were written while he was thinking 'under Félix's spell' (240), Guattari would, without a doubt, have felt the same about Deleuze, although there were also differences. Deleuze mentions Guattari's speed, as opposed to his own slowness. 'He never *ceases.* He has extraordinary speeds. I am more like a hill' (237), he notes, and when he mentions that Guattari's 'ideas are drawings, or even diagrams', he adds that 'concepts are what interests me' (238). One aim of my text is to carefully compare and contrast Guattari with and Guattari without Deleuze, to chart some of the similarities and differences of Guattari's diagrams and Deleuze's concepts, and to show that Guattari has his own conceptual slowness.

Deleuze's friendship, which shines through every one of his texts on Guattari, is mirrored in the deep gratitude that pervades Guattari's reminiscences of their both kairotic and catalytic meeting in 'Everywhere at Once' (SS: 81–7). Here was someone whose thought resonated deeply with Guattari's, and who proposed that they work together. 'Then there was the miracle, my meeting Deleuze, which opened the way to a whole series of things. How did it happen? I told him my ideas about group subjectivity, about transversality, etc. I was very pleased. He was very encouraging. And then he said, "Why don't you write all of this down?" To tell the truth, writing always makes me a little uncomfortable; talking with people, discussing things, that's okay, but writing . . . Then he said, "We can do it together"' (SS: 83–4) [→ **Deleuze 88**].

When Edward P. Butler (2008) makes a compelling case for an elective affinity between Naess's ecosophy and Deleuzian philosophy, although the more obvious choice would be to posit such an elective affinity between Naess and the work of Guattari, he can do this because, although they came from different fields, there is a similarly ecological strain in Deleuze's and Guattari's thought. Perhaps this ecological baseline is the deepest level of resonance between their works; the ground that allowed them to work together so seamlessly. Also, both Deleuze's philosophy and Naess's ecosophy have such a high degree of conceptual and ethical valence that they can easily come to suffuse other conceptual assemblages. In Naess's and Deleuze's recourse to the notion of the intrinsic value – a somewhat unfortunate translation of the initially mathematical term eigenvalue (*Eigenwert*) that denotes the value a being has in and of itself as opposed to the value it has for somebody else (*Fremdwert*) – of all living beings, 'the Deleuzian ethic of individuation and the deep ecology ethic of intrinsic value are functionally indistinguishable' (2008: 145), Butler writes, arguing further that 'the ecosophical concept of intrinsic value derives its ethical force from affirming an individuative striving in natural beings that is *at once* and *as such* the striving to recognize others, to constitute a plane of immanence whose intensive complexity expresses the maximal multiplicity of values' (149). To this, I wholeheartedly agree, although I would, for reasons that will become clear later on, either change the term plane of immanence to plane of consistency, or, if I were to retain the former, omit the last two words. Also, I would underscore Butler's belief that for both Guattari and Deleuze, in 'the absolute positivity of nature there is a plenitude, as well as an anonymity, of "natures"' (150).

If Naess enriches Guattari's thought, Guattari's takeover can in turn come to enrich Naess's concept of ecosophy because, despite the differences between the two ecosophies, Guattari's horizontal, or, more precisely, fractal ecology – in light of this fractalism, which I will deal with in detail in 'Ecosophic Spaces' (pp. 152–82), it is as inaccurate to call Guattari's ecology a flat ecology as it is to call his ontology a flat ontology – shares the love of the non-human world that suffuses Naess's deep ecology, as well as the overall objective to not only conceptualize but also to live according to a both non-metric and metric adequation between the world and its creatures, from sponges to humans and from coral reefs to megacities.

If both of these milieus have become increasingly toxic today, that has different reasons and it concerns equally different modes of toxicity. Still, the whiteout of coral reefs is perhaps adequate to the sterile high-rise architectures of Dubai's tourist resorts, and, as Guattari states in *The Three Ecologies*, in 'taking over entire districts of New York and Atlantic City', Donald Trump is adequate to a 'species of algae', while the evicted renters are adequate to 'the dead fish of environmental ecology' (43). According to a similar adequation, this time between a natural and a media ecology, while 'monstrous and mutant algae invade the lagoon of Venice, . . . our television screens are populated, saturated, by "degenerate" images and statements' (43). Although today many milieus are stressed more than ever, and in many places to their very limits, the overall planetary milieu has not quite stopped maintaining itself.

Apart from Naess's ecosophy, a number of other ecologies that defined the 1970s and '80s had enriched Guattari's thought, such as those that developed from the Gaia hypothesis developed by James E. Lovelock in 'The Quest for Gaia' from 1975. Despite the connotation of a nurturing, caring planet evoked by the reference to the Greek Earth goddess Gaia – a name suggested to Lovelock, perhaps unfortunately so, by his friend William Golding – the hypothesis develops an extremely sober and clearheaded argument about climate change in a world considered as an organism of which man is 'the equivalent of a central nervous system' (Lovelock 1975: 306). While John Tinnell and Gary Genosko rightfully highlight the differences between Naess and Guattari, I would perhaps not go as far as Genosko, who notes that 'instead' of Naess's deep ecology, 'Guattari used as a foil the Gaia hypothesis advanced by Lynn Margulis and Lovelock – their conception of the biota as the sum of living things on Earth' (2009: 19); not as far not because I think Genosko is wrong to point to Margulis and Lovelock, but because Guattari tends to take up many different influences at the same time. Not either-or, but and. In both *The Three Ecologies* (40) and *Chaosmosis* (132), for instance, Guattari also mentions Ilya Prigogine and Isabelle Stengers, whose notion of dissipative systems was another inspiration. Also, he was following and integrating into his thought the implicitly ecological work of biologists Humberto Maturana and Francisco Varela. Still another influence, with which I will deal in detail in my first chapter, was the early ecology of Lucretius' *De Rerum Natura*, which had come to Guattari by way of Deleuze's early work, as well as by way of the work of Michel Serres; two sources from which Lucretius' ecology was to find its way into *A Thousand Plateaus*.

A basic tenet of the conceptual milieus Guattari's schizoanalytic ecology draws on is that not only adjacent milieus but all milieus are related. In fact, even before Ernst Haeckel coined the term ecology – a compound of household (*oikos*) and account (*logos*) – in his 1866 *Generelle Morphologie der Organismen* (*General Morphology of Organisms*) to designate the study of 'the household of nature [*Naturhaushalt*]' (188), the 'economy of all nature' (286, quoted in Stauffer 1957: 141; Cooper 2003: 4), or, as Charles Darwin called it, nature's polity (as in: organized society), ecological thought *avant la lettre* had invariably been aware of the deeply networked nature of the system of the planet.

Haeckel, who, following Darwin, envisioned ecology as 'the whole science of the relations of the organism to the environment including, the broad sense, all the "conditions of existence"' (286, quoted in Stauffer 1957: 140; Cooper 2003: 5), differentiates quite sharply between organic and inorganic nature. While both are 'of the greatest significance for the form of organisms', the former, which encompasses 'the entire relations of the organism to all other organisms with which it comes into contact, and of which most contribute either to its advantage or its harm', exert 'a much more profound transforming action on organisms than do the inorganic', which consist of 'the physical and chemical properties of its habitat, the climate (light, warmth, atmospheric conditions of humidity and electricity), the inorganic nutrients, nature of the water and of the soil, etc.' (286).

In Gregory Bateson's ecology – which is yet another ecological influence on Guattari that Verena Andermatt Conley traces in 'Artists or "Little Soldiers?" Félix Guattari's Ecological Paradigms' (2009) – this separation into the organic and the inorganic is already less pronounced, and the interactions between organism and milieu, and thus of culture and nature, become less categorical and increasingly dense. As Bateson notes about a polluted Lake Erie and the people living around it, 'you decide that you want to get rid of the by-products of human life and that Lake Erie will be a good place to put them. You forget that the eco-mental system called Lake Erie is a part of your wider eco-mental system – and that if Lake Erie is driven insane, its insanity is incorporated in the larger system of your thought and experience' (1991: 7.2). Already in 1911, John Muir had programmatically stated that 'when we try to pick out anything by itself, we find it hitched to everything else in the Universe' (110).

Guattari's late work is in intimate conversation with all of the the above-mentioned ecologies, as well as with many others. Invariably, however, it does more than simply integrate or adopt them. Rather, it transmutes them into elements of the larger project that he calls ecosophy and that I will designate, among others, as fractal ecology, synaptic ecology, process ecology or expressionist ecology. It is the term schizoanalytic ecology, however, especially in the way it echoes *Schizoanalytic Cartographies*, that I feel comes closest to the conceptual core of the project of a Guattarian ecology.

Schizoanalytic Cartographies: Ecology without 'Ecology'

Although *Schizoanalytic Cartographies* is not explicitly ecological, in *Guattari's Diagrammatic Thought: Writing Between Lacan and Deleuze* Janell Watson proposes to think of it, together with *The Three Ecologies* and *Chaosmosis*, as part of a 'triptych' (2011: 102). This felicitous image I would only specify further by proposing that *Schizoanalytic Cartographies* should be considered as the triptych's central panel, in that it provides the 'conceptual framework' (102) that pervades the two slimmer volumes [→ **Deleuze 78**]. In *The Three Ecologies*, its presence is noticeable but faint. Although that text's conceptual frames are predominantly political, with references to 'military-industrial complexes' (TE: 29) and to Guattari's concept of an 'Integrated World Capitalism' (31), it also brings into play central concepts from *Schizoanalytic Cartographies*, such as 'incorporeal Universes of reference' (38), 'existential Territories' (40), 'existential refrains' (50), 'expressive a-signifying rupture[s]' (45), '*heterogenesis*' (51) and 'meta-modelization' (57). As Guattari does not provide the larger conceptual contexts of these references, however, many of them remain opaque, if not downright enigmatic. The same holds for *Chaosmosis*, which centres more on subjectivity and 'psychological metamodelisation' (C: 11) than on the directly political and ecological. With *Schizoanalytic Cartographies* having been published at that point, however, Guattari can add to *Chaosmosis* explicit references to the book's central diagram. (I should note that although calling this diagram a fourfold casts a long Heideggerian shadow over it, I would maintain that despite Heidegger's early ecology, which is centred around his concept of the care for the world, conceptually, the two fourfolds – Heidegger's fourfold relates earth, sky, mortals and divinities – are worlds apart.)

Schizoanalytic Cartographies is perhaps the most crucial and at the same time the least critically rehearsed of Guattari's texts, although Genosko, O'Sullivan, Elliott and Watson provide immensely useful introductions and explications. One reason for this academic neglect is that it is easily his least accessible and his most demanding text. It is a relentlessly abstract solitaire that provides the most detailed account of the form of Guattari's thought. Although it echoes the structure of *The Machinic Unconscious* in that it also groups a number of short pieces around a central text, it has, more than *The Machinic Unconscious*, the feel of a monograph. As all of Guattari's earlier books are collections of articles, it might in fact be considered as Guattari's first book-length study. It is also his true conceptual legacy.

Schizoanalytic Cartographies provides a conceptual map of a world that is, paradoxically, both indifferent – in both senses of not caring and, more importantly, of being without difference – and at the same time infinitely differentiated. A detailed reading of *Schizoanalytic Cartographies* considered as an ecological text is central to my project because, although it mentions the word ecology only three times and each time merely in passing, its diagrammaticism develops the conceptual ontology, the epistemology as well as the topology from within which it is possible to adequately think that eminently ecological paradox. The book, which Raymond Bellour considers the most important of Guattari's 'grand conceptual reveries' (2011: 220), provides an extremely elaborate and highly abstract diagram of this paradoxical world. In the midst of a plethora of urgent ecological problems, and programmatically with only a very small number of references to the increasingly unsettling and depressing state of the world in its introduction, Guattari, who had always been deeply involved in the current political and cultural debates around him, and who had never stopped intervening directly in the political arena, develops a conceptual diagram that allows us to read both sponges and humans as expressions of the world, and thus as agents in and of that world's moment-to-moment creation: *living as inevitably ecological, whether that ecology is good or bad.*

Flanked by the side-panel projects of the relatively accessible and interventionist *The Three Ecologies* and the more theory-driven *Chaosmosis*, both of which develop their arguments from within ample political and cultural contexts and examples, *Schizoanalytic Cartographies* does not direct the reader to the urgencies of our world's deeply endangered natural and cultural milieus. (Chapter 7 of *Chaosmosis*, which is written from under the shadow of *Schizoanalytic Cartographies*, deals with some of the latter's political and cultural implications and ramifications.) If we generally tend to think of ecology as a form of doing science that immediately and programmatically addresses environmental problems, and that leads to practices of life vis-à-vis those problems, its rigorous diagrammaticism and meta-modelization asks us to abstract from these urgencies in order to think about how to adequately face and administer them. In the ecological race to save the planet by means of political activism, *Schizoanalytic Cartographies* asks us, for a moment, or, more specifically, for 173 pages of intensely formalized argumentation, to stop and hold our breath.

Constructing Ecology

For many newcomers to Guattari's work, the sustained formalism of *Schizoanalytic Cartographies* will come as a surprise because, as I have noted, Guattari is often considered to be, especially in comparison to Deleuze, a very restless, and by some scholars even a dangerously haphazard thinker. In his journal, Guattari often says so himself. Still 6 October 1972: 'When it works I have a ton to spare.... I lose it as fast as it comes, and I get more. Active forgetting! What matters is interceding when it doesn't work, when it spins off course, and the sentences are fucked up, and the words disintegrate, and the spelling is total mayhem.... And I have to make a *text* out of that mess and it has to hold up: that is my fundamental schizo-analytic project. Reconstruct myself in the artifice of the text' (2006: 401).

One of my aims is to show that under Guattari's insecurities, under his often überabstract, seemingly eclectic writing, below his staccato style, his sometimes hectic and seemingly hysterical speeds and his conceptual acrobatics, lies a very calm, legato consistency. A deep conceptual rigour that is tied to an insistent question and demand. In *Schizoanalytic Cartographies*, Guattari might in fact be said to achieve something like the 'sovereign distance' (SS: 166) he himself attributes to Deleuze's style. Once again 6 October 1972: 'I don't even take the trouble of expressing myself so that when I reread myself I can understand whatever it was I was trying to say. Gilles will figure it out, he'll work it through ...' (2006: 401). Despite all these self-doubts, in *Schizoanalytic Cartographies* extremely precise arguments assemble heterogeneous elements into carefully constructed conceptual machines. In the supercharged terminologies and references that Guattari uses to assemble his planes of consistency and composition, something emerges that reverberates through all of his texts. That something is a deeply ecological concern: *a conceptual urgency.*

A closer look at Guattari's schizoecology reveals that this concern forms the extraordinarily rigorous and consistent conceptual spine of Guattari's oeuvre. From the implicit ecology of his work at the La Borde clinic to the explicit ecosophy of the later work, Guattari invents figures of thought that allow us to think the relation between the world and its creatures in a way that is adequate both to the complexity of each of these notions as well as to the complexity of their interplay. Invariably, the question is how to adequately express and, in doing so, to adequately intervene in the world, or, perhaps even more fittingly and paradoxically, to adequately create and construct it.

Indeed, the perhaps most fundamental tenet of Guattari's schizoecology, which is a tenet that he never puts into question or abandons, is the notion of constructivism. This notion resonates in many ways with his concept of the general machinism of the world and in particular with his concept of an inherently constructive, or machinic, desire. As Guattari and Deleuze note in *A Thousand Plateaus*, 'there is no desire but assembling, assembled desire' (399). In ecological terms: from the potentialities provided by a deeply indifferent world, its both differentiated and differentiating creatures are called to construct viable, sustainable modes of living. In Guattari and Deleuze's terminology, the difference between the world as indifferent and as both differentiated and differentiating is that between two paradoxically both identical and differentiated planes. 'The field of immanence *or* plane of consistency must be constructed' (157, emphasis added), Guattari and Deleuze note in *A Thousand Plateaus*. While the indifference of the two planes – also considered as the plane of diversity and of difference respectively – is captured in their use of the word *or*, in *What is Philosophy?*, Guattari and Deleuze note that this constructivism is at the same time what differentiates the two planes. At that late moment, they stress quite programmatically that 'philosophy is constructivism, and constructivism has two qualitatively different complementary aspects: the creation of concepts and the laying out of a plane' (36). In a similar vein, when Guattari talks about the pragmatic operations of his meta-modelling in *Schizoanalytic Cartographies*, he notes that the problem lies in 'trying to construct ordinary consistencies and temporalities from infinitely slow speeds of separability and infinitely rapid speeds of continuity' (129). In *The Three Ecologies*, 'the agenda is a "futurist" and "constructivist" opening up of the fields of virtuality' (38). (To capture its various shades of meaning and connotation, I will differentiate between the plane of consistency and the plane of consistencies. While the former pertains to that plane's abstract aspect, the latter pertains to its concrete aspect [→ **Deleuze 2**].)

What keeps this constructivism from turning into a utopia of unlimited agency and cybernetic control is that it operates – like history, chemistry and everything else – within the given contingency of a field in which chance is itself constructive as the ultimate agent of the production of unqualified and ceaseless change. As Guattari and Deleuze note in *What is Philosophy?*, echoing Stéphane Mallarmé, 'a throw of the dice: constructivism' (75). This constructivism, which extends from the smallest actual building blocks of the system of the world to the most minute virtual modulations of the system of thought, forms the ungrounded ground of Guattari's schizoecology.

Although the history of the natural sciences is everywhere pervaded by constructivisms, Guattari's schizoecology relies in particular on a notion of constructivism that developed midway through the twentieth century from within an interdisciplinary conversation whose platforms were a number of conferences, in particular the Macy Conferences that took place between 1946 and 1953 in New York. Part of the core group of attendants were Heinz von Foerster, a leading figure in second-order cybernetics, and Gregory Bateson, a leading figure in the fields of anthropology and ecology. A further conference held in San Francisco on the theme of the construction of reality was convened in 1978 by von Foerster and Chilean biologist Francisco Varela, who in turn functions as a link to the Lindisfarne Conferences that began in 1972 and the Mind and Life conferences that have run from 1978 until today, bringing together, amongst other unlikely constellations, scientists and the Dalai Lama.

It is one of the strengths of Guattari's thought that he never separates the logic of science from its practice. While this is particularly important in his critique of psychoanalysis, it also pertains to scientific theories, which not only trace processes of actual and virtual constructivism, but are themselves their result. In this context, the various conferences that helped to bring about the notion of constructivism might themselves be considered as part of the process of the coming-into-being and subsequent consolidation of a specific theory in that they contributed directly and practically to the construction of that theory's conceptual spine. In fact, any scientific theory – what von Foerster calls an eigentheory as a theory whose internal structure does not stop maintaining itself and that thus achieves a certain measure of consistency – might be said to assemble itself from within an initially vague, shifting self-survey of heterogeneous elements. Suddenly, in an indeterminate place and at an indeterminate time, singular conceptual elements orient themselves along a communally created vector or axis. As if a conceptual field were slowly magnetized, its elements begin to accrue around a both conceptual and infrastructural spine.

The first conceptual premise of the constructivism that I have contoured above seems to be anything but ecological. Living beings, it maintains, are operationally and informationally closed off from the world around them. In other words, their internal reality is constructed from within cybernetic and cognitive processes that take place in complex but closed networks, such as the nervous or the neuronal ones. At the same time, the second, equally important premise of that constructivism, which cuts across the first one, is eminently ecological. Although all living beings are operationally and informationally closed, they are energetically open to and immersed in the milieu within which their life unfolds. They are immanent to and in constant energetic exchange with the world in which they live and which they bring about.

This immersion concerns what Maturana and Varela call structural couplings between the living being and the milieu, from metabolic processes to modalities of movement and barometric pressure; in short: all the ways in which the being is a part of and attuned to the milieu as a field of indifferent intensities rather than as a field of differences. A basic ecological premise is that these structural couplings go both ways. The living being is structurally coupled to the milieu and vice versa. In fact, on this level, there are no clear-cut boundaries between being and milieu. In the terminology of *Anti-Oedipus*, on this level of what I will later call quantities rather than qualities, everything is a question of ceaseless production.

To be energetically open to the world, living entities need membranes and receptor surfaces such as the skin. Such membranes, Lynn Margulis notes, are 'a precondition for cell metabolism' (Margulis and Sagan 1995: 67). These membranes, however, do not need to be surfaces in a strictly topological sense. They can be any interface that functions as a surface of sensation. (I will use the term sensation to designate the quantitative aspect of how entities register this irritating landscape, and the term perception to designate the qualitative aspects of that registration.) Even though language, as a surface of both sense and sensation, might also be considered to be such a receptor surface, for humans, the surfaces that register irritations are usually aligned with the five senses, although there are many other modes of sensation such as thermoception, proprioception, nociception, equilibrioception or kinesthesioception. Even these, however, are just samples of a potentially infinite variety of human and non-human modes of sensation, such as those that pertain to the ability to sense electric or magnetic fields, to feel faint shifts in natural media, such as subtle changes in the pressure and faint modulations of currents in water or air. Honeybees 'orient themselves by light polarization in the sky' (119), Margulis notes. In fact, the world might be described as an infinite variety of surfaces of sensation, many of which are, from a human perspective, wonderfully surprising. In *Pilgrim at Tinker Creek* Annie Dillard notes that butterflies 'taste with their feet' (1976: 255). Often, humans do not even have words for these forms of sensation and perception, even less concepts.

The function of a being's perceptual and cognitive networks and surfaces is to turn incoming stimuli into patterns, and to extract concepts from these patterns. To turn quantities into qualities, that is. From the multiplicity of quantitative irritations that impinge upon them, a battery of both perceptual and cognitive agencies create qualitative distinctions, and from these distinctions, concepts and diagrams. They register the mode and the intensity of the irritation, compare and contrast it to earlier irritations, and then use the resulting shifts in the overall pattern to create cognitive and affective maps that help navigate the specific landscape of life – their existential milieu, Guattari will say – to which they are immanent. In terms of the beings' living, the ultimate objective of these processes is to construct a qualitative, meaningful world from a quantitative, irritating one: A world that is adequate to the quantities or, as ecologists might say, a world that is adequate to the household of nature.

For constructivisms, therefore, there is no truth in the wild. There are only recurrent energetic processes that provide perceptual and cognitive operations within the living being with food for internal qualification. From sets of stimuli, entities construct objects with equally constructed qualities such as colour, hardness, elasticity or movement. In other words, living beings register recurrent stimulations, isolate them from the set of overall stimuli that is constantly provided by the milieu and call the result of these cut-outs objects. As von Foerster notes, an object, as opposed to a thing-in-itself, is precisely not something in-itself but merely 'a "sign for stable behavior"' (1993: 103). In fact, objects are not even a sign of their own qualities and behaviour, but rather, as the title of one of his articles states, 'Tokens for (Eigen-) Behaviours' (2003: 127).

Bateson maintains in *Mind and Nature: A Necessary Unity* that 'experience of the exterior is always mediated by particular sense organs and neural pathways. To that extent, objects are my creation, and my experience of them is subjective, not objective' (2002: 31). Already this might be said to soften up that constructivist stance, or at least to qualify it: To that extent. Guattari, while he subscribes to the formal differentiation between informational closure and energetic openness, goes even further than Bateson in suspending that formal, epistemological differentiation into an eco-ontology and eco-epistemology in which it is treated according to a logic of complementarity. The shift is from what Maturana and Varela call autopoiesis to what Guattari calls, in an ecologized variation of the term that stresses the heterogeneity of the elements of genesis, heterogenesis.

What remains uncontested in Guattari's ecological modification of the logic of constructivism is that cognition is not only about pattern recognition but also, and more fundamentally so, about pattern production. It is about the extrapolation and extraction of objects from a given landscape of quantitative stimuli. This extraction, which is reductive in that it entails the conversion of an infinite experiential and causal nexus into a finite one, is operationally necessary for what Guattari calls the giving to exist in the given: for entities, or, in Guattari's terminology, for consistencies, to exist in their given world. (In the following, I will, where applicable, talk of living entities or simply of entities as consistencies and vice versa. As Guattari notes in *The Anti-Oedipus Papers*, 'instead of substance: *consistency*' (2006: 267) [→ **Deleuze 17**]. In accordance with these two registers, Simon O'Sullivan situates the folding of 'the relationship between virtual and actual, between infinite and finite' (2012: 99) and of 'a continuum of sorts (a "reciprocal determination") between what Deleuze calls "virtual ideas" and "actual" states of affairs' (89) at this meeting of the actual given and the virtual giving; at a point that Guattari calls, in *Schizoanalytic Cartographies*, the Point of Contingencing. (Rather than reciprocal determination or mutual determination, I will use the term reciprocal presupposition (*présupposition réciproque*) that Guattari and Deleuze use in *A Thousand Plateaus*.) According to this logic, 'the infinite is not barred, nor deferred, but is in fact folded into the finite' (O'Sullivan 2011: 11). Already at this point, one might provisionally conceptualize this folding in ecological terms: *finite actual resources, infinite virtual potentiality.*

If there is no truth in the wild, there is, similarly, no truth in the entity. There are only sets of stimuli and informational as well as operational reactions to these sets. As these are different for every mode of living, there is no common, given ground or reality. There is only constant change and production. Without the modulation of the energetic landscape that both surrounds and traverses a being, that being would in fact not be able to exist. If there are no more changes in the landscape of stimulation, the senses stop operating. In a desert of perception, the being's perceptual and cognitive machines literally dry out: no perception, no differences; no differences, no perception. One of Guattari's most basic ecosophic propositions is that there is a reciprocal presupposition between beings and milieu, which form two aspects rather than two parts of an infinitely machined world. Consider, for instance, the famous tick, tree, temperature and dog machine Guattari and Deleuze describe in *A Thousand Plateaus*, or their example of the wasp-orchid machine (TP: 238). If the being's operational and informational closure is why there is no truth in the wild, this overall machinism of the world is why there is also, somewhat paradoxically, no wild in the wild. Later, I will argue that only one aspect of the plane of immanence is truly wild.

A third conceptual premise of the above constructivism is that every actual and virtual entity is made up of elements that range from infinitely small to infinitely large plateaus of construction above and beyond it. (I will talk in more detail about the notion of infinity later on). To all of these it is connected through its immanence in the world. Every consistency, in other words, is infinitely constructed from heterogeneous elements that form assemblies by way of heterogenetic processes. According to Guattari and Deleuze such assemblaging happens simultaneously on a thousand plateaus, from the atomic to the cellular and further to the cosmic level. This radical form of constructivism, in which both actual and virtual operations are conceptualized from within the complexity and communality of countless, recursively nested assemblages, forms another fundamental given of Guattari's ecosophy. As the world is infinitely machined, nothing in and of it is in any way essential, natural, or pre-established. In fact, nature itself is never natural, in the sense that it would follow stable and essential rules and regulations. Everything in nature is process and experiment. The conceptual ramifications of this idea, to which very few scientists would object, are far-reaching, and to remain true to their implications at all times is perhaps the most challenging task of all forms of ecology. As all beings are both elements and aspects of the machined world, Guattari suggests in *The Three Ecologies* that 'environmental ecology' should be renamed 'machinic ecology' (66). As Genosko notes, this ecology is neither 'posthuman nor . . . post-natural' (2009: 19).

Ecosophy: Ecology before 'Ecology'

A major implication of the logic of a machinic ecology is that no entity can uncouple itself from its milieu's affordances and constraints. In fact, each entity can be defined by listing its specific abilities to move within such sets of affordances and constraints.

That is, by drawing up the complete list of its abilities and inabilities. This is why Guattari and Deleuze do not believe in either genres or genders. Another basic ecosophic lesson is that ecology is not something done to the world by humans, but by the world to itself. Everything is already given. One does not need to create multiplicity, as multiplicity is already given and remains given, although it might be reduced, at certain moments and in certain places, to a degree that is no longer healthy. But then, healthy for whom? If in an infinitely machined world everything is always already ecological, it is, even in the anthropocene, never a question of creating ecologies but rather of intervening in and 'administer[ing]' (SC: 19) already given ecologies and situations in ways that allow them to be viable and liveable rather than toxic. But then again, liveable and toxic for whom? These choices and responsibilities are, invariably, ours.

Today, these choices often have to do with whether one follows radical forms of constructivism that focus equally on all three premises of constructivism, or cultural, sometimes called linguistic constructivisms, that focus mainly on the first premise. The distinct logics of these two versions of constructivism have led to the implementation of very different and often contesting modes of thought that formed the conceptual background and milieu of Guattari's ecosophy and that still today define modes of conceptualizing the world. In this context, cultural constructivisms often define themselves against what they feel is radical constructivisms' too strong allegiance to and belief in natural-science empiricisms, while radical constructivisms consider cultural constructivisms as too idealistic. My argument is that Guattari refuses to choose between these positions, and that his thought bears, at all moments, the conceptual tensions and stresses that result from this refusal. While Guattari is critical of the tendency to conceptually reduce life to culturally constructed life, he is, at the same time, equally critical of a reduction of consciousness to a physics of thought. The ultimate challenge is to travel between the Scylla of a culturalist belief in a direct emanation of material life from thought, and the Charybdis of a naturalist belief in a direct emanation of thought from material life. Not empirical or idealist constructivism, but rather the full spectrum of constructivisms: *more empiricism, more idealism*.

In their practice, cultural constructivisms – what Guattari sometimes scoffs at as postmodernism – have concentrated on human language and the cognitive agency of what cybernetics calls the observer, who looks at the scenes of life from a quasi-outside position, while for radical constructivisms, the observer is both apart from but at the same time invariably a part of the observed scene. As Henry David Thoreau, the patron saint of American ecology, noted in *Walden*: 'we are not wholly involved in Nature . . . I only know myself as a human entity; the scene, so to speak, of thoughts and affections; and am sensible of a certain doubleness by which I can stand as remote from myself as from another. However intense my experience, I am conscious of the presence and criticism of a part of me, which, as it were, is not a part of me, but spectator, sharing no experience, but taking note of it; and that is no more I than it is you. When the play, it may be the tragedy, of life is over, the spectator goes his way. It [life] was a kind of fiction, a work of the imagination only, as far as he was concerned' (1995: 88). Even in being separated from the world, entities are part of being in the world and of the world.

In this context, consider Guattari's take on the use of video technology in psychiatry. Against the notion of objective observation, Guattari stresses that the elements captured in video-monitored scenes do not simply 'interact (as systems theorists imprudently declare) but enter into existential agglomeration' (SC: 184). If all situations are moments of 'heterogenesis' (184), which means that they consist of assemblages of heterogeneous elements coming-into-being and dissipating, the scene to which all actors are immanent forms an 'intensive' ecology that includes the actors' being-looked-at as well as a multitude of other actors. 'The scene functions like a sponge, if you like, which soaks up a certain type of scattered, deterritorialized being-there' (184). While the cybernetic and systems-theoretical observer has an important place in Guattari's system of thought, that observer must always be ecologized, as when Guattari replaces it with the inherently much more dispersed concept of an '"observer" Assemblage' (54): *not only heterogenesis, therefore, but ecogenesis.*

The same ecologization applies to language. As Guattari and Deleuze note with an ironic stab at Jacques Lacan's reliance on Saussurean linguistics, 'a language is never closed upon itself, except as a function of impotence' (TP: 8). If Lacan famously noted that there is no metalanguage, with which Guattari would agree, Guattari notes in *The Machinic Unconscious*, even more telegrammatically but equally critical of Lacan, that '*there is no language in itself*' (27). Like video monitoring, acts of language are invariably immanent to an ecogenetic field, and as such to a comprehensive media ecology that includes an infinite amount of both signifying and a-signifying semiotics; to what Deleuze calls 'signaletic material [*matière signalétique*]' (1989: 33) and Guattari 'signaletic matter' (SC: 40) [→ **Deleuze 77**].

In this context, one way radical constructivisms widen the conceptual scope of linguistic constructivisms is that they extend processes of perception, cognition and even consciousness infinitely deep into the assemblages that are the world, which they consider to be pervaded, down to its most microscopic levels, by perceptual and cognitive machines, and thus by virtual processes of discrimination and differentiation. When Varela argues that even cells have rudimentary brains, one can begin to comprehend radical constructivisms' trust in a sentient world to which all entities are immanent, as well as, in analogy, the scope of Guattari's notion of heterogenesis. Already Thoreau noted that 'the subtle powers of Heaven and of Earth' make up 'an ocean of subtle intelligences' that 'are every where, above us, on our left, on our right; they environ us on all sides' (1995: 87). At the same time, radical constructivisms formally separate, on all levels, and according to all possible parameters, the actual and the virtual series. The question posed by radical constructivisms, therefore, is twofold: How to maintain a formal distinction between the categories of the actual and the virtual even while maintaining that both series operate simultaneously, and to a similar degree, within every living being?

Ultimately, what radical constructivisms argue is not that cultural constructivisms have it all wrong, but that, by limiting the scope of their field of interest, they do not include enough of the world into their conceptual field of vision, such as the myriad of perturbations and irritations that at every moment disturb the clear oppositions created by the differential technologies of human perception and cognition. (I will differentiate between the term perturbation, which I use to designate the movements of the milieu as such, and irritation, which, as I noted, designate these movements in relation to and as experienced by individual living beings.) They ignore the often imperceptible, unconscious forces that cannot be easily integrated into a cultural calculus. While in terms of media studies, cultural constructivisms are based on a clear and present digital logic whose symmetrical beauty shines through even their most complex conceptual architectures, the beauty and grace of a radical constructivist logic lies in the reciprocal determination of digital data and analog intensities that the entities cannot stop integrating. In other words, if cultural constructivisms are logical, radical constructivisms are ecological. Ultimately, what cultural constructivisms exclude are the infinitely many and complex ecologies that make up the productive phyla to which every living being is immanent, and that provides an energetic reservoir that is eminently and everywhere alive: *their unconscious.*

The Subject of Schizoanalytic Ecology

Guattari's ecologizations imply that even while the subject he is concerned with is by default the human subject – depending on the conceptual context, this can be the Cartesian subject, the Lacanian subject, the mad subject, the worker, us – his thought includes, long before theories of non-human agency would become popular, the full diversity of entities such as snails, trees, viruses or molecules, all of which are part of, and in actual fact make up the situation of, or that is, the world.

In terms of the human subject, Guattari's question is invariably about its processualization: how to make it 'drift from systems of *statements* and preformed subjective *structures* towards *Assemblages of enunciation* able to forge new coordinates for reading and to "bring into existence" new representations and propositions' (SC: 17). In terms of the genesis of Guattari's thought, the notion of assemblages of enunciation, as well as that of 'group-being [*l'etre-en-groupe*]' (TE: 34), are conceptually more powerful versions of his earlier, more narrowly political notion of groupuscules.

How can one think an individual entity's relation to the world, and how can one make this relation viable? From the first page of *Schizoanalytic Cartographies*, on which Guattari wonders '[h]ow should we talk today about the production of subjectivity?' (SC: 1), to the final page of *Chaosmosis*, which states that 'among the fogs and miasmas which obscure our *fin de millenaire*, the question of subjectivity is now returning as a leitmotiv' (C: 135), questions of subjectivity hold a privileged position in Guattari's work, and, as he notes, in contemporary culture in general. 'Questions of the production of subjectivity no longer only concern a handful of visionaries' (SC: 13).

Although Guattari ecologizes the notion of autopoiesis by considering it as a heteropoiesis, theories of self-organization are among the most basic and sustained references in his ecosophy, as when Guattari notes that one of the central notions of schizoanalysis, understood as 'the analysis of the impact of Assemblages of enunciation on semiotic and subjective productions in a given problematic context', is 'the idea of an existential circumscription that implies the deployment of intrinsic references – one might also say, a process of self-organization or singularization' (18). In psychoanalytic terms: how to free the subject from the relentlessly oedipal machines and their both familial and familiar fault lines? In economic terms: how to free the subject from its insertion into a ruthlessly capitalist machine? How to take the subject and allow it to be once more open to change, movement and experimentation? According to Guattari, the potential for such a deeply emancipatory project of re-invention and re-invigoration lies in learning to make use of the affordances provided by the more molecular and collective movements within the cracks of the molar machines into which subjects are, at various times and in various ways, inserted. How, in general terms, to conceptualize moments of change and the possibility of change as an increase in grace, considered, in both actual and virtual registers, as *the practice of elasticity*?

On this simultaneously aesthetical and ethical background, Guattari's conceptual enemies are all actual and virtual assemblages that keep the subject cramped up. These range from psychoanalysis, capitalism, repressive political regimes or mass media cultures to today's societies of control. How to administer given ecologies that are inevitably to some degree constrained in ways that make it possible to evade cramps? How to make life on this planet more liveable, more in tune and in resonance with or adequate to the planet? The planet which, as its creatures, we express and literally are. How can we do this without false romanticism or misty-eyed nostalgia? What are the machines we might need for such a paradoxical project?

Ecosophy at La Borde

The La Borde clinic was a testing ground for the project to involve the milieu in the cure. If familial machines kept the subject so cramped up that it developed neurotic or even psychotic responses in order to escape the pressure, the classic psychoanalytic approach was to make the subject accept what Lacan called the symbolic order and thus to subject itself, at least to a healthy degree, to the cultural logic that created the cramp in the first place. This involved to break up the subject's imaginary phantasm in order to facilitate its more mediated insertion into the cultural machine. While this insertion kept the symbolic machine intact, Guattari wondered why one would not change that machine rather than its subjects? Instead of making the subject submit to the cultural machine, which was constructed in the name of the father and from within a logic of lack, why not start from the idea of opening up the cultural or, in terms of semiotics, the symbolic machine to all the other machines that operate in and as the world? Why not open up the psychoanalytic milieu, which quite literally consisted of two equally hierarchical sites – the divan-chair arrangement and the clinic-doctor arrangement – to the multiplicity of these machines.

For this project, La Borde provided a milieu that was conceptually constructed in such a way as to make it possible for doctors and patients to live in a more communal, non-hierarchical manner. In this both analytic and lived-in milieu, the project was no longer to uncover the subject's unconscious, but to literally construct the subject's unconscious in a more connective and, as Guattari calls it, transversal manner. Its both intensive and extensive architectures and infrastructures allowed the La Borde machine not only to construct the patients' unconscious, but also to map it by asking the patients to track and record their movements by way of technological media devices such as cameras, microphones and typewriters. The idea behind this sculpting of the given infrastructures and environments was to facilitate more graceful and elastic movements. To make movements faster in terms of what Guattari, in *Schizoanalytic Cartographies*, calls the speed of determination. La Borde, then, may be read as an experiment: take the logic of radical constructivism, ecologize it and then apply it to the field of psychoanalysis. See how that introduces, inevitably, a new aesthetics and ethics into the practices of thought and of life. In ecological terms, let the patients, quite literally, take walks within an open, both actually and virtually less hierarchically architected analytic machine that is situated within a similarly less hierarchical machine to live in. Let them use video cameras to monitor themselves in specific situations: *videoanalysis meets media ecology*.

And further: if the default definition of media ecology is an assemblage of technical media, why stop there? Why not include natural media, such as the elements, into that ecology? Why not think of any loosely coupled arrangement of heterogeneous elements, regardless of whether these arrangements are actual or virtual, as a medium for formation? If, as Guattari notes in the context of the practice of the video-monitored scene, 'everything happens not through composition or the play of elements *partes extra partes*, but through a setting out [*disposition*] in which each point is the centre of reference for the whole' (SC: 184), why not widen the technical media ecology into an extended media ecology in which not only a video camera, but everything from atoms to water is a medium that underlies and carries processes of formation, subjectivation or, as Guattari also calls it, processes of crystallization: *ecoanalysis*.

'Drawing, Cities, Nomads' from 1992 transposes the changes in the milieu of La Borde to the scale of the modern city. In the text, which I will deal with in more detail later on, Guattari develops a project for the ecologization and singularization of life in the city, a project in which every constructivist action is conceived as an act of invention and thus inherently future-oriented. If structural couplings are considered to make up the unconscious practices of urban life, every intervention in and administration of the given ecology of the city concerns all levels of the urban situation, from the subjectivity of its human inhabitants to the 'partial subjectivity' (119G2) of its non-human inhabitants, such as animals, patches of grass or its climate. Its haecceities. From a habitation to the fleeting childhood memory triggered by a traffic overpass. From the 'multiple material and social constraints' of the overall milieu to the architect's personal 'signature' (121G4): *the more individual, the more collective.*

| ECOGENESIS

> The soul is a material body, the body is a thing, the subject is just an object, physiology and psychology is just physics. And, consequently, the senses are reliable.
>
> Michel Serres, *The Birth of Physics* (49)

> Either I am seriously mistaken, or this is materialism.
>
> Michel Serres, *The Birth of Physics* (121)

> We are almost all naturalists today.
>
> Heinz von Forester, *The Beginning of Heaven and Earth Has No Name* (134)

The Crystal World, Crystal Ecology

IN ORDER TO be considered an eigenecology, which is a neologism that echoes the concept of eigentheory, any ecology needs to rest its political and cultural pragmatics on an overarching ontology and epistemology. Although Guattari was perhaps more famous – and sometimes notorious! – for his many political and cultural interventions and for his co-authored texts with Deleuze, his solo writings, first and foremost *Schizoanalytic Cartographies*, attest to the fact that all of his activist pyrotechnics rely on a very sober and level-headed conceptual architecture: *schizoecology as eigenecology*.

Quite adequately, the theoretical spine of Guattari's schizoecology – its conceptual eigenvalue, one might say – includes a delineation of the ontological moment of ecogenesis understood as the genesis of living beings from within a fundamental multiplicity. Guattari's delineation of the modes in which living beings are immersed in the larger ecology of the living takes the form of a *crystal ontology*.

Guattari's idea that the world is infinitely machined and thus infinitely constructed leads inevitably to the question about the specific modes of construction. Guattari calls the most general of these modes crystallization. As he notes in *Chaosmosis*, every process of individuation is a '*crystallization* of intensity' (30, emphasis added). Similarly, in reference to the strategy of videoanalysis, he talks of heterogenesis as the creation of 'crystals of self-organization' (SC: 184). (At this point, I should note the twofold conceptual register in which Guattari and Deleuze conceptualize intensity. As the measure of different levels of energy, it is an attribute of the actual. As the opposite of actual extensity, however, it denotes the virtual. Within the field of the living, for instance, the extensive, corporeal aspect of a consistency operates as both a carrier medium and as a pick-up machine for energetic perturbations, while its intensive, mental aspect functions as a machine of what I have called pattern production and pattern recognition.)

While one background of Guattari's crystallography is Deleuze's conceptualization of the meeting of the actual and the virtual as a becoming-crystal, the concept of crystallization can also be traced back to the primal scene of ecology: Already Ernst Haeckel, in his 1917 *Kristallseelen, Studien über das Anorganische Leben* (*Crystal Souls, Studies on Inorganic Life*), talked of 'crystal souls' (92). Haeckel was particularly interested in 'liquid crystals' (1), which he considered as the link between organic and inorganic life-forms as fields without a 'sharp border' (17) between them. Although Haeckel differentiated between sterrocrystals, collocrystals, biocrystals and rheocrystals, the latter of which he considered to be most fully alive and thus the threshold between anorganic and organic life, he maintained that ultimately, in the continuum of nature – '*natura non facit saltus*' (26) – all crystals were 'alive' (38). (For more on liquid crystals, see my 'Motel Architectures'.)

In such an eco-crystal world, processes of crystallization denote the passage from chaos to structural stability, from disorder to order and from formlessness to form, and thus the emergence of individual, singular life from a communal, or, perhaps better, from an anonymous, living multiplicity. They allow us to conceptualize how form follows from and emerges within the informal. In other words, crystallizations are figures of the various processes of formation and individuation that constructivisms set out to describe and to explain. According to Guattari, entities that result from such processes show an 'autopoietic consistency' (C: 78) that unfolds in the field of 'intensive and processual becomings' (117) to which they are immanent. In denoting all forms of both actual and virtual machines, crystals are figures of the individual entities that make up the allover crystal machine that is the world. (In the following, I will sometimes use the term allover instead of overall to evoke the abstract expressionist strategy of allover painting.) Guattari's conceptual turn to crystals and crystallization should be read from within this notion of a crystal world and life. In very abstract terms, Guattari considers crystals as forms, and crystallizations as formations. As he notes in *Schizoanalytic Cartographies*, 'certainly it is not possible to determine a clear frontier between "spontaneous" chains and crystalline, proto-vital, proto-machinic forms of organization. But this passage is only envisaged here in a speculative fashion so as to bring to light certain constitutive steps in machinic processes' (81).

Ecosophic Semiotics

It is one of the most striking characteristics of Guattari's schizoecology that he does not restrict the logic of crystals and of crystallizations to extensive, actual forms and formations. He also considers it to preside over the consolidation of ideas and concepts. When he describes the genesis of language as a mode of crystallization in *The Machinic Unconscious*, this is done with the explicit aim of ecologizing it. Codes form, or, perhaps more precisely, inform the meaningless intensities of a given sonorous milieu into meaningful linguistic patterns. 'Every signifying statement crystallizes a mute dance of intensities' (32), Guattari notes. Although human language is a seemingly closed system made up of a finite number of differential elements, Guattari argues, it draws on and is in constant exchange with the milieu of these sonorous but mute intensities, as well as with any number of non-human — as in: nonlinguistic — semiotics. In other words, the meaningless multiplicity of the spectrum of sound is the medium that carries meaningful and thus no longer mute language. The semiotic world consists of any number of linguistic and thus signifying materials and operations, but also of nonlinguistic, and thus a-signifying materials and operations levels. In fact, Guattari will maintain that an ecological semiotics should always be aware of the expressive register within the representative register.

Guattari's notion of an a-signifying semiotics is the most important aspect of his critique of the logic of the signifier, which represses precisely the emergence of human language from the field of noise, as well as its implication in various modes of a-signifying, expressive signaletics. While a-signifying, signaletic materials have not yet congealed into an autonomous, linguistic sign-system, a signifying semiotics operates from within the idealistic assumption that it does have an autonomous existence. From within different contexts, both Manuel DeLanda and Maurizio Lazzarato have addressed this level of a-signifying, non-autonomous machinic semiotics. As Lazzarato argues, 'in a rock, in a crystalline structure, the "form" is conveyed by the "material" itself, such that expression and content are inherent to each other. There is no differentiating between a mineral, chemical, or nuclear stratum and a semiotic stratum organized into an autonomous syntax' (2014: 67). While this is true, one of the most important strategies in Guattari's schizoecology is to look for such a-signifying semiotics not only in non-human entities, but also within humans. As I argue in the next chapter, it is in this context of 'a more expanded semiotics'

(O'Sullivan 2012: 103) that Guattari stakes Louis Hjelmslev's semiotics, with its differentiation into expression and content, against Saussure's and Lacan's differentiation into signifier and signified.

While human beings have developed a linguistic code, the idea is not to set the human against the non-human – Guattari does not categorically differentiate between them – but rather to argue that beyond the level of signification humans also operate on levels of non-autonomous semiotics. Despite readings to the contrary, the level of a-signification does not denote the loss of meaning within a signifying system, and thus a subversion or a destruction of meaning from within. Rather, a schizoecologic semiotics concerns transfers that operate on levels of a-signifying signaletic materials rather than on those of an autonomous human language; the ways the former percolate into the latter: *the semiotic unconscious.*

On a purely formal level, most of Guattari's interventions into psychoanalysis and capitalism concern this ecologization of the semiotic. Except in moments of onomatopoeia, for instance, Saussure considers language as a signifying system that is uncoupled from sonorous intensity. Famously, rather than seeing language as expressive of the sonorous world by giving it a voice, Saussurean semiotics considers language as an arbitrary code that is representative of a referent that is excluded from it in that the referent comes to the speaker as an always already semiotic object. Within such a semiotics, language's generative intensity is silenced, cancelled or reduced to the white noise of information theory rather than the pink noise of ecology: *ecosemiotics*. (For more on white and pink noise, see my 'Vibes: Tape-Recording the Acoustic Unconscious' (2015).) Lacanian psychoanalysis, which deals with this silencing as the process of primal repression and with the return of the repressed in terms of involuntary misfirings of language, is one instantiation of the attempt to close off the realm of representation and information from the allover milieu of given sound. In fact, the difference between Lacanian psychoanalysis and schizoanalysis is that the latter is based on an ecosemiotics that keeps language, at all times, tied to the intensities of the sonorous milieu and to the many levels and modes of a-signifying semiotics. How could it not be so tied, Guattari would argue, when it has emerged from and within that sonorous milieu in the first place?

The notions of crystals and crystallization, then, describe processes of contraction, conglomeration, compression and solidification in the sense that heterogeneous elements come together in the organization of an actual consistency, such as a molecule, a plant, an animal, a human or a city. At the same time, they describe processes of contemplation in the sense that heterogeneous elements come together in the organization of a virtual consistency such as a thought or a concept. There are actual crystals and virtual crystals. Crystal bodies and crystal thoughts. When Guattari talks of the virtual 'crystal of an event' (SC: 185), he stresses that not only actual, but also virtual consistencies are both spatially and temporally cohering entities. As the process of crystallization is a constructivism and as such machined, Guattari maintains that '[i]n so far as it is a crystallization of the real, the possible and the necessary, Being is essentially a machinic product' (91).

Gilbert Simondon, whose work is another element that enriches Guattari's schizoecology, argues that any process of individuation or crystallization takes free-floating or loosely coupled blocks of energy from its milieu. In feedbacking with that milieu, crystallizations inevitably administer and change it. Although most exchanges take place between crystals and their adjacent milieu, both the crystal and its local milieu operate within and are part of the allover milieu. That more general machinic assemblage – ultimately, the machine of nature – changes, sometimes only to an extremely small degree, with each operation that takes place within it. Sometimes, however, minute changes in one place have immense effects in another, far-away place, which underlines that in a milieu, everything is connected to everything else. It stands to reason that nothing in such a machinic milieu is universal or general, which in turn implies that there are no easy ecological questions and no easy ecological answers. Without the option of generalization, every answer is invariably an answer to a specific question and problematics: *hetero- or ecogenesis.*

Although at any given moment no part of an individual machine can be completely closed off from the rest of the allover machine, this does not imply that closed systems cannot be thought, or that there aren't attempts to create and implement such closed systems, from atomic shelters to national borders. One of the most consistent conceptual refrains in Guattari's work is a critique not so much of systems that involve some degree of closure, but of systems that categorically value closure over openness, or, even worse, that aspire towards complete closure. Before any ethical evaluation that might be attached to such systems, their inherent fault lies in that they are not in tune with or adequate to a world in which nothing is completely closed off from anything else.

In talking about closed systems, Guattari repeatedly returns to Saussure's programmatic exclusion of the referent from the field of semiotics and of psychoanalysis. In fact, a decisive difference between psychoanalysis and schizoanalysis is that the latter thinks of existential qualities as invariably inserted into site- and time-specific milieus. Despite certain similarities, this differentiates schizoanalytic objects 'from Kleinian "part objects" or from the Lacanian "object little a" . . . Rather, they are like crystals of singularization, points of bifurcation outside the dominant coordinates, on the basis of which mutant universes of reference can spring up' (SC: 36). If the universal function of objects in psychoanalysis is to stand in for the same given lack, and to function within a universally given oedipal matrix, this predetermines the spectrum of their use, and it leads psychoanalysis to read them according to unduly generalized parameters. This is how Lacan's *object a* ended up as 'a general function stripped of all traits of singularity' (SS: 224).

Guattari contrasts this closure, which also underlies Georg Wilhelm Friedrich Hegel's notion of alphabetical script as the best system of notation because it is the most arbitrary and generalized one, with other semiotic systems that are more directly in touch with the allover machine that is the world. If, as Guattari proposes, the function of objects varies with their use in specific local and temporal milieus and situations, one can no longer interpret them in relation to pre-established conceptual architectures such as those provided by psychoanalysis. Rather, they should be interpreted, in every specific situation, according to their functions for and within invariably singular existential entities. There are reasons to pick up an old portable television at a flea market that go beyond the fact that it stands in for my lost youth and the evenings when the family huddled around it in the camper at the coast. While these reminiscences might be relevant for my decision, there are many other reasons why I pick it up just then and there. Amongst these, many are indistinct, and many might not easily fit the psychoanalytics of lack, or the rumbling background noise of what Guattari would come to call 'World Integrated Capitalism' (SS: 77).

To draw this section together: In Guattari's crystal ecosophy, the term crystal designates existential consistencies that have emerged within and that move through constantly changing, processual milieus. In terms of evolution, a characteristic of crystals is to be composed of smaller crystals and to form larger entities, which means: to assemble heterogeneous elements into larger arrangements by way of operations of consistencing. As the main elements of a theory of formation, crystals and milieus are the two most important elements of Guattari's ecological theory of the subject and of subjectivation: *crystal ecology*.

Out of Turbulence, Ecology

If, as Erwin Schrödinger proposes, matter is either amorphous or crystalline, the question about the relation between these two states of aggregation, and about the ways in which form emerges from the informal, cannot be answered without answering the question of how the amorphous comes into being in the first place. In *Capitalism and Schizophrenia 1 and 2*, this question leads Guattari and Deleuze to scientific conceptualizations of the moment of the world's coming-into-being; to moments of genesis that decide much about how to conceptualize an ecology that is analogous to the world. The passages in which Guattari and Deleuze conceptualize the ecogenesis of the world come from *A Thousand Plateaus*, which develops much of what will flow into *Schizoanalytic Cartographies*. While the book thematizes processes of crystallization, its conceptual consolidation might itself be described as a process of crystallization in the way it constantly enriches itself by using not only the surplus energy provided to both Guattari and Deleuze by the thought of the other, but also the surplus energy provided by its adjacent practical, discursive and conceptual milieus. Ironically, this openness was one of the more common accusations against Guattari's and Deleuze's overall project. Many readers were suspicious of their recourse to scientific, such as chemical and biological, registers. As if they had crossed a line separating a philosophical universe from a non-philosophical universe that had no place in the world of a culturally constructed philosophy in which the natural universe was considered to be a cognitive vacuum, in that it was always already mediated by human language and thought. As if the protected philosophical knowledge that was bred in the closed-off laboratories of thought was under siege. From these immensely diverse milieus and their conceptual tableaus, Guattari brings to Guattari and Deleuze in particular the field of nonlinear dynamics or, in more popular terms, chaos theory; a field that had a strong cultural impact in the 1970s and '80s, and which Guattari would continue to use in all phases and across all aspects of his work.

The way Guattari and Deleuze pick up science and integrate its concepts and terminologies into their own conceptual architectures is one of the reasons for the conceptual and terminological oscillations and vibrations that define *A Thousand Plateaus*. While at this point Guattari was somewhat of a free agent whose work profited immensely from the injection of the philosophical, Deleuze felt the full pressure of philosophy, which saw the conceptual openness of the book as a betrayal of philosophy's conceptual purity. It didn't help that Guattari and Deleuze would not always follow the various sciences to the letter and that, on top of such infidelities, they were, at some moments, openly critical of science. In *Schizoanalytic Cartographies*, for instance, Guattari notes that '[n]ot only do the cartographies of subjectivity have nothing to gain from aping science, but the latter can perhaps expect a great deal from the problematics that they carry along in their wake' (34).

Lucretius' Venus: The Figure of Ecosophy

Despite these betrayals, their use of the natural sciences as conceptual launching pads can help to anchor Guattari's and Guattari and Deleuze's conceptual machines and terminologies. In *A Thousand Plateaus*, one of these launching pads is Lucretius' scientific poem *De Rerum Natura*, which, a bit like an early version of *A Thousand Plateaus*, folds poetry, philosophy and the natural sciences into one another. The text, which is one of the first proto-ecological essays in that it is about the economy of nature and about the genesis and functioning of the world, provides a long, slow zoom into the moment of the birth of the world. Deleuze had already dealt with

Lucretius' text in his 1969 essay 'Lucretius and the Clinamen'. At that time, Lucretius had been seminal in the conceptual crystallization and consolidation of Deleuze's philosophy. As Guattari remembers in 'The Schizoanalyses', when he and Deleuze returned to *De Rerum Natura* in *A Thousand Plateaus*, it was its celebration of process, 'this processual option, this refusal of a generalized economy of equivalences, this choice of the "clinamen", that led us to challenge fixed cartographies, the unvariables by right in the domain of subjectivity' (SS: 215). By the time it enters *A Thousand Plateaus*, Lucretius' text had been further enriched for Guattari and Deleuze by the philosopher and historian of science Michel Serres, whose books *The Birth of Physics* from 1977, *Hermes V* from 1980, and *Genesis*, which was, like *A Thousand Plateaus*, published in 1982, were all extended meditations on Lucretius from under the conceptual shadow of nonlinear and fluid dynamics; *The Birth of Physics* more explicitly so than *Genesis* and *Hermes V*. Serres had found three eminently contemporary scientific projects in Lucretius: a nonlinear dynamics *avant la lettre*, a nonlinear semiotics, and a physics of immanence. As all of these projects are seminal for Guattari's schizoecology, let me follow Guattari and Deleuze's negotiation of Lucretius and Serres in *A Thousand Plateaus* in more detail.

Multiplicity and the *Clinamen*

Serres provides extremely concise scientific investigations of Lucretius' conceptualization of the moment of the beginning of the world against the background of what contemporary science calls a deterministic chaos. That concept, which Serres calls, in reference to Lucretius, an ordered multiplicity, together with the concept of a complete chaos, which Serres calls a pure multiplicity, will come to form one of the fundamental conceptual backbones of Guattari's schizoecology.

In *A Thousand Plateaus*, Guattari and Deleuze relate the question about adequate models of the birth of the world to the difference between what they call major or 'royal' (361) science on the one hand, and minor or 'nomad' (362) science on the other [→ **Deleuze 110**]. The former tends towards organization and axiomatization, the latter towards experimentation and pragmatism. In a terminology picked up from Simondon, one is tendentially molar, the other tendentially molecular. Minor science is first pragmatic and then axiomatic, major science is first axiomatic and then pragmatic. Lucretius' text enters *A Thousand Plateaus* by way of the atomism of 'Democritus and Lucretius' (361), which Guattari and Deleuze consider as a minor science that deals explicitly with the genesis of the world. It is also, as Serres argues, an early form of what would become the scientific field of nonlinear or fluid dynamics. 'Rather than being a theory of solids treating fluids as a special case; ancient atomism is inseparable from flows, and flux is reality itself, or consistency' (361). As such, the logic of atomisms 'is one of becoming and heterogeneity, as opposed to the stable, the eternal, the identical, the constant. It is a "paradox" to make becoming itself a model, and no longer a secondary characteristic, a copy' (361). This very paradox will define Guattari's diagram in *Schizoanalytic Cartographies* considered as a formal diagram of an ultimately informal, but simultaneously everywhere formal, constantly becoming, processual world.

In the way a liquid is reduced, one might reduce the ecological to the two related questions that I introduced earlier. How to be adequate to the world? and: If ecology aims at such an adequation, then how to be ecological? As these questions imply that ecology rests on an image of the human's relation to the world and, as I noted above, the challenge is to develop not only adequate images and figures of the world, but also adequate figures of thought from within which to conceptualize this world and this adequation, the questions raised by both Lucretius' and Guattari's work might be formulated as: How would an ecology look that rests on the logic of non-linear dynamics? and: How can such an ecology be used as a guide for a practice of living that is adequate to our world and our living within it?

The figure of nature that underlies Lucretius' ecopoetical science or ecoscientific poetry is Venus Anadyomene, the mythical goddess of beauty, love and creativity, who is born from the foam of the sea and thus quite literally a figure of the crystallization of form from foam. Emerging from the sea, she is the figure of a liquid crystal life. Serres follows Lucretius in his celebration of Venus, whom he reads as the figure of a physics of turbulence. 'One must imagine Venus turbulent, above the noise of the sea' (G: 122), he notes. As the muse of Lucretius' proto-ecology, she 'is not transcendent, like the other gods, she is immanent to this world, she is the being of relation' (BP: 123). Serres reads Lucretius' physics of immanence as the conceptual precursor of any form of an ecology of the living. Venus presides over nature, which is the most fundamental multiplicity from which every science emerges, and which every science needs to address. As Serres notes in his reading of Honoré de Balzac's story 'The Unknown Masterpiece' in the first chapter of *Genesis*, the ground of nature is 'the *belle noiseuse*, a naked Aphrodite resplendent in her beauty, rising fresh from the troubled waters, as the model Gillette who comes forth naïve and aborning from the canvas of the dying old master' (G: 15).

When Guattari and Deleuze take up Serres' argument, they link it to their notion of the war machine as the conceptual figure of the inherent strife that defines any natural process – in mythological terminology: of the figure of Venus' lover Mars – and to the space of Venus as smooth or deterritorialized. 'Serres states what he considers to be Lucretius's deepest goal: to go from Mars to Venus, to place the war machine in the service of peace. But this operation is not accomplished through the State apparatus; it expresses, on the contrary, an ultimate metamorphosis of the war machine, and occurs in smooth space' (TP: 490). In this light, Marsilio Ficino's statement that 'Venus dominates Mars, and he never dominates her' (quoted in Grafton et al. 2010: 564) is the perfect motto for an adequate ecology. In fact, one of Guattari and Deleuze's fundamental beliefs is not that Mars should or could be silenced once and for all – 'From time immemorial "nature" has been at war with life!' (66) Guattari exclaims in *The Three Ecologies* – but that Mars should always be put into the service of Venus. Never the other way around. To follow this vector wherever possible, and trusting in the ultimate supremacy of Venus, would already ensure that one's practice of life is adequate to the world.

Like Lucretius', Guattari and Deleuze's approach is both mythological and scientific. Moreover, it is deeply pragmatic. There will always be strife and war. To believe in the end of war is a phantasm that disregards the nature of nature, and thus is, as Charles Olson would maintain, unequal to the real itself. If war could be stopped, one might assume that it would have been stopped by now. In every war, however, one should always be on the side of Venus, although this has to be the true Venus rather than the co-opted Venus that pilots paint onto the noses of their fighter planes. If the ground of nature and of the natural sciences is a pure multiplicity, the natural sciences can be judged by how adequate their concepts are to that ground. From this premise, the strength of Lucretius' work lies in its considering nature to be infinitely varied, everywhere alive, fundamentally productive, and inherently joyful.

The ontological question, then, is 'how is Venus born from the sea, how is time born from the noisy heavens? How are forms born from the formless?' (G: 26). It is in order to answer this question that one needs, both chronologically and conceptually, to return to the very beginning of the world. Lucretius defines this first moment by way of a conceptual diagram that aligns two givens. The first is a rain of atoms that falls vertically through an inherently empty space. In Lucretius' account, this atomic rain designates an eternally unchanging and thus timeless, strictly ordered state before the birth of the world. The second given is the infinitely small deviation of one single atom from this vertical vector. Lucretius calls this contingent, symmetry-breaking deviation the *clinamen*.

This minimal angle triggers a cascade of further atomic collisions which leads to a state of allover atomic disorder. In more positive terms, it triggers a movement that leads to a state of pure atomic multiplicity. As all forms of order emerge from this atomic multiplicity, they will invariably bear witness to it. 'That when bodies are borne straight down through the void by their own weight, | At just about an instant uncertain and place likewise not set, | They shift position slightly veering off course plumbed directly, | To the extent, you might say, that their movement is altered effective. | And unless they were wont to slant a bit, everything straight down, | Just like raindrops in showers, would fall plunging through the void depthless. | So not careening they'd never collide nor would blows and buffets | Happen to atoms; thus, nature would not have created aught ever' (Lucretius 1973: 53).

In Serres' more mathematical wording, 'at some point, that is to say by chance, a deviation, a very small angle is produced' (BP: 11). This unpredictable swerve of one atom happens '*incerto tempore incertisque locis*' (112). As 'the minimum angle of formation of a vortex, appearing by chance in a laminar flow' (6), this deviation brings about 'aleatory scattering' (112), 'collision' (126) and 'turbulence' (6). As Guattari and Deleuze comment, 'in atomism, just such a model of heterogeneity, and of passage or becoming in the heterogeneous, is furnished by the famed declination of the atom. The *clinamen* ... constitutes the original *curvature* of the movement of the atom' (TP: 361, emphasis added). Two principles of nonlinear dynamics follow from Lucretius' genetic diagram. The initial conditions of processes that develop from such an uncertain, 'stochastic' (BP: 6) origin can never be fully known; and any system will remain sensitive to and dependent on these uncertain, and thus uncomputable, conditions.

At this point in his reading of Lucretius, Serres might have proceeded to show how and by what means islands of order emerge from these chance collisions. The deeper Serres zooms into the moment of the *clinamen*, however, the more complex he finds its logic to be. Although the *clinamen* denotes the initial moment of the emergence of order from disorder, this process seems in actual fact to proceed in reverse, because the emergence of order happens by way of the disordering of the completely ordered rain of atoms. The 'laminar flow, the figure of chaos, is at first sight a model of order ... Turbulence seems to introduce a disorder into this arrangement' so that 'disorder emerges from order' (27). In Lucretius' image of the sudden, unexpected shift from a literally timeless rain of atoms – which, as a continuous stream of rain made up of single drops, describes with great precision what Guattari defines in *Schizoanalytic Cartographies* as the co-presence of a continuous logic of Flows and a discontinuous logic of Phyla – to a turbulent and further to a vortical world, it is only from this secondary, turbulent disorder that vortical orders emerge, in a shift from, as I noted earlier, the white noise of pure chaos to the pink noise of a deterministic chaos. In terms of fluid dynamics, 'the origin of things and the beginning of order consists ... in the narrow space between *turba* and *turbo* ... between *turbulence* and vortex' (28): *flow, turbulence, vortex*.

For Lucretius, as for Guattari and Deleuze, all formations emerge from the turbulence of pure multiplicity, which means that any notion of an inherently stable being, or of stasis in general, is an idealization. A structure, Guattari would note with subtle irony, is merely the name we give to a dynamics that has been decelerated to zero; a statement that is surely one of the most laconic definitions of process philosophy. Guattari and Deleuze relate the narrow space between pure multiplicity (*turba*) and ordered multiplicity (*turbo*) to their idea of a smooth space of becoming, arguing that the passage from the *clinamen* to the vortex follows an inherently smooth logic, which is, as noted above, the deeply pragmatic logic of minor sciences: 'One goes from a curvilinear declination to the formation of spirals and vortices on an inclined plane. . . . From *turba* to *turbo*: in other words, from bands and packs of atoms to the great vortical organizations. The model is a vortical one; it operates in an open space throughout which things-flows are distributed, rather than plotting out a closed space for linear and solid things. It is the difference between a *smooth* (vectorial, projective, or topological) space and a *striated* (metric) space' (TP: 361–2). I will return repeatedly to the differentiation that Guattari and Deleuze introduce here; that between the logic of smooth space that operates with and from within a topological, non-metric space, and the logic of striated space, which considers space as reduced to, and under the condition of its being metric.

While Guattari will ecologize the notion of smooth and striated space, the important differentiation Guattari and Deleuze introduce at this point is that between a Cartesian space that is empty and homogeneous, and a topological space that is a heterogeneous force-field. Lucretius, Guattari and Deleuze argue, provides a mathematical model of the creation of order from within an inherently topological, heterogeneous and even turbulent space which, if one were to plot it within a vector space, would show a multiplicity of random, inherently asystemic and aperiodic vectors, while a vortical movement, in which minimally formed systems have already emerged from pure turbulence, would show a minimum of order and systematicity. At this point, the vectors would show a faint orientation. In Guattari's terminology, they would show a minimal degree of consistency. In a mathematical notation, they would have become eigenvectors. While turbulent space is 'simply disorder' (BP: 28) and thus movement without form, vortical space contains 'a particular form in movement' (28; see also 175–6). One can think of vortices, therefore, as faint aperiodic crystals that develop within a turbulent field that is defined, in Lucretius, as a foam or aerosol made up of air and water: *Venus rising*.

From this point of view, one of chaos theory's favourite slogans about the genesis of the world – islands of order emerge in a sea of chaos – might be rewritten as: singular consistencies emerge in an anonymous, everywhere at least faintly ordered aerosol that, at the same time, is everywhere pervaded by pure chaos. Later, I will argue that the interplay of the planes of immanence and consistency will negotiate precisely these modes of chaos as pure disorder and of order as a consistency within that chaos. The shift from pure turbulence to the vortex – from a (*turba*) to o (*turbo*) – contains, *in nuce*, the birth of the system of the world. Every genesis proceeds from a turbulent multiplicity that does not stop pervading our seemingly ordered world. The rewriting of the difference between fluid sea and solid land into the more ambiguous space of an allover aerosolic world is taken up in Serres' notation that 'the cosmos is not a structure, it is a pure multiplicity of ordered multiplicities and pure multiplicities' (G: 111), which can be taken as one of the most concise shorthands for a Guattarian ecology. Translated into Guattari and Deleuzian terminology, the cosmos is a plane of immanence made up of planes of consistency and planes of immanence.

How to read this strange loop? Somewhat counter-intuitively, the shift from turbulent disorder to vortical order seems to be 'precisely the reverse' (BP: 27) of that from laminar flow to chaotic multiplicity. In the latter case, disorder emerges from order; in the former 'several orders emerge from disorder' (27). Already here, however, Guattari and Deleuze note a seeming paradox that Guattari will build on and develop further in *Schizoanalytic Cartographies*: Flows are striated. Lucretius' image of a laminar rain, Guattari and Deleuze stress, implies that 'homogeneous space is in no way a smooth space; on the contrary, it is *the form of striated space*' (TP: 370, emphasis added). Homogeneous space is 'striated by the fall of bodies, the verticals of gravity, the distribution of matter into parallel layers, the lamellar and laminar movement of flows' (370). It is only when one single atom deviates from this laminar flow that a smooth space comes into existence: 'Smooth space is ... the space of the smallest deviation' (371).

Like the space of Lucretius' atomic rain, striated space is organized and ordered. It is the space of the plow that furrows the earth, the space of grids, such as the mathematical grid, the urban grid, as well as the cartographic grid that measures the urban grid. It is also the space of striated muscles; sets of muscles ordered in parallel bundles that are under conscious, voluntary control. Smooth space is the non-grid landscape of the nomad who wanders the earth, the madman whose mind is unfurrowed and the poet, whose language undoes the grids of grammar, syntax and meaning. The space of smooth muscles; sets of more disordered muscles that are not under conscious, voluntary control. But then, things are not quite that clear-cut. The apparent contradiction between order and chaos – which is, I will argue, in actual fact a complementarity – is owed to the temporality of the *clinamen*, which contracts, in the sense of both drawing together and of establishing a natural contract between, three conceptually and chronologically consecutive moments. An ideally infinite zoom into this contraction would, at infinity – that is, when the three moments are chronologically infinitely close together – reach a point at which the three successive moments become the one, single, infinitely short moment of the *clinamen*. In conceptually contracting these three moments into one, the logic-at-infinity of the *clinamen* pays tribute to the infinite complexity of that moment, as well as to the infinite speed of change from one moment to the next.

The three moments happen simultaneously, however, only at such a chronological point-at-infinity, which is a moment that can be thought, but that cannot be perceived.

It is possible to think infinity but not to experience it. In every perceptual zoom, the three moments remain successive, with the vertical atomic rain designating a state minimally before the origin of the world, the turbulent moment of atomic multiplicity designating the moment of the birth of the world, and the vortical moment the emergence of different atomic orders from the moment minimally after the birth onwards as the time of the emergence of ordered multiplicities from within a pure multiplicity. In *Lucretius I: An Ontology of Motion*, Thomas Nail rightly considers such a momentous eternity before the creation of the world 'a total abstraction. If there was such a time, nothing would be, which is obviously not the case. Matter curves and bends by its own autonomous change of motion' (2018: 195).

What exactly, then, is a logic-at-infinity? Serres stresses specifically that the logic of chronological contraction includes the infinite. The spiral order of vortical space begins already 'in the infinitely small declination' (BP: 91) of the *clinamen*. Within the chronological contraction, however, it is important to maintain a crucial differentiation. Conceptually, the shift from the angular moment of genesis and the curved moment of the formation of a vortex happen simultaneously. In an infinitely short moment. From that point-of-view, the creation of disorder from order and of orders from that disorder happens at the same time. Perceptually, however, which means as embodied, the Lucretian dynamics imply a minimal chronology and duration. In this light, the twofold logic of the *clinamen* might be said to plot the creation of time itself. Of a time that is, from its very beginning, split into two separate but ultimately complementary chronologies. One mathematical, immaterial and conceptual, the other physical, material and perceptual. One virtual, the other actual. According to the mathematical image that models successive temporal moments spatially as consecutive points on a continuous line, the *clinamen* contracts these moments into a point at which the temporal intervals between them are infinity small. According to this logic, the three phases of the *clinamen* contract into one abstract, extensionless mathematical point. In an embodied world, however, time is invariably durational, although at a point at which the duration between any two moments becomes too small to be perceived it seems to be infinitely small and thus momentous. From this perspective, moments contract into a physical, and thus always to some degree extended point. As such, perception recapitulates the mathematical difference between point and line as the one between instant and duration.

In terms of perception, the time it takes for the *clinamen* to interfere in the laminar flow remains a duration whose length is inversely proportional to the ratio of the respective speed of its perception. Depending on the increase of the perceptual speed of discrimination, the duration is contracted into increasingly shorter temporal intervals. In analogy, with the decrease of the perceptual speed of discrimination, the intervals expand more and more. As every perceived instant can be zoomed into by increasing the speed of perception, the time of the *clinamen* is, according to the specific perceptual point of entry, either perceived as a discrete instant or as an extended, continuous interval. Although there is always duration in perception, that duration is either unconscious or conscious. Either imperceptible or perceptible.

In embodied time, the moment of the *clinamen* can never be reduced to a completely extensionless and thus purely immaterial, intensive point. Even as imperceptible, the embodied time of the *clinamen* is always only quasi-immaterial and quasi-punctual. It is invariably as if it were immaterial and as if it were punctual. The paradox of perceptual time, therefore, is that in order to perceive an infinitely short duration one would have to imagine an infinitely fine perceptual apparatus; a paradox to which I will return in more detail later on, as I will to the complementarity of the two temporal modalities of a mathematical and a physical, embodied time. Abstract and logical time on the one hand; concrete and perceptual time on the other. For now, let me just note that in living beings, the two modalities are in operation simultaneously without, on a formal level, ever becoming identical. Digital time and analog time. Actual time and virtual time: *temps and dureé, chronos and aion*.

The infinitely short moment of the *clinamen*, as the moment of the passage from disorder to order and thus of the birth of the world, lies, as the 'potential infinitely small and the actual infinitely small' (BP: 4), at the end of two zooms, one mathematical and noumenal, the other perceptual and phenomen(ologic)al. Serres explicitly links this complementarity to the distinction between the digital and the analog. As a discrete instant, the *clinamen* denotes an infinitely short digital 'differential or fluxion' (4). As an infinitely short duration, it denotes a minimal flow or fluctuation. As an infinitesimally small angle it is digital; as the beginning of turbulent flow it is analog. While the angular case concerns the mathematical relation between point and line, the vortical case concerns the perceptual relation between an ideal pulse of being and an empirical duration of becoming.

From the paradox that 'the vortex arises by a *fluxion* in the first hypothesis ... and by *fluctuation* in the second' (31) Serres extrapolates two modes of science and their respective epistemologies. The digital hypothesis leads to the 'solid mechanics' (7) of Leibniz and Newton. To 'infinitesimal calculus ... [and to] the science of fluxions' (31). The analog hypothesis, which Serres considers to be the more contemporary one, leads to 'fluid mechanics' (11), to nonlinear dynamics and to the scientific conceit of a turbulent sea in which islands of order emerge through complicated processes of self-organization. As Serres notes, 'order by fluctuation has become our problem' (31). This separation touches on a basic premise of minor and royal science and their respective conceptual spaces. Royal science sets a solid axiomatics against a fluid pragmatics and 'all the dynamic, nomadic notions – such as becoming, heterogeneity, infinitesimal, passage to the limit, continuous variation' (TP: 363).

The differentiation between fluid and solid tends to have an adherent politics. As the analog, continuous variations of the fluid are much harder to control than the digital similarities of the solid, a royal science is, more often than not, in the service of systems of control and of profit, if not of greed. The 'State needs to subordinate hydraulic force [which belongs to smooth space] to conduits, pipes, embankments, which prevent turbulence, which constrain movement to go from one point to another, and space itself to be striated and measured, which makes the fluid depend on the solid, the flows proceed by parallel, laminar layers' (363).

As major sciences subsume everything under the law of the solid, Guattari and Deleuze consider psychoanalysis, in that it subsumes everything under the law of the solid signifier, to be a royal science. Solid-state physics, and solid-state linguistics. Against this 'despotism', nomad science 'consists in being distributed by turbulence across a smooth space, in producing a movement that holds space and simultaneously affects all points, instead of being held by space in a local movement from one specified point to another' (363). At this point, Guattari and Deleuze seem, at least rhetorically, to set the solid-state, striated axiomatics of psychoanalysis against the fluid, smooth pragmatisms of schizoanalysis. While this is an inviting proposition, I will argue later on that such a symmetrical differentiation is ultimately not adequate to Guattari's ecosophy.

Turbulent Semiotics

Lucretius' text is pervaded by a conjunction of physics and linguistics. The nonlinear dynamics that Serres excavates from Lucretius' text, therefore, do not only concern the formational aspect of a material atomism. One might well argue, in fact, that the real strength of Serres' reading lies in excavating from Lucretius' text a nonlinear semiotics *avant la lettre* that is complementary to its *avant la lettre* nonlinear dynamics. If the latter is based on a material, the former is based on an immaterial atomism. In his reading of that immaterial atomism, Serres makes a larger point about the reach of semiotics that will be seminal in Guattari's schizoecology. In an extended argument, Serres shows that the complicated logic of the *clinamen* reverberates through the analogy Lucretius sets up between atoms and letters; an analogy that becomes, in extension, an analogy between things and words. Formation and information follow a similar assemblage theory. For Lucretius, Serres notes, atoms 'are letters, or are like letters. Their interconnection constitutes the tissue of the body, in the same way as letters form words, empty spaces, sentences and texts' (BP: 141). By way of this twofold assemblage theory, the *clinamen* marks not only 'the birth of things' but also the complementary 'appearance of language' (23).

Lucretius' analogy, which revisits the rain of atoms as a rain of letters, considers the multiplicities of atoms and of letters as two distinct but complementary media, a term I will comment on in more detail in 'Expressionism in Ecology 4: Squaring Media Studies' (pp. 118–24). For now, let me just note that in this context, media are sets of loosely coupled elements that can be formed into larger assemblages. On this background, while atoms are the medium of actual formation, letters are the medium of virtual information. Atoms are the seemingly unorganized carriers of organizations, letters are the seemingly meaningless carriers of meaning. By way of this conceptual isomorphism, Serres transposes the logic of the *clinamen* from a physics of formation to a metaphysics of information. If the rain of atoms designated a cataract of the materially formless, the semiotic rain of letters designates a 'cataract of the meaningless' (78) that implies 'the absence of a sign, the absence of a signal' (144). The cataract of the meaningless is 'without code', Serres notes, as 'nature does not code the universal' (150). In nature, there are only concrete universals, never abstract ones. In the same way that there is only an anonymous, momentous time without any duration in the pre-genetic, universal rain of atoms, there is no code in the universality of the semiotic cataract, which stands for 'the zero state of information, redundancy. . . . the indefinite repetition of letters' (109).

If this semiotic extreme denotes the complete absence of change by virtue of complete and universal order, the similarly uncoded extreme of semiotic turbulence denotes constant and ubiquitous change by virtue of complete and universal disorder. In terms of redundancy, which will become an important concept in *Schizoanalytic Cartographies*, while the first extreme is defined by minimal probability and maximal redundancy, the second is defined by 'maximal improbability' and 'minimal redundancy' (146). Within the framework of material formation, the laminar and the turbulent states had designated the extremes of pure order and pure chaos respectively. Only the vortical state in-between these equally ideal positions had designated a state of aperiodicity. In analogy, within the semiotic framework, the states of minimum and of maximum redundancy designate the semiotically impossible extremes of a complete difference of data on the one hand, and a complete identity of data on the other. The semiotic extremes are, like the physical ones, impossible because 'the singular and the whole either produce no information or infinite information, which has no sense either' (147). Only the in-between state allows for coding, and can thus become the arena in which what I have called elsewhere an intelligent materialism can unfold. Information and meaning can only be generated in the semiotic state in-between these equally ideal positions.

By way of his parallelism of atoms and letters, Lucretius develops a far-from-equilibrium semiotics that emerges from a multiplicity of signaletic elements that reach deeply into the biological phylum. In Lucretius, while the moments of complete order and complete disorder – the rain of atoms and turbulence respectively – are timeless or infinitely short, vortical 'nature is coded' (140) from its very beginning and down to its infinitely small elements. As Margulis maintains, 'mind and body, perceiving and living, are . . . self-reflexive processes already present in the earliest bacteria' (Margulis and Sagan 1995: 32). In fact, already 'the clinamen sets the first coding, it introduces a new time, writing, memory, the reversible of the negentropic' (BP: 150).

All entities that emerge from and that consolidate within the state of originary turbulence are simultaneously 'unstable and stable, fluctuating and in equilibrium, . . . order and disorder *at once*' (30, my emphasis). Serres stresses, however, that the initial turbulence is not only the genetic ground of living entities but also the state into which they will once more dissolve. In the same way that turbulence is both 'productive and destructive' (92), the *clinamen* is both 'formative and declining' (92). While formation refers to the *clinamen* as a generative, negentropic force, declination refers to the fact that, if one looks at it from a hydraulic and embodied rather than a geometric and abstract point-of-view, the *clinamen* introduces a first, minimally entropic inclination into the horizontal plane of creation. All systems slide down this inclined slope towards a 'final equilibrium from which no genesis can emerge' (37). In these twofold dynamics, the *clinamen* contracts the birth and the death of entities as immediately dependent on each other: 'theorem of the world: neither nothingness nor eternity. Neither straight line nor circle. Neither laminar flow nor stable cycle. Nature, that is to say birth, that is to say death, is the line inclined by the angle that produces a global vortex, which the wear of time brings back to the straight' (58).

The Joy of Ecosophy

The concept of a nonlinear, both genetic and destructive nature leads Serres to introduce, in an amalgamation of the philosophical and the scientific, a 'physics of immanence' (BP: 54) that operates by way of a *'combinatory topology'* (98). This physics of immanence is the third important conceptualization Guattari and Deleuze share with Lucretius and Serres. The logic of the *clinamen* implies the fundamental multiplicity, or 'plurality' (98) of the world as a complex system that has no outside because 'nothing is exterior to things themselves' (54): *ecosophic immanence*.

Ultimately, what Lucretius gifts to science is a joy that is generated by the fundamental positivity and multiplicity of a productive nature. According to this physics of immanence, the world is a fundamental positivity that operates without a universal, transcendental plane that would order it from without. Rather, the orders that emerge from its multiplicity are administered from within the world itself. As I noted earlier, for both Lucretius and Serres the embodiment of the creative force is Venus as a figure of 'nascent nature in joyous pleasure' (111). Even in times of deepest depression, which Guattari knew all too well, this affirmative pleasure of a creative, dissipative desire will, everywhere and at all times, define his thought.

All operations in and of this world are defined by this originary, joyful multiplicity, which is why 'the logic of ... dualism ... must be opened to plurality' (98), and why it is fatal to bring down 'the multiple to two, and the specific to the general' (98). This is why an ecological ethics should not be general, but both infinitely abstract and infinitely concrete. If Hans Jonas proposes in *The Imperative of Responsibility* that one should act so that the effects of one's 'actions are compatible with the permanence of genuine human life' (1984: 11), Guattari's ecosophic ethics aim, in less anthropocentric terms, to retain, at all costs and at every moment, the largest number of possible choices. In each situation, ethics must be the guardian of potentiality and of the possibility of choice. The guardian of diversity and pure plurality.

An important implication of an immanent physics is that science, like ecology, cannot be reduced to the theoretical. As it is immanent to nature, it cannot be contained in the ideally uncontaminated space of the laboratory, in the same way that it cannot be contained in pure mathematics. If 'the laboratory, and every closed system, are a protection against turbulence' (BP: 68) and thus disconnect science from a world considered as inherently contaminated, science must, in a move against this artificial closure, accept and even seek its own contamination. It has to get its hands, as well as its minds, dirty. This is why Guattari and Deleuze maintain that science, as minor science, cannot help but be practical. Without giving up its logical and conceptual purity, science should open itself up to the world and to all of its biomaterial processes and assemblages. In fact, it must think its involvement in the complementarity of conceptual purity and actual contamination. If it accepts, in its deepest conceptual implications, that the 'senses are faithful' (49) it will become a 'physics' that 'is faithful to the world, since the formation of its text is isomorphic with the constitution of the natural tissue' (159). The *clinamen* in fact contains in itself a '*passage from theory to practice*' (83) in that its first contraction aligns the digital and the analog. The logics of thought and of life.

A radically pragmatic 'physics of open systems' (79), which operates according to the logic of the *clinamen*, allows one to think the self-organization of infinitely many finitely complicated entities, the genesis of 'auto-productive forms' (106). All of these forms have their own politics that they operate within what we consider to be human politics. In terms of materiality, these are the non-human bodies of photons, molecules, microbes, viruses and more complex non-human consistencies. At the same time, in terms of virtuality, they are the non-human thoughts of photons, molecules, microbes, viruses and more complex non-human consistencies. All of these non-human thoughts operate within what we consider to be human thought. These two parallel series, Serres and Guattari and Deleuze argue, are complementary.

To recapitulate: the *clinamen* operates according to a logic of nonlinear dynamics *avant la lettre*. It is based on a differentiated notion of chaos, it describes systems that are far-from-equilibrium, it accounts for their sensitivity to initial conditions, it incorporates an overall systemic hydraulics, a theory of self-organizing production and a theory of natural coding. The logic that makes Lucretius a minor scientist is that of order(s) from multiplicity and the notion of a universal systemic ecology in which everything is connected to everything else; an ecology that is a witness to the fundamental multiplicity and the creativity of nature.

Although Guattari agrees with both Lucretius and Serres, and although both can help to contour his thought, he goes a crucial step further. Despite his interest in Lucretius' nonlinear semiotics, Serres stresses physics, as when he notes that 'every non-physical interpretation of the *clinamen* remains essentially idealist' (113). As Serres is interested mainly in the birth of physics, he tends to work from within the actual system of the world, which is the field Guattari will call, in *Schizoanalytic Cartographies*, the given. Although the field of the human subject and thought, which Guattari relates to the field of the giving, are everywhere implicitly implicated in Lucretius and Serres, in Guattari, that field becomes an explicit structural element on a par with the field of the given. The given world is always related to, and always needs to be thought of, in its relation to the giving as the field of individual entities and individual thought. In fact, the two are complementary. I will deal with a further difference – the fact that Serres conceptualizes pure multiplicity as a state of fluid turbulence, while in Guattari the image of turbulence is taken over by that of the aerosolic plane of immanence – in more detail in 'Process Ecology' (pp. 45–50).

At the same time, Guattari would agree that from the moment of the birth of the world onwards, the world is a dynamics of continuous flows and discontinuous cuts, and thus of a game of diverse, analog indifference and digital difference, that plays itself out on or in the plane of consistency as (the other side of) the plane of immanence. In 'Ecosophic Spaces' (pp. 152–82), I will explain why one should talk of being in rather than on a plane. Like Lucretius, Guattari conceptualizes the world as fundamentally processual. 'There is no initial state or terminal state with it. And consequently, there is no zero time of Big Bang, nor any rebounding on itself of the expansion of the cosmos. It is becoming processualizing itself, the heterogeneous in the process of differentiating itself' (SC: 94).

Consistencies: Invariance in Process

From a mathematical perspective, the moment of the *clinamen* might be said to describe the beginning of a vortical orientation within a vector space, and as such the birth of crystal orders from a stochastic chaos by way of the gradual orientation of heterogeneous vectors within that space. By way of recursive operations, which are operations that reproduce the same value upon every re-entry into a functional formalism, a field begins to accrue around a number of invariant values. According to these dynamics, the ecogenesis of entities can be visualized as the gradual coming-into-being, by processes of both actual contraction and virtual contemplation, of a field of density, or as the coming-into-being of a vortex around a centre of attraction. After the initial deviation of the *clinamen*, such recursive operations bring about the crystallization of more or less invariant sets. The result of such processes of consolidation or consistencing, which take place on even the infinitely small, most molecular levels, are consistencies that are in actual fact nothing but the set of invariant values that result from such recursive operations. In this context, invariance refers to the fact that these values keep the system within a specific computational envelope, creating what Bateson calls, in *Mind and Nature*, 'pattern[s] through time' (2002: 14). By way of such iterations, which might also be described as computational habits or routines, consistencies contract around a nucleus that Guattari calls, in *Schizoanalytic Cartographies*, an existential attractor. They separate themselves from the infinitely complex multiplicity of the processual space that surrounds them. They actualize specific vectors from a milieu that contains an infinite number of virtual – as in: potential – vectors. This extraction of a vectorial territory from a vectorial milieu is what makes it possible to define the emergence of consistencies as a process of crystallization. While such habit-formations make it possible to conceptualize entities without recourse to the notion of essence, at the same time, habits can easily harden into quasi-stable, and thus quasi-essential, routines. If certain habits become addictive – that is, if a habit becomes too much of a habit – the entity loses its plasticity.

If one assumes that entities are defined by the invariants that remain while they undergo changes, invariance can also be used to model entities in relation to the changes they undergo. Or, if one stresses the processual rather than the systemic side, habits isolate entities within processes by defining invariants within these processes. If no invariant can be identified within a specific process, the process is not *system*atic or *object*ive, because it is impossible to identify an invariant element that could be said to have undergone the process. In other words, to identify an invariant vector is to define an object in process by way of its invariant characteristics within that process. To identify, in other words, a systemic spine. The minimal definition of a consistency, then, is: something that undergoes change. From this perspective, it is only within the parameters of continuous change that a consistency can be defined as the invariance in undergoing transformational processes. Even where one cannot detect them because they might be infinitely faint or subtle, there are, in any kind of process, such invariants. This is why for the sciences, which see the world as an infinitely complex machinic system, the question about the presence of these invariants is epistemological rather than ontological. As they might exist for only infinitesimally short durations, or on the level of infinitesimally small levels of extensity, the ability to perceive them depends solely on the particular scale of temporal and spatial observation, such as that of a human eye, an electron microscope or the surfaces of sensation that allow a fish to perceive a current in the water or subtle changes in temperature. In other words, the world is both infinitely processual and infinitely consistent, although in terms of perception and operation it is only finitely so: *infinite ontology, finite epistemology*.

Once the notion that an entity has a structural or ontological essence is replaced by the notion that it is literally the set of invariants within a larger processual field – or, from the systemic side, a set of invariant characteristics within a process of constant transformation – truth is replaced by viability and essence by consistence. Any process of consistencing implies, however, processes of deconsistencing. In ecological terms, consistencies can only maintain an overall, operationally integrated consistency as long as they remain within the energetic ranges that allow them to remain coherent. If in the medium that it inhabits an entity can no longer operate within the tolerances that define its range of acceptable structural change, it will lose its overall coherence. As Varela stresses in *The Embodied Mind*, 'organism and medium mutually specify each other' (Varela et al. 1991: 197): *the pragmatics of ecology*.

This '*mutual specification* or *codetermination*' (198) of entity and milieu is what Guattari and Deleuze call 'reciprocal presupposition' (TP: 44). As they are 'mutually unfolded and enfolded structures' (Varela et al. 1991: 199), every change is dependant on the systemic history and the overall weather – as the set of probabilities – of that milieu: 'pattern formation and morphogenesis are highly constrained cellular choreographies that drastically delimit the scope of possibilities for change' (189). The entity's combined pasts lead up to its present and define its pattern of potentiality. As Varela notes, the 'historical formation of various patterns and trends in our lives is what Buddhists usually mean by *karma*' (116). A *caveat*, however: although I have argued that consistencies are defined by sets of invariants within processes of transformation, let me also stress that true, ideal invariance does not exist, as every entity is defined by constant, often imperceptibly subtle changes. Invariance, therefore, is a pragmatic and epistemological rather than an ontological value. This impossibility of true invariance lies at the centre of the 'ontological pragmatics' (SC: 35) that Guattari develops in *Schizoanalytic Cartographies*: *ontoecology*.

Process Ecology

If the recursive operations that underlie the gradual consolidation of both actual and virtual consistencies explain how consistencies come to cohere, they do not say anything about what kind of consistency consistencies have – including the consistency that is the world. Guattari's answer to that question can explain some of the most intriguing aspects of his notion of schizoecology. At the same time, it allows us to re-evaluate a number of common assumptions about Guattari and Deleuze's philosophy and politics. Earlier, I noted that vis-à-vis Lucretius, Serres conceptualized the world's fundamental multiplicity as a state of fluid turbulence. In Guattari, the state of fluid turbulence is aligned with that of aerosolic dispersion. This seemingly negligible shift in the multiplicity's aggregate state has immense consequences for Guattari's ecosophy, as well as for readings of Guattari and Deleuze as a variation of process philosophy.

An aerosol is a dispersed, colloidal system of solid or liquid particles in a gas, or, more abstractly, a mixture in which one substance of microscopically dispersed insoluble particles is suspended throughout another substance. The term, which is an abbreviation of aero-solution, was first used in the 1920s to describe clouds of microscopic particles in the atmosphere. Dust, fume, mist, smoke and fog are aerosols. When Deleuze compares the event 'to a mist rising over the prairie' (1990a: 24) he evokes an at this point virtual, aerosolic state: events form a 'faint incorporeal mist which escapes from bodies' (9–10). In contrast to such a virtual aerosol, an actual aerosol has an, if only infinitesimally subtle, extensity, such as the one that has in the history of science and philosophy defined, amongst others, the æther, electricity or light. While aerosols, as important agents of global warming, tend to have a bad press in today's ecologies, in Guattari's process ecology, the aerosolic has immensely positive connotations, and it fulfils a crucial function. As the world's ungrounded ground, it ensures that world's fundamental processuality. In *Schizoanalytic Cartographies*, Guattari notes that at some uncertain point in time and space, consistencies appear in the 'powdery diversity' (111) of the plane of immanence which lies '[l]ike an aerosol ... in a state of suspension at the heart of the "chaosmic" Plane of Consistency' (155).

For many readers of Guattari and Deleuze, this might be a somewhat surprising image. In readings of Guattari and Deleuze as a version or variation of process philosophy, it is the fluid rather than the aerosolic that tends to be championed over the solid. While it is uncontested that the fluid has an important function in Guattari's process ecology, I will propose that to trust in the fluid might not be adequate to the complexity of Guattari and Deleuze's thought [→ **Deleuze 31–5**]. Already in *The Anti-Oedipus Papers*, Guattari seems to have been thinking about the differences and similarities between the fluid and the aerosolic. The body without organs, he notes, is 'the epitome of all flows – ultimately, recourse to the punctum: weightless and infinitely divisible atom' (2006: 368).

According to Guattari's process ecology, both the physical world and the world of thought can only be administered in their aspect of being aerosolic. One of the more outrageous propositions Guattari brings to ecology, in fact, concerns a twofold aerosolics: If it is easy to imagine a living body as an auto-assembled ecology of a multitude of living cells that are enfolded and implicated within each other, it is perhaps more difficult, or at least more unusual, to imagine every thought as an auto-assembled ecology of smaller thoughts that are equally enfolded and implicated within each other. This, however, is precisely what Guattari's process ecology does when he maintains that a thought has the consistency of an aerosol, and as such forms a plane of consistency. If one takes seriously the idea that every thought is an embodied assemblage or ecology of dispersed, discrete drops or particles of thought – that it is, in terms of its state of matter, an aerosol that is animated and permeated by both conscious and unconscious changes, inflections and movements – it is difficult to fully comprehend, as in grasp, such a thought. If Deleuze notes in *Cinema 1* that there is a gaseous perception, in *Schizoanalytic Cartographies* Guattari proposes that there is also a gaseous thought.

Henry James's careful, slow-motion tracing of the complex movements, coagulations, solidifications and dispersions of the heterogeneous assemblages that literally are his characters' thoughts, and of the most subtle movements of lives constructed from an undifferentiated multiplicity of events, instantiates such a virtual aerosolics. His late work especially is written from within a deeply aerosolic poetics. As he notes in 'The Art of Fiction', 'the novel is in its broadest definition a personal impression of life; that ... constitutes its value, which is greater or less according to the *intensity of the impression*' (1984: 392, emphasis added). Not qualitative clarity of impression, but quantitative intensity of impression. To witness life, writing should be adequate to life in the quantities.

James uses an implicitly ecological image to express that every form of the measurement and of the administration of life should be based on perceptual and mental machines that are themselves infinitely aerosolic. 'Experience is never limited and it is never complete; it is an immense sensibility, *a kind of huge spider-web, of the finest silken threads, suspended in the chamber of consciousness and catching every air-borne particle in its tissue*. It is the very *atmosphere* of the mind; and when the mind is imaginative ... it takes to itself the *faintest hints of life*, it *converts the very pulses of the air into revelations*' (393–4, emphases added). There are particles floating in the air, experiences form an airy atmosphere, art translates quantitative pulses of air into qualitative, mental revelations: an aerosolic art that attempts to be adequate to an equally aerosolic world.

If Henry James creates a literary aerosolics, his brother William develops a psychological, philosophical and even a cosmic one. In his process philosophy *avant la lettre*, he uses the equally compelling, perhaps even more explicitly ecological image of a twofold, both physical and mental, aerosolics: 'If evolution is to work smoothly, consciousness in some shape must have been present at the very origin of things. Accordingly we find that the more clear-sighted evolutionary philosophers are beginning to posit it there. Each atom of the nebula, they suppose, must have had an aboriginal atom of consciousness linked with it; *and, just as the material atoms have formed bodies and brains by massing themselves together, so the mental atoms, by an analogous process of aggregation, have fused into those larger consciousnesses which we know in ourselves and suppose to exist in our fellow-animals*' (1890: 149). (See also his reference to M. Janet's notion of 'mental dust' (1890: 229).)

At first sight, this image of an aerosolic world seems to clash with James's famous remark that consciousness 'does not appear to itself as chopped up in bits ... it flows. A "river" or a "stream" are the metaphors by which it is most naturally described' (239). In talking of 'the stream of thought, consciousness, or subjective life' (239), James seems to conceptualize experience, at least in terms of human consciousness, from within a fluid rather than an aerosolic medium. Similarly, Guattari seems to subscribe to a fluid ontology when he notes that 'schizoanalytic subjectivity is established at the intersection of Flows of signs and machinic Flows' (SC: 20). With both William James and Guattari, however, the case is more complicated, and it is precisely this complication that differentiates Guattari's version of process philosophy from many recent readings of process philosophy, especially ones that are, somewhat ironically, inspired by Guattari and Deleuze. (On Guattari and William James, see also Pelbart 2011: 78–9.) By default, these readings relate the fluid to the smooth, the deterritorialized and the molecular, and the solid to the striated, the territorialized and the molar, making the fluid the favoured term. Nail's reading of Lucretius, for instance, which is informed by 'the waveform theory of matter' (2018: 212) and 'quantum field theory' (1), argues that 'all particles are fluctuations or effects of more primary field processes' (1). Like Lucretius, Deleuze and Serres before him, Nail celebrates Venus as 'the fluid kinetic conditions for philosophy itself. Venus is the watery encircling of the air' (27). While I find Nail's reading convincing, from a Guattarian perspective, his stress on Lucretius' fluid materialism, like Serres', is perhaps slightly too one-sided. If Venus is indeed 'the fluid multiplicity of foam' (27), one might equally describe her as the airy encircling of the water or as the aerosolic multiplicity of foam. While Nail stakes, like Serres, the morphogenesis of matter against idealist accounts of the birth of the world, Guattari and Deleuze propose the potentiality of the virtual plane of immanence as what Nail calls the inherent *voluptas* of motion. Nail and Guattari would agree, however, that the shell on which Venus stands 'does not grow like a plant grows, but like a crystal' (28).

The reason I stress Nails's fluid ontology is that Guattari would caution such fluid readings not to put too much trust in the image of process as a continuous flow, or, if these readings are Deleuzian, as the movement of pure becoming. In many ways one would be right to do so, but one should also remember that, famously, already in *A Thousand Plateaus* Guattari and Deleuze had cautioned their readers in the final sentence of 'The Smooth and the Striated' not to put too much trust in smooth, fluid space. 'Never believe that a smooth space will suffice to save us' (500). Such a fluid space needs to be aerosoled, Guattari will argue in *Schizoanalytic Cartographies*, because politics can only operate and take place in an aerosol. Against many readings of Guattari and Deleuze, in fact, there are no politics in and of the fluid in *Schizoanalytic Cartographies*.

Guattari is not only wary of any too-easy celebration of the fluid and of fluidity in process philosophies, he in actual fact reverses it. Somewhat counter-intuitively, in the fourfold, Flows are territorialized. It is not that good, deterritorialized and analog flows harden into bad, territorialized and digital assemblages. Rather, a process of fractalization that brings about the coming-into-being of difference aerializes Flows into the misty atmosphere of an infinitely differentiated network of crystal machines; into the aerosolic foam from which Venus rises. In the fourfold, the elements – Flows, Phyla, Territories and Universes – denote aspects of the world, and as such none of them can be favoured or taken to be more fundamental. As I will describe in detail in the next chapter, Flows and Territories are fluid and territorialized, while Phyla and Universes are aerosolic and deterritorialized. Crucially, while Flows are actual and real, Phyla are actual and possible. Although in terms of the fourfold Guattari notes that the 'actual real' (SC: 28) world shows itself first as 'Flows of matter and energy' (2), and then as Phyla, this does not imply a fluid ontology such as Nail's. From Guattari's position, Nail favours, perhaps too exclusively, the aspect of Flows.

Nail's fluid ontology implies the both temporal and philosophical antecedence of the fluid over the solid. While this is a fair move from the position of ontology, Guattari's fourfold does not stop at the ontological moment, and it does not develop from it an overall fluid ecology. Rather, the fourfold opens up a space in which the aggregate states of the fluid and the solid are in a state of complementarity. As such, it models an ecological weather, considered as an assemblage of the elements, in which the fluid and the aerosolic define two aspects of the world's dynamics. If the fluid aspect is inherently territorialized while the aerosolic is deterritorialized, that does not imply, however, that Guattari favours, in that context, the aerosolic over the fluid. Rather, the fourfold aligns the two aggregate states in an infinitely complex field of de- and re-territorialization that is invariably at the edge of chaos and far-from-equilibrium. A field of fluid atoms and particular fluids. Because what is a drop but a particular, miniature ocean, and a particle but a fluid quantum of energy within a field of forces?

William James comes close to a twofold, both actual and virtual aerosolics when, with his notion of a continuous flow of discontinuous experience, he sets the concept of a discrete continuity against the image of a fully fluid world. Perhaps Alfred North Whitehead's description of reality as drops of pure experience that have a neutral status as concerns subjectivity and objectivity in *Process and Reality: An Essay in Cosmology* echoes James's and foreshadows Guattari's aerosolics. Singular, atomic experiences of singular facts assemble into clouds. As Whitehead notes, 'the final facts are, all alike, actual entities; and these actual entities are drops of experience, complex and interdependent' (1978: 18). In this context, Whitehead's prehensions might be said to concern processes of comprehending (*Erfassen*) aerosolic systems. When he notes that these prehensions are 'not atomic' (235), this does not concern ontology or structure. Rather, in an affirmation of an experiential atomism, it means that atoms are invariably collections or congregations and thus that they 'can be divided into other prehensions and combined into other prehensions' (235): *aerosolic swarms*.

I will deal with the relation Guattari sets up between Flows and aerosolic Phyla in more detail in '1st Vector: From Flows to Phyla (Fractalization)' (pp. 75–80). For now, my argument for a both ontological and epistemological aerosolics rests on the fact that Guattari conceptualizes the plane of immanence as an aerosol that animates the plane of consistencies, which invariably contains forms, although these might be infinitely subtle. If the pure aerosol of immanence is in and of itself timeless and thus without history, every actualized, more or less consistent aerosol on the plane of consistency has a history that is intimately tied to the movements and interactions of all of the drops that make up that aerosol, as well as to the dynamics that relate it to its adjacent milieu. As Guattari notes in *The Anti-Oedipus Papers*, 'the plane of consistency is *historical reality*' (2006: 270). On the plane of consistency, the fully inconsistent, ultrafast, ultralight and dispersed aerosol of the plane of immanence is actualized in and runs at all times and in all places through the slowed-down aerosols that make up the plane of consistency. In 'Synaptic Time' (pp. 148–50), I will show how the virtual aerosol of concrete thought is aligned with the actual aerosol of the abstract machine by way of what Guattari calls the synaptic moment. The both abstract and concrete aerosols of thought emerge in this eminently ecosophic overlap. Ernst Mach uses a beautiful image for such a twofold, both given and giving aerosolics. 'On a bright summer day in the open air, the world with my ego suddenly appeared to me as *one* coherent mass of sensations, only more strongly coherent in the ego' (1914: 30): *aerosolic life, aerosolic thought, aerosolic ecology*.

Mach's image shows that one does not have to be a scientist or a philosopher to get an impression and an idea of an aerosolic ecology. All it needs is to look carefully at what goes on inside and around oneself. To take a walk. In fact, already at this point, here is the gist of Guattari's ecology: From Thoreau's 'Walking' to Varela's 'Laying down a Path in Walking', taking a walk is the perhaps best figure of Guattari's schizoecology. To the walker and thinker, the tableau of forms of life, of modes of living and of perceptual surfaces, while a constant source of wonder and surprise, is also a cause of concern. While scientists catalogue the experiments of nature in an attempt to understand their internal mechanisms, while artists transmute them into affects by way of painting, writing, music, film or architecture, in *Schizoanalytic Cartographies* Guattari creates their conceptual diagram. In this diagram, all forms and modes of life are registered on abstract levels of speed, movement, density and connectivity, as well as on concrete levels of entitarian affects and thoughts.

2 SCHIZOECOLOGIC CARTOGRAPHIES

> Félix reached an unusual level that contained the possibility of scientific functions, philosophical concepts, life experiences and artistic creation. This possibility is homogeneous while the possibles are heterogeneous. Thus the wonderful four-headed system in his *Cartographies*: 'Territories, flows, machines and universes.'
>
> Gilles Deleuze, 'For Félix', *Two Regimes of Madness* (382)

> What admixture, what interactions ought to occur between the flux (and resurgence) of the 'natural moment', in Henri Lefebvre's sense, and certain artificially *constructed* elements, introduced into this flux, perturbing it, quantitatively and, above all, qualitatively?
>
> 'The Theory of Moments and the Construction of Situations', unsigned, *Internationale Situationniste* no. 4 (June 1960)

[In]formal Diagram, In[formal] World

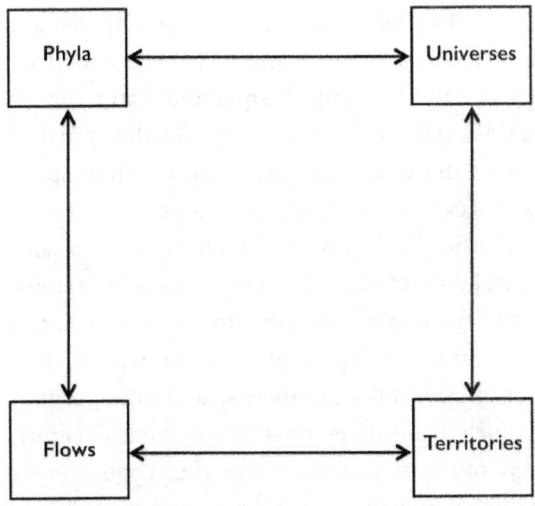

The Four Functors

ACCORDING TO GUATTARI, the fourfold is not a model of one specific process or structure, but rather a 'meta-model' (SC: 17) that should function as 'an instrument for deciphering modelling systems in diverse domains' (17). The complexity of this übermodel calls for an extended commentary. A reader's guide. Perhaps, in some aspects, *Anti-Oedipus* and *A Thousand Plateaus* might be read as such reader's guides. In my own commentary, in order to keep Guattari's overall argument in sight at all times, I will approach *Schizoanalytic Cartographies* at what might be called a medium level of entry. Below this level, many more levels define the fourfold in even more detail.

After a short introduction, all *Schizoanalytic Cartographies* does is to explicate, in often painstaking detail, the immensely complicated diagram that makes up the book's conceptual spine. As Guattari was a card-carrying Lacanian until his gradual and complicated fall-out with psychoanalysis, the book's many formalizations and the numerous diagrams of specific positions and conceptual vectors within the overall diagram must inevitably evoke the diagrams Lacan uses to formalize psychoanalytic axioms. For some, it might even evoke Lacan's growing obsession with ever more complicated mathemes, as well as his increasingly formalist interest in and use of knot theory.

One difficulty of explicating the fourfold is that a formal diagram, which is a diagram that conforms to the conventions of what we understand, by default, a diagram to be, does not in itself have a narrative along which one might structure one's analysis or commentary. Usually, a formal diagram provides a system's or a situation's structural, abstract blueprint, into which an infinity of potential stories may be inserted and whose possibilities it defines, in the way that the diagram of a subway network defines the abstract possibilities of the diversity and simultaneity of an infinite number of concrete, singular trips. In other words, a formal diagram subtracts from a structure or situation any form of context. Rather than tell a story, it provides a spatial and conceptual frame for the possibility of the telling of stories. In the case of the fourfold, one might say that it provides the space to conceptually square any structure or any-situation-whatever (*situation quelconque*). At the same time, Guattari provides the fourfold with a narrative in that his own explication goes along a both temporal and conceptual vector that concerns processes of heterogenesis and singularization. Earlier, I could talk of the Flows as the first and of aerosolic Phyla as the second aspect of the world because this temporal vector proceeds from the lower left (Flows) to the upper left (Phyla), then across to the lower right (Territories) from where it ascends to the upper right (Universes). This chronological progression sequentializes and thus separates the four aspects of the world that, in their spatial superposition, form the conceptual space within which it becomes possible to think Guattari's schizoecology. In fact, one might think of this sequentialization as analogous to the one that defined the moment of the *clinamen*. Like that sequence, this one sequentializes what is, at infinity, one simultaneous instant. When I talk about that sequence using temporal qualifiers such as first, later, then or before, this should always be taken as a gesture that introduces a formal, epistemological distinction that qualifies something that, from an ontological perspective, cannot be distinguished.

The structure of this chapter takes up this twofold logic. After positioning the fourfold in relation to the notions of formal and informal diagrams, and after a short introduction to the terms that are aligned in the fourfold, it first proceeds by way of a number of conceptual foldings, and thus by way of spatial superposition and implication (*im-plicare*). (Even though these foldings are by necessity sequentialized, they should ultimately be thought of as simultaneous.) This series of foldings traces the construction of the complex conceptual topology of the diagram and, by extension, of Guattari's schizoecology. After these foldings, the chapter follows the fourfold along its temporal, narrative vector from Flows to Universes (*ex-plicare*). This twofold analysis of the fourfold ends with a look at the way the fourfold squares the notions of striation and smoothing, which provides the most direct conceptual figure of Guattari's schizoecology. Taking up the overall structure of *Schizoanalytic Cartographies*, the chapter ends with four shorter sections on specific squarings that are performed by the fourfold. These squarings concern Guattari's conceptualization of philosophy, of psychoanalysis, of aesthetics and of media studies.

One of the most important questions raised by *Schizoanalytic Cartographies* is how to adequately diagram Guattari's general ecosophy, in the original sense of marking out by lines. How to develop a conceptual milieu in which to think both an eco-ontology and an eco-epistemology. Together, the two sides of the fourfold provide this conceptual, onto-epistemological milieu. The mode in which it does this, however, is unusual. Although it might look at first sight like a formal diagram, the fourfold does not adhere to the default function of such a diagram, which is to provide the schematic rendering of a system's abstract structure that disregards specific, concrete situations within that structure; to subtract these situations from the structure. All formal diagrams are based on such a logic of reduction that Jorge Luis Borges has ironized in his short story 'On Exactitude in Science', in which an abstract map becomes as concrete, and thus identical to, the territory. The function of the fourfold is more paradoxical. It is to provide a simultaneously abstract and concrete rendering of a system and its situations: *meta-modelization*.

Programmatically, in the context of his both terminological and conceptual shift from subject to assemblage of enunciation, Guattari stakes the fourfold against two of contemporary culture's most influential formal diagrams: psychoanalysis and capitalism. For Guattari, what is generally known as the subject or the individual is inevitably part of a milieu of 'collective apparatuses [*équipements*] of subjectification' (SC: 2). In this milieu, 'all machinic systems, whatever domain they belong to – technical, biological, semiotic, logical, abstract – are, by themselves, the support for *proto-subjective processes*' (2, emphasis added). As elements in and of such a constantly changing machinic milieu, assemblages of enunciation are both processual and inherently ecological. This being-processual and being-ecological is why they cannot be captured by the 'fixed and invariant' (24) maps that are provided by formal diagrams. 'In the domain of subjectivity' (24), such fixed maps 'are established in certain areas of an Assemblage (as is the case for the Oedipal triangle in the Capitalist field of production)' (24). Already here, the square of the fourfold is staked against the formal diagram of the triangle of psychoanalysis, which provides that system's structural blueprint by way of subtracting from that system all of its concrete and structurally superfluous characteristics. It reduces the concrete situations of its subjects to the abstract form of the oedipal triangle. A second aspect of a formal diagram is that it provides an overview of a system from a position outside of that system, which is a transcendental position Guattari and Deleuze often abbreviate as $n+1$. Again, the psychoanalytic diagram is a case in point in that the form of psychoanalysis that underlies that diagram lies on a level outside of the diagrams that it produces. It establishes what Guattari and Deleuze call a plane of transcendence. This is why, as Jacques Derrida noted, wherever psychoanalysis looks, it finds itself.

If it is not a formal diagram, it would be inviting to identify the fourfold with what Deleuze, as well as Guattari and Deleuze, call an informal diagram, which is a term that is easily misunderstood and, at first, eminently counter-intuitive and paradoxical. Although it shares some of the aspects of an informal diagram, however, the fourfold also differs in important ways. Perhaps it might be considered to be the formal, virtualized version of an informal diagram. In fact, the conceptual beauty and challenge of the fourfold, in particular its challenge to other theories and practices of ecology, resides in its position in-between a formal and an informal diagram.

Although Guattari and Deleuze sometimes use formal diagrams to visualize specific conceptual constellations, the more interesting diagrams are informal, $n-1$ diagrams, which do not presuppose, as do formal diagrams, a given formalism. They are diagrams of a Lucretian world made up of pure multiplicities and ordered multiplicities. Diagrams under the condition of a given multiplicity. In this light, the question raised by informal diagrams is how to capture a given world that cannot be reduced to a set of stable forms and laws, that is always both abstract and concrete, and that, as part of the milieu it describes, itself forms the milieu within which it is constructed. In this light, the challenge of the fourfold is how to share Borges' logic of being both utterly abstract and utterly concrete, without, however, coming to crush the territory.

In Guattari and Deleuze's terms, a diagram that is adequate to such a task would have to provide a *survol* – which is a term they take from Raymond Ruyer – from within that world rather than from without. It would have to be a low-flying diagram that models the infinitely many and complex operations in-between all of that world's fractal layers – the world's coagulations, stratifications and destratifications – from within that fractal space. Ultimately, it would need to model an always time- and site-specific blueprint of the energetics and the intensities of the world and of its changes under the condition that there is no dimension outside of that modelled world.

In the work of Guattari and Deleuze, the informal diagram is linked to the virtual and the actual as the most general of these mutual presuppositions in which, despite the logic of that symmetrical presupposition, the virtual often seems to have a conceptual and even a chronological primacy over the actual that echoes the primacy of the fully virtual aspect of the world as the plane of immanence over its actualized aspect as the plane of consistencies. Like the virtual during the inevitable moment and process of its actualization, for instance, 'the informal diagram is swallowed up and becomes embodied ... in two different directions that are necessarily divergent and irreducible' (38). It is at this point that the world is split into the two aspects of the virtual as actualized and the actual as virtualized. Or, in a variation of Spinoza that evokes the relation between the plane of immanence and the plane of consistency, virtual and actual are one and the same thing, conceived first under the attribute of thought, secondly, under the attribute of extension. In other words: *diagrammatic complementary.*

Although the fourfold takes up many of the conceptual elements of the informal diagram, Guattari gives it a crucial twist. When in *The Logic of Sensation* Deleuze reads Francis Bacon's first brushstrokes as the informal diagram that corresponds to the storms of light that it actualizes in coloured pigment, the strict formalism of the fourfold is almost diametrically opposed to such an informal diagram. While Bacon's brushstrokes stress the actual aspect of the informal diagram, the fourfold – as a conceptual diagram of the world's ecological forces considered as the dynamics of both formalizing and informalizing processes that pertain to the existence in the world to whose functionings it conceptually corresponds – stresses its virtual aspect. In its very formal and conceptual exactitude and rigour, it captures the world's simultaneous informality and formality. As this is done from within the logic of virtual conceptualization rather than actual embodiment – from within philosophy rather than art, that is – its deceleration of the aerosolic plane of immanence is perhaps even fainter than it is with Bacon. If Bacon actualizes the world's ultrafast informality in faintly decelerated, actual pigment, Guattari virtualizes a world that is both actual and virtual in a diagram that provides a lined, faintly actualized image of concepts. Paradoxically, in its actualization of virtual concepts in abstract lines, it brings the full force of virtualization to bear on that world. As a formal diagram of the both time- and site-specific, both formalizing and informalizing processes that take place in a world that is at the same time infinitely formal and infinitely informal, the fourfold is both extremely abstract and extremely concrete. Is it not, however, an informal diagram in formal clothes, nor is it a formal diagram in informal clothes. Rather than opting for one register, or setting these registers against each other, one should think of the fourfold as conceptually raising both registers to their highest possible potential: *full informality, full formality.*

If the beauty of Bacon's paintings lies in an artistic transmutation of actual pigment into affective form, the beauty of Guattari's diagram lies in how it transmutes, or, as Deleuze might say, how it philosophically spiritualizes the world into a conceptual aerosol or powder: *ecosophy.* (Genosko notes that Guattari's notion of aerosolic affect differs from Deleuze's Spinozism: 'and he notes as much, referring to the effect on his thinking of affective "atmospherics" (hazy yet comprehensible) borrowed from phenomenological psychiatry; specifically, Guattari gleaned this from Arthur Tatossian' (2009: 160).) Perhaps one might say that in the fourfold, an informal diagram is present in a seemingly formal one in the same manner in which the plane of immanence is present in the plane of consistency as an excess that does not stop pervading it. In its ecologization of the informal and the formal, the fourfold is both transcendental and empirical. Both abstract and concrete: *fully abstract, fully concrete.*

In *Schizoanalytic Cartographies,* Guattari reorganizes the relation between these two aspects. He retains the idea that entities emerge within this almost blind and mute informal diagram, which would be a diagram of the world in and for itself, by and in which that world expresses itself. He stresses, however, that these entities are aspects of this world and thus that it is from within a logic of expressionism that one has to diagram the way in which the world is given a voice, or, more accurately, a multiplicity of voices. The fourfold diagrams this ecological polyvocality of an in itself almost mute world. As the strictest of actualizations of the infinite, irreducible virtual multiplicity of the world, as well as of that world's modes of formation, the fourfold does not only model that complementarity, it is itself a figure, or perhaps more precisely a diagram of that complementarity.

While all of the above concerns the diagram as a form, let me, in what follows, provide a first overview of its content. What are the aspects of the world that are aligned within the fourfold? What are the four functors mentioned by Deleuze – Flows, Phyla, Territories and Universes – that, taken together, make it possible to delineate Guattari's schizoecology? And, how exactly are these aspects related?

Guattari's Figure 1.1 shows the complex relation of the four functors. In telegrammatic shorthand, in the fourfold's conceptual quadrophonics – what is known in acoustics as 4.0 surround sound – the abscissae align, on the left side, 'material and signaletic Flows' with 'abstract machinic Phyla' and, on the right side, 'existential

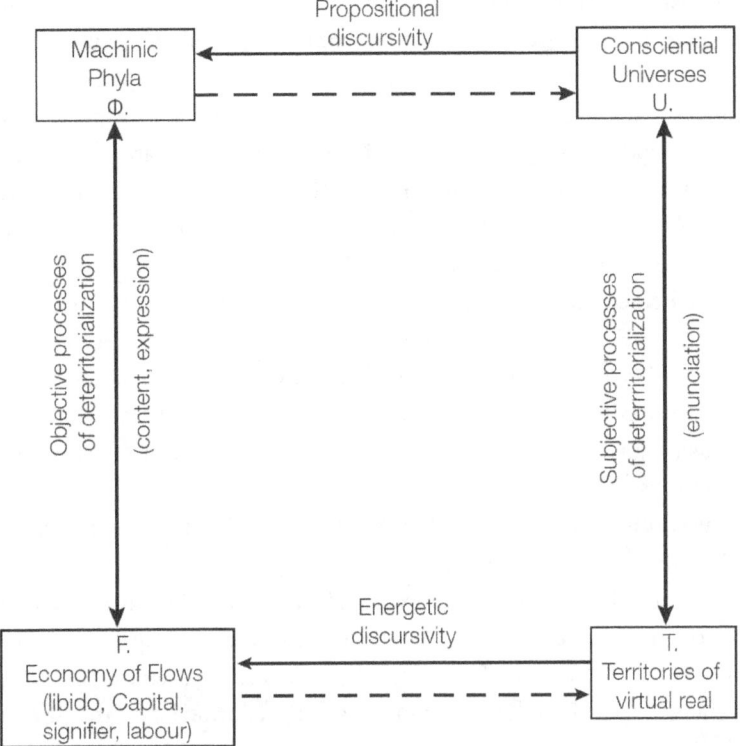

FIGURE 1.1 Discursivity and deterritorialization

Territories' with 'incorporeal Universes' (SC: 26). Accordingly, the lower ordinate aligns Flows and Territories, while the upper ordinate aligns machinic Phyla and Universes. In Guattari's most economic notation, which he will use throughout the book, the fourfold aligns the fields of F, Φ, T and U. As I noted in reference to Nail, Flows designate the world as actual and real, Phyla as actual and possible. Territories designate the world as virtual and real, Universes as virtual and possible. The positions on the fourfold's left side define the given, actual world in its aspects of how it is given to itself, which is first as Flows and then as Phyla. The right side defines the world as the giving – that is, as its consistencies – in the aspects of those consistencies' creation of virtual Territories and Universes. The two sides taken together chart the ecological relations between the anonymous world, individual life and individual thought.

Along the fourfold's vertical axis, Flows and Phyla are actual and thus extensive, while Territories and Universes are virtual and intensive. Although the actual real world shows itself first as Flows of matter and energy, this fluid world is only one of the world's aspects, and although the genesis of a schizoanalytic subjectivity takes place in Flows, in the process of creating from that actual real aspect of the world, the aspect of the world as a field of 'actual possibilities' (28), these Flows undergo a process of fractalization that atomizes them into Phyla. From its aspect and aggregate state of being fluid, it changes into aerosols. As Guattari describes this shift from the real to the possible, 'fractalization concerns the systemic articulations and lines of possibility relative to the discursivity of Flows' (177). (According to context, I will call Phyla, following Guattari, abstract machine, rhizome or, more generally, network.) On the actual side, which concerns a field that is objective, quantitative, extensive and abstract: '1) Flows of matter and energy; 2) the abstract machinic Phyla that preside over *objective* laws and changes' (52, emphasis added). While the actual side of the fourfold designates the world as the given, the virtual side, which designates the world as the giving, the 'virtual real' (28) aspect of the world that shows itself in fluid, continuous Territories also opens up, by way of a virtual fractalization, to its aspect as discontinuous, aerosolic Universes: the world in its aspect of 'virtual possibility' (28) and aerosolic virtuality.

On the virtual side, then, which concerns a field that is subjective, qualitative, intensive and concrete: '3) existential Territories, considered from the angle of their self-enjoyment (their "for itself") and, finally, 4) incorporeal Universes, which escape from the energetic, legal, evolutionary and existential coordinates of the three preceding domains' (52). As I argued earlier, it is in the field of the giving that the hope for an ecological ethics lies, not in the fluidity of the given world in its aspect of being actual and real, although all four aspects are equally important for a consistencing, and thus ecologization, of the allover world. As Guattari notes, 'by virtue of their relations of reciprocal presupposition (indicated on the abscissae), and their relations of composition (indicated on the ordinates), the four functors ... deploy four domains' (26). Within this reciprocal presupposition, the fourfold diagrams two complementary assemblage theories. One of the central ideas of schizoecology follows from this: a virtual thought is as assembled and composed – as constructed, that is – as an actual assemblage.

These two fields are layered onto each other in that the diagram is not only partitioned into an actual and a virtual side but also in that these two sides also separate it into the side of the world as such and the side of its concrete entities or consistencies. 'There is the Given, thus there is the Giving' (58), Guattari notes, modulating Deleuze's differentiation of the given and the given as given from *Difference and Repetition*. 'Difference is not diversity', Deleuze had noted. 'Diversity is given, but difference is that by which the given is given, that by which the given is given as diverse' (1994: 222).

If one looks at the fourfold from the perspective of the hetero- or ecogenesis of entities, one might maintain that on the plane of consistencies, the given comes, both temporally and conceptually, before the giving. While the virtual plane of immanence comes before the plane of consistencies, on that plane, the actual world seems to come before its creatures. When one considers the four functors as different aspects of the world, however, the temporal sequence turns into a logical relation: thus there is the Giving. Although the given presents itself, as the given, to the giving, which might imply a temporal sequence, from the very beginning the two sides cannot be separated. 'There is the Given, there is the Giving, but neither the one nor the other should be considered as subjected to compartmentalized domains of consistency' (SC: 59). In fact, domains and degrees of consistency are distributed along the horizontal axis, which cuts, in both the actual and the virtual fields, across the vertical one. While Flows and Territories have a high degree of consistency and are given in the mode of the continuous, Phyla and Universes have a low degree of consistency and are given in the mode of the discontinuous. As Guattari notes, 'the Phyla will constitute the "integrals" of Flows, as it were, and the Universes, the "integrals" of Territories' (28). Given this fourfold organization, one always needs at least two cursors to chart a specific position within the fourfold; one that moves along the horizontal and one that moves along the vertical axis. Degrees of mutual presupposition and of consistency that apply to all kinds of milieus and situations are defined in the movement of these two cursors. In terms of psychoanalysis, for instance, as shown in Guattari's Figure 1.4 (p. 105), the actual side concerns the libido, while the virtual side concerns the unconscious.

Consistencies are constructed within the four heterogeneous domains according to the 'diverse modalities of "transversality"' (52) that pertain between them. In fact, *Schizoanalytic Cartographies* is an investigation into the different modes of such transversality. Originally a mathematical term that defines the geometrical treatment of the intersection of spaces, Guattari took up the term many years before it became famous in cultural studies in the context of the notion of intersectionality, to describe complex situations from within topological registers. As Guattari writes, 'The "transversalist" function' affords the 'possibility of traversing the districts of time and space, and of transgressing identitary assignations'; it 'is found in the heart of the Freudian cartography of the unconscious and also, although in a different sense, in the preoccupations of linguists concerned with enunciation' (2009b: 297). As I will explain in more detail in 'Fractal Space: Guattari's Leibniz' (pp. 155–80), Guattari relates transversality to the fractalization of dimensions into a dimensional multiplicity that allows for quasi-continuous passages between and intersections of levels that remain mathematically, as in formally, distinct. Despite the fundamental transversality of the fourfold's fields, however, Guattari sets up a number of spatial and thus logical constraints, such as '*a principle of exclusion* that forbids direct tensorial relations between, on the one hand, the consistencies F and ∪ and, on the other hand, the consistencies T and Φ' (SC: 58).

The content of the four functors is suspended within their logical and formal positions. In very abstracted terms: Flows denote movements that are given, continuous, actual and real. According to the recursivity of the fourfold in terms of covering different plateaus and its applicability across plateaus, these can be all kinds of flows, from flows of lava or libido to flows or money or tears. Phyla, which are analogous to what Guattari and Deleuze at other moments call rhizomes, denote discontinuous networks made up of given, discontinuous, actual and possible elements. These networks also pertain to very different plateaus and contexts, such as atoms, musical notes, colours or people. Although both Territories and Flows denote continuous movements, movements in Territories are giving, virtual and concrete. They define the affective relations consistencies have to their environment. A flower produces a Territory, as does a tick, a beaver or a chemical composition. In fact, every consistency comes with an affective Territory that is created by living in a specific milieu, which might in fact be described as a complex layering of shifting, concrete Territories.

In *Schizoanalytic Cartographies*, consistencies rely in their existential consolidation on habitual, recursive routines that create self-similarity. Guattari's term refrain captures this coming-into-being of a structured field – that is, a Territory – through the gradual emergence of an orientation by way of iteration, regardless of whether that routine is mathematical, physical, biological or narratological: 'Under the generic term "refrain", I will group reiterated discursive sequences, closed on themselves, having as their function an extrinsic catalysis of existential affects' (207). A refrain – which Guattari describes in *The Machinic Unconscious* as a '*nomos*' (107) that in its original meaning of habit or convention, denotes a kind of 'sonorous seal, a short melodic formula' (107) – stakes out a Territory in a song. So does a repeated route one takes to work, or, generally, any habit that creates a habitat. A Territory describes a lived and lived-in space, or a perceived system in which a subject 'feels at home', Guattari notes in *The Anti-Oedipus Papers* (2006: 421). The transversality of Guattari's meta-model implies that such refrains can be found in different conceptual regimes and on different plateaus. 'Refrains can take rhythmic or plastic form, be prosodic segments, faciality traits, emblems of recognition, leitmotifs, signatures, proper names or their invocational equivalents; equally they can be established transversally between different substances . . . They can be of a sensible order . . . or a problematic order . . . just as much as of the order of faciality' (SC: 207). To complete the circuit from lower left to upper right, Universes denote, in analogy to Phyla, deterritorialized networks made up of discontinuous elements. Unlike Phyla, however, these networks are giving, discontinuous, virtual and concrete. Universes concern mental rather than material life.

Together, the two vertical columns form the two assemblage theories of the world in its aspect of for itself and in its aspect of its consistencies as spiritual automata that, as the giving, express and create this given world; in Louis Hjelmslev's terms, the world in its aspects of content and of expression. On this level of description, the fields taken together also provide the space for overall movements of smoothing and striation, and of the construction of more or less ordered consistencies and multiplicities within them. The ecologically most important and fascinating aspect of the fourfold is that the fields of the given and of the giving, and thus those of content and expression, are conceptually and topologically superposed. It is in this superposition, or folding, that Guattari's schizoecology emerges and resides.

Folding the Fourfold

Guattari choice of the figure of a fourfold is symptomatic in that he aims to evade both a binary logic, which tends to work according to digital either-or operations, as well as a triangular logic, which defines in particular psychoanalysis and which still underlies most of the diagrams in *The Machinic Unconscious*. As he notes in *Schizoanalytic Cartographies*, 'axiomatics with two terms ... necessarily result in a "depotentialized" representation and an inaccessible "grund", whilst dialectics with three terms lead to pyramidal, arborescent determinations ... It is only with 3 + n entities that one can establish: 1) a trans-entitarian (matricial) generativity, without any essential priority of one essence over another ...; 2) a principle of self-affirmation, auto-retroaction, a self-transcending ... or auto-poietic (Francisco Varela) foundation' (69).

Let me start my delineation of Guattari's fourfold thought by looking at the diagram's overall conceptual and spatial topology. Guattari calls the conceptual plane laid out by the fourfold 'an infinitely proliferating phase space of possibility' (134). To describe the space of thought from which and within which to think the world as a phase space is a very conscious and mathematically informed decision. It evokes the mathematicians Ludwig Boltzmann, Henri Poincaré and Willard Gibbs, who developed the term in the late nineteenth century to represent, by way of mathematical diagrams, all possible states of a particular system.

Echoing that definition, the fourfold diagrams a logical rather than a chronological space – which mathematicians call state space or state diagram – that would track the movement of dynamic systems through a temporal sequence. As in Boltzmann, Poincaré and Gibbs, in Guattari the notion of phase space denotes a fundamental, given space within which all potential and possible states of the system of the world can be modelled. Already on this level, the fourfold is decidedly ecological in its superposition of two planes or surfaces; in its setting up of a complementary relation between a chaotic surface of unlimited potentiality and of a surface on and in which the construction of both actual and virtual consistencies commences. As Guattari notes, the relation between these two surfaces is one of mutual expressionism. 'Concretely, it is a question here of all the expressive matters open to the facets of mutation and creation: genetic, ethological, semiotic codes, semiologies and the ensemble of situations in which a "constructivist" Expression is grafted onto material – phonic, scriptural, organic – chains, by starting to play the double game of being-for-itself what it is, through the modular relations that articulate it, and of being-for-something-else, elsewhere and after, as a function of a variety of memorial and possibilistic pro-positions' (134). Depending on the aspect that he stresses at a particular moment, Guattari will talk of the given space within which formations occur and on the background of which these formations are conceptualized, as the chaotic plane of immanence and as the plane of consistency or of consistencies.

1st Folding: Immanence | Consistencies

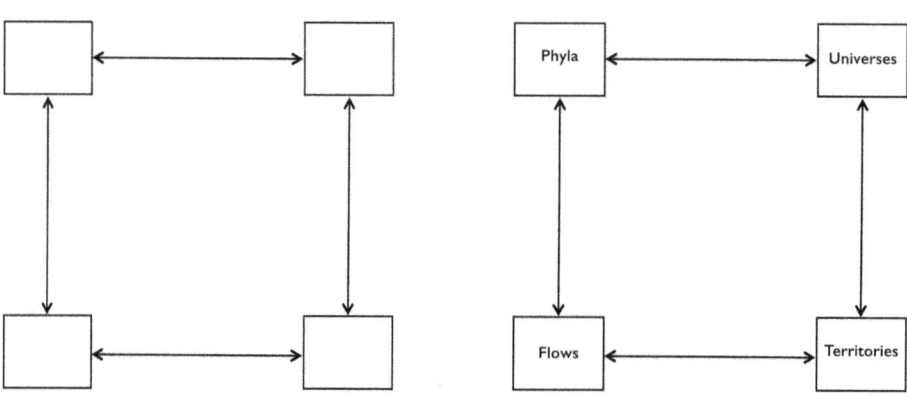

In Serres' terminology, the complementarity of these two planes, which are equally central in the work of Guattari, of Deleuze and of Guattari and Deleuze, is that of the plane of pure multiplicity and of ordered multiplicity respectively. According to this distinction, the immanent aspect is related to a chaotic state that Guattari in *Schizoanalytic Cartographies* defines in terms of the infinite speed at which states appear and disappear in it [→ **Deleuze 164**]. Evoking a later argument from *What is Philosophy?*, in which Guattari and Deleuze state that unlike philosophy, science gives up the notion of infinity, and without too much concern for the laws of physics, Guattari maintains that this infinite speed transgresses even the scientific limit set by the speed of light as the point-at-infinity of acceleration. On this plane things happen 'at an infinite speed of transformation . . . , transgressing the sacrosanct principle of contemporary physics based on the speed of light, which consists in fixing a threshold limiting the size of the ensemble of possible speeds' (SC: 105). The only characteristic of this plane is that it has absolutely no characteristics. That is, it is without consistency and without consistencies. It is, in mathematical terms, radically uneigen and informal. It has no eigenvalue and it does not contain forms. The only and basic principle that defines it are its constant, infinitely fast changes. (On infinite speed, see Plotnitsky 2006: 40.) As it is strictly without qualities, it should not even have its own possessive pronoun. According to Guattari, the plane of immanence cannot even be said to be, because there is no state of being in it. In all of Guattari's work, the dynamics of this completely deterritorialized and ceaselessly deterritorializing plane, whose multiplicity is denoted in Lucretian terms as turbulence, in Deleuzian terms as diversity, in Guattarian terms as an aerosol and in ecological terms as absolute wildness, make up the most fundamental and persistent forces in and of the world. It denotes a positive, active principle of ceaseless change that runs through all actual and virtual assemblages, and that provides the infinite potentiality needed to allow for and to create lines of flight in even the most decelerated and controlled of circumstances. It guarantees the potential openness of the future. As it is genetic, all forms and modes of territorialization are not prior to it, but rather concrete answers to its given force of deterritorialization. The plane of immanence is not a reservoir of change, however, that would store a potentiality for change. It is not an archive. Without consistency, and thus without memory and history, it is the site of the production, at each infinitely short moment, of an infinite potential for change in relation to the consistencings that happen on and in the fourfold in its aspect of the plane of consistency or of consistencies. The plane of immanence continuously charges that plane of consistencies with an ontologically given and thus inevitable potential for change and deterritorialization.

Guattari considers this ceaseless force of infinitely fast change, positively and affirmatively, as a source of infinite potentiality; as the productive ground of the world. If it is defined as a chaos, it is not chaos in its classical aspect of an apocalyptic, dark void, but as a genetic, ultralight aerosol. 'It is worth retaining a certain mistrust of overly static representations of chaos, especially those which would try to illustrate it in the form of a mixture, of holes, caverns, dust, even of fractal objects. What is particular about the chaos of the "primordial soup" of the Plane of immanence is that it can only exist in and as the process of "chaotizing" and in such a way that it is impossible to circumscribe a stable configuration in it and to maintain its consistency. Each of the configurations that it can outline has the gift of dissolving, at an infinite, if not absolute, speed. In its essence, chaos is rigorously ungraspable' (SC: 103).

As a space without states, this aerosolic chaos is fundamentally processual, although it would, more precisely, have to be defined as the infinitely fast succession of unconnected, heterogeneous moments of equally uneigen states. It is 'essentially glischroidic, without limit, without contour, without any possible internal displacement or division into subsets. Existence here is still only co-existence, trans-existence, existential transitivity, transversality' (105). Serres had described such a state as that of a pure energy exchange or Brownian motion. As Guattari notes, it is in 'the "originary" state of "Brownian" dispersion of redundancies of entity [sic]' as 'a place in which nothing referred to anything so as to refer to everything, at such a speed that nothing remains of these references. One might say that the memory ... of the arrangements of the soup of chaos equals zero' (119).

How are these two planes, as two aspects of the world, related? Although the planes are formally distinct, they should, at the same time, be thought of as ontologically complementary. As I noted, at infinity the planes of immanence and of consistency are in actual fact the same plane. Perhaps this is why Deleuze would talk about nature as 'the plane of immanence *or* consistency, which is always variable and is constantly being altered, composed and recomposed, by individuals and collectivities' (1988: 128, emphasis added). One way to conceptualize the connection between the planes is in terms of speed. The link is that, as Guattari points out, the primordial slowing down manifested in finite speeds is already present in chaos. 'We will be led to superpose the immanence of infinity and finitude onto the immanence of complexity and chaos; we will have to assume that the primordial slowing down manifested in finite speeds, proper to limits and extrinsic coordinates and to the promotion of particularised points of view, inhabits chaos just as much as the infinite entitative speeds which attempt to domesticate philosophy with their conceptual creations' (C: 112). As Guattari states, 'infinite speeds are loaded with finite speeds, with a conversion of the virtual into the possible' (112). From this perspective, 'chaos is not only the bearer of "pre-programmed" morphogenetic potentials, it harbours the processual embryos that enable mutant morphogeneses to be brought to light. It is seeded with "bifurcation points", with "mutant filters" for which no calculation can predict the position or the potentialities' (SC: 104): the informal diagram is already present in the plane of immanence.

Although Guattari differentiates formally between this 'chaotic hyper-complexity (virtual, non-discursive and constantly on the way to dissolution)' (104) that is without consistency because 'the very same compositions that I just said appear and disappear at infinite speed' (103), and 'ordinary complexity (which is proper to real Flows and possibilistic Phyla)' (104), there are forms of connection between these two complexities, one of which is, as I just argued, speed. Another way to connect them is to make use of the concept of superposition, which implies describing the two planes as complementary. 'Thus, we will be led to superpose the immanence of infinity and finitude onto the immanence of complexity and chaos; we will have to assume that the primordial slowing down manifested in finite speeds, proper to limits and extrinsic coordinates and to the promotion of particularised points of view, inhabits chaos just as much as the infinite entitative speeds which attempt to domesticate philosophy with their conceptual creations. The movement of infinite virtuality of incorporeal complexions carries in itself the possible manifestation of all the components and all the enunciative assemblages actualisable in finitude' (C: 112). There is no difference in kind, therefore, between the two planes. Already 'the "primordial soup" of the Plane of immanence is . . . populated by two types of entitarian state' (SC: 108). The difference is that between 'chaotic multiplicities composing and decomposing complex arrangements at infinite speeds', which is what Serres called unordered multiplicities, and 'existential filters selecting relatively homogeneous sets of arrangements characterized by the iteration of local and localizing decelerations' (108), which is what Serres called ordered multiplicities. The difference between quantities and qualities is tied to this logic. The latter never leave the space of quantities. On, or in, the plane of immanence 'filters are constituted as interfaces between: 1) the virulent virtualities of chaos, stochastic proliferations; and 2) actual potentialities that can be listed and consolidated' (109). As O'Sullivan notes, 'chaos already contains complexity and that complexity is always already composed out of a chaos from which it emerges and towards which it returns' (2012: 99). While O'Sullivan defines the relation between chaos and complexity from within a chronological chiasm, according to the logic of complementarity, which is the same as that of the virtual and the actual, the virtualities of chaos are, at one and the same time, complex actualities: *the possibility of ecology.*

In the informational terms Serres has excavated from Lucretius, the chaotic state of 'hyper-complexity' (SC: 104) denotes a state without redundancy. It is without form and formation. In sonorous terms, it is a state of constant white noise; in visual terms, a state of pure whiteness. In semiotic terms, it is a state of turbulence that equals infinite information. Somewhat counter-intuitively, all constructivisms are based on this plane's power to bring about change. In another of Guattari and Deleuze's terminologies, it is the ultimate war machine. Although the image is not fully adequate to the topology of complementarity that defines the two planes, one might think, for now, of the plane of consistency as the other side or, more concisely, as another aspect of the plane of immanence and vice versa. In Serres' reading of Lucretius, the chaotic plane was instantly transformed into a plane of consistency that was defined by a fundamental constructivism and that was everywhere populated by consistencies, even if these were, in the beginning, fleeting and germinal.

In order for the world to go on, however – symptomatically, Lucretius' image of the history of the world was that of an entropic slope – the differential plane of consistencies must be continuously charged with the potentiality that is provided by the state of pure diversity. If I talked of transformation, therefore, this does not mean that the chaotic plane of immanence vanishes in order to give way to the plane of consistencies. The transformation is conceptual rather than chronological. For Guattari and Deleuze, the plane of consistency is an aspect of the plane of immanence and vice versa. In scientific terms, the former is the figure of a pure chaos, the latter is the figure of a deterministic chaos. That is why Guattari noted, evoking the terminology of quantum physics, that the two planes are in a state of superposition.

The threshold between chaos and construction runs along the plane of immanence's aspect of being the world's most chaotic ground, and its aspect of being the carrier-medium of formations and consistencies. In relation to consistencies, the world's plane of immanence as the plane of consistencies is no longer completely neutral, but both destructive and constructive, as well as both deterritorializing and territorializing. In this double definition, the plane of immanence forms the ungrounded ground of the fourfold that in turn models the operations of consistencing and deconsistencing, or, in another of Guattari's terminologies, those of territorialization and deterritorialization that take place within it. Again, however, within is not quite the right word. As they stand in a relation of complementarity, at the same time that the two planes are formally distinct, the plane of immanence is the plane of consistencies and vice versa.

Topologically, the position of the plane of immanence might also be defined as the most interior outside of Guattari's fourfold. In fact, its spatial position is harder to describe than its logical position, which defines it, formally, as the fourfold's other side, while ontologically, it is the space of the fourfold. Again: the two planes are formally distinct, which is why one must differentiate between them, but ontologically indistinct, which is why one cannot differentiate them. Like particle and wave, the two planes are two complementary aspects of one and the same plane. Conceptually, the plane of immanence is the given space in which constructions take place. It designates the space in which the fourfold's four sections emerge as an overall plane of consistency.

Two axioms follow from this. The first is that the plane of consistencies is everywhere constructed except at a point of complete deterritorialization that lies at infinity. Wherever it seems to be amorphous, therefore, it is only apparently so. Any logic applied within the plane should be adequate to this infinite constructivism, which is pervaded by an equally infinite force of deterritorialization. The second axiom is that if all heteropoietic processes happen in far-from-equilibrium milieus – which is a term Guattari takes from nonlinear dynamics and Guattari and Deleuze take from the work of Gilbert Simondon – concepts such as truth need to be treated by way of a similarly far-from-equilibrium logic rather than by way of a formal logic, although that logic has its place on the plane of consistencies as well.

If both physical and psychic worlds are defined by the logic of consistencies, a fully chaotic space – that is, the plane of immanence – might be considered to be an idealization. The fourfold itself, however, precludes such an idealization. The solution to that problem concerns once more the complementarity or reciprocal presupposition of the two planes. While Deleuze uses these terms specifically to define the relation of the actual and the virtual as the most fundamental mode of complementarity, in Guattari this pertains generally between any relation of seemingly separate but in actual fact mutually determining fields, such as entity and environment. No environment without entities, no entities without environment, which is a logic that will come up again in terms of Hjelmslev's fields of content and expression.

In the fourfold, the most fundamental complementarity is that of the planes of immanence and of consistencies. According to the definition of complementarity in quantum physics, the two planes are either in a state of ontological superposition (in this case, they are one plane), or, once they are collapsed by an observer, they are epistemologically unfolded into either one of their aspects (in this case, they are formally two planes). In terms of topology, the notion of two sides of one plane is the collapsed version of a one-sided, spatially indifferent plane. If one collapses the plane, the informal plane of immanence provides an uneconomical, and thus unecological state of pure multiplicity as the world's foundation, while the formed plane of consistencies is defined by economies and ecologies. As in Lucretius, the plane of immanence, as the plane of consistency and vice versa, is the ontological plane to which everything on or also in the plane should be adequate. All constructions and consistencies are contained within the virtual plane of immanence, as 'the primary matter of virtuality, the inexhaustible reserve of an infinite determinability' (SC: 103). As I will show in 'Speeds of Determinability' (pp. 141–7), for something to have the infinite potential to be determined it must itself be infinitely undetermined. Itself infinitely unaffiliated, it must have an infinite availability for affiliations.

While the virtual has specific functions within the plane of consistencies, where it is always to some degree actualized, it literally is the plane of immanence. As I noted, however, there is always a moment-at-infinity where the two aspects of the plane converge. 'If one has come to accept that life, mind, desire and truth today exist "far from equilibrium", this is because they had to exist already, *in the night of time*, in the form of *powdery metamorphic bifurcations* at the heart of the most apparently amorphous of states' (52, emphases added). The plane of consistencies, in fact, is the plane of the actualization of these reserves and potentials: 'Chaos is not only the bearer of "pre-programmed" morphogenetic potentials, it harbours the processual embryos that enable mutant morphogeneses to be brought to light' (104). The fourfold, then, is the map of the plane of consistency as the plane of immanence, which together denote the two complementary planes of the chaotic and the 'chaosmotic' (155) sides of the world and of subjectification. It models the chaosmotic side of that world and of its creatures, but it is, for lack of a better image, pervaded by the aerosolic intensity of the plane of immanence. On the plane of consistencies, the ratio of determinability is spanned out between the two ideal extremes of the infinite stasis of being, and the infinite speed of the succession of unconnected states. Between existential intensification and immediate abolition. 'Let us note in passing', writes Guattari, 'that from such a point of view, the status of the virtual for an entity would consist in finding itself caught between two infinities: that of an absolute existential intensification and that of its immediate abolition' (103).

The notion of a fully virtual chaos in *What is Philosophy?* echoes the notion of chaos in *Schizoanalytic Cartographies*. In the former, it is again defined 'not so much by its disorder as by the infinite speed with which every form taking shape in it vanishes' (WP: 118). It is a void 'that is not a nothingness but a *virtual*, containing all possible particles and drawing out all possible forms, which spring up only to disappear immediately, without consistency or reference, without consequence. Chaos is an infinite speed of birth and disappearance. Now philosophy wants to know how to retain infinite speeds while gaining consistency, by *giving the virtual a consistency specific to it*' (118). Partly on the background of Gilbert Simondon, Guattari and Deleuze argue in *What is Philosophy?* that philosophy aims to retain the open, unformed milieu in which and by which the virtual is embodied in its actual. As Simondon had noted, 'the participational relationship connecting forms to their background is a relationship which straddles the present and brings the future to bear upon the present, that which brings the virtual to bear upon the actual. *This is so because the base is a system of virtualities, of potentials, and of moving forces, whereas forms are a system of the actual*' (1980: 51, emphasis added). While science deals in functions and reports about the actual, philosophy deals in concepts and it reports about the virtual. If actualization cancels out the purity of the virtual, it also brings about the shift from infinite potentiality to finite possibility. 'In general, a state of affairs does not actualize a chaotic virtual without taking from it a *potential* that is distributed in the system of coordinates' (WP: 122). Guattari and Deleuze argue that each consistency is literally in and of the both energetic and intensive milieu. 'From the virtual that it actualizes it draws a potential that it appropriates' (122). This appropriation of potentiality is why there are, according to Guattari and Deleuze, no closed systems. Not only is every system inevitably in touch with the plane of immanence as the plane of pure potentiality; more fundamentally, every system is, quite literally, one of its aspects. Even 'the most closed system still has a thread that rises toward the virtual' (122): *ontological and ecological expressionism*.

In *What is Philosophy?* the surplus virtuality is contained in the Guattari and Deleuzian event: 'if we go . . . from states of affairs to the virtual, . . . the virtual is no longer the chaotic virtual but rather *virtuality that has become consistent*, that has become an entity formed on a plane of immanence that sections the chaos. This is what we call the Event, or the part that eludes its own actualization in everything that happens' (156). That is, something in the event invariably exceeds its actualization. 'The event is not the state of affairs. It is actualized in a state of affairs, in a body, in a lived, but it has a shadowy and secret part that is continually subtracted from or added to its actualization: in contrast with the state of affairs, it neither begins nor ends but has gained or kept the infinite movement to which it gives consistency' (156).

From the point-of-view of having been actualized, the virtual is the name for the surplus intensity and potentiality that is embodied in and thus cancelled out by the crystallization of consistencies. It is in order to mark this difference that Guattari and Deleuze differentiate between the actual and the real. 'It is the virtual that is distinct from the actual, but a virtual that is no longer chaotic, that has become consistent or real on the plane of immanence that wrests it from the chaos – it is a virtual that is real without being actual, ideal without being abstract. The event might seem to be transcendent because it surveys the state of affairs, but it is pure immanence that gives it the capacity to survey itself by itself and on the plane' (156).

According to one of Guattari and Deleuze's basic conceptual gestures, this surplus intensity on the plane of immanence as the field of ultrafast quantity is an ideal, rather than the embodied intensity on the plane of consistency as the field of the idea and of quality; the ideal of an ultrathin, ætherial, living aerosol. 'What is transcendent, transdescendent, is the state of affairs in which the event is actualized. But, even in this state of affairs, the event is pure immanence of what is not actualized or of what remains *indifferent* to actualization, since its reality does not depend upon it. The event is immaterial, incorporeal, unlivable: pure *reserve*' (156, italics added). The pure event is the infinite potentiality that rushes through every form of actualized life: *full potentiality, all of the time.*

2nd Folding: Virtual | Actual

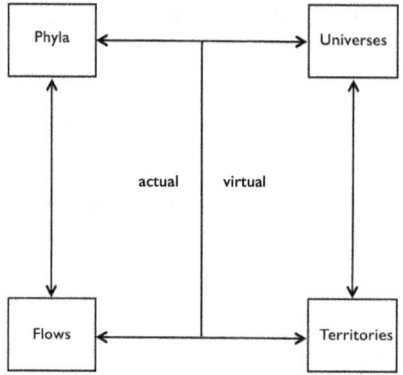

On or in the plane of consistencies, the decisive complementarity is that of being for itself and of being for something else, and thus of presenting itself to something other. Ecologically, the idea of a world for itself designates the deep paradox of a world without its entities. This world – as Guattari would say, the world in its aspect of being actual and real (Flows) or actual and possible (Phyla) – is simply as it is. All we can say about this world is that it is indeterminate, and as such neither helpful nor vengeful. This world will never choose sides in what we consider to be good or bad. It will never help us. The responsibility for our world as aspects of that world resides fully in us. In this responsibility, only multiplicity and change are on our side, although both of these can, have been and will be co-opted.

The paradox of being for itself and of being for something else concerns the fourfold's formal split into the sides of the given and of the giving; a formal differentiation that is forever undercut by the ontological and ecological complementarity between the two fields. There is the indeterminate, given world, and there are the concepts that its creatures epistemologically mine and extract from their measurements of that given world's purely quantitative states. I stress this because the notion of an indeterminate and indifferent world underlies, at all moments and from all aspects, Guattari's ecology. All notions about or images of the given world are assembled on the side of the giving, and as such all are phantasms or measurements projected onto a fundamentally indeterminate state of affairs; qualities projected into quantities, quantities measured by qualifying them.

Although I mentioned that Guattari takes the notion of complementarity from quantum physics, where observers collapse complementarity by qualifying and measuring it, I have used the term somewhat loosely and intuitively. In quantum physics, the foundational complementarity is that of particle and wave or entity and energy. In the following, I will ask whether this complementarity can be folded onto that of the actual and the virtual, or, which would be the same, onto the pair of extensity and intensity. In other words, can the two sides of the fourfold be folded onto each other along its vertical axis?

In quantum physics, complementarity is less about the indeterminate and indifferent world as such as it is about a logic of measurement as a process of the determination of that world. In this context, measurements enact the shift from an indeterminate to a determinate state. For Erwin Schrödinger, this concerns what has been called the collapse of the wave function. Consider Schrödinger's famous mathematical fable or thought experiment about a cat put into a black box wired up in such a way that a deadly amount of hydrocyanic acid gas is released or, with a similar probability, not released into its system, the random trigger of that release being dependent on the rate of decay of a radioactive substance. Schrödinger maintains that before the box is opened in order to find out which probability has actualized itself, the cat should be considered to be simultaneously both dead and alive. Schrödinger's conceit illustrates the idea that during the time that the cat is unobserved, it is in an indeterminate state in relation to being dead or alive. While it is unobserved, the cat cannot be said to be in a specific state of either being dead or of being alive, because the system of the cat is dissolved in the general indeterminacy of the box, which is at this point defined, like waves, as a communal, unparticular superposition of eigenstates. That is, the cat does not have its own eigenstate. Until its observation or measurement, therefore, the cat is indifferently or indeterminately both alive and dead. From within the conceptual given of superposition, the cat's states should be imagined as being equally mixed or smeared within the box before it is opened in order to see which of the cat's states has actualized itself. 'The Ψ-function of the entire system would express this by having in it the living and dead cat (pardon the expression) mixed [*gemischt*] or smeared out in equal parts' (1935: 157). Schrödinger's conceit shows that complementarity does not concern the object in and of itself, but rather the conceptualization of the act of measuring it. Only after systems have been identified and thus actualized through their measurement can they be said to be, like particles, in a specific state. In fact, before the measurement one cannot even talk of singular particles or systems. In other words, the process of measuring literally constructs particular systems: *quantum constructivism*.

If one considers the perceptual apparatus as a complex measuring device, it is not so much that given systems are measured, but that systems are constructed through their measurement. The measurement collapses the given indeterminacy in that a general state of indeterminate and indifferent superposition is reduced to a specific eigenstate. It is only at the moment of measurement that the eigenstate of the superposition – the Ψ-function – is collapsed in the sense that it is reduced to an individual eigenstate, or, more precisely, to one eigenvalue. Guattari's wager is that the logic of complementarity – the logic of the wave function and its collapse – is adequate to model the logic of how to address a fundamentally unknowable, indifferent and indeterminate, given world. Quite categorically, Schrödinger maintains that there simply are no values before the measurement. Measurements turn a quantitative, indifferent world into a qualitative, differential one. If 'a variable has *no* definite value before I measure it; then measuring it does not mean ascertaining a value that it has'. As 'reality does not determine the measured value' (1935: 158), it is only the repetition of the measurement that allows us to determine its accuracy. This is why the truth is only ever probabilistic or, in Deleuzian terms, false. All ecology is false in this way: *false ecology*.

In recapitulating Schrödinger's logic, the fourfold aims to be adequate to such an indeterminate world. As Manuel DeLanda notes in *Intensive Science*, the virtual 'leaves behind traces of itself in the intensive processes it animates, and the philosopher's task may be seen as that of a detective who follows these tracks or connects these clues' (2002: 44). If the tracing is adequate, 'the intensive will then be revealed to be behind both the extensive and the qualitative' (46). For DeLanda, this calls for philosophy to no longer 'perform this task via a set of propositions which refer to the virtual'. Rather, 'it must construct a thought which is *isomorphic with the virtual*' (174, emphasis added). For DeLanda's argument to accord to Schrödinger's logic, revelation would have to denote that this revelation concerns the virtual as hidden behind the actual. If it means that the virtual itself will be revealed, however, that would exceed the range of the knowable. The fourfold should not provide an explication of the true state of the world. What it should provide is a model that allows one to adequately address its indeterminate state, which means a model that does not fall back onto what Schrödinger considers to be a simple representational model. In this context, thought should perhaps not so much aim to be isomorphic with the virtual – in fact, thought is from the beginning virtual – but rather to be adequate to the world. Adequate to the world in its aspect of the quantitative. To be, in other words, ecological: *quantitative ecology*.

To sum up: Within the fourfold, a vertical complementarity concerns the reciprocal presupposition of the actual and the virtual. This complementarity is collapsed into a formal, measured difference between them, which is captured in their separation into the fields of the actual and the virtual. However, although these two sides are formally distinct, they are ontologically complementary in that they reciprocally presuppose each other.

3rd Folding: Particle | Wave

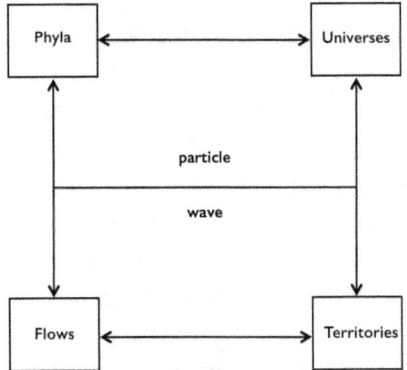

Although it is fundamental, the complementarity of the two levels of the virtual and the actual is not the only one that is operative in the fourfold. In fact, the fourfold might be described as a conceptual machine for the multiplication of complementarities. As there are any number of transversal relations between the four fields, one should in fact no longer talk of one general complementarity but rather of a multiplicity of complementarities. The complementarity that comes closest to that of quantum physics is that of particle and wave, which plays itself out along the fourfold's horizontal axis in the dynamics between Flows and Phyla and between Territories and Universes.

Guattari notes that on the actual side, the first functor implies going 'back up to the starting point: there are Flows; *the world presents itself in the form of fluctuation*' (SC: 75, my emphases), adding that 'flows only exist as intensive fluctuation'. Perhaps one might say that, in terms of quantum physics, Flows are figures of the indeterminate state of the wave function, while Phyla are figures of the state of the collapsed wave function. It is only in Phyla that machines exist that can measure states – if at that moment only potentially, because these machines are not yet of the giving – and that can themselves be measured. Again, the fourfold does not choose between Flows and Phyla. Waves and particles, one might say, are one and the same unknowable thing or state, conceived now under the attribute of thought, now under the attribute of extension. There is no relation of antecedence or precedence between them, that is, but one of complementarity. Even the notion of the ante- and precedence of continuity over discontinuity will lose its evidence when the two terms are squared in the fourfold. In terms of Nail's reading of Lucretius, this concerns the formal distinction between field and particle. The difference between Flows and Phyla, then, is one of aggregate state, not of ontology, and it is as different aggregate states that they concern specific aspects of the world. In Phyla, everything has a possible value.

Instantiating that possible value, however, which means measuring it, implies, in terms of the fourfold's conceptual logic, crossing over to the side of the giving. On that side, Schrödinger's logic also plays itself out horizontally between the complementary registers of virtual, immaterial and intensive states of continuous Territories and discrete Universes, with Territories being analogous to Flows and Universes being analogous to Phyla. At this point, the plane of immanence and the plane of consistencies, as well as all four functors, have been folded onto each other. The surface of the diagram has been folded into what Guattari will describe as its transversal, or fractal space. It is within these fractal foldings that the aspects of the fourfold are aligned and take place. In this fractal space, the fourfold diagrams the plane of consistency and consistencies as the constructivist aspect of the plane of immanence. One has to imagine, however, the positive force of deterritorialization of the plane of immanence to run, at all times and in all places, through that plane and all of its constructions. Within that plane, the four sections of the fourfold are 'radically heterogeneous domains' (18) that are related not so much by way of one overarching logic – Guattari distinguishes between four causalities that operate in it: formal, final, efficient and material – as by 'diverse modalities of "transversality"' (52), by fractal layerings of and movements between its four 'domains of consistency' (56). As Guattari states in 'Transversality', stressing its both fractal and oblique character, 'transversality is a dimension that strives to overcome two impasses: that of pure verticality, and a simple horizontality. Transversality tends to be realized when maximum communication is brought about between different levels and above all in terms of different directions' (MR: 18). At La Borde, this state was brought about by the famous grid (*la grille*), an inherently topological plan that allowed for the rotation of tasks that broke up the hierarchy between doctors and patients. In the passage '"Framing" the deregulation' of 'La Grille', a talk Guattari held on 29 January 1987, he describes it in the same terminology he used to describe the fourfold. It is a 'crossroads [*carrefour*]' (1998: 3); a 'hypercomplex operator' (10) that functions as 'a sort of instrument to regulate the necessary institutional deregulation' (4).

The foldings have shown that the world is indifferent, and by way of this indifference, it brings about a distinction into oppositions that are in actual fact complementarities, such as Flows and Phyla, Territories and Universes, Flows and Territories, as well as Phyla and Universes. Within these functors, the complementaries of extension and intension, actual and virtual, objective and subjective as well as waves and particles: from an ecological perspective, the complementarity of *the world and its creatures*. What counts for all of these is, as Niels Bohr noted, *contraria sunt complementa*: quantum ecology.

Vectorism: In the Fourfold

1st Vector: From Flows to Phyla (Fractalization)

	Actual	Virtual
Possible	Φ.: Phylum of actual possibility	U.: Universe of virtual possibility
Real	F.: Flux of actual real	T.: Territories of virtual real

FIGURE 1.2 The matrix of cross-relations of the four categories

In the next sections, I will shift from spatial to temporal registers. Within the fourfold, the specification of the four domains is not only in terms of actuality and virtuality, but also, within the actual, in terms of the real and the possible, as is shown in Guattari's Figure 1.2 [→ **Deleuze 47**]. Real actual Flows are complementary to possible actual Phyla. The same holds for the virtual side. Real virtual Territories are complementary to virtual possible Universes. Everywhere, particles and waves. While these complementarities are considered from within spatial and conceptual registers, Deleuze, as well as Guattari and Deleuze, also describe the actualization of the virtual that defines the vertical axis of the fourfold as a cancellation, and thus as a temporal process. A similarly temporal logic defines the shift from fluid to aerosolic along the horizontal axis. Although in *Schizoanalytic Cartographies* Guattari considers both of these shifts as changes of aspect – once from virtual to actual, once from real to possible – he replaces the somewhat tragic rhetorics implied by the notion of cancellation by the more ecological notion of the complementarity of potentialities and possibilities inherent in processes of fractalization from Flows to Phyla and from Territories to Universes. From this angle, these dynamics are no longer tragic. In fact, the shift from territorialized Flows to deterritorialized Phyla opens up the ecological field in the first place. The birth of the possible from a real world of Flows entails the birth of abstract machines [→ **Deleuze 90**]. Although Flows remain important, and although the vocabulary is still one of envelopment and subsumption, the shift is genetic and at first counter-intuitive in that the discontinuous is more powerful than the continuous. From the point-of-view of 'inter-entitarian' (SC: 27) processes, 'the Flows and the Territories of the real [are not] on an equal footing with the Phyla and Universes of the possible – the latter envelop and subsume the former in such a way that *the reality of the possible always has primacy over the possibility of the real*' (28, emphasis added): *rhizomatic ecology*.

As I noted in relation to process philosophy, the instigation of the realm of the possible does not entail a tragic hardening of Flows. Rather, it is a process of making Flows countable and measurable by turning them into aerosolic networks, within which one can formally differentiate between terms or nodes and relations or lines. In *The Fold: Leibniz and the Baroque*, Deleuze defines such a process, in terms of perception, as a process of aerosolization; of 'pulverizing the world but also of spiritualising its dust' (2001: 87). In mathematical and perceptual terms, Phyla and Universes integrate Flows and Territories. As Guattari notes, 'the Phyla will constitute the "integrals" of Flows, as it were, and the Universes, the "integrals" of Territories' (SC: 28). In 'Fractal Space: Guattari's Leibniz' (pp. 155–88), I will deal in more detail with the long Leibnizian shadow that looms over Guattari's conceptualization of how exactly fractalization turns the real actual into the possible actual; of how integration brings about the possibility of administering the world and thus the possibility of ecological interventions.

In describing these processes, it has been almost impossible to escape an implicit temporalization. In fact, the very notion of process implies a chronologics. As I noted earlier, Guattari himself implies and invites such a chronologics by inscribing a narrative vector into his explication of the fourfold that goes first from Flows to Phyla, which is why I could argue that the real and actual world shows itself to itself first as Flows and is then atomized into an aerosol that consists of particular elements that Guattari calls 'particle-signs' (158). Again: this atomization allows one to treat the world as a complex machine whose parts are differentiated from each other and which thus might, on the side of the giving, be described, modified and administered. Along the vertical vector, 'the bipolarization of Flows into semiotic Flows and . . . [purely material] Flows is inseparable from the putting into play of smooth machinic Phyla in the neighbouring register F' (78) (see Guattari's Figure 1.1, p. 57). Unlike a world of pure Flow, a machinic and coded world can be designed. Although at this point fractalization still pertains only to the given world, it is already the first step in the birth of the false from the unknowable truth of the world, because already the shift from real Flows to possible Phyla implies the secretion of code. In shifting the material world to the signaletic world, the fractalization of the given marks the first internal differentiation between the given and the given as given. Already here, the birth of the powers of the false: *a-signifying ecology*.

While abstract machines are the result of the deterritorialization of Flows, Flows remain an important aspect of the world as what might be called the medium of abstract machines. Somewhat paradoxically, in fact, pure Flows are, like uncoded noise, both infinitely less and infinitely more differentiated than networks. Although formally, Flows might be conceptualized as approaching, asymptotically, a state of potentially infinite difference, one cannot make distinctions within a fluid. In informational terms: one cannot make digital distinctions within an analog Flow without losing the Flow. Symptomatically, a Flow comes in the singular. Even if there are many Flows, each of these is once more a Flow rather than a mixture or a multiplicity of drops.

Guattari's argument is that in order to make digital distinctions within a Flow, that Flow has to be turned into a network by way of the putting-into-practice of an infinitely complicated process of fractalization. Symptomatically, already the chaotic phase space of the plane of immanence was defined by a 'proto-fractalization' (SC: 103). This transversal sliding from one aspect to the other is taken up on the plane of consistency, on which 'one will never encounter FT contingency in the pure state and even less so ΦU transcendence, but only degrees of contingencing and degrees of deterritorialization, associated within expressive Assemblages E^cC^φ (136). For Guattari, contingencing measures processes of territorialization; as opposed to singularization, which measures processes of deterritorialization. As such, contingencing refers to Flows and Territories, while singularization refers to Phyla and Universes.

If chaos describes a space of pure inconsistence, the cascades of fractal unfolding happen on the plane of consistency, and thus according to the ordinary complexity proper to real Flows and possibilistic Phyla – from within the field of chaosmos rather than chaos as a field of a fully decontingenced, as in deterritorialized, multiplicity. That is, from within the field of ordered multiplicity or complexity. These contingencings happen on the plane of consistency. In the light of the plane of immanence's aspect of proto-fractalization, however, virtual contingencings are already part of the process that constructs the plane of consistency. As Guattari notes in relation to the fractalization of Territories into Universes, 'at the "end" of an infinite process of fractal unfolding . . . the phase space becomes identical to the general Plane of Consistency (PoC), or chaosmos, which itself *corresponds* to a state of infinite determinability' (151, emphasis added), to a 'molecular-fractal chaosmos' (157) that is finitely determinable, while infinite determinability denotes a state of pure openness and freedom as a state that can be determined, with infinite speed, into any-machine-whatever.

When the continuous, territorialized aspect of the world as Flows is fractalized, it turns into the discontinuous, deterritorialized, proto-metric aspect of the world as a rhizomatic network that Guattari also calls the abstract machine, while he calls the dynamics that are responsible for this shift expressionism. Somehow, at an unspecified time and space, a domain and a dynamics of 'expressive fractalization' (134) comes into existence within a Flow. At this moment of expressive fractalization, the world begins to express itself to something, which at this point still means to another aspect of itself as actual, by way of becoming infinitely differentiated. This expressionism turns Flows into aerosolic quasi-Flows. The cascade of expressive fractalizations of Flows is 'essentially correlated to a deterritorialized and fractal smoothing of the set of striations of Flows' (138): *expressive ecology before ecology.*

To sum up: Fractalization breaks up an unmeasurable volume into a measurable network. Like a liquid is atomized in a moisturizer, it atomizes or pulverizes the fluid world. To remain adequate to the Flow, however, the space of the aspect of the world as pulverized must be infinitely fractalized, which implies that not only space itself but also everything in it must be infinitely scaled. In other words, both container and contained must be defined by a logic of infinite recursion. In this putting-into-relation of machines by way of fractalization, 'the traits of intensity constitutive of abstract machines cease to be pro-positional so as to become trans-positional. They sweep across their paradigmatic Phylum of origin and can, at any moment, leap from one Phylum to another' (93). Abstract machines are rhizomatic, and as such they allow for transversal movements across plateaus: *the birth of transversality.* Although Flows remain as an actual and real reservoir, only abstract machines bring about relationality. 'So, exit the manifest configurations of Flows: only the deep structures of abstract machinic Phyla remain. Consequently, the landscape changes radically because these deep structures no longer respond to the logic of clearly and distinctly exo-referred sets of objects' (93). At first sight, it seems to go against the spirit of Guattari and Deleuze to say that the striation of Flows brings about the world's aspect of a field of actual possibilities. However, as I will show in 'Striation and Smoothing: The Figure of Schizoecology' (pp. 95–100), in *Schizoanalytic Cartographies* one needs to carefully distinguish between processes of territorialization and processes of striation-as-complexification. 'We will call this putting into interaction of possibilistic Phyla ... at the most deterritorialized levels, "rhizomatic striation". For their part, the operators of this selection will be called "abstract machines"' (90).

The rhizomatic network makes up a fractal surface in which an infinity of relations and causalities interact transversally, which is why its internal structures cannot be axiomatized: 'One will not be able to arrange them in the manner of the arborescent diagrams of Chomskyan generative grammar, each articulation of which is duly hierarchized and even less assimilate them to mathematical statements supported by an axiomatic foundation' (93). The rhizome itself cannot have a scientific axiomatics because its structures 'are constituted by abstract machines without any fixed identity, which – although expressed through formulae and laws – nevertheless escape from any transcendent coding inscribed on a bedrock of scientificity ... These abstract machines ceaselessly explore and work the variations-derivations-integrations proper to the fields of possibility (operations characterized here as trans-positional), outside of any testifiable temporality' (93).

Against many readings of the rhizome as an inherently anarchic space, therefore, one should set Guattari's stress on the constructive element of the rhizomatic machine. It is not enough to state that everything is connected to everything else, it is similarly important to realize that and how the rhizomatic machine striates spaces. 'But if nothing, neither God nor structure, can impose its law on laws, then is not our striation of machinic Phyla condemned to sink into anarchy and powerlessness, each machinic monad interfering with everything and nothing only to close up on itself in the last instance? By examining the subsequent stasis, we will see that this is not the case because abstract machinism is, on the contrary, the instance par excellence of the capitalization of processual powers' (93). Rhizomes are capitalist as in: constructivist. They profit from and exploit the inherent force of deterritorialization – whose negentropic source I will identify as solar in 'Solaris: Photonic Ecology' (pp. 183–7) – that allows for their far-from-equilibrium singularizations: 'This machinism responds to other principles, not those of the endo-ordination of sensible Flows or the relative ordination of instantiated Flows, but a processual trans-ordination, because it is through its intermediation that enrichments of complexity, re-orderings far from territorialized equilibria and singularizing bifurcations pass. Each supplementary degree of deterritorialization of an abstract machine thus corresponds to an increase in its power of effect, which will no longer be expressed in terms of a quantity of energy but in terms of a reinforcing of the potentiality for singularization, or, in other words, a reduction of entropy' (93).

The both actual and virtual integrations of Phyla and Universes, however, operate on Flows and Territories, and they are in constant processes of being determined by them. 'Machines and machinic fields are engendered on the basis of striated Flows' (84) and there are passages from the 'proto-machinic smoothing of Flows to the deterritorialized machinic Phyla' (78). Also, both Phyla and Universes can at any time decompose into Flows and Territories. A coded language, for instance, can dissolve into uncoded, fluid sounds and affects in cases of a wailing voice. In both of these forms of expression – a maximum of real expressive force and a minimum of possible expression in Flows and Territories; a minimum of real expressive force and a maximum of possible expression in Phyla and Universes – the wager is to be adequate to something fundamentally unknown and unknowable: *to be adequate to the world; to be, in other words, ecological.*

As expression entails signalings, and signalings entail iterations, Guattari notes that the surplus in the process of the fractalization of Flows is the coming-into-being of codes and codings. Fractalization 'produces an added value, it secretes a surplus value of code' (134). This actual discursivity, which Guattari opposes to virtual enunciation, pertains to the forms of communication that Guattari treats under the aspect of the creation of particle-signs, or, as Guattari and Deleuze also call it, of a-signifying, signaletic material. The truly ecological gesture is that Guattari installs the birth of a fundamentally expressive semiotics that he will stake against the representational semiotics of Saussure already at the vector between Flows and Phyla. On the given rather than the giving side of the fourfold, that is: *abstract code, abstract ecology*.

2nd Vector: From Phyla to Territories (Affect)

For most readers of *A Thousand Plateaus*, the first moment of the coming-into-being of semiotic Flows that Guattari describes in *Schizoanalytic Cartographies* as the disruption of territorialized Flows by way of a cascade of 'irresistible' (145) fractalization might come as a surprise. As I noted, in *A Thousand Plateaus*, in which smooth, deterritorialized spaces are set against striated, territorialized strata, Flows tend to have a positive value. Now, in *Schizoanalytic Cartographies*, Flows are considered as territorialized because they are inherently indifferent. Fractalization deterritorializes by breaking up the given, continuous volume of Flows and thus creating a space that is inherently differential and differentiated. As quasi-voluminous, fractal spaces and machines can be administered much easier than fluid spaces and machines (if these can even be said to exist). 'Everything plays out around the springing up of the rupture . . . , the point of emergence of expressive fractalization, from which the conversion of certain material Flows into signaletic Flows will make itself felt' (SC: 133).

The differential, expressive space of Phyla forms the field from within which the perceptual machines of concrete consistencies, which themselves come into being through that very fractalization in the first place, can relate to the actual world through operations that happen by way of codes considered as systems of making distinctions, measuring and digitalization. It is on the giving side of concrete machines that, at the first moment when something given opens itself up to a giving-in-construction, the true possibility of an expressive ecology comes into being. The primal scene of ecosophy. Guattari finds an adequate model of these expressive semiotics in the work of Hjelmslev. While Deleuze turns to Spinoza to show how the world expresses itself in and through its creatures, Guattari, staying close to the problem of coding and discursivity, turns to Hjelmslev's notation of the complementarity of expression and content. As he notes at the beginning of *Schizoanalytic Cartographies*, 'the discursive chains – of expression and of content – only respond very distantly, or against the grain or in a disfiguring way, to the ordinary logic of discursive sets' (4). Hjelmslev is set against Saussure: *expression vs. representation*.

For Guattari, Hjelmslev's semiotics are the most important counterweight to Saussure's because Hjelmslev ties language to a consistency's creation of an existential milieu by way of his stress on using codes as forms of practising its life: 'the primary purpose of their expressive chains is no longer one of denoting states of facts or of organizing states of sense in the axes of signification, but ... of enacting existential crystallizations' (4). In this context, ideologies, myths and cults do a much better job of linking the affective aspect of entities and milieus than the Saussurean couple of signifier and signified, or, for that matter, Lacanian psychoanalysis. In Guattari's model, it is always a question of 'setting in motion a function of existentialization ... which consists in deploying and putting into intensive concatenation specific existential qualities' (35): *existential semiotics*.

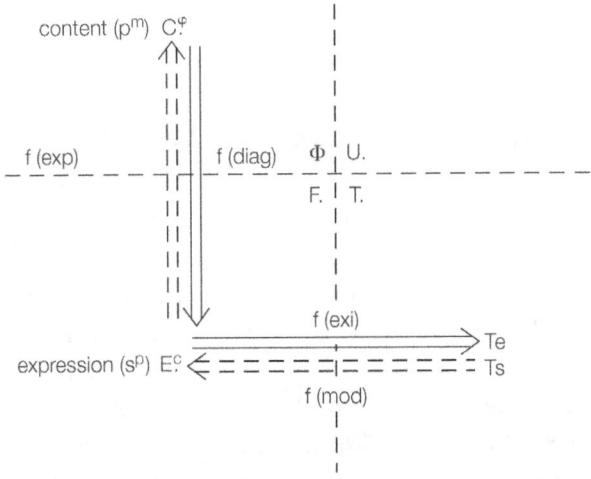

FIGURE 6.8 The inversion of deterritorialization

This expressionism is based on the fact that Hjelmslev sets up a 'relation of *reciprocal presupposition* or of solidarity between the form of Expression and the form of Content' (207, my emphasis). Within the fourfold, this reciprocal presupposition operates by way of the expressive and diagrammatic functions that move like shuttles between Flows, which correspond in Guattari's view, as is shown in his Figure 6.8, to Hjelmslev's level of Expression, and machinic Phyla, which correspond to Hjelmslev's level of Content. 'Let us note that this reversal of the form of Expression/form of Content relation ... conforms with one of the fundamental intuitions of Hjelmslev' (145), Guattari notes. '[E]xpressive fractalization' starts 'the double game of being-for-itself ... and of being-for-something-else' (134). And further, 'expression has thus become essentially correlated to a deterritorialized and fractal smoothing of the set of striations of Flows. Machines of Expression somehow have the function of making the possible ooze out of all the encysted modular forms that

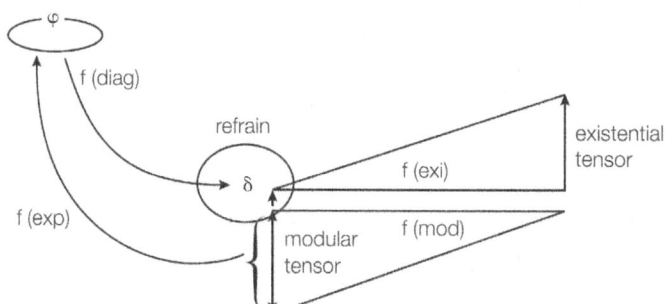

FIGURE 6.11 Existential refrains (repetition of Figure 6.8 as a function of Figure 6.10)

harbour it' (138). It is within this process of an inherently constructivist, expressive fractalization that the registers of codes and coding are created, in a process that will ultimately allow the opening up of the given to the giving. The volume of Flows is broken up into a fractal space that can be registered, or: that is the result of an as-yet-anonymous self-registering.

The side of the giving comes into existence by way of a territorialization of the fractal dynamics that happens simultaneously and that is performed according to a diagrammatic function that allows a concrete entity to affectively access the deterritorialized field of Phyla; to create, already at this point of its genesis, a link between itself and the world. In fact, Guattari considers these functions as two aspects of the same overall function. 'By inverting itself, by becoming a diagrammatic function f(diag), the expressive function f(exp) meshes directly with material flows, and becomes capable of catalysing machinic "choices", such as feedback, and of bringing about changes of state correlative to energetic conversions' (168). This genesis of entities is evolutionary in the sense of a pachinko evolution, in that the machinic propositions and with them 'the status of f(diag) [are] always precarious, aleatory, problematic, confined, contingenced by the margin of manoeuvre that is authored by existential refrains' (145). Guattari's Figure 6.11 illustrates these dynamics, in which the refrain holds a central position.

In its feedback-loops with existential Territories, the registers of objective discursivity and subjective enunciation meet at 'the point where expressive discursivity no longer just refers to itself through the mechanisms of paradigmatic commutation, where it puts its relationship of neutrality and arbitrariness with regard to the referent into suspense so as to engage forcefully with reality', which means 'with the modular stratifications of the everyday world' (142). As Guattari notes, a 'diagrammatic function, f(diag), corresponding to the relations between matter of Expression and

Referent' (208), brings about a 'diagrammatic distance ... between expression and content' (236). In crossing the fourfold's vertical divide, the diagrammatic function, in creating feedback loops between Phylum, Flow and concrete Territory, creates a relation between, or perhaps better, a superposition of, the discursive and the enunciative realm: *ecological superposition*.

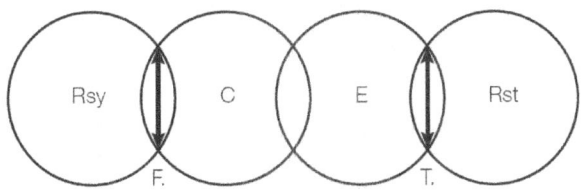

FIGURE 2.5 Intersection of the Given and the Giving

The reason that Guattari stakes Hjelmslev's distinction of content and expression against Saussure's distinction of signifier, signified and referent (see AO: 242; also Guattari's Figure 6.8) is that, as Guattari's Figure 2.5 shows, the logic of content and expression allows for this ecological superposition. 'An intrinsic systemic Referent [that] corresponds to the Given (Rsy)' and 'an intrinsic structural Referent [that] corresponds to the Giving (Rst)' (SC: 60). As Guattari stresses, 'if, under certain conditions, there are systems proper to the Given-non-Giving and structures proper to the Giving-non-Given, there is also an intersection between Given-Giving and Giving-Given (Figure 2.5), which constitutes what Hjelmslev calls the semiotic function (or Solidarity) and the two functives of which – Content [C] and Expression (E)' (59): *ecological solidarity*.

Hjelmslev's expressive semiotics are not only set against Saussure's representative semiotics, however. By extension, they are also set against their use in Lacan's representative psychoanalysis. Despite the fundamental formal differentiation between the given and the giving, an ecological semiotics and 'the schizoanalytic undertaking will never limit itself to an interpretation of "givens"; it will take a much more fundamental interest in the 'Giving', in the Assemblages that promote the concatenation of affects of sense and pragmatic effects' (19). As is shown in Guattari's Table 2.1, both the vectors of the Given and the Giving, as well as those of Content and Expression, reach across the formal divide between the world and its creatures. It is this crucial conceptual crossing that allows us to ecologically tie the world's creatures to the world; to tie the enunciative registers of Territories and Universes to the discursive registers of Flows and Phyla. Formal difference and ontological identity: *ontological ecology as formal ecology and vice versa*.

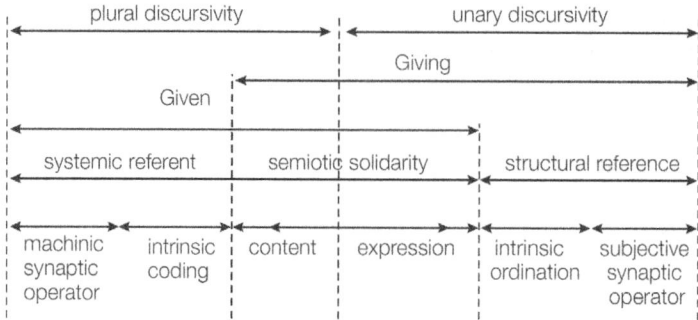

TABLE 2.1 Relationship between categories of discursivity

As complementary, the sides of non-entitarian, actual Flows and Phyla and entitarian, virtual Territories and Universes are two aspects of the same overall space. The world expressed by its creatures, the creatures creating their world. As I have shown, a first conceptual gesture to topologically model this deeply ecological complementarity was to fold the two sides of the fourfold onto each other along its vertical axis. At the same time, the squarings performed by the fourfold invariably involve both axes. One way Guattari addresses this double folding is in terms of endo- and exo-reference, as well as endo- and exo-consistency. As Guattari defines the second, 'we will call "exo-reference" the serial arrangement resulting from the putting into discursive connection of n terms of the multiplicity. We will call "endo-reference" the intensive, that is to say, non-discursive, proto-existential operator from which the preceding arrangement results' (113) [→ **Deleuze 94**].

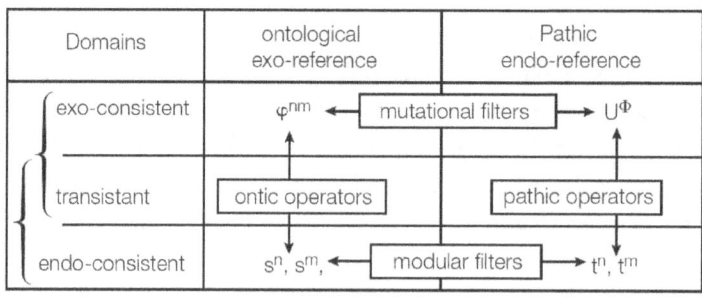

FIGURE 4.8 Ontological exo-reference and pathic endo-reference

As Guattari's Figure 4.8 shows, the difference between ontological exo- and pathic endo-reference is that between the actual and virtual and is thus organized along the vertical divide between the abstract and the concrete. As always in the fourfold, this difference is further differentiated along the horizontal divide, in this case into the fields of exo- and endo-consistency. In the actual, ontological register, Flows are without outside, while in Phyla everything causes everything else from the outside, although, strictly speaking, there is no outside because there are no insides, as that difference only comes into being within concrete, pathic entities. Here, Territories are, like Flows, endo-consistent, while Universes are, like Phyla, exo-consistent.

As it denotes an abstract, given world without perceiving entities, Flows and Phyla are without concrete forms and indifferent, while the concrete, giving field of sensible Territories and existential Universes is both formed and formal. This field, which is made up of entities that have developed an inside – 'extensity imposed the framing of an inside and an outside on each entitarian circumscription' (98) – is endo-referential: 'the soul of code, of the sign, language, catalysis, the imprint, the image, the tracing, the plane, the programme of concrete machines, what I call their diagrammatic function, associates two modalities of evaluation. One is exo-referred and attached to the materiality of process; the other, endo-referred, confers on it its complexity, its singularity, its existential consistency' (95). While the horizontal vector concerns exo- and endo-reference, at the same time, the difference between exo- and endo-consistency concerns the horizontal axis. Flows and Territories have an endo-consistency in that they are continuous and durational, while discontinuous and momentous Phyla and Universes have an exo-consistency. (Remember also the endo-ordination of sensible Flows on p. 79.) In-between those two determinations, ontic and pathic operators allow processes of fractalization that link modular to mutational, and thus territorialized to deterritorialized registers. Modes of abstract ontology on the left side of the fourfold, modes of concrete epistemology on the right, although, once more, the two fields and processes are complementary.

It is first in the recursive feedback-loops between Flows, Phyla and Territories that rudimentary, germinal enunciative entities and states, and with them, proto-subjective domains come into being. Somewhat like Freud's libido, these proto-entities, which Guattari calls existential 'graspings' (77), are defined by a certain 'existential stickiness' (C: 115). Later, the epistemological register will be added to the pathic register of existentialization. On the actual side, expressive and diagrammatic functions operate between actual, objective Flows and Phyla (the given, quantity). On the virtual side, they operate in relation to virtual, subjective Territories, as the domain of sensible entities (the giving, quality) that come-into-being in feedbacks with the fractalization of Flows into Phyla. In these feedbacks, which cross the vertical divide, the expressive deterritorializations that develop between Flows and Phyla are diagrammatically reterritorialized in the creation of concrete, sensible Territories. As such, the diagrammatic function forms 'the "other side" of the expressive function' (SC: 164). As Guattari notes, 'when an existential requalification f(exi) happens to succeed an expressive fractal rupture f(exp), the question of the existence of an operation of intermediary reterritorialization is posed' (145).

In the same way that cybernetics models the creation of a system as the shift from an objective, infinite causal complexity to a subjective and finite one, this reterritorialization causes, in Guattari's terminology, a shift from infinite to finite determination.

The fractalization of Flows that results in deterritorialized Phyla originates in 'the deterritorializing expression of f(exp)' (145) which 'developed a fractalism everywhere, in an expansive mode within the phase spaces of the domain φ' (145). This fractal expressionism also causes a machinic smoothing in the space between Flows and Phyla. 'It is a question here of all the expressive matters open to the facets of mutation and creation: genetic, ethological, semiotic codes, semiologies and the ensemble of situations in which a "constructivist" Expression is grafted onto material – phonic, scriptural, organic – chains, by starting to play' (134). This play is that of crystallization and evolution.

To recapitulate this decisive moment: With all heterogeneous elements in place, the world begins to play, at first with itself as fractalized and integrated into Phyla. The result of the initial machinic smoothing is the creation of Phyla as a field of machinic rather than entitarian propositions by way of the expressive function. 'The decisive turning point, with the surplus value of possibility generated by the instantiation of Flows, is that it is no longer only the manifest being-there, the attested locality of a figure of redundancy, that is taken into account, but also the integral of its possible dis-positions, before, after, next to and beyond its actual manifestations' (84). While the expressive function creates Phyla, the diagrammatic function concerns the passages from this field of machinic propositions back to Flows and further to Territories; with the actual world folding over into the world of the giving, and thus into its creatures. This is where the first instance of contingencing as territorialization takes place. As the first territorial impulse in the allover field of the deterritorialized, the Point of Contingencing, on whose ecological and territorializing aspects I will concentrate, marks the possibility of the birth of concrete entities: 'The articulation of the Point of Contingencing . . . is the cornerstone of th[e] conjunction between being-there, closed on itself and proto-alterity, *which links together the things of the world and life*' (136, emphasis added). At this point, 'heterogeneous components of Expression' and 'diverse substantial consistencies relative to the multiple incorporeal referents on which it [Expression] is inscribed' (138) are superposed: *crystal ecology*.

Stressing once more that these processes are going on at the same time, the actual territorialization of Phyla in the field of Territories follows the '*diagrammatic function* f(diag)' (145), which is 'like *the reverse side* of the expressive function' (145, emphasis added). In some way and to some degree this intermediary diagram folds up the infinite potentialities that expressive fractalization had unfolded. This folding, however, is productive and necessary in that it brings the 'surplus value of possibility δ to the sensible surface' (145). By enfolding and reterritorializing the continuously unfolding, deterritorializing fractalization and 'heterogeneification' (87) that defines Phyla around a sensible surface, the diagrammatic function creates the reduced and slowed-down mode in which the world reaches and creates a sensible, modular entity. At the end of that diagrammatic process lie what Guattari calls sensible territories.

The slowed-down code that comes into being as the surplus value of territorialization allows the sensible surfaces of endo-entities to read out the actual side's machinic propositions in relation to themselves and to their own functioning. Guattari calls this the shift from actual, anonymous discursivity to virtual, entitarian enunciation. If Flows have a proto-signaletic character that is instantiated by Phyla as deterritorialized Flows, it is only in and by endo-entities that the given discursivity of the world is enunciated. These are the first voices of the mute and clamorous world.

The shuttling between and superposition of expression and content created, on the actual side, a 'machinic smoothing' that 'breaks with the uniquely proximal type of discursivity specific to Flows, so as to introduce a caesura, a completely new opening of "possibilization"' (86); while the first codings on the actual side put to work 'encodings and diverse modes of semiotization' (86). When these semiotic dynamics of encoding cross over to the virtual side, they are used to construct existential refrains. From the position of the existential territory, 'refrains . . . are established at the junction of two existential and diagrammatic functions' (145). On the virtual side, these dynamics create first sensible Territories; surfaces of sensation that, at the end of the feedback process, become what Guattari calls existential modules. An unoriented sensible surface, one might say, becomes an oriented eigensurface. Codings help to stabilize such existential Territories by way of recursive iterations: 'processual, active, aspects, imported via diagrammatic determination f(diag) could come to be added to the passive, "hysterical" aspects of existential grasping f(exi)' (145–6). These determinations, which shuttle between the given and the giving, and thus between the actual and the virtual, emerge and reach back – passing through the functions of existential territories – to the side of Flows and Phyla. Already in his Figure 1.1 (see p. 57), Guattari had related energetic discursivity to the triangle of enunciation made up by abstract Flows and Phyla and concrete Territories (the given-giving triangle). It shows that Guattari develops an energetic and existential semiotics that operates without the register of Universes that denote the domain of individual consciousness. This is the instantiation of Guattari's unconscious: *an expressive, ecological semiotics.*

This given-giving triangle is set against the double articulation of Saussurean linguistics and its claim of pure representation within a linguistically constructed world. 'These logics, which I also call logics of bodies without organs, or logics of existential Territories, have this particularity: that their objects are ontologically ambiguous, they are bifaced objects-subjects that can neither be discernibilized nor discursivized as figures represented on a background of coordinates of representation' (40). According to Guattari's expressive semiotics, the signs that a representational semiotics situates on the side of Territories and Universes are intimately related to and in fact emerge from the side of Flows and Phyla. Together, the expressive and diagrammatic functions create a relation of transversal, expressive feedback loops rather than a relation of representation. Even while representational signs denote one level of signalization, they are invariably related to material Flows and their organization into Phyla, and thus to the fourfold's actual side. In this way, representational signs are inevitably related to the field of expression, in the same way that psychoanalysis is related to schizoanalysis. For Guattari, all forms of signs are inherently ecological.

The heterogenesis of entities brings all of these levels into play. In fact, the coming-into-being of codes and codings is correlative to the coming-into-being of entities. The genetic operations of this creation relate three Guattarian concepts that are also prominent in texts by Guattari and Deleuze: expression, diagram and refrain. In relation to these texts, the surplus-value of *Schizoanalytic Cartographies* lies in defining these terms in more detail and in providing them with a more contoured position within the overall field of processes of subjectivation. As I noted, the expressive function shows that language is invariably tied to the field of an energetic semiotics. The diagrammatic function ensures the reduction of an overall field of machinic propositions to the construction of refrains in the register of subjective Territories. In these processes of contingencing, signs operate as affective surfaces that are intimately tied to existentializing operations. This moment marks the superposition of material, given life, with the virtual, existential and aisthetic practices of giving, concrete entities: *affective ecology*.

3rd Vector: From Territories to Universes (Concepts)

Although any operation in the fourfold puts all of its four attractors into play, the creation of Universes from Territories uses the fractalization of Flows into Phyla to construct another triangle, which this time stresses the feedback-loops between actual Phyla, virtual Territories and Universes; between rhizomes, existential modules, and what Guattari calls monads. This triangle adds a further superposition: that of code, of Alexander Gottlieb Baumgarten's notion of aesthetics as a mode of *aisthesis*, and thus as the theory of sensuous and affective judgements of taste that refer to Territories, and of more artwork-oriented, conceptual aesthetic practices concerning Universes [→ **Deleuze 194**]. From contingencing as territorializing to singularization as deterritorializing.

On the horizontal axis, Territories fractalize into Universes in analogy to the way Flows fractalize into rhizomes. First, however, Territories come into being by looping through expressive rhizomes, and by bringing back to themselves virtual diagrams of these rhizomes. In fact, these feedback loops are the very mode of their creation.

In other words, by way of iteration and differentiation, they inscribe concrete, bounded and virtual Territories into the allover abstract and actual milieu of rhizomes. They cut out the operational space of a concrete entity from within the overall milieu, which is why in Table 2.2 (p. 95), Territories are related to Cutouts. Stressing the dynamics of this process, one might say that Territories are refrained milieus. Entities slow their milieu down by refraining it. The 'concatenation of Flows' that created sequences 'is correlative to a striation, a heterogeneization (or hetero-genesis) of the sensible world' (78) of subjective, existential Territories.

In my discussion of the 2nd vector, I showed how, along the horizontal axis, sensible Territories develop into existential Territories by way of diagrammatic processes of habit-formation (iteration) and striation (complexification). Within the milieu, they carve out concrete habitats. Architectures of living. 'At the end of this toing and froing and after an enrichment of their potentialities, the old modular sensible Territories Ts find themselves converted into a new species of existential Territory Te' (143). In these dynamics, the force of expression is decelerated and delimited. Having crossed into the field of the giving, it is bound into 'existential refrains' (148). Taking up this conceptual crossover in a terminological crossover to Guattari and Deleuze's pair of molar and molecular, which are terms that entered their work by way of Gilbert Simondon, Guattari states that 'with this coiling back of Expression onto Existence we have returned from the fractal-molecular register to the molar-modular register' (144): From molecular Phyla to molar Territories.

The molar-molecular pair, which I have used without much specification until now, is often read in terms of scale. At the same time, however, Guattari and Deleuze relate them to grades of consistency. Diffuse fractalized assemblages, in which the single elements have more valences, and thus more options to move, are related to the molecular, while more strictly organized assemblages are related to the molar register. As with the smooth and the striated, in both *Anti-Oedipus* and *A Thousand Plateaus* one can often sense a valorization that stakes the liberating forces of molecularization against the oppressive forces of molarization, as when, in the opening chapter of *A Thousand Plateaus*, molecular blocks of short-term memory are set against the molar narratives of long-term memory, or when light and fast ad-hoc groupings are set against heavy, überstructured bureaucracies. Again, however, one should be wary of such a judgement, at least in relation to the Guattari of *Schizoanalytic Cartographies*, where molecularization and molarization are less concerned with questions of scale or what Guattari calls speed of determination, than with questions of internal measure. Every assemblage has a specific, albeit constantly shifting value of molarizations and molecularizations that marks relative values in terms of its overall consistency. More importantly even, in *Schizoanalytic Cartographies* the two terms are in a deeply ecological way asymmetrical rather than oppositional. Molecularization has to do with smoothing, which concerns inter-entitarian space. Its measure is a deconsistencing that pertains to operations of smoothing instigated by the ecological milieu in which entities move, which in turn has to do with the possibilization of change and modulation. In other words, molecularization is related to processes of becoming-medium or becoming-milieu, while molarization has to do with intra-entitarian organization, formation and operation, and is related to processes of becoming-form and becoming-territory. In this light, the field of modules and Territories is one of molarization and of the construction of pathic forces and currents that define an entity's home.

The ecological lesson of this is that while 'machinic molecules' are 'more deterritorialized and more abstract' (16) than molar arrangements, the latter, as they are composed of molecules, can never fully repress the molecular level. Even though it is imperceptible, 'the molecular phylum is thus found traversing individuals, species, and milieus' (MU: 127). In the fourfold's chronologics, molar modules, which, although they have molarized the molecular codings in and of rhizomes in order to come into being, are still traversed by these molecular codings. At some point at which the existential registers are stable enough, the existential registers open themselves up to the forces of deterritorialization. By way of concrete deterritorialization, they add to the register of molar modules and modulations those of molecular monads: First, a sensible surface becomes an existential surface. In a second step, that virtual entity, by more feedbacks with the material and the sensible, creates, gradually, a deterritorialized field of concrete possibility. The feedback loops create the register of Universes. If the real of actual Flows is what the real of virtual affects are to Territories, the possible of actual rhizomes is what the possible of virtual thought is to Universes. The gradual shift from sensible modules to existential modules and further to monads takes place from within the field of the refrain, which functions as a modulator from affect to thought according to a Spinozist logic of the superposition of quantitative irritation and the qualitative idea of that irritation. Part of the creation of a cognitive monad from a sensible module has to do with codings, which add, along the horizontal axis, a deterritorialized and deterritorializing field of thought to a more territorialized and territorializing field of sensibility and perception.

As I noted earlier, the fractalization in Phyla allows for the creation of diagrammatic, decelerated Territories, which are in turn accelerated into Universes that are defined by an infinite virtual fractalization that frees the entity from the spatio-temporal constraints of Flows and Territories. 'With heterogenesis, two types of relations are thus differentiated: ... modular, serial and finite relations (FT); fractal, non-proximal and infinite relations (TU)' (SC: 184). The moment of heterogenesis puts into play the contraction of actual and virtual fractalization within and into an entity. 'The scene functions like a sponge, if you like, which soaks up a certain type of scattered, deterritorialized being-there' (184) Guattari had noted in terms of the videography at La Borde. Actual fractalization links up with virtual fractalization. The given links up with the giving. On an infinity of levels, the actualities of the world link up with the virtual minds of its spongy creatures: *soak-up ecology*.

In both modular and monadic cases 'one is dealing with modes of self-existentialization' (184). While the first are intrinsically territorializing, however, the second are 'intrinsically deterritorialized (or deterritorialized-deterritorializing)' (184). The aim is the construction of a virtual field of fractalization in which a monad 'is no longer territorially enslaved to extrinsic coordinates but has become tributary to processual ordinates. In so doing, its forms have become infinitely transposable and translatable, separated from the status of structure to become a matter for abstract machines. It is no longer just the topological dimensions that are fractalized here but also the dimensions of time and substance. By this new fractal procedure, sensible and abstract qualities invent original relations of transversality' (184–5). Guattari stresses the constructivist aspect of this shift. 'We [sic] not dealing here with the simple observation of heterogeneity but with a labour of heterogenesis; each dimension demands to be discernibilized, deployed in all its virtualities. Whilst the energetico-temporo-topographical coordinates implied legal transcendent constraints, the scopic dis-position, on the contrary, accommodates aleatory factors in the immanence of the Assemblage. The link that it institutes is an existential glue steeped in molecular bifurcations and degrees of freedom, which it owes to the fact that its fractal folding is no longer formal but operates as an aporetic junction between heterogeneous qualities each one bearing a destiny' (184). In other words, a Territory is fractalized into a deterritorialized Universe. The refrain, as a minimal spine of a specific song of existence, is opened up to a more rhizomatic music that is free to move wherever it wants, without having to ensure itself of and being immediately involved in its own existential registers. Or, even more directly, the thought that defines an entity can be a testing-ground that is much more free than the thought that is immediately concerned with the existential complex of that entity. For Deleuze, this freedom, which is the freedom of philosophy, is also the promise of a Proustian poetics and aesthetics, while Guattari stresses the superposition of aisthetic and aesthetic registers. For both, however, when a fictional world comes into being whose creation is not based on the exigencies of one's own life and subjectivity, like that created from within Proust's corked-off room, this world is precisely not the world of *l'art pour l'art* but *l'art pour le monde*. It is the art of the world considered as an abstract machine by one of its concrete entities.

The interplay of expressive and diagrammatic operations pertains also to the shift from passive connection to active disjunction and thus from quantity to quality: 'a genesis of consistencies putting into play entitarian ensembles with a heterogeneous ontological status: besides modular components, discursive phase spaces, non-discursive enunciative basins, etc. With this relation, the more and the less are no longer inscribed "between" entities, but incrusted in their very being. It is no longer a matter of an extensive but of an intensive relation, and separation ceases to be passively connective so as to become actively disjunctive, that is to say, generative of processes of complexification' (130): *schizoecology*.

At the end of this tour along the vectors of the fourfold, all four functors are in operation within a field of allover heterogenesis and singularization. In a deflection from cybernetic to biological registers, this vectorial heterogenesis of consistencies concerns the genesis of living entities as autopoietic systems. As Guattari and Deleuze note in *What is Philosophy?*, 'what is truly created, from the living being to the work of art ... enjoys a self-positing of itself, or an autopoetic [sic] characteristic' (WP: 11). According to Guattari, all processes of individuation and singularization rest on 'existential qualities that self-organize at the root of being' (SC: 179). In accord with the theory of nonlinear dynamics, these self-organizations happen without an agency situated outside of the field of self-organization. Stressing its surprising, uncomputable element, Guattari notes that 'a self-organizing process can be set off where nothing precise could be expected' (189): *incerte tempore, incerte loci*.

Guattari posits two fields of generation, which pertain to the milieu and to the entity respectively: 'a trans-entitarian (matricial) generativity, without any essential priority of one essence over another (without the infrastructure–superstructure relation, for example' (69) and, as I noted earlier, a principle of 'self-affirmation' whose foundation is 'auto-poietic' (69). Mirrored into the virtual side of the giving, the force of expression allows Territories to be fractalized into Universes. The 'practices of putting into refrain don't just shake up encysted references and certainties. They indicate the potential lines of a many-headed fractalization, a multidirectional and transversalist fractalization that can carry its effects to the heart of fundamentally heterogeneous domains' (148). The truly fractal spaces, then, are those of Phyla and Universes; the space of an entity as what Guattari calls, in *Chaosmosis*, an 'incorporeal ecosystem' (94). As the virtual, subjective analogues to Phyla, Universes are the domain of deterritorialized thought. They refer to cognitive pattern production, which Guattari also calls the creation of constellations. This is the milieu of philosophy. If Phyla denote the actual world as an abstract machine, Universes denote the virtual and concrete world as a constellation.

As virtual, entitarian rhizomes, Universes are point-of-viewed by the entities that create them. An anonymous, rhizomatic consciousness that permeates singular Universes is perspectivized and embodied by existential Territories. 'By themselves, incorporeal Universes have no means at their disposal for recentring themselves, to belong to or position themselves in relation to one another. Heterogeneity and alterity are thus for them essentially generated on the basis of crystals of ontological self-affirmation (or hyper-complexity) that existential Territories constitute' (166).

As the space of entitarian thought processes, 'Consciential Universes' (20) are subjective rather than objective, and as such concrete universals, 'not abstract universals' (160). In fact, Universes are immaterial crystals. 'What gives Universes consistency, what striates them, is the crystallization within them of a singular-singularizing Constellation' (160). As 'the enunciative instances of the phase surfaces of possibility' (151), Universes are the enunciative, giving complement to discursive, given Phyla. In short: Universes are virtual abstract machines, point-of-viewed by concrete entities. Singularized and virtualized Phyla. The world of Spinoza fractalized into and by its monads. As such, they posit 'the paradox of a non-discursive complexity, arising from incorporeal Universes of reference' (98).

As rhizomatic, Universes give space to 'the radically deterritorialized and virtual act of enunciation' (169). It is in relation to this field that the paradox of enunciative assemblages is most clearly stated. The field of Universes is 'at the same time both the locus of an actualized enunciation and of an infinity of virtual enunciations' (153). As such, the paradox that defines Universes is that they are both completely determined and completely undetermined. 'Each enunciation articulating a minimal determinability $d^{+\infty}$ is haunted by a virtual divisibility $d^{-\infty}$ (virtuality of a Universe). It is enunciative intentionality that, at its very root, sets off a process of continuous fractalization' (154). Universes imply 'the coexistence of an infinite fractal process and of a contingent determination that, in some way, snags, fixes, ballasts it' (1).

From within the fourfold's chronological vector, the creation of Universes marks the final step in the process of heterogenesis. 'In setting itself out to the exclusion of all other Constellations, a Constellation of Universes does not situate itself in relation to them in terms of a figure/ground relationship. It doesn't affirm its difference against the others but from its own interior, in an intensive mode of existential autonomization. It is from this taking on of ontological autonomy, this pure affirmation of a being-for-itself – the importation of which results from a requalification coming from the domain T – that the enunciative matrix of a heterogeneity, which one will find at work again in the four corners of the cycle of Assemblages, is born' (165–6).

In other words, although Universes are actual(ized) in and by concrete entities, they are, at the same time, fully virtual. As Guattari notes, a Universe is 'something that repeats, that affirms itself, that is neither localized, finite nor discursive but is nevertheless singular or, rather, irreversibly singularizing: this is what constitutes incorporeal Universes, which I have equally characterized as Universes of reference or Universes of enunciation' (159). Universes are the concrete, virtual milieus of assemblages of enunciation. Crucially, before it is the field of the consistency of meaning, the field of Universes is, like that of Phyla, the field of deterritorialization. Paradoxically, it first of all deconsistencies meaning. It smooths every thought – considered as a virtual striation-as-complexification – even while that thought emerges in it. As such, it is the field of the potentiality of change: 'this smoothing by the incorporeal enunciators U finds its diagrammatic grasp, its root of singularization (the fact that it is not a matter of Platonic Universals cut off from every sensible hook) in the points of contingencing, Pc, where the expressive foldings originate and where the diagrammatic foldings-up are snagged' (157). On the plane of consistencies, Universes allow for a recuperation of the infinite determinability of the plane of immanence from within the register of concrete entities. They show the freedom of the virtual as a field that is separated from the actual world. This is the power of the false and thus of art: to construct fully virtual universes that are, at the same time, adequate to the world: *universal ecology*.

At this point, let me sketch a conceptual portrait of the fourfold. To some degree, the fourfold is a response to Lacan's formalizations of psychoanalysis. However, while Lacan formalizes the form of psychoanalysis, Guattari formalizes a world that is both infinitely formal and infinitely informal. The wager of the fourfold is to formalize the given diversity of the world, as well as the parameters of how forms emerge from within this diversity according to a logic of pure construction rather than according to an always already assumed, a-priori logic such as the logic of psychoanalysis.

How, then, do forms come into being from within the informal? In the preceding sections, I have shown that the ungrounded ground of any form of the assembly of forms is a plane of pure chaos that does not stop pervading every form as a ceaseless force of deterritorialization. Even while it is used to create these forms, it is, in its actualization in these forms, partially cancelled out. There remains, however, an excess of the informal over the formal, and thus of irreducibility over reduction. Conceptually, that excessive plane – the informal, irreducible set within which forms and reductions are assembled – is the fourfold's implied plane of immanence, while its explicit structuration is concerned with that plane as the plane of consistency. Within the positions that define the fourfold as marking aspects of the formation of an ultimately informal world, the most general distinction is between one side as that of the given, abstract and assembled world, and the other as that of its giving, concrete and assembled creatures. This basic differentiation provides the ecological parameters within which to think the world. As they delineate a phase space, all positions in the fourfold should be considered as operating simultaneously. In fact, the positions might be said to function as what nonlinear dynamics calls attractors. If a vortex is defined by a one-point attractor that is situated at the centre of the vortex, Guattari's fourfold is based on a four-point attractor into whose hypercomplex milieu each singular, spatially situated and dated state is suspended, and into whose transversal field it is diffracted. Unlike Lacan's diagram of the discourses of the

		Discursivity	
		• plural • continuous • fusional	• unary • discontinuous • of mixtures
Deterritorialization	• Infinite • Irreversible • Far from equilibrium	Φ. Processual machinic *phyla* (Rhizomes)	U. Incorporeal *universes* (Constellations)
	• Finite • Reversible • Close to equilibrium	F. Energetico-signaletic *flows* (Complexions)	T. Existential *territories* (Cutouts)

TABLE 2.2 Values and characteristics of the four domains F, Φ, T, U

hysteric, the master, the university and psychoanalysis, the fourfold does not provide a psychoanalogical grid across which specific patterns rotate. Instead, it models a field of the living within which processes of individuation and singularization take place. From within this attractor-space, the fourfold, as shown in Guattari's Table 2.2, describes 'four domains of consistency: energetic-signaletic Flows . . . , the entities of which are arranged in Complexions; abstract machinic Phyla . . . , the entities of which are arranged in Rhizomes; existential Territories . . . , the entities of which are arranged in Cutouts; incorporeal Universes . . . , the entities of which are arranged in Constellations' (56–7). Complexions denote states of real, exo-referential and objective Flows; Rhizomes (Phyla) states of possible, exo-referential and abstract networks with their separation into terms and relations; Territories states of concrete, subjective endo-references; and Constellations states of concrete, subjective, endo-referential networks. Territories are cut out from Complexions, Constellations are constructed in Rhizomes: *four-point ecology*.

Striation and Smoothing: The Figure of Schizoecology

The figure of Guattari's schizoecology emerges most clearly, perhaps, from within the relation between striated forms and smooth media that is set up in the fourfold. In reference to his work with Deleuze, Guattari's realignment of '*striated and smooth*' (TP: 484) space is arguably his most far-reaching conceptual innovation. The asymmetry of the dynamics of smoothing and striation that Guattari develops in *Schizoanalytic Cartographies* encapsulates, in perhaps its purest form, the programme of Guattari's move into ecology. In particular, this move concerns the redefinition of striation and smoothing as processes of hardening and softening in *A Thousand*

Plateaus. Guattari's proposition in *Schizoanalytic Cartographies* is that any complexification of a consistency is a striation, while any movement of a consistency through its medium is a smoothing, in that it asks the consistency to adapt to always new circumstances. It asks it to move within the milieu in the most viable and elegant manner, in the same way that in a mathematical formula viability and elegance are one and the same thing: *more elegance, more viability*.

On this background, *Schizoanalytic Cartographies* allows us to retroactively throw into perspective *A Thousand Plateaus*, as well as many readings of Guattari and Deleuze that have emerged from it. The *Capitalism and Schizophrenia* project is often defined by the rhetorical slant that both captures and envelops Guattari and Deleuze's arguments. According to this slant, which might well have been introduced by the more politically oriented Guattari but which is also the result of the overall historical setting around 1968, smoothing is considered as liberatory and revolutionary, while striation is considered as an act of state power that debilitates its subjects. In 1989, the strength of *Schizoanalytic Cartographies* lies partly in its rhetorical sobriety. As I noted earlier, it is an extremely level-headed text.

Because of its rhetorics, many readers of *A Thousand Plateaus* have come away from the book with the impression that striation is tendentially negative while smoothing is tendentially positive. While much of this is the result of how the book says things rather than of what it says, in *Schizoanalytic Cartographies*, the notions of smoothing and striation are not only less rhetorically charged, they are also related in a less symmetrical and oppositional manner. It is on both of these levels that *Schizoanalytic Cartographies*, although it takes up many of its tenets, retroactively re-contours and perhaps even changes *A Thousand Plateaus*.

In *A Thousand Plateaus*, smooth space is related to landscapes such as the 'desert, steppe, sea, or ice' as figures of a multiplicity that is 'non-metric, acentered, directional, etc.' (484). This relates it to the minor geometry that the book sets against royal geometry. While this invites readings that favour the minor over the major, already in *A Thousand Plateaus* the relation between these two is more complicated. Minor geometry makes major or royal geometry possible in the same way that, mathematically, an unmeasured and thus unnumbered space allows for the spectrum of numbers to emerge from it in the first place, and as such provides, as the unnumbered medium of numbers, which would be designated in *Schizoanalytic Cartographies* as actual and real, the possibility of numbers. This also implies that from the perspective of major science the 'inferiority' of minor geometry 'is only apparent, for the independence of this nearly illiterate, a-metric geometry is what makes possible the independence of the number, the subsequent function of which is to measure magnitudes in striated space (or to striate). The number distributes itself in smooth space; it does not divide without changing nature each time, without changing units, each of which represents a distance and not a magnitude. The ordinal, directional, nomadic, articulated number, the numbering number, pertains to smooth space, just as the numbered number pertains to striated space. So we may say of every multiplicity that it is already a number, and still a unit. But the number and the unit, and even the way in which the unit divides, are different in each case' (484–5). Rather than standing in opposition to major science, minor science provides its ungrounded ground. As such, it is 'continually *enriching* major science, communicating its *intuitions* to it, its way of proceeding, its itinerancy, its sense of and taste for matter, singularity, variation, intuitionist geometry and the numbering number' (485, emphases added). Minor science, one might say, is *the unconscious of major science, not its enemy.*

Although it attests to its ecological immersion in a specific cultural milieu, it is almost against itself that the revolutionary rhetorics of *A Thousand Plateaus* have clouded over, at least for many of its readers, its conceptual complexity, according to which striation is always both negative and positive. It is 'an operation that undoubtedly consists in subjugating, overcoding, *metricizing* smooth space, in neutralizing it, but also in giving it a milieu of propagation, extension, refraction, renewal, and impulse without which it would perhaps die of its own accord' (486). Already in *A Thousand Plateaus*, minor and major science, as well as processes of smoothing and striation, are symbiotic, as 'smooth space allows itself to be striated, and striated space reimparts a smooth space, with potentially very different values, scope, and signs. Perhaps we must say that all progress is made by and in striated space, but all becoming occurs in smooth space' (486).

While it fully endorses this symbiotic and complementary view, a striking conceptual shift in *Schizoanalytic Cartographies* is that Guattari considers striation to pertain less to a disabling stratification than to an enabling complexification. As such, striation, which can of course be co-opted in the same way that abstract machines can be co-opted, is not only inevitable, it is as positive as smoothing. It should be affirmed, that is. As Guattari notes, 'striation reveals itself to be synonymous with processes of the enrichment of the possible and the virtual' (SC: 98). In analogy, smoothing pertains less to an invariably liberating destratification than to any change in the relation between entities, or between entities and their milieu. Any new route I take down the road smoothes my practice of living in that it makes me more subtly aware of the milieu. The ecological lesson is that every new navigation of a given milieu implies processes of smoothing. As Guattari proposed at La Borde, the patients should monitor their movements and *path*ologies. According to the logic of transversality, in fact, skipping a stone or doing a little quick-step can have similar effects of smoothing as do unexpected changes in the chemistry of a specific molecular arrangement in my knee. The shift from intra-entitarian striation to the smoothings implied by the entity's movement through its milieu or by inter-entitarian relations makes the operational theatre of the two terms both equivalent and asymmetric. 'Every heterogeneity developed in an entitarian register is a striation', while 'every inter-entitarian transformation of the neighbourhood between two registers is a smoothing' (78). According to this deeply ecological conceptualization, striation pertains to the amount of a consistency's internal complexity, and thus to its operational and informational closure, while smoothing pertains to its movements within the milieu, and thus to its energetic openness and its structural coupling to that milieu, which concern the totality of the resonances between entity and milieu at each infinitely short moment of that entity's existence. In evolutionary terms, these structural couplings denote processes of adaptation, as when one enters a room and automatically adapts to its milieu both in terms of physical and psychic tensors, stressors and tenors. How one enters a room not considered as an environment, which means as a computed and perceived reality, but as a milieu with which one is in resonance, has a lot to do with what we call grace, which, as Heinrich von Kleist explained in 'On the Marionette Theatre', functions mostly on unconscious, automatic levels. It denotes the ability of an entity to open itself up and automatically adapt to as many of the constantly changing tensions and forces within its milieus as possible. To get its dark precursors into action. To become imperceptible. It is only in this sense that Guattari promotes a *dark ecology*.

If one breaks ecology down to the entitarian level, for an entity to remain operative, changes in the milieu and adaptations to these changes must lie within a range that is provided by that entity's abstract structural blueprint, as well as by the specific forms of its embodiment. If perturbations and changes exceed this range and can no longer be integrated, the network of structural couplings between the entity and the milieu or medium dissolves. The milieu becomes first unhealthy and ultimately lethal. Structural couplings, then, concern the extremely complicated resonances and calibrations between entities and the given multiplicity of the milieu; a dynamics in which the entity's aim is to keep its own systemic organization and structure intact in terms of formal invariance. In other words, its aim is to stay alive. Expressed less dramatically and more ecologically, its aim is to create an 'adequate conduct' (Maturana 1987: 76).

The fact that the entity and the milieu experience each other as sets of quantitative irritations has immediate ecological implications. The difference between intensive and informational, as in a-signifying and signifying registers, is analogous to that between a continuously changing set of dynamics and their integrated version, and thus to that between a medium that touches and irritates entities on a quantitative level and an environment that operates on a qualitative level. This parallelism goes through all levels of the recursive assemblage of objects, down to its smallest elements. In the words of von Foerster, 'no [cell] codes the *quality* of the cause of an irritation, only the *quantity* of the irritation' (1993: 56). Objects, therefore, are merely tokens of the entity's eigenbehaviour: 'our sense organs continuously "report" only the more or less severe bumping against an obstacle, but they never convey features or characteristics of that which they bump against' (von Glasersfeld 2011: 21). In ultimately addressing the realm of the energetic and of impulses – the *'intensity* of the irritation' (von Foerster 1993: 274) – structural couplings cause or pilot structural changes. They trigger changes in the entity's operational architecture, which in turn feedback into further structural couplings. As observers have no conscious knowledge of most of these structural changes, they perceive them as behavioural changes. As such, structural couplings are the dark precursors of behavioural change.

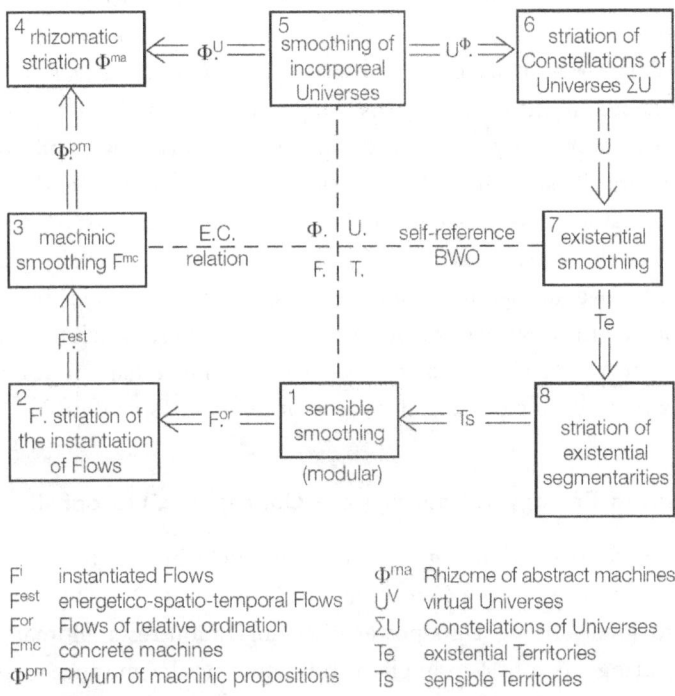

FIGURE 3.7 Cycle of the Assemblages of enunciation

In terms of how unconscious systemic histories are related to the notations of these histories from within the cognitive platform that is responsible for behavioural changes the question is how to think Guattari's programmatic statement that '[t]*here is no language in itself*' (MU: 27), which mirrors Maturana's statement that 'everything that is said is said by an observer' (1987). Guattari's stress on a-signifying semiotics has to do with the idea that language should also be seen as a mode of structural coupling. Signification, which is extrapolated from the internal observation of structural change is, invariably and at the same time, an attribute of a-signifying structural coupling. The level of language does not replace structural couplings, therefore; it is one form of structural coupling among an infinity of others. On this background, while language has to do with the complexification and thus striation of entities in terms of its signifying function, it also has to do, to a similar degree but in terms of its a-signifying function, with operations of smoothing. It is implicated in the general ecosophic logic that, as Guattari's Figure 3.7 shows, striation happens within functors, while smoothing happens between them: *striated functors, smooth passages.*

In this conceptual rear-view mirror, one can see how much of *A Thousand Plateaus* already points to this asymmetry rather than to the perhaps too simple politics of smoothing that many, especially many political readings, have distilled from the book. In more general terms, *Schizoanalytic Cartographies* allows one to critique any easy evaluation of Guattari and Deleuze's conceptual pairs, as when readers valorize lines of flight over habits, in the same way that they valorize smoothing over striation or horizontality over verticality. As Genosko notes, 'the Guattarian and Foucauldian senses of transversality share in the valorization of horizontality (over the "verticality of thought", as Guattari noted while remaining wary of valorizing just one orientation)' (2009: 65). While this is true, one should go even further and re-evaluate these pairs from within their overall asymmetry and deeply ecological complementarity. At this point, therefore, let me rewrite *less striation, more smoothing!*, which is a slogan many scholars of Guattari and Deleuze would subscribe to, as the perhaps more contentious, but eminently more ecological slogan *more striation, more smoothing!*

Expressionism in Ecology I: Squaring the Concept – Chlorophyll

From within the fourfold, thinking schizoecology might be said to involve or, even stronger, to consist of creating a conceptual quadrophonics. Quite literally, the fourfold asks us to square thought. Its power of ecologization rests, ultimately, on this expressive squaring. As a first example of this squaring, let me turn to what is by default seen as an unbridgeable rift between the subject and the world [→ **Deleuze 178**]. In his 1944 essay 'Mind and Matter' Erwin Schrödinger deals with this rift in terms of light, which is two different things simultaneously: electromagnetic radiation, and how a certain spectrum of electromagnetic radiation is perceived by the optical machines we call eyes. What disturbs Schrödinger is the incommensurable gap between these two registers; the gap between the experience of being 'hit by and receiv[ing] light quanta' (1976: 123) and, for instance, the experience of the luminous beauty of what is called golden hour.

This gap splits the medium of light up into what Schrödinger calls objective 'rays of light' (123) and subjective 'rays of vision' (123). What bothers Schrödinger is that there is no immediate relation between these two modes of rays. While 'the sensation of colour cannot be accounted for by the physicist's objective picture of light-waves' (154), the 'color in itself tells you nothing about the wave-length' (160). Throughout his text, Schrödinger searches unsuccessfully for a way to conceptually heal this 'horrible antinomy' (122), which is also mentioned by Varela in *The Embodied Mind*: 'If we actually measure the light reflected from the world around us, we will discover that there simply is no one-to-one relationship between light flux at various wavelengths and the colors we perceive areas to have' (1991: 160). Despite this difference between 'perceived color and locally reflected light' (160), and thus between subjective colour and the electromagnetic wavelengths measured by an objective apparatus such as a camera or a spectrometer, there is a correspondence or resonance between the entity and its medium. This correspondence, however, has nothing to do with the extraction of an objective truth or a stable reservoir of knowledge from that medium. Rather, it concerns an enacted correspondence, in which the designation of colour functions as a communal, pragmatic value that is useful to negotiate, in terms of evolution, the relation between entity and medium. It is an evolutionarily tested mode of navigation within the optical world. As Varela notes, 'our perceived world of color is ... a result of one possible and viable phylogenetic pathway among many others realized in the evolutionary history of living beings' (183). At the same time, other entities have developed completely different viable phylogenetic pathways, such as the whale, whose wondrous optical worldview Herman Melville marvelled at in *Moby Dick*, or the compound eyes of the fly in David Cronenberg's *The Fly*. As Cornelius Castoriadis notes, 'we live in a world of colors that we create, but that we do not create entirely arbitrarily because they correspond to something, namely to the shocks that we receive from the outside world' (2000: 114, quoted in Hansen 2009: 141)

If this asymmetry pertains to the difference between the fields of the given and the given as given in Deleuze, in Guattari it pertains to that between the given and the giving. Both of these differentiations rely on the notion that no actual is without its virtual and no virtual without its actual. While Guattari and Deleuze agree on this, in *Schizoanalytic Cartographies* Guattari sets out to square this well-rehearsed Deleuzian pair. This squaring shows that the fourfold cannot itself be considered as an informal diagram. In the guise of the abstract machine, the informal diagram is in actual fact situated within the fourfold in the position of Phyla and thus less comprehensive than the allover informal diagram in Deleuze's pairing. In particular, it is actual and abstract, although it pertains to the virtual, the concrete and the real by way of its relation to the three other attractors of the fourfold.

It might be read as a marker of the ecosophical in *Schizoanalytic Cartographies* that Guattari negotiates the implications of this squaring by way of the difference between different aspects of green. But then again, chances are that the choice of colour is contingent. What is ecosophical, however, is that in its squaring, Guattari's diagram of a green world dissolves the binary antinomy – objective, actual measurement will never coincide with subjective, virtual perception and vice versa – within its overall topology. There is an actual and real, given green. A green as Flow. Then there is, from within a more bio-chemical context, the green that plants use to procure nutrition, which means a green that has become, in some aspects, part of a plant-nutrition rhizome. A green of Phyla. Then there is the green that carries affect, such as Gatsby's green light at the end of Daisy's dock. This is the affective green of Territories. And finally, there is chlorophyll or, metatheoretically, the diffracted green that is constructed by Guattari in his text: The immaterial concept of green constructed within the field of Universes. While Schrödinger considers the difference between an objective green and a green that is constructed and filtered by an entity's biological or technical machines of perception to be a tragic antinomy, Guattari sees the diffraction of the green into the four functors as productive: 'Being-green-there, clinging on to the plant, is certainly not nothing! But being green by a detour through the Virtual Universe of colours or through algorithms and technico-scientific procedures capable of presiding over the wavelengths of luminous Flows is something completely different! But is it really necessary to repeat that the one does not happen without the other?' (SC: 136). Like Deleuze, Guattari proposes to align rather than to separate an actual green in the given and a virtual green in the giving. While Deleuze's alignment of the world as given and the world as given as given leaves it at that, however, Guattari unfolds the green into four rather than two greens. Each of these greens accords to one of the four functors – F, Φ, T, U – respectively: 'Thus the same serial trait – the "green" – can be circumscribed in a modular relation mf or circulate in φ in an "atmospheric", fractal state' (136). In Flows and Phyla, that is. In Territories, it exists 'in an infinitesimal discursive form' (136), in Universes 'in a non-discursive incorporeal form' (136). The green, then, circulates within the fourfold in dynamic constellations that play themselves out between and in both the given and the giving. Any specific green will always have to be determined within this fourfold field. The difference between or rather the complementarity of the actual and the virtual must, therefore, be determined further. 'Must it be inferred that the two worlds – of contingent territorialities [FT] and of transversal, fractal and deterritorialized entities [ΦU] – overlap and interpenetrate? That would be a little too simple!' (136), Guattari states. In this complementarity of a given and giving green along the fourfold's vertical axis, as well as in its further determination along its horizontal axis, lies *the birth of schizoecology*.

The challenge is to find an adequate topological model for this fourfold circulation, which forms the underlying ground of any form of ecology; to find an ecological model that adequately expresses the relation between the world and its creatures. At some moments, Guattari takes up the Deleuzian vocabulary of matters-of-fact or states of things and of events to delineate the ecological quadrophonics implied by this circulation. 'Doubtless one cannot avoid postulating the existence of a level of pure abstract incorporeal reference [the green of the giving], which we will call the Plane of Consistency (PoC), traversing the ensemble of states of things [the green of the given]' (136, my brackets). In the fourfold, matters-of-fact lie on the side of Flows and Phyla, while events lie on that of Territories and Universes. 'Traits of singularization ... date, eventalize, "contingentialize" states of fact' (4), Guattari notes. Similarly, in his essay 'Architectural Enunciation' he defines architecture as 'a process of eventization, that is to say, of the historical enrichment and re-singularization of desire and of values' (SC: 239).

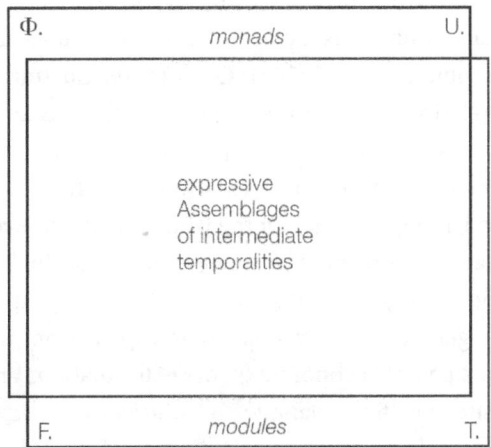

FIGURE 6.6 Overlapping of monads and modules

The two internal assemblage theories Guattari sets up by supplementing the vertical vector in the fourfold with a horizontal vector are echoed in Deleuze's differentiation between pure events and assembled events on the one side, and pure matters-of-fact and assembled matters-of-fact on the other, which means that the difference between Deleuze and Guattari is ultimately one of degree rather than of kind. Still, it is important that Guattari positions every situation within a field defined simultaneously by four equally powerful attractors. In order to position and gauge a situation, Guattari notes, the vertical axis between the actual and the virtual that defines the fourfold needs always to be brought into conjunction with the horizontal, constructive axis. Guattari's Figure 6.6 illustrates that in relation to this constructive axis, the 'two extreme zones of contingency FT and of virtuality ΦU' are, from a strictly 'cartographic point of view', invariably linked together in a 'zone of intersection' (136). It is only in this double exposure that 'expressive Assemblages' (136) can be adequately, which means ecologically, conceptualized. While there is a vertical distinction between the actual and the virtual on the level of FΦ and that of TU, a similar, horizontal distinction pertains between FT and ΦU which concerns 'modules of finite contingencing' and 'monads of infinite determinability' (138). Modules define the territorializing field between Flows and Territories, while monads define the deterritorializing field between Phyla and Universes. Modules are 'substantial' (82). They are related to 'the domain of sensible and signaletic Flows' (171) and denote the realm of 'sensible territorialization' (78). Their position is that of 'territorialized proto-enunciation' (118).

Guattari puts two analogous processes into play to differentiate between modules and monads. There is contingencing on the side of modules, and singularization on the side of monads. The question is 'how can degrees of contingency, as well as the symbiosis of incorporeal Universes with sensible modules, be established?' (156). In monads, 'singularization . . . is the deterritorialized equivalent of contingencing operating within sensible modules' (164). Once more, Guattari processualizes and thus ecologizes the relation between the terms. Not chaos and order, but contingencing and determining. Not actual and virtual, but actualizing and virtualizing. Although the formal distinction pertains, it does so only as a function within a larger processuality. Not green, but greening. Not the world, but *process ecology*. As each situation, such as the situation of greening, is squared in the fourfold, processes and situations cannot be reduced to generalities. The situation of a patient in a mental clinic is irreducible to a generalized psychoanalytic explanation, the situation of a worker is irreducible to a general economic theory. All situations are impervious to general, not time- and site-specific explanations: *situationist ecology*.

Somewhat ironically, in fact, the one thing the fourfold cannot model is a strictly formal situation. If a situation is looked at through the lens of the fourfold, the result will never be an explanation of or a solution to that situation, but rather a lining of that time- and site-specific situation that might facilitate an intervention in the situation, hopefully with a heightened awareness of the dynamics that define the situation as one element of the larger set of any-situation-whatever. In the sense that the situationists define the constructed situation as 'a moment of life concretely and deliberately constructed by the collective organization of a unitary ambiance and a game of events' (Ivain 2006b: 51), the fourfold is inherently situationist: *situgram*.

It is invariably the user's job, therefore, to delineate the specific roles the various actors have in the situation in order to adequately administer it. What the fourfold provides is a painstakingly abstract figure of thought that lines the parameters of any given situation as invariably site- and time-specific. Every one of these situations, and thus any administration, implies a singular and constantly changing arrangement.

As an axiomatics of how to adequately administer the world, therefore, the fourfold is an immense wager, but then, all theories are such wagers and they can be reduced to diagrams. Very few theorists, however, put as much work into providing their diagram and into abstracting their thought into such an immensely complicated conceptual figure as Guattari: *the fourfold as ecogram*.

Expressionism in Ecology 2: Squaring the Unconscious

A second ecological squaring performed by the fourfold concerns the formal diagrammatism of psychoanalysis; its use of 'fixed and invariant' maps, of 'universals' and of 'structuralist mathemes' (SS: 302). Early on in *Schizoanalytic Cartographies*, in fact, Guattari uses the difference between Freudian psychoanalysis and schizoanalysis to illustrate the operation of the four functors. Where, within the fourfold, are the positions of the libido and the unconscious? Is there even only one libidinal field, or are specific libidos constructed in different fields? As Guattari's Figure 1.4 illustrates, although the libido emerges in the actual field of Flows and Phyla as an anonymous, productive force, it comes to involve all four functors when it is considered under the aspect of individual entities and their unconscious. In order to align the two sides of the fourfold, and thus the libido and the unconscious, one needs to conceptualize an energetic semiotics that, in terms of psychoanalysis, can be found in Freud more than in Lacan, who initiates, in O'Sullivan's wonderful phrase, 'a wholesale signifier enthusiasm' (2012: 106).

In his talk on 'Semiotic Energetics' given at the Cerisy Colloquium in France, June 1983, Guattari traces Freud's shift from the *'initial hypothesis of an energy whose effects were simultaneously physical and psychic'* (B: 394; slightly altered in SC: 50) to his 'second topography', in which 'the energy metaphors are gradually dispelled in

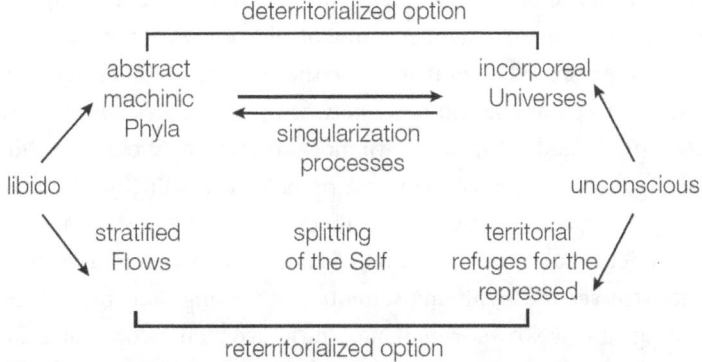

FIGURE 1.4 The optional matter Libido-Unconscious

favor of more anthropomorphic models' (394). Guattari's 'psychophysics' (396) aims to reconnect the actual libido and the virtual unconscious along what he calls 'the various energetics that are brought into play, which I would call "semiotic energetics"' (400). These connect 'transformations that are established simultaneously between the most heterogeneous domains that one could conceive'. A psychophysics, therefore, 'presupposes various modalities of "transversality" between those domains' (397). In his discussion in *Schizoanalytic Cartographies*, which is to a large extent a rewriting of that talk with some added information on the fourfold, Guattari stakes, against Lacan's foreclosure of the actual, 'the stroke of genius, if not the stroke of madness, that led Freud to invent a *semiotic energetics*, the first theorizations of which were, all things considered and despite their naively scientistic character, less reductionist than those that he was later to develop in the context of the institutionalization of psychoanalysis' (SC: 47; slightly altered in B: 392). Although Guattari does not directly mention this particular context, let me relate these semiotic energetics, or perhaps energetic semiotics, to Freud's early neurological concept of breaching (*Bahnung*) that he develops in 'Project for a Scientific Psychology', if only because it involves the synaptic moment as a moment that creates an overlap between the actual and the virtual. At this point, Freud's model of the psychic apparatus is still that of a neurological circuit that processes stimuli, with the concept of breaching describing the paths and the pathologies of energetic excitations running through that network. In this context, Freud initially differentiates between two sets of neurons that deal with stimuli coming from the outside and from the inside respectively: 'The system Φ . . . receive[s] external stimuli, while the system Ψ . . . receive[s] endogenous excitations' (1954: 364). While the Φ neurons are permeable, allow quantitative excitations to pass through them without resistance, and remain unaltered by these passages, in the latter, the 'contact-barriers make themselves felt, so that they allow quantity . . . to pass through them only with difficulty or partially. This second class may be left in a modified condition after each excitation, and thus afford *a possibility of representing memory*' (360).

According to this model, memory is first of all a direct property of the actual neural network. It is represented – comparable to the cracks in Marcel Duchamp's fractured *Great Glass* or the paths in a computer network – '*by the facilitations existing between the Ψ neurons*' (Freud 1954: 361). Memory, therefore, should be thought of as a structural organization rather than as a psychic reservoir. In fact, Freud considers the ego as nothing but 'a network of cathected neurons' (358). Later, this scientific, energetic model that stresses the level of an a-signifying semiotics will be replaced by one that stresses the signifying semiotics of writing and traces. The logic of the mystic writing pad takes over from that of the neuronal network. 'Guattari's modelling of a processual and ecological subjectivity contra Lacan' (O'Sullivan 2012: 90) has to do with the various conceptual take-overs involved in this shift.

To come back, however, to Guattari's Figure 1.4. If until now I was concerned with the folding of the actual and the virtual onto each other along the fourfold's vertical axis, that folding is supplemented by a second folding that defines the fourfold along its horizontal axis and that complicates the first folding. According to that horizontal folding, Guattari proposes that there are two modes of the libido and of the unconscious within the analytic field. 'The libido finds that it has two statuses conferred on it. That of a processual energy making dynamic relations drift far from their equilibrium position, or that of a static energy contributing to the stratification of psychic formations' (SC: 30).

On the actual side, the libido can remain in the shadow of reterritorialization when it is considered, as it is in psychoanalytic doctrine, as a stratified, territorialized Flow that is 'first encysted in the somatic part of the drives (the drive and the source, by contrast with the aim and the object), then organized in psychogenetic stages, to finally be made prisoner of a timeless face-to-face confrontation with an entropic death' (30). On the virtual side of the fourfold, the unconscious can be considered, in analogy to stratified libidinal Flows, as a stratified virtual unconscious that functions as 'a *refuge-Territory* for the repressed' and that is, in reference to Freud's topographical model of subjectivity, 'kept on a leash by the censor of the Conscious-Preconscious system in the first topography, and by the Ego-Superego system in the second' (30). This territorialized unconscious causes a splitting of the self in that it prohibits fractalization and thus does not allow for the interplay of the dynamics of territorialization and deterritorialization.

In contrast to psychoanalysis, schizoanalysis brings into play the notion of a deterritorialized, fractalized and rhizomatic libido that is linked to the position of Phyla and that functions as 'the integral of the (material and signaletic) transformational Flows of desire' (30). In analogy, it brings into play a deterritorialized unconscious of and in Universes that is unrepressed, rhizomatic and far-from-equilibrium; 'a Universe of reference of an ensemble of lines of alterity, virtual possibilities, unprecedented new becomings' (30): *an unconscious-in-production*. Importantly, however, both options are part of the diagram and both forms of the libido and the unconscious can be constructed in it. There are gases and snowstorms, but also geological strata and sheets of ice. There are impressions and fluctuations. Faint reveries. Turbulent concepts. But also fixed, territorialized thoughts and stabilized references.

According to the two foldings described above, when Guattari differentiates between an 'absolute' and 'molecular' unconscious that is expressive and a-signifying, and a 'relative' and 'molar' (22) one that is representational and signifying, these two forms of the unconscious are not in a state of simple opposition and exclusion, and it is impossible to simply choose one over the other. As O'Sullivan reminds us, however, one should not 're-privilege the signifying over the asignifying but ... note that the signifying element cannot be ignored (and in fact Guattari is always at pains to point out that signifying semiotics play their part in schizoanalysis). A confrontation with chaos then, but also the concomitant construction of an assemblage to give the latter consistency, to make it workable' (2012: 108). Again: *more signification, more a-signification.*

In relation to the internal architecture of the fourfold, the space of human reality is defined by both a-signification and signification. In this context, Guattari's critique of Lacan is not that he is in any way wrong, but rather that he is only interested in the second mode of the unconscious, while he should also be interested in the first. 'We will start, then, from the broadest hypothesis, namely, that of the existence, for humans, of an unconscious domain associating, on an equal footing, facts of sense borne by structures of representation and language, and very different systems of coding, moulding, tracing, imprinting, relative to organic, social, economic, components, etc.' (SC: 21). Even more than Freud, Guattari notes, Lacan reduces the influence of the libido on the unconscious by focusing on the virtual sector of the unconscious and on the materiality of the signifier rather than that of the libido. From the point of view of a Lacanian semiotics, one might think of that level as a semiotics of the Real; a Real that Lacan can think of, however, only as a lack, or, more precisely, as being included in psychoanalysis only as its excluded. While a linguistic semiotics pertains to the informational closure of the entity and thus to sets of qualities, the fourfold includes the register of an energetic semiotics that is expressive and that pertains to the openness of the system to constantly changing sets of quantities. To signaletic matters and to particle-signs. Only such an expressive semiotics, which links the actual semiotics of the world and the virtual semiotics of the world's creatures, can be truly ecological.

An energetic semiotics ties the anonymous materiality of Flows to that of Phyla in the same way that a theory of affects ties an individual body to an individual mind. Again, however, the logic is fourfold. Any consistency is defined by the actual semiotics of the given world as well as by the virtual semiotics of the world of the giving. The analogy of the two, in fact, is what causes consistencies to be a part of the world and at the same time to be apart from it. It is what allows them, as that world's creatures, to be equal to that world.

If Lacanian psychoanalysis is centred on the consistency's operational and informational closure, Guattari proposes to consider the field of the libido as machinic and to align its dynamics with an unconscious that is equally deterritorialized. As such, he aligns the consistency's operational and informational closure with its energetic openness to and involvement in its milieu. Programmatically, in the fourfold the subject's modes of existence concern both fields as seemingly exclusive but in fact complementary. As Guattari notes, the subject is 'at the outset ... *indifferently* material and/or semiotic, individual and/or collective, actively machinic and/or passively fluctuating' (18, emphasis added).

Guattari's arduous and in many aspects painful separation from Lacan has to do with this ecologization of psychoanalysis. It is directed against the notion that the unconscious is structured like a language – for Lacan, the unconscious concerns quite literally 'the level of symbolic overdetermination' (2007: 88) – as well as against the ontology of the lack of the Real, which Guattari and Deleuze submit to a radical critique in *Anti-Oedipus*. In *A Thousand Plateaus*, which is less of a critique, they open up Lacan's linguistically constructed unconscious to an unconscious that is radically constructed on all levels, in all of its aspects implicated in both actual and virtual registers, and open to all of the physical, chemical, biological, linguistic and other registers within which a subject's life unfolds. This has wide-ranging implications. Most importantly, 'the issue is to *produce the unconscious*' (TP: 18) rather than to uncover it: *schizoanalytic constructivism*.

Expressionism in Ecology 3: Squaring Aesthetics

On Sunday, 28 December 1986, which is a date that, in reversing 1968, literally turns the moment of the student revolution into the middle of Ronald Reagan's presidency, Guattari, on a panel of the Modern Language Association Convention in New York that commenced at 13:30 p.m., delivered a talk on three paintings by Balthus, which was entitled 'Cracks in the Street'. That title is Guattari's re-write of 'Cracks in the Text', which was the title originally proposed to him by the organizers of the panel. In the programme of the convention, Guattari's paper, which was presented in a session hosted by the Division on Sociological Approaches to Literature, was advertised as 'The Existential Ruptures of Discursivity'. It was the third paper to be presented, following two revolutionary papers: Cornelius Castoriadis's 'Historical Creation and Revolution' and Remi Clignet's 'The Structure of Literary Revolution'.

Already in 1975, Guattari had been a participant, together with Gilles Deleuze, at a very chaotic and by now notorious conference on schizo-culture at Columbia University, hosted by Semiotext(e) and chronicled in a two-volume publication, during which he had cancelled, half-way through the presentations, the session he himself chaired. Guattari and Deleuze had left the conference early in protest. Eleven years later, in 1986, he was going straight into the belly of the beast, because the Modern Language Association was, at that time, at the heart of cultural and linguistic constructivism and thus fully invested in the logic of the signifier that was embodied, most importantly perhaps, by the work of Jacques Lacan, Jacques Derrida and Michel Foucault. Knowing this full well, Guattari begins his talk, quite programmatically and scandalously, by putting the field of discursivity into perspective for and in this specific situation: 'In response to the invitation to your conference, I had suggested calling my paper "The Existentialising Functions of Discourse". But after having crossed the Atlantic this proposition became "Cracks in the Text of the State". Already that gives us quite a lot to think about! Subsequently, it was explained to me that for a meeting placing itself under the auspices of an organization devoted to literature, it would be a good idea to stick to the idea of the text' (SC: 253).

Guattari's answer to what one would have to imagine as more or less gentle reminders by the conveners to stay in line is wonderfully ironic. 'OK!', he notes, only to add 'but it nonetheless remains that when I speak of discourse, it is only incidentally a question of text or even of language', after which he provides some short examples of what he calls a 'discursivity outside the text' (253): Lenz's schizo-stroll in Büchner, the grasping of a Zen garden, a scene from Renaud Victor's movie *Ce gamin-là* in which an autistic child observes the slow formation of drops of water. It is only on the background of such non-textual semiotics that he agrees to the initial letter of invitation. 'So, I'm OK with the title "Cracks in the Text" that was suggested to me and with the diverse modalities of textual discontinuity that your letter of invitation enumerated: gaps, ruptures, interstices, slippages, margins, crises, liminal periods, peripheries, frames, silences ... OK to all that, on condition, though, that it is not taken as a pretext to definitively silence the other forms of discursivity that persist in inhabiting our world!' (253–4).

One can only surmise what the audience must have thought and felt when Guattari went on to talk, only three pages later, about 'the plague of the signifier [that] has so ravaged the human sciences and our literature' (256), and how lost they must have been when the talk moved on, in a number of vertiginous conceptual sweeps, from Balthus' inherently fractal paintings to a conceptualization of fractal space as the adequate topological model to conceptualize the space of the world. Throughout, Guattari's argument is relentlessly abstract and relies on the listeners' knowledge of advanced geometrical concepts such as homothety, which concerns the topological transformation of spaces in which a number of parameters remain invariant. (One of the reasons why reading Guattari is often so excruciatingly difficult – perhaps even more difficult than reading Deleuze – is that unlike Deleuze, who provides extended readings of the philosophies from which he develops his thought, Guattari never provides extended readings of the hard sciences he draws on.) At this point, after a fractal reading that must have been completely enigmatic to people interested mainly in literature – in the same way that most of Guattari's ecological texts must have remained completely enigmatic to people mainly interested in ecology – most of the listeners were presumably in utter confusion.

Against the privileged, hegemonic position of the signifier, Guattari argues that 'the signifier has no ontological priority over the signified' (256). In fact, he maintains,

Balthus, La Rue
(1929) © 2019 Artists
Rights Society (ARS),
New York / ADAGP,
Paris

Balthus, La Rue
(1933) MoMa, New
York, James Thrall
Soby Bequest
Copyright © 2019
Artists Rights Society
(ARS), New York /
ADAGP, Paris

Balthus, La Rue
(1959) © 2019 Artists
Rights Society (ARS),
New York / ADAGP,
Paris

against the prevalent beliefs of theory in 1986, that the latter 'can pass into the position of "trump card"' (256). In its soft subversion of the signifier, whose Saussurean semiotics Guattari replaces with Hjelmslev's logic of expression and content, Guattari's paper argues for a 'strong comeback of the Signified, of the "iconic", of the non-digital, of the symptom, in short a certain "democratic" liberation of molecular populations' (261, my modified translation). No superego, no control, no castration, no lack.

As the signified is an image, and as such part of the visual field, Guattari substitutes 'for the statement proposed, a *composite memory* of three paintings by Balthus on the theme of the street' (254, emphasis added). Guattari uses the word *souvenir* rather than *memoire*, perhaps to stress the materiality of the mnemonically superposed paintings that form his talk's conceptual storyboard. (On Guattari's Balthus, see also Elliott 2012.) The conceptual topology of that storyboard is a countermodel to Lacan's Borromean Knot, which diagrams the psychoanalytic triad of the Symbolic (the signifier), the Imaginary (the signified) and the Real (the referent). Famously, for Lacan, the referent, which Guattari replaces by what he calls the world in and for itself, is excluded from the realm of the sign and of signification. By way of this shift Guattari's model replaces the psychoanalytic, representational model with a schizoanalytic, expressive one. On this storyboard, Guattari lays out the conceptual plane on which he assembles an aesthetics that goes beyond the signifier, in that it considers that signifier as a result rather than as a beginning; as the end product of a process of semiotic reduction rather than the agent that opens up a significant world in the first place.

In Guattari's complex expressive machine all three Lacanian realms function as equally positive and present attractors. In addition, the Real is no longer excluded and forms a further aspect of the world. The Imaginary – which Lacan relates to the iconic and to the phantasm, whose alignment with the law of the Symbolic proceeds from within a dynamics of symbolic castration in which the Real marks the excluded lack that the phantasm does not stop aiming to fill – is replaced, in Guattari, by the realm of existentialization and affect (sensation). The Symbolic is redefined as the realm of thought (sense). In fact, in terms of aesthetics, one might easily fold Deleuze's books *The Logic of Sensation* and *The Logic of Sense* onto the fourfold. In this superposition, the former would proceed from the position of Flows and Territories to Phyla and Universes, while the latter would proceed from the position of Phyla and Universes to Flows and Territories, sensation being to sense as Flows and Territories are to Phyla and Universes.

When it was published in *Chimères* in 1987, the text of Guattari's talk contained not only reproductions of the three paintings, but also a photograph taken by Joséphine Guattari of the actual site (*L'état actuel du passage*) that is presented most accurately in the third painting. What I will argue is that Guattari's conceptual and mnemonic

The actual state of the passage.
Photo by Joséphine Guattari.

superposition of these four images is, although Guattari never mentions it, an aesthetic recapitulation and instantiation of the conceptual superposition of the four functors in the fourfold along a chronological vector that is similar to the one Guattari uses in the fourfold. In its progression from Flows to Phyla, Territories and Universes, that diagram (p. 114) comes to function as the conceptual storyboard not only of a Guattarian ontology, but also of a Guattarian aesthetics: *Becoming Balthus*.

The photograph, which is, for reasons I will discuss later, the final illustration in the article, instantiates the first position of the fourfold; the world considered as the paradox of territorialized Flows. The given, actual and real world expressing itself to itself, here symbolized by the objective image of the camera considered, for this purpose and very foreshortened, as an anonymous recording machine. The progression from the photograph to the first painting follows the fourfold's progression, in that the painting instantiates and belongs to the position of the world's aspect as a deterritorialized abstract machine. Significantly, Guattari had positioned the beginning of codes and codings in the shift from Flow to Phyla; from Josephine's empty street to a first allover expressionism of a still anonymous, but now heterogeneous,

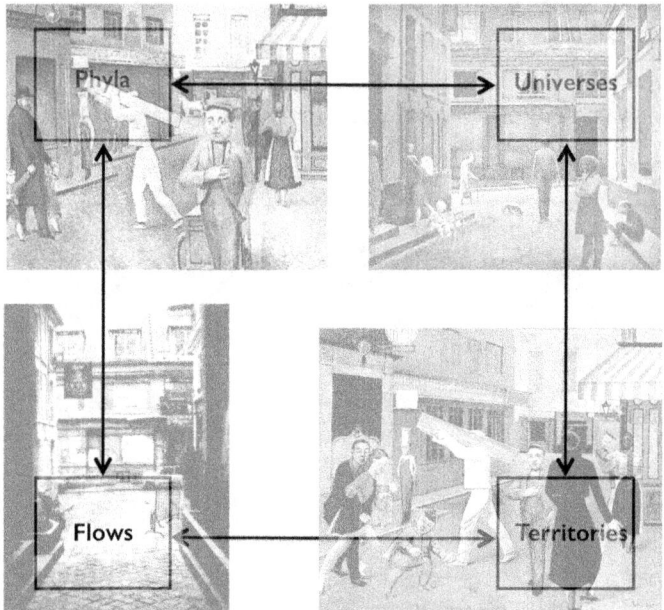

aerosolic world. The heterogeneous world as given to itself. In the oxymoron of an arrangement of unrelated singular figures, the first painting reaffirms 'the irreducible polyvocity of the components of expression that contribute to the production of an aesthetic effect' (SC: 255). This given heterogeneity, which concerns signifying and a-signifying components equally, such as figures and colours, forms the irreducibly deterritorialized ground of the world that subverts all forms of psychoanalytic aesthetics: 'No hermeneutics, no structural overcoding can compromise the heterogeneity and functional autonomy of these components, the guarantors of the processual opening of the work, no signifying operation can "resolve" the interlaced paths of aesthetic discursivity' (255–6).

The photograph and the first painting concern the two aspects of the actual world as given: the world as continuous Flow and the world conceptualized as an integrated, or fractalized abstract machine. (As shown earlier, the first secretion of codes and codings happened in the shift from one to the other.) It is in the crossover from the allover heterogeneity of the abstract machine to the virtual, individual heterogeneity of the virtual side that concrete machines, or entities, emerge: 'The aesthetic rupture of discursivity is not undergone passively, the heterogeneity of registers to which it leads must be conceived as a *heterogenesis*. It is enacted by operators that I characterize as *concrete machines*' (256). The second painting marks this crossover to the aspect of the world as the giving, which is the world in its aspect of being made up of concrete machines, of entities with their affective Territories and conceptual Universes. The empty and rhizomatic street of the left side is now populated and perceived by individual, singular and related beings. These 'concrete machines ... at one and the same time, dissociate and gather together matters of expression, "polyphonize" them, as Bakhtin would have it, and transversalize them, that is to say, make them shift between their diverse levels of deterritorialized forms and processes, which I call abstract machines' (256).

In the conceptual storyboard developed in *Schizoanalytic Cartographies* Territories denote the affective, existentializing organization and composition of an individual space that is cut out from the allover, deterritorialized, abstract machine that is the anonymous world, in a movement from a world to my world. The beginnings of an ecological aesthetics that trails the anonymous world behind, and that encompasses both *aisthesis* and aesthetics, lie in this crossover. By way of an existential function and a 'pathic operator' (257), part of the deterritorialized machine is captured by an emergent self that constructs a territory by cutting figures and correspondences out of it. Balthus' second painting concerns this 'existential function when it is organized in aesthetic Assemblages' (257): *aisthesis*. The painting embodies, recapitulates and artistically expresses (the creation of) such an existential and affective territory, tracing a vector from its fragile beginnings and defences against dissolution to the moment when it opens itself up to the freedom of thought. Unlike in the first painting, Guattari writes, the figures, no longer completely unrelated, form a fragile milieu that 'answer[s] to an enigmatic play of correspondences' (254): fragile, because the arrangement of the figures is ambiguous (as with the hand of the woman front right), the perspective is out of joint (somewhat as in a de Chirico painting), and even the aggregate state of the territory is not clear-cut. (As if the street were under water, Guattari compares the position of the girl in the red sweater to that of a Cartesian diver.) The key to these secret correspondences lies in the figures' movements and gestures as well as in an overall, 'depersonalized' (258) 'strategy of gazes' (254) that draws the spectators into the street, where they become a mobile part of its unsettling spatial and affective organization and carve out their own territories. 'Our own gaze has ceased to be contemplative; it is captured, fascinated and henceforth functions as a transmission belt between a gaze-machine at work in the painting and the unconscious processes that it triggers in us. A curious trans-human, trans-machinic relation of inter-subjectivity is established' (258). The scene, Guattari notes, could come from 'a Robert Wilson play' (255), and it feels like 'a Zen composition for the city' (255). It is in this affective street and its cracks – artistically rendered in the painting's cracked structure – that processes of existentialization and territorialization take place. 'Existence is not a given by rights, a gain, it is a contingent production that is constantly called into question, a rupture of equilibrium, a headlong flight establishing itself in a defensive mode, or in a regime of proliferation, in response to all these cracks, these gaps, these ruptures ...' (257). However, although the spectators' own territories are disrupted in the confrontation with the painting, the overall vector remains one of reterritorialization. Guattari stresses that both signifying forms and a-signifying affects are part of the painting's territorializing effect. 'The rutilant relations of surface and colour and ... the dance of gazes [generate] a systematic disordering of the coordinates of our ordinary world (to illuminate it anew but so as finally to bring us back to it)' (255).

This return to a territorialized world is why Guattari maintains that on the affective, aisthetic level, the painting captures our gaze in the name of a molar system of surveillance; of a Freudian, 'panoptic superego' (255) that presides over the cityscape, capturing us within 'the hegemony of a seeing without a subject, without any object, with no purpose' (254–5). In other words, the painting asks us, like Althusser's policeman, to identify our position within the painting's given territory. It brings back 'the ancestral fear of disintegration.' It 'takes on this fear, absorbs it like blotting paper, *then relays it back to us*' (258). (In this context, see also Guattari's reference to the 'Ego-Superego system' (30) in Freud's second topography, and the reference to the '*refuge-Territory* for the repressed' (30; also Guattari's Figure 1.4) that I mentioned earlier.)

Although this affective scene is, like the position of Flows, territorialized, it opens itself up, once it is consistent enough, to the final position of Universes. As such, it functions as a conduit from a defensive position to a position that is open and future-oriented. In fact, the very process of territorialization sets off, like a fractal cascade, 'what, following Jakobson, I will call a phatic operator. Through it, certain ruptures of form, certain dissolutions of pre-established perceptual schema, certain diversions of sense find themselves converted into new enunciative cutouts' (257). This fractalization of the territory forms the threshold to the third painting, whose composition comes closest to the *état actuel*, the actual state provided by the photograph a that moment, and which shows a 'much more molecular treatment of [its] plastic elements' (255): *aesthetics*. This shift from the molar and modular to the molecular and monadic composition 'initiates a soft topology' (255). It is at this point that 'the impact of the "cracking" is displaced from molar ensembles to molecular intensities; the powdery grain of pictorial matter takes primacy over the structurally qualified relations. The breaking down of the dynamic of gazes throws facts and gestures, which to that point had been hooked onto the eyes of the characters like a garland, off centre. It is the painting itself, taken as a whole, which makes itself into a gaze and an originary instance of sense, implanting a "becoming Balthus" at the heart of our ways of seeing the world' (259).

At this fractal moment, the painting becomes a catalyst for an analogous movement of the dispersion and fractalization of the spectator's subjectivity. It triggers a 'subjective mutation, taking us far from well-worn paths' (259). As Guattari notes, 'the enigmatic power that the Passage by Balthus is loaded with resides in the fact that its real "subject" is, precisely, nothing other than this operator ... of passage, transversality, of the transfer of subjectivity' (259). In the conceptual move from and superposition of the actual world to the pathic world and further to the world of thought, this point of the overlap of Territories and Universes is the ultimate moment of art and aesthetics. At this moment, however, the other three functors are not eclipsed. Rather, at this moment, at which all four functors are superposed, the fourfold is at its most comprehensive.

Guattari's affirmative, productive, unsettling and deterritorializing schizoaesthetics are staked against a psychoanalytic aesthetics that is based on a fundamental, productive lack in and of representation, and with that, against a Freudian hermeneutics. Compare Guattari's reading to a psychoanalytic perspective, from which art is approached by way of a figure of thought that sees a fundamental but productive lack in and of representation. Art is born from an inherently impossible desire to represent the unrepresentable Real, and it circles around and tries to bring into representation repressed desires and primal scenes. Overall, it is a machine of compensation and substitution. It is as such that it calls for a Freudian hermeneutics. Guattari sets art as affirmative, productive, unsettling and deterritorializing against such an art of lack. In spatial terms, it fractalizes the three psychoanalytic dimensions into a topology that allows one to think processes of subjectification in a more complex, transversal manner.

As Guattari notes 'the principal characteristics of the fractal impulse convertor put to work by Balthus can be summarized in three points' (260–1). The first is that fractalization allows for quasi-continuous shifts between spatial and conceptual levels that Guattari calls the option of transversality. It fractalizes clear dimensions and allows formerly separated fields, such as those of art and politics, to intersect. 'The stakes of such a fractalization of the psyche are not lacking in ethico-political repercussions. It is a question of the constraining, "one way", discursivity of capitalist subjectification, which can thereby find itself expropriated by multi-centred, heterogeneous, polyphonic, polyvocal approaches established far from "pre-coded" equilibria' (260–1). The other two functions of art are to be a catalyst for resingularization and for the heterogenesis of subjectivity. In the social field, art intervenes in and subverts closed systems of representation – here: systems that follow the logic of the signifier – and turns them into open, expressive systems. The shift from a logic of representation to a logic of expression takes place on the background of a replacement of an axiomatic ground, such as the structure of psychoanalysis, by the processual ground of schizoanalysis. It stakes an existential, affective sense against a logical sense: '1 It permits an escape from *systems of representation closed in on themselves*; it eats away at their limits in such a way as to make them work as a "strange attractor" of transversality. 2 Its intrinsic processuality leads to a constant repositioning of its ontological references and to a modification of *the existential dimensions of its enunciation*, dimensions that are synonymous with permanent resingularization. 3 The fact that it escapes from the pre-established circumscribing of sense leads to its deployment in *self-referenced fields of expression that can be considered as so many instances of the self-production of subjectivity*' (260).

Not surprisingly, these three points are directly related to the main topics of the fourfold. A field of open systems of expression versus a field of closed systems of representation. A processual versus an axiomatic ground. As Guattari notes in *Chaosmosis*, art can bring about a 'controlled chaosmotic deterritorialization . . . under the sign of social, aesthetic and analytic practices' (C: 56). It can energize consistencies in order to let them escape their too-routinized attractors and to bring them into new states of metastability and disequilibrium. Guattari's reading of Balthus shows how art can bring about such a destabilization, in that it implies 'an activity of unframing, of rupturing sense, of baroque proliferation or extreme impoverishment, which leads to a recreation and a reinvention of the subject itself' (C: 131).

The way Guattari softens up and subverts the panel of the MLA is the perfect analogue to Balthus' softening of the topology of the street and his soft subversion that Guattari conceptualizes in his talk. From this angle, Guattari's presentation of 'Cracks in the Street' might itself be seen as an example of conceptual art, or as a performance piece. As a short-term installation, perhaps, of a both signifying and a-signifying machinic aesthetics. His audience must have been irritated, unsettled, deregulated but also, perhaps, animated. In some listeners, his performance might have, like a work of art, brought about, within the environment of the MLA and thus literally under the sign of social, aesthetic and analytic practices, such a controlled chaosmotic deterritorialization. In this light, encounters with art, but also the encounter with Guattari's situationist, ecological schizoaesthetics during the 1986 MLA convention, might generate, perhaps, an aesthetics-to-come: *becoming Balthus, becoming Guattari*.

Expressionism in Ecology 4: Squaring Media Studies

In November 1985, one year before the MLA paper in New York, Guattari had presented the paper 'Postmodern Deadlock and Post-Media Transition' (2009b) in Tokyo. Two other texts – 'Entering the Post Media Era', a manuscript published in *Soft Subversions*, and 'Towards a Post-Media Era', a 1990 text that was published in *Chimères* in 1996 – also deal with the 'junction of television, telematics and informatics' (2013c: 27) in an increasingly 'media-driven world' (2009a: 302).

In these papers, Guattari stakes his vision of a post-media era against against the environmental, mediatic and mental pollutions that define the present moment: 'irreversible ecological damage', the 'mass-mediatic pollution of collective subjectivity' (2009b: 300), and the 'desingularizing and infantilizing leveling of the capitalist production of signifiers' (296). Perhaps the new developments in the media landscape harbour the potential for deterritorializations that will bring about a 'a post-media era of collective-individual reappropriation and an interactive use of machines of information, communication, intelligence, art and culture' (279); a post mass-media media ecosophy. Perhaps the new media platforms are planes of potentiality that should be embraced and administered in an ecosophic manner. That the 'production of our signaletic raw materials is increasingly dependent on the intervention of machines does not imply that human freedom and creativity are inexorably condemned to alienation by mechanical procedures' (297), Guattari claims. In fact, 'nothing prohibits that, instead of the subject being under the control of the machine, the machinic networks are engaged in processes of a healthy subjectivation. In other terms, nothing prohibits machinism and humanity from starting to have fruitful symbiotic relations' (296; see also TE: 31). As Michael Goddard notes, 'the generation of a media, or rather post-media, ecology' might lead to 'an unforeseen processual production of subjectivity amplifying itself via technical means' (2013: 48).

Against any form of pre-media nostalgia, Guattari argues that an unmediated reality has never existed. There were no '"good old days" when things were as they were, regardless of their mode of representation'. Already, 'during the Paleolithic age – with its own myths and rituals – expressive mediation had distanced itself from "reality"' (2013c: 27). The potentiality of the 1985 media moment lies in the pervasive presence of a-signifying media machines by which 'all prior formations of power and their particular ways of shaping the world have been deterritorialised. Money, identity, social control fall under the aegis of the smart card.' In this 'almost delirious universe of mass-media subjectivity' the state of reality 'is way more cracked than it seems. It can blow up like a windshield under the impact of molecular alternative practices' (27).

This mediatic deterritorialization might be read as an updated version of the shift from television to video, in which Guattari had also seen the potential for dissensual, or as Marshall McLuhan might say cool, interventions into an originally strictly one-way, consensual, hot medium. Now it is the promise of a shared information platform and the 'miniaturization and the personalization of equipments' (2009b: 298) that might allow for a 'resingularization of the machinic mediatized means of expression' (298; see also Berardi 2008: 29). While this promise would soon be eclipsed by the intervention of data-driven forms of power and control, a line of potentiality might be drawn that leads Guattari from his involvement in the free pirate radio stations of the '70s – he wrote 'Millions and Millions of Potential Alices' to serve as a preface to the French edition of *Alice e il Diabolo*, a situationist account of these experiments – to the affordable super 8 and video cameras used at La Borde, and further to the contemporary smartphone softwares that allow users to realize film projects, which Guattari would have considered as another potentiality from within which to construct a singularized media politics. As he notes in *Schizoanalytic Cartographies*, 'the passage from the consensual mediatic era to a dissensual post-mediatic era ... will allow each person to take on fully his or her processual potentialities and perhaps to transform this planet, which is lived as a hell by four-fifths of its population today, into a universe of creative enchantments. I imagine that this language will ring false to many jaded ears, and that the least badly intentioned will accuse me of being utopian' (13). In 2019, one might add: to each potential diversification of the media ecology, its winter years.

Today, these shifts would be described as changes of the media ecology, which we tend to think of as the superposition of various technical media in a given situation. While Guattari is immensely interested in such technical media-assemblages, his use of video in La Borde shows that his notion of the media ecology that would be able to diagram a situation in all of its complexity is much more comprehensive. Some of this opening up of media to the allover milieu – one might speak, perhaps, of media studies in the expanded field – reverberates through 'Towards a Post-Media Era', as when Guattari notes that 'through this transformation the classical triangulation – the expressive chain [*chaînon expressif*], the object of reference [*l'objet référé*] and the meaning [*signification*] – will be reshaped' (2013c: 27). Media practices, and thus media studies, should open themselves up to the a-signifying levels that open up when the signifying language 'leaves itself' (2009b: 298). Any 'pragmatic of the "bringing into being"' – 'to crystallize pragmatic singularities' and to 'catalyze the most diverse processes of singularization' – is 'not the exclusive privilege of language; all the other semiotic components, all the other procedures of natural and machinic encoding are competing for it' (299). Within technical media ecologies, the divide between the analog and the digital tends to run between analog media such as vinyl, and digital media such as the hard drive, or, in a more structural context, between the analog reality of the actual, abstract world and the coded, digital reality of the virtual, concrete world. By way of the media, facts are translated into 'facts of languages and these, in turn, to binarisable or "digitalisable" signifying chains' (295).

By default, to talk about media means that one is talking about technical media. While Guattari's notion of a post-media ecosophy shows how involved he was in the aspect of media as technical media, the fourfold supplements the level of his activist interventions in the field of cultural pressures and potentialities that are instantiated by technical media with a more expanded notion of mediality that adds the levels of natural media and perceptual media to that of technical media. In this context, as it does with all binaries, the fourfold fundamentally complicates the binary divides between analog and digital media, as well as between the analog and the digital in general. In the fourfold, already the actual world is both analog and digital, as Phyla are fractalized and thus digitalized versions of analog Flows. The same applies to the virtual world. While Territories are analog, Universes are digital. At the end of the process of the fractalization of Flows, the digital. At the end of the process of the fractalization of Territories, the digital. While digitalization as a function of aerosolic possibilization goes from the bottom to the top of the fourfold, it goes, at the same time, from the left to the right as a function of virtualization. 'Unary values, corresponding with the Giving, ... introduce an irreducible dimension of discontinuity and ontological appropriation (grasping)', while 'plural values corresponding to the Given, ... introduce a dimension of continuity and processual multiplicity into Assemblages' (SC: 58–9). Already here, the functors have both digital and analog aspects according to specific contexts and aspects. This inherent contextualization is why the fourfold is not a formal diagram. While territorialized states imply continuity according to the vertical vector, deterritorialized states imply discontinuity. This distinction, however, is not categorical. When Guattari's Table 2.2 (p. 95) defines Flows and Phyla as continuous, this accords to the horizontal scanning.

In other aspects, even this twofold scanning is not enough. In Guattari's Figure 3.1 (SC: 70), for instance, which relates exo-referred modelling and endo-referred meta-modelling, Flows and Territories are discontinuous while Phyla and Universes are continuous. The explanation for this reversal of the logic of the vertical vector is that 'continuous discursivity Φ marks the infinite multiplicity of a state of fact or a state of things' (70) when it is looked at from an exo-referential angle. This exo-referred continuity, however, is 'only given in "contingenced" (territorialized) Assemblages' (70) which are endo-referred, and, from that conceptual aspect, discontinuous. As actual and deterritorialized, Phyla might perhaps be understood to be quasi-continuous, while virtual Territories might be understood as quasi-discontinuous.

Overall, while one should no longer consider 'that the continuous and the discontinuous are passively given, but that they participate in processes of continuation-discontinuation' (156), even more fundamentally, the digital and the analog follow, like all binaries, the logic of complementarity. From within this logic, three 'orders of paradoxes and aporia can coexist' (119): physical, semiotic and aesthetic. While the semiotic paradox concerns 'the relations between Expression and Content, the Semiotic and the "material", the contingent and the universal, the immanent and the transcendent', the aesthetic paradox concerns the 'a-significance' that is 'at work in the "existentializing function" inhabiting diverse forms of discursivity' (119). The physical paradox, finally, concerns 'relations of exclusion and yet of co-occurrence ... between the continuous and the discontinuous, the wave and the particle, the aleatory and the determined' (119): *analog and digital in the quantum field.*

As assemblages of enunciation are defined within all three fields simultaneously, they partake in all aspects of this complementarity. 'Not only can the same concatenation of entities engage in consistencies with antagonistic definitions, but it is the way that infinitely "rapid" and absolutely deterritorialized, null consistencies are twinned with and adjacent to tardy and relatively deterritorialized consistencies ... Once again, another series of paradoxes from contemporary physics – when the same quantum of energy is incarnated in forms that are simultaneously wave and particle, discontinuous and continuous, separable and inseparable – come to mind' (110): *digital analogicity; analog digitality.*

In this superposition of analog and digital registers, the notion that digitalization cuts into continua and thus excludes analog *glissandos* in favour of digital intervals such as yes and no, or 0 and 1, no longer categorically means that given Flows and Phyla denote the world under the aspect of analog quantity, while giving Territories and Universes denote the world under the aspect of digital quality. While that distribution would imply that the actual world is more comprehensive than the virtual world – as Guattari notes, his alignment of a vertical and a horizontal scan of the fourfold concerns 'the paradox of the continuous that envelops the discontinuous and the intensive, the discursive' (112) – what digitalization loses in *glissandos* in this horizontal distribution, and thus in terms of the range of expression of the given continuum, it gains in both differential possibility, as in clarity and administrability. The digital is more robust and error-resistant than the analog. At the same time, while the analog is susceptible to small errors, it is more open to mutations, variations and modulations, and thus allows for newness to come into the world. Once more, it is not that one of these aspects is better than the other. What the fourfold diagrams is the complementarity of the two: *full analogicity, full digitality.*

The fourfold's conceptually superposed spaces allow us to think the ecological adequation between the world and its entities. The ecological superposition is instantiated spatially by the various ways in which the spaces of the fourfold overlap. Although Guattari maintains that 'we are forbidden a digitalized, binarized access to the molecular unconscious' as that unconscious is a-signifying, already Phyla are differential, which is why that impossibility of access 'doesn't mean that we are condemned to fall into an entropic abyss of disorder' (23). The plane of consistency is not organized according to the formal distinction between disorder and order, but according to a dynamics of disordering and ordering. If according to a formal distinction the uncoded is continuous and analog while the coded is discontinuous and digital, it is 'an everyday experience' that 'flows of energy are intimately mixed with signaletic Flows' (89). In other words, in the fourfold, the digital and the analog cannot be categorically distinguished. The fact that the registers of virtualization and digitalization are scanned crosswise instantiates this impossibility.

Guattari's squaring of the digital and the analog allows for a true ecologization of media studies. To be ecological does not imply deciding between the analog and the digital, as between ecological vinyl and non-ecological hard drive, or between a-signification and signification. In fact, from within the logic of a media ecosophy, at a moment-at-infinity, a concrete, entitarian and thus a digital perception would become infinitely fine, as in quasi-analog, while an abstract, anonymous and thus an analog, fluid reality would become infinitely subtly differentiated, as in quasi-digital: *becoming medium, becoming form.* At this deeply ecological moment of the folding of the giving onto the given and vice versa, the digital concept would comprehend the analog world and the analog world would comprehend the digital concept: *media-ecosophy at its point-at-infinity.*

Although Guattari's post-media texts do not directly reference the fourfold, apart from the squaring of the analog|digital divide, the fourfold provides a productive field for a recalibration of the notion of media ecologies that involves an expansion of the range of media that adds natural and perceptual media to technical media. Perhaps one might conceptualize such a squaring of media ecology, if somewhat provisionally and speculatively, by way of a superposition of the four natural elements onto the four functors of the fourfold. Such a superposition, which takes up and implicitly comments on the aesthetic squaring that Guattari performs in relation to Balthus, ties Guattari's media ecosophy back to Lucretius, and not only by way of Empedocles, who related the four elements (*rhizomata*) to the two opposing forces of love and strife, and thus to Venus and Mars, but also to Lucretius' theory of simulacra. As Hartmut Böhme writes, according to that theory 'everything that exists is at the same time the medium of its representation. The world is ordered toward its perception [*auf Wahrnehmung hin geordnet*]' (1997: 28). In other words: *aistheton.* In that Lucretius considers the elements as 'media of perception', he provides 'the first media-theory in history' (28).

In this superposition, Water would be in the position of Flows while Air would be in the position of Phyla. Although both of these are actual media, Phyla might be considered to be proto-perceptual, in that the shift from fluid to aerosol brings about a-signifying, material codings that are then virtualized in Territories: *media ecosophy*. In the giving, virtual media are defined by a similar vector that goes from perceptual, affective media to conceptual media, with Earth in the position of Territories, and Fire, in particular considered as the multiplicity of virtual light, in the position of Universes. Within this field, technical media should be thought of as developing and operating within all four functors; staking out a transversal field of actual media, as analog Flows and digital Phyla, and virtual media, as aisthetic Territories and aesthetic Universes. Reverberating through all four of these elements is the aerosolic æther of the plane of immanence.

3 ECOSOPHIC TIMES AND SPACES

> Subjectivity needs movement, directional vectors, ritournelles,
> rhythms and refrains that beat time to carry it along.
> Félix Guattari, *Soft Subversions* (69)

> I do not trust metaphors from thermodynamics.
> Félix Guattari, *Soft Subversions* (2)

> to try to reconcile the irreconcilable
> Félix Guattari, *Soft Subversions* (34)

Ecosophic Times

A Short History of Time

IN 'PRELIMINARY', THE fifteen-page introductory chapter to *Schizoanalytic Cartographies*, Guattari sketches, in very broad strokes and in a style that echoes the sweeping historical narratives woven into *A Thousand Plateaus*, a panoramic history of the times of Western culture. The chapter, at the end of which Guattari does address, for some five pages, some of the economic and political urgencies we live in today – including references to a 'postmedia era' and to 'the Greens in Germany' (SC: 13) – is not only about time, however, it is also part of the internal chronologics of *Schizoanalytic Cartographies*. It marks the moment of the drawing in of breath before that breath is held for 173 pages. Breathe in. After these central pages, the book exhales into seven short case-studies of literature, painting, theatre and architecture. Breathe out.

Differentiating between the stages of European Christianity, Capitalist Deterritorialization and Planetary Computerization, Guattari delineates the different ways in which each stage constructs a period-specific time. As Guattari would note in *Chaosmosis*, both 'space and time are thus never neutral receptacles; they must be accomplished, engendered by productions of subjectivity' (102–3). Both are the products of processes of constructivism and thus open to the future. They are milieus that are invariably administered in ways that have created either good or bad ecologies. In other words, Guattari maintains that the stages are not about taking a natural time that they stress or compress in different ways. Rather, time itself is radically time- and site-specific. Each historical moment constructs its specific time. As Serres notes in *Hermes V*, 'space as such, the one and global space, is a philosophical artefact. . . . time as such, the one and universal time, is also an artefact' (1994: 68).

As constructed, time is inherently heterogeneous. As Serres describes it in *Conversations on Science, Culture, and Time*, time is 'crumpled' (Serres and Latour 1995: 60). As living entities are assemblages of heterogeneous elements, and as each element constructs its own time – the time of bone marrow, the time of the liver – they are composed of a heterogeneity of fractal times and temporal plateaus that are entrained into the overall, integrated time of the specific entity. In fact, in terms of time each entity is itself the result of this entrainment, organization and regulation of a temporal heterology.

While entitarian time is assembled through what DeLanda calls 'the ability of nonlinear oscillators to synchronize or entrain one another's temporal behaviour' (2002: 92), the cultural time of Christianity is synchronized and thus entrained by the strictly linear, religious oscillators of 'clocks, which beat the same canonical time throughout Christendom' (SC: 8). Consider that in Roman times, the twelve hours of the day were measured, more ecologically, according to the daily rising and setting of the sun, which meant that within a 24-hour cycle, every day had differently long hours. Christian time, which quite literally rang through and thus organized both rural and urban space, put an end to this modulated, directly time-specific time. It introduces a strict rhythm into time that never wavers and that is everywhere the same. It presses, one might say, the modulated contours of Roman time into a tight chronological corset. (On Roman time, see Rovelli 2018: 40–1.)

The introduction of a measured, universal time that has been uncoupled from the seasons and from specific geographies is taken up and can literally be heard in the strict notation that, simultaneously, came to define the production of music: the 'step-by-step invention of religious musics enslaved by their written support' (SC: 8). In different registers, the Christian construction and administration of time brought about an increasingly steady organization of life whose subtle modulations were forced into a strictly serial rhythm. While the beat of that rhythm was religious, the rise of the capitalist phase was defined by a construction, manipulation and administration of time that recapitulates its religious organization from within economic registers. Factory whistles replace church bells. Time 'finds itself literally emptied of its natural rhythms by: chronometric machines, which will lead to the Taylorist dividing up of work; techniques of economic semiotization, by means of credit money, for example, which imply a general virtualization of capacities for human initiative and a predictive calculus bearing on the domains of innovation – sort of writing cheques on the future – that allow the imperium of market economies to expand indefinitely' (10). Guattari describes the third stage of temporalization, which defines today's time, as computerized and computational. With the help of ultrafine chronometrics that work on almost infinitely fast and accurate levels, time is cut up into increasingly smaller intervals, which allows it to be measured and manipulated on increasingly microscopic plateaus.

This three-step narrative could easily be misread as a somewhat predictable critique of the growing colonization of time by more and more intrusive technologies of measurement, and of the adherent politics of a more and more pervasive regime of chronological control. As Guattari does not consider the technical intrusion as a manipulation of a naturally given time that might be seen, in retrospect, as more leisurely, slower and more human, however, it is not in itself frightening or negative. Why not read the increased potential of chronological administration positively? 'With the acceleration of the technological and dataprocessing revolutions, we will witness the deployment or, if you will, the unfolding of animal, vegetable, cosmic, and machinic becomings' (TE: 133).

There is, then, neither a temporal nostalgia nor a chronological Luddism in Guattari. How could there be, when he puts all of his trust in the infinite speed of pure time as the ground of world's ceaseless potentiality for change? Rather, Guattari's question is why, from within our chronological condition that allows for the überfast construction and manipulation of time on electronic plateaus, have we not caught up with the potentialities and possibilities of that condition? Rather than criticizing technological progress, Guattari criticizes our inability to put this progress to good use. Somehow, the new potentialities of minute, subtle interventions into the complex machinics of time have not been taken up in any positive, ecological manner. As if we hadn't learned yet to live up to this still too-fast and too-powerful means of the manipulation, or again, more adequately, of the construction of new times. 'With the temporality put to work by microprocessors, enormous quantities of data and problems can be processed in minuscule periods of time, in such a way that the new machinic subjectivities keep on jumping ahead of the challenges and stakes with which they are confronted' (SC: 11).

Why are we still caught in our old, much coarser constructions of temporalities and their adherent subjectivities? 'In the matter of dreams and utopias, the future remains largely open! My wish is that all those who remain attached to the idea of social progress – for whom the social has not become a trap, a "semblance" – turn seriously towards these questions of the production of subjectivity' (15). Why are we still lagging behind the potentialities of constructing new times and the adherent potentialities of constructing the world? Why do 'the immense processual potentialities carried by all these computational, telematic, robotic, bureaucratic, biotechnological revolutions so far still only result in a reinforcement of previous systems of alienation, an oppressive mass-mediatization, infantilizing consensual politics. What will enable them finally to lead to a postmedia era, setting them free from segregational capitalist values and giving a full lease of life to the beginnings of a revolution in intelligence, sensibility and creation?' (12). From within the light of these potentialities, Guattari imagines a truly progressive, ecological administration of temporality that will lead to a new world 'as prefigured in the phenomenal growth of a computer-aided subjectivity' (TE: 38, my emphasis).

If we are at a moment when the speed of the manipulation and administration of time by way of the computer and its adherent technologies is, although forever asymptotically, approaching the temporality that governs the plane of immanence on which things change 'at an infinite speed of transformation' (105), why does that acceleration not release the potentialities of infinite speed? Why, at this potentially liberating moment, do the older forms of administering the world persist in employing and co-opting these potentialities for inherently regressive projects? Why can we not think positively of a computer-aided subjectivity, like we think, in architecture and elsewhere, of computer-aided design? Why, in other words, is the twenty-first century torn by religious wars that are, simultaneously, cover-ups for deeply capitalist agendas? What would happen if we were to succeed in releasing the new temporalities, and with them new forms of machinic subjectivity, into the world from within a truly ecological project and horizon? If that was what is meant by today's accelerationism, then, by all means, let there be accelerationism!

While these questions address some of the urgencies of the use of technology in the design of dissensual temporalities, the acceleration of the construction of and interventions into time can also be read in terms of the more abstract conceptualization of time proposed in *Schizoanalytic Cartographies*. In fact, Guattari cautions us, both conceptually and in terms of the structure of the book, that we should slow down and understand more about the abstract notions of an ecological time, temporality and chronology before we attempt to politically administer these urgent questions. We should spend some time on how time and temporality are negotiated in the relentlessly abstract, but simultaneously concrete logic of the fourfold.

Fractal Time

Guattari's ecological squaring of time is based on the concept of a time that is fundamentally diverse and chaotic. In terms of the fourfold: the ground of time given in terms of the infinite speed with which states appear and disappear in and on the plane of immanence. At the same time, the time of the plane of consistency is decelerated and fundamentally constructed in terms of modes of time as well as in terms of the relation between speed and slowness. Guattari's ecologization of time on the plane of consistency also implies thinking of time as being infinitely scaled. The way the imperceptible or the unperceived can be made perceptible in relation to such temporal scalings is, despite our technologies of ultra slow-motion, perhaps a bit less rehearsed than the way that spatial imperceptibilities can be made perceptible by way of zooming into smaller spatial plateaus with the help of magnifying glasses, telescopes or electron microscopes.

In *What is Philosophy?*, Guattari and Deleuze stress such temporal scalings when they note that in order to relate the brain-mind complex to 'vital ideas', one has to enter 'the deepest of synaptic fissures, in the hiatuses, intervals, and *meantimes* of a nonobjectifiable brain' (209, emphases added). As Guattari notes in *Schizoanalytic Cartographies*, 'to clarify this enigmatic intersection between intermediate temporalities, we must return to the fractal nature of their texture' (177). As with space, then, a basic characteristic of schizoanalytic time is that it has to be thought of as infinitely scaled. Especially when it concerns very stable temporalities, such fractal, molecular temporalities and changes in speed might seem, from an operational perspective, to be negligible. Like cars absorb very small bumps in the road, entities absorb the shocks of changes of speed until these exceed a critical point and cascade onto the macrolevel. Both from a lived and from an aesthetic perspective, however, such molecular chronological plateaus are seminal. In the same way that each spatial plateau constructs its own temporalities, time itself is a constructed assemblage of media and forms. Very fast movements on very small levels make up the temporal media for larger and slower forms of time or temporal forms.

If temporal changes on smaller or finer plateaus were unimportant on larger, coarser scales, this would introduce a chronological arbitrariness into the logic of media. Both in art and in life, however, such arbitrariness is a sad idealization. In reality, diverse plateaus of speed and slowness form complex fields of temporal resonance, feedback and interplay, as with Proust's involuntary memories and the appearance of the fully virtual world of Balbec and the Guermantes. From an ecological perspective, every temporal plateau, however subtle, is relevant to the overall temporal field.

Chronos and Aion Revisited

In *Schizoanalytic Cartographies*, time is present on all of the fourfold's conceptual levels. The most general of these concerns its processual character; the fact that stasis is not an essential characteristic of entities but rather the effect of an undue deceleration of a process. All temporalities constructed within the fourfold are implicated by this temporality of the fourfold in and of itself. Processuality does not only find its way into the fourfold in that it diagrams a multiplicity of temporal processes and movements, however. Its very terminology aims to be adequate to this allover processuality. One of the ways in which Guattari pays a conceptual tribute to the fundamental processuality of the world within the fourfold is to verb nouns, such as talking of consistencing instead of consistency or, even more radically, necessitation instead of necessity. As Guattari notes in *The Anti-Oedipus Papers*, 'maybe we shouldn't make multiplicity [*multiplicité*] a substantive but a verb: multiplicitate [*multipliciter*]' (361). (See Margulis on Vladimir Ivanovich Vernadsky's 'use of the gerund "living"' to stress that 'life was less a thing and more a happening, a process' (Margulis and Sagan 1995: 45). See also her statement that 'life on Earth is more like a verb' (22) than a noun.)

In general, Guattari's conceptualization of time in *Schizoanalytic Cartographies* is developed from within a matrix Guattari and Deleuze had developed in *A Thousand Plateaus*. That matrix, in turn, was based on Deleuze's twofold logic of Chronos and Aion as the two complementary modes of time and temporality that are analogous to the complementarity of the actual and the virtual. In this theory of time, one can in turn feel the conceptual reverberations of Bergson's differentiation into *temps* and *durée*. Again, the temporal relations between an actual and a virtual time need to be constructed at every moment. 'The intersecting of discursive temporalities with existential durations does not go without saying. It is not mechanical, it must be brought about, assembled' (SC: 175–6).

In *A Thousand Plateaus*, Chronos denotes Cartesian time as 'the time of measure that situates things and persons, develops a form and determines a subject' (262). Chronos is extensive, Aion intensive time. In Guattari's terms, given time and giving time. One is the time of metrics and of 'interpretation', the other that of non-metric 'experimentation' (267). Christian time is chronic in that its strict, digital measure organizes the world without regard for the milieu through which it rings, and for the chronological modulations that are linked to shifting seasonal rhythms and durations. It is as if a temporal grid were laid over the landscape of time, similar to the grid a map's coordinate system lays over a landscape. Aion, in opposition, denotes what might be called topological time, as 'the indefinite time of the event, the floating line that knows only speeds and continually divides that which transpires into an already-there that is at the same time not-yet-here, a simultaneous too-late and too-early, a something that is both going to happen and has just happened' (262). While Chronos is 'pulsed' and circular, Aion is a 'non-pulsed' and linear (262).

If many readings favour aionic over chronic time, one should once again resist the temptation to evaluate what are really two aspects of time, in the same way that one should resist favouring smoothness over striation, or becoming over being. Light cannot do without darkness. The world comes as *chiaroscuro*. Particles cannot do without waves and vice versa. If any of these terms could do without its other, this would put an end to the logic of complementarity [→ **Deleuze 148**]. Each of the two times cannot do without its other, in the same way that minor science cannot do without major science and vice versa. In fact, in certain aspects, such as metric Chronos and non-metric Aion, one might well speak of Chronos as major and Aion as minor time.

Although the theory of time in *Schizoanalytic Cartographies* is developed from within the conceptual shadow of Deleuze's differentiation, it also deviates from it in a number of important aspects. Similar to the way Guattari's differentiation between the given and the giving is developed from within Deleuze's differentiation between the given and the given as given, but gives that differentiation an ecological spin, in the fourfold Guattari gives a deeply ecological spin to the theory of time that Deleuze, as well as Guattari and Deleuze, had developed elsewhere.

The Squaring of Time

In the fourfold, the vertical vector of time takes up the temporal modes of Chronos and Aion. In the context of the given and the giving, however, these two temporal modalities are positioned on the abstract and the concrete side respectively. To this positioning, Guattari further adds the process of the assemblage of both chronic and aionic time. The former concerns the way the continuous time of Flows is fractalized into the discontinuous time of Phyla. As Guattari notes about the 'fractal nature' (SC: 177) of that time, the relations between the times of real Flows and possible Phyla depend on 'a passage between molar structures and the molecular operators that work them indirectly by means of the establishment of an *infinitesimal deterritorialized continuum*' (177, emphasis added). The molecular operators fractalize a continuum into a quasi-continuum. As I noted earlier, the time of Flows is continuous, while the time of Phyla is aerosolic, which means that it is deterritorialized by way of the dispersion into drops, which do not exist in Flows as single entities, into the atmosphere, where they have a singular existence outside of their anonymous existence as part of a continuous Flow. The relation between the continuous time of Territories and the deterritorialized time of Universes defines the establishment of a similar infinitesimal quasi-continuum. In analogy to the fractalization of Chronos in the abstract, discursive field of Flows and Phyla, the existential, subjective 'register of enunciations' is defined by an 'Aïonic fractalization' (177). To both sides, then, Guattari adds a temporal assemblage theory of time.

A further element of Guattari's squaring of time is that Chronos has to be thought of as a time that is unrelated to concrete entities, and thus is without the parameters of perception or memory. Although Deleuze also argues that in the actual everything is a cause to everything else, which means that chronic time does not know of the relation between cause and effect – whether that is understood horizontally and thus temporally or, as with the Stoics, vertically and thus causally – he tends to think of both modes of time in relation to concrete entities. In Deleuze, both Chronos and Aion are entitarian times. Although the shift Guattari introduces might at this point seem to be negligibly small, it marks a fundamental shift from philosophy to ecology. In Guattari, chronic time is not only actual but also abstract and thus radically non-entitarian. In this pure form, Chronos designates the time of the world in its aspect of being actual and real as well as actual and possible. Aion, the entitarian, concrete complement to Chronos, is related to the virtual times of Territories and Universes. As the time of entities, Aion is the time of affect, perception, memory and of thought: *chronic and aionic ecosophy*.

As with all parameters of the fourfold, even while the time of the world and the time of its subjects are formally and operationally distinct, they are ontologically one. 'There isn't any effect, counter-effect or interaction between the two types of temporality. All that can be said is that *one is the existential condition of the other*' (177, emphasis added). Like the other registers that pertain between the actual and the virtual, Chronos and Aion follow a logic of reciprocal presupposition. In Guattari's reconceptualization, however, their being 'intermediate' (173) makes them inherently ecological. They are both of the given and of the giving. On the side of the given, 'behaviours of pure discursivity ... are knotted together around ... machinic Propositions that are "chronic"'; on the side of the giving, entitarian behaviours 'are set out/arranged in a single non-discursive block as an existential Territory (durations)' (173). Chronic time, in the field of the Given, is an 'objective time', while Aionic time, in the field of the Giving, is related to 'subjective temporalization' (174).

Up until here, despite the addition of a fully objective, abstract time of the world to the concrete time of its entities, as well as of the notion of temporal fractalization, the general registers of a Deleuzian and a Guattarian theory of time remain the same. Guattari, however, further ecologizes Deleuze's twofold time by introducing temporal modalities and movements between the actual and the virtual. While Deleuze maintains that duration is of the event and thus of the virtual, Guattari relates it to the space between Flows and Territories rather than to the virtual Aion *per se*, and thus to a space between abstract|actual and concrete|virtual time. The complement to that duration is the similarly intermediate, momentous time that operates between Phyla and Universes; 'fecund "synaptic" moments that singularize a presence in the present' (173). Although Guattari does not use the word, these opportune, fecund moments are a version of the kairos from Greek antiquity, which is the opportune time to intervene in a situation. How to read these intermediate times? Do they belong to both the actual and the virtual? Guattari's Figure 8.4 shows these intermediary times – which Guattari couples to Aristotle's four logical modalities: formal, material, efficient and final – in relation to the abstract time of the given and the concrete temporalization of the giving. Both Flows and Territories are durational, while Phyla and Universes are momentous. Between the temporal aspects of Chronos and Aion, and thus between the world and its entities, the durational time of affect is the result of the complementarity of Flows and Territories, while the synaptic time of kairos is the result of the complementarity of Phyla and Universes: *not fully worldly, not fully entitarian, both times are both.*

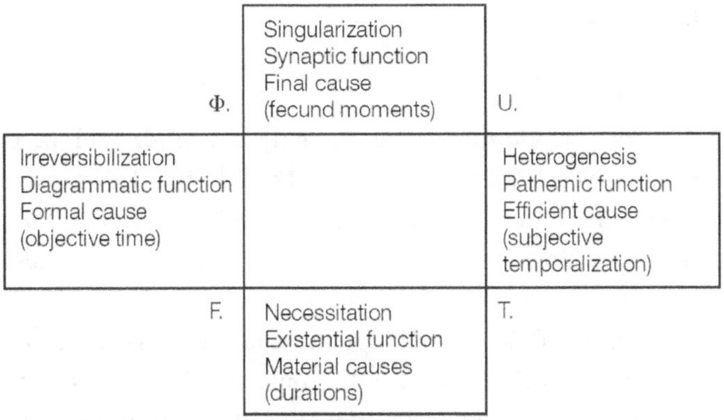

	Φ.	Singularization Synaptic function Final cause (fecund moments)	U.
Irreversibilization Diagrammatic function Formal cause (objective time)			Heterogenesis Pathemic function Efficient cause (subjective temporalization)
	F.	Necessitation Existential function Material causes (durations)	T.

FIGURE 8.4 Temporality in four dimensions

On the backdrop of George Bataille's *The Accursed Share: An Essay on General Economy*, which sets an excess of energy against the scarcity of restricted economies, Guattari's ecosophy relates kairos to the uses of that energetic superabundance, which Bataille relates to solar energy and to the energetic surplus of life's chemical reactions, while Guattari relates it to what I will later describe as the excessive, luminous plane of immanence. That excess can be squandered in sacrifice, war or luxury, the latter of which are the two main modes of capitalist squandering. 'It expresses a circuit of cosmic energy on which it depends, which it cannot limit, and whose laws it cannot ignore without consequences. Woe to those who, to the very end, insist on regulating the movement that exceeds them with the narrow mind of the mechanic who changes a tire' (Bataille 1988: 26). That energy can also be squandered, however, in artistic creativity. In this context, kairos is not a given political resource, but related to the ecological, adequate administration of an unlimited cosmic potentiality. How to adequately administer the excessive plane of immanence on or in the ecological plane of consistencies? How to squander excess energy wisely, which means according to an ecological ethos and mode of life. As Guattari notes, final causes are related to this '"accursed share that the initiated can transform into a fecund moment of creative freedom", in the domain U' (SC: 175).

Guattari's fecund moment moment is somewhat different from the way that Antonio Negri, in 'Kairòs' (2003), sets kairos up as the adequate time of a revolutionary materialist politics. As O'Sullivan notes, 'Negri develops the concept of kairos as an attempt to think through and against th[e] spatially and temporally complete system [of capitalism]' (2012: 118). In the fight against Integrated World Capitalism, Negri puts his trust in the disruptive power of kairos as 'the time of the instant, the moment of rupture and opening of temporality. It is the present, but a singular and open present' (2003: 156). As 'the ontological fabric of materialism; the affirmative power of being; and the subjectification of becoming' (161), it provides the potentiality of a people and of a politics to come.

Although Guattari's synaptic moment is similarly disruptive, and although it also operates in the present, Negri's ascetic politics – to be understood, perhaps, as a political version of the artistic *Arte Povera* movement in Italy – differ from Guattari's ecosophy. By relating Universes and Phyla, Guattari's synaptic kairos aligns, as in Bataille's general economy, the world and its creatures rather than monads with other monads. Although there are ecological elements in Negri's argument, as when he relates kairos to the irreversible time of the world – 'kairòs is the only real [*vero*] point of ontological irreversibility. It is so because kairòs is the force [*vis*] that advances' (164) – or when he notes that 'the construction of a common name cannot be indeterminate: the product of the expression of kairòs is indeed always singular (the hæcceitas)' (171), Negri's kairos remains ultimately a political concept that allows a community of monads to be free and experimental because 'subjectivity is not something that subsists: it is – on the contrary – produced by kairòs, and ... depends on the connection of monads of kairòs' (175). Kairos allows one to bring about, *hic and nunc*, a material multitude. As Negri notes, we 'give kairòs a corporeal form, we give it weight and colour, that is to say we consider the body as the incarnation of kairòs' (177).

The difference between a political and an ecological kairos can help explain the difference between Negri's idea of an ascetic politics and Bataille's and Guattari's notion of cosmic plenitude. While both are answers to a state of Integrated World Capitalism, only Bataille and Guattari stake the world and its operation against the inherent pathologies of capital. While Negri sees the antidote to capitalism in poverty, as the direct repudiation of capital, consumption and wealth, for Bataille and Guattari the kairotic concerns the question of an ecological administration of the given wealth of the world. In fact, *Schizoanalytic Cartographies* might be considered as adding a new, Leibnizian connotation to the term 'integrated' in Integrated World Capitalism, insofar as it evokes not only its global reach, but also its inherent complexity: fractalized world capitalism, perhaps. In Guattari's ecosophic writing, as if he had re-evaluated the long march through the institutions, one cannot remain outside of the reach of capitalism. Anarchy is less of an option than the creation and administration of ecological infrastructures. To find the right moment to actualize lines of flight afforded in and by specific capitalist situations and institutions; a strategy I will talk about in more detail in 'Ecosophy: In the Cracks of Capitalism' (pp. 209–14): *excessive ecology*.

Guattari's rhetorical question 'what use is a temporality with four dimensions?' (SC: 173) highlights the general conceptual set-up of time in the fourfold, in which, as Guattari's treatment of kairos shows, time is not conceptualized according to a specifically entitarian or human perspective. Rather, the fourfold charts a deeply ecological time that is spanned out between all four of its attractors. 'When I propose here a description with four dimensions . . . I only intend to indicate that one cannot tackle this domain in the style of naïve or philosophically "armed" phenomenologists' (SC: 175). The fourfold is suffused by this ecological, everywhere constructed and experimental time. 'Times are composite and call incessantly for recompositions on the basis of the most diverse instrumentations and experiments' (175).

To recapitulate: The time of Flows is the abstract time of the pure flow of the world. Time in its aspect of bare time, one might say. Somewhat paradoxically, this is a time without temporality in that it is strictly for itself. Time in its aspect of being real and actual. In Phyla, time opens up to the field of possibility. In-between the two functors, it is fractalized into a possible, as in administrable and administrative, time. Both flow time and machine time are actual and abstract. It is only in the virtual field of the giving that the aspects of time that are generally considered as temporal unfold. Virtual time is time in its aspect of entitarian time. Time as lived by the world's entities. On this side, Territories are defined by the existential, durational time of the refrain, while the time of Universes is the momentous and deterritorialized synaptic time of thought considered as a concrete virtual rhizome. In this squaring of time, its different aspects come to fundamentally implicate each other.

The Tetrahedron of Abstract Machines

As I have noted, Guattari processualizes a number of his terms. His Figures 8.4 and 7.9 show how abstract machines are related to individuated entities as concrete machines. Guattari installs a number of processes in the intervals between the functors that are marked terminologically as processes by letting three end in -ion while the fourth, heterogenesis, is sufficiently processual in itself to not need such a marker. Although Guattari deals with necessitation and heterogenesis before he covers singularization and irreversibilization, I will, in order to highlight his implicit ecologization of time, begin with irreversibilization.

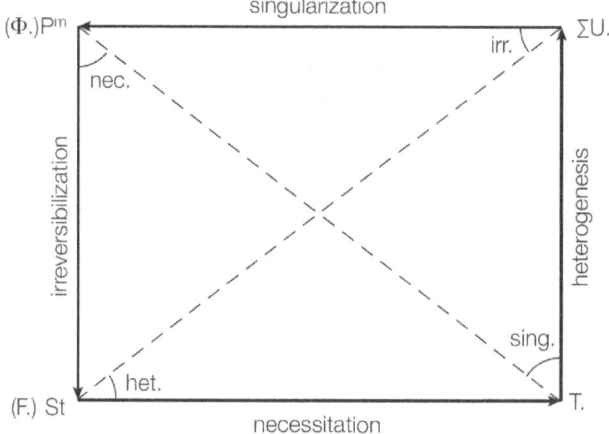

FIGURE 7.9 The tetrahedron of abstract machines

Although the other terms also concern temporal aspects, irreversibilization is the only explicitly temporal concept of the four. As Figure 7.9 shows, it concerns the vector from Flows and Phyla. From an entitarian perspective, irreversibilization is by default read in terms of the arrow of time, which links it to the experience of individual death. At this point, however, the discursive side has not yet been folded onto the enunciative, entitarian side. Irreversibilization, therefore, concerns a purely actual time that is assembled between the real and the possible. Abstract irreversibility refers less to individual death, therefore, than to entropy – as in Lucretius' image of the inclined slope – but also, more importantly for Guattari, to the negentropic, dissipative dynamics described by Prigogine and Stengers. Apart from these dynamics between closed, entropic systems and open, dissipative ones, irreversibilization is related to the fact that in a universe defined as a deterministic chaos, processes cannot run backwards in time because of their sensitivity to initial conditions. Processes cannot be reversed because their dynamics are defined by a multiplicity of bifurcations that happen on an infinite number of scales. The very dynamics that make it impossible to recreate the past make it possible to have a future, that is. As I noted earlier, Guattari does not tire of stressing that the future, for the better or for the worse, remains largely open. It is only when Flows are looked at in terms of the durations of existential Territories – which in turn unfold into deterritorialized Universes by way of processes of machinic heterogenesis – that the world's structural irreversibility is aligned with an entitarian, concrete one. 'One can now see that the ontological status of concrete machines implies not only the entry of abstract machinic functions but equally existential operators allowing them to be aggregated with the incorporeal Universes and existential Territories that confer on them a self-consistency' (SC: 97).

Both the notions of entitarian death and of enunciation, then, should be seen in complementarity to a worldly discursivity, and thus according to the overall chronologics that define the fourfold. Entitarian time cannot be reduced to the fourfold's virtual side and it cannot completely cover the time of the world, although it also cannot be uncoupled from that time. In its twofold connotation and vectorial direction, irreversibilization shows how entitarian time is implicated in and complementary to the abstract time of the world. As time is diffracted into the four fields respectively, and assembled within the logical space defined by their interplay, entitarian time becomes truly consistent only when all four attractors are brought into play simultaneously. In order for the assemblages of time to work, entitarian time must be coupled to the time of the milieu of the actual world. In other words, it needs to be part of an allover temporal ecology. It must, in fact, itself construct such a temporal ecology. All processes of becoming slower or faster, or of time-axis manipulation, must take place between the times of the world and those of its entities. Even if the entity disavows it, its time invariably takes place in that ecological superposition.

The ecologization of time, then, should be thought of from within the superposition of the given times of the world and the giving times of its entities. This is shown in the way that although the time of irreversibilization concerns fractalization and the 'expressive function ... f(exp)', it is linked, by way of existentialization and the 'existential function ... f(exi)' (143) that pertains to the relation between Flows and existential Territories, to the time of necessitation and thus of the refrain, which denotes the construction of duration that defines the pathic, affective time of entities. In Territories, the abstract times of Flows and Phyla are entrained into the concrete temporal rhythms of virtual refrains that bring about – that construct and assemble – modular durations.

If the intermediary times are no longer positioned between the four functors in Guattari's Figure 8.9, this is owed to the fact that it describes temporal registers from within the enunciative, entitarian position and that the temporalities are positioned according to the domain of their origin. It diagrams the enunciative dimensions and

	Necessitation	Heterogenesis	Singularization	Irreversibilization
Domain of origin	F	T	U	Φ
Recession	existential f(exi)	pathemic f(path)	synaptic f(syn)	diagrammatic f(diag)
Causality	material	efficient	final	formal
Mythographic reference	Ananke	Hubris	Moira	Dike
Determinability	$d^{+\infty}/d^{-\infty}$	$d^{-\infty}\int d^{+\infty}$	$d^{\pm\infty}$	$d^{+\infty}\int d^{-\infty}$
Temporalization	durations	dates	fecund moments	objective times

FIGURE 8.9 Enunciative dimensions

the various parameters that define them, such as temporality, causality and mythography. In Figure 8.9, the time of duration and material causes is shifted to the register of real Flows, objective time and formal causes to the register of possible Phyla. The time of Territories is that of dates and efficient causes, while that of Universes is that of fecund moments and final causes. (The mythographic references are Ananke, the Goddess of necessity; Dike, the Goddess of Justice; Hubris, the Goddess of Insolence; and the Moira, goddesses of Fate.) At this point, Guattari has assembled the full diagram of schizoecologic time.

The Proust Refrain: Becoming Proust

In 'Refrains and Existential Affects', which is one of the essays that mark the phase of exhalation in *Schizoanalytic Cartographies*, Guattari returns to what might be called his own Proust refrain, which he had begun to develop in *The Machinic Unconscious*, and which groups, somewhat like *Schizoanalytic Cartographies*, a number of shorter texts around one central essay; in this case an essay on *In Search of Lost Time* [→ **Deleuze 96–8**]. Already at this point, Guattari uses Proust's writing to illustrate that both time and memory are assembled. 'Universal time is abolished in favor of a thousand assemblages of temporalization, corresponding with infinitely varied styles of deterritorialization. One never bathes in the same impression twice as soon as the micropolitics of assemblages of enunciation leads to the liberation of living, heterogeneous and singular matters of expression' (MU: 305). In the context of this temporal diffraction, facialities and refrains play important roles in that they 'do not belong to space and time "in general"' but rather 'effectuate particular spaces and times' (138). Although the refrain 'holds the assemblages and their heterogeneous components together' (146) and thus creates an individual time, this time is in turn '"beaten" by concrete assemblages of semiotization be they collective or individuated, territorialized or deterritorialized, machinic or stratified' (107). For instance, 'in the universe of capitalistic refrains' everyone lives, as I have shown earlier, 'in the same rhythm and the same accelerated cadences' (109): *factory time then, stock-market time now.*

If Guattari's reading of Proust in *The Molecular Unconscious* precapitulates 'Cracks in the Street', his reading in *Schizoanalytic Cartographies* might be said to recapitulate it. In fact, like 'Cracks in the Street', 'Refrains and Existential Affects' can be read as an instantiation of the fourfold's heterogenetic logic by way of an argument that follows its narrative vector: *squaring Proust*. As in real-life, in order to activate the forces of deterritorialization and singularization that can develop from a refrain's initially existentializing function, the work of art needs to free its a-signifying components. In this shift from signifying to diagrammatic registers, it must treat the refrain as an existential occurrence rather than as a type. Proust performs such a singularization of the refrain; its slow 'ungluing' (111) from both the existential and the cultural beats that surround it.

According to the narrative vector of the fourfold, when actual 'expressive chains' cross over into the field of the virtual, they are territorialized by processes of 'existential crystallizations' (SC: 4). They become 'intensive traits' (4) that date, on the plane of consistency, the birth of an entity as a concrete virtuality from within the field of the abstractly actual. They date, one might say, the moment at which the plane of consistency becomes the plane of consistencies. Guattari's Figure 8.9 shows that datings, in that they denote processes of existentialization, belong to and are of Territories. 'Traits of singularization – kinds of existential stamps – ... date, eventalize, "contingentialize" states of fact, their referential correlates and the Assemblages of enunciation that correspond to them' (4). This birth, in which the abstract world is concretized first into sensual surfaces and further into affective existentializations, already contains the possibility of the fractalization of the virtual into Universes. These twofold dynamics, Guattari remarks, escape a purely signifying semiotics: 'This double capacity of intensive traits to singularize and transversalize existence, to confer on it a local persistence, on the one hand, and a transversalist consistency – a transistency – on the other, cannot be fully grasped by rational modes of discursive knowledge. It is only given through an apprehension of the order of the affect' (4). It can only be known by affect: *aisthetic ecology*.

In relation to Proust, Guattari notes that 'like an existential stamp, heterogenesis marks the fractal dating of the regime of de- and re-territorialization of an Assemblage of enunciation' (185). In *Remembrance of Lost Time*, this aisthetic dating, which is relative to 'an abstract formula, the crystal of an event, regulating transversal passageways between different registers' (184–5), refers to 'the instant that the narrator's foot steps onto the wobbly paving stone in the courtyard at Guermantes, allowing passageways between the different expressive components, harmony, polyphony and melody together, that inhabit Proust' (185). At this moment, 'a matter of expression will find itself invaded by a whole worldliness [*mondanéité*], as if haunted by an enunciating subjectivity' (185). In reference back to Guattari's reading of Balthus, that wobbly paving stone might also be found on *Le passage du Commerce Saint-André*. On that background, while the photograph and the first painting of the scene had instantiated the two aspects of the actual, the moment that Proust's narrator steps into the courtyard prefigures and instantiates the shift from the actual to the virtual, affective registers of Balthus' second painting. As if the moment of that stepping into the remembered world was at the same time the moment that pen meets paper, it marks the birth of literature.

From that moment onwards, Proust's affective crystal starts to grow and to gradually suffuse the overall narrative field. 'Vinteuil's little phrase' (MU: 233) forms the nucleus of a refrain that 'becomes enriched from one assemblage to the next' (269) until it has gained a '*synchronic*' (280) and '*diachronic consistency*' (279). This affective process of gradual consistencing goes hand in hand with the refrain's fractalization into the transversal spaces of the narrative. 'An abstract machine has begun to take on consistency and crystallize multiple and heterogeneous potentialities' (251). At this point, the text has become a Proust machine that covers the overall, fractalized textual universe. 'We have come to the point where the same type of abstract machinism henceforth traverses the world of the "Young Girls", Vinteuil's music, Elstir's painting, and Proust's phrases' (287). The slow expansion of this both aisthetic and aesthetic machine is everywhere performed under the sign of artistic deterritorialization. Like Balthus' third painting, the text has, from an existential, molar affect, created an allover molecular constellation.

A personal, affective memory is transmuted, by way of writing, into a deterritorialized literary constellation. 'The subject refuses being passive with regard to his or her past. As actual intensities, memories must be folded onto the work of creative semiotization' (319). This semiotization, which Guattari also calls 'becoming graphematic' (286), 'releases an extremely effective component of *perceptive reading* and *creative writing*' (286). Like Balthus' *molecularized* pictorial space, Proust's narrative space forms a fractalized, deterritorialized mnemonic landscape and atmosphere. As such, the set of novels, like the fourfold, 'can and must be read in all directions: from the end towards the beginning, but as well as diagonally by traversing spaces, times, faces, characters, intrigues' (320). By way of the intensification, dispersion and fractalization of an affective refrain into the multiplicity of the literary text, Proust has written a 'schizoanalytic monograph' (231); a 'prodigious rhizomatic map' (231): *becoming Proust*.

When Guattari returns to Proust in *Schizoanalytic Cartographies*, he highlights that the process of fractalizing the refrain is transversal, and that it concerns any number of situations, registers and conceptual plateaus simultaneously. 'It is no longer just the topological dimensions that are fractalized here but also the dimensions of time and substance. By this new fractal procedure, sensible and abstract qualities invent original relations of transversality. The pathic operators of the Proustian "Search" clearly indicate to us the recursive paths of temporal passage between "times" that are distant from one another and between heterogenesized substances' (SC: 185). The memory is no longer that of an individual, but of a world. The superposition of the affective, modular time of Territories and the deterritorialized, monadic time of Universes goes along a 'trans-monadic axis, or axis of transversality, which confers a transitive character on enunciation, making it drift constantly from one existential Territory to another, generating singularizing dates and durations from it (once again the privileged example here is that of the Proustian refrains)' (212). From an existential date, Proust's writing creates a fractal space of virtual memory. This field of virtual memory is the site of creative freedom. At this point, let me quote once more Guattari's notion that incorporeal Universes 'escape from the energetic, legal, evolutionary and existential coordinates of the three preceding domains'. From an aisthetic refrain, Proust has created a molecular aesthetics that trails the aisthetic refrain behind: *schizoecologic aesthetics*.

Speeds of Determinability

Guattari's Figure 8.9, which ends the text on the fourfold in *Schizoanalytic Cartographies*, contains the register of determinability, which Guattari uses to further delineate his conceptualization of time and temporality. Guattari ties the 'speed of determinability' (SC: 172) to the logic of speed in *A Thousand Plateaus*, where Guattari and Deleuze note that on a very abstract level, movements on a plane are defined purely in terms of speed and slowness. One of the more complex conceptual notations in *Schizoanalytic Cartographies* concerns the squaring of these registers, which brings together a number of registers that do not immediately seem to be related to each other, and even less to time. Before I define these speeds in more detail, however, another word of caution. Many studies of Deleuze and of Guattari show a tendency of evaluation that echoes the ones I have already mentioned: that of smooth and striated space. This time, speed is inherently good, while slowness is inherently bad. Taking up Guattari and Deleuze's rhetorics of speed, these readings argue that the allover project should be to speed things up. This accelerationism is based on the argument that encrusted, slow-moving entities can be saved from themselves and their slownesses by various modes of acceleration. Again, although this is to some extent true, it is too easy to reduce an eminently complex problematic to a simple dynamics because things are again more complicated. In fact, the value of Guattari lies in what one might call his relentless complicationing. As I have noted, in the same way that ecology cannot trust in a simple temporal retardation that would imply a regressive nostalgia for more natural and slower modes of existence, it cannot trust in a simple acceleration and a belief in a happily sped-up subject. In the fourfold, the logic of speeds and slownesses is once more paradoxical: *more speed, more slowness.*

Guattari's first conceptual move is to relate ratios of speed, and thus of time, to ratios of determinability and thus of consistency. This alignment refers back to the plane of immanence. The conceptual connection between the temporal and formal registers is that the infinite determinability of the plane of immanence is analogous to the infinitely fast changes that define it, while the finite determinability of the plane of consistency implies finitely fast changes. If something is not determined at all, it is free to be determined at a maximum speed. As it has no determination in and of itself, it can be determined by the lightest and smallest of determinations. It offers no resistance to being determined, like Lucretius' atom offers no resistance to the *clinamen*. As with the *clinamen*, in fact, the change from a state A to a state B is infinitely fast. So fast, one might say, that the notions of 'it' and of 'something else', as well as 'state' do not even apply.

The plane of immanence is defined by such an infinite determinability, infinite speed, infinite change and a fundamental a-temporality, while processes of consistencing are defined by finite determinability, deceleration, stratification and temporalization. This shift in speed from infinite to finite is part of that from the amorphous to the crystalline, although at the beginning of crystallization, there is not yet a clear limit between the two, which is why Guattari noted that 'it is not possible to determine a clear frontier between spontaneous chains and crystalline, proto-vital, proto-machinic forms of organization'. In terms of ordering, this shift involves 'the transformation of aleatory chains of the "primitive soup", or redundancies, into smoothed, proto-machinic sequences that have been brought under control' (81). Symptomatically, the term control is used here without the rhetorical dark-weather cloud that surrounds it in, say, *A Thousand Plateaus* or in *Anti-Oedipus*.

'It is on the basis of the notion of a reference speed that we will try to redefine consistency' (105), Guattari notes. If consistencies emerge, they 'will be affected by two fundamentally different types of iteration: that of infinite speed and that of "decelerated" speed. "Deceleration" (or reterritorialization), which leads us to draw out consistency as a fundamental new dimension of Assemblages, whose operations begin in chaos' (105–6). This initial slowing-down is noted in the minute deceleration brought about by the informal diagram. Consistencies emerge at the edge of chaotic immanence and constructed consistency. As I have noted, although Flows, Phyla, Territories and Universes belong to the finitely fast plane of consistency as the plane populated by consistencies, they are pervaded by the infinite speeds that define the plane of immanence as the plane of pure, ultrafast intensities that animates the plane of consistencies.

The birth of assemblages, however, does not solely consist of a simple deceleration. It is defined by a paradoxical process that ecologically aligns infinite and finite speeds according to different modalities. 'Infinite speed is synonymous with the absolute lability of iteration and, as a consequence, with zero consistency. . . . the reiteration sequences here are infinitely short', while the '"decelerated" speeds' that define assemblages 'are synonymous with an intensification of consistency' (106). The slower the entity, the more consistent it is. It is from within this general formula that Guattari notes that a structure is merely the name for a dynamics that has been decelerated to zero. Finite speeds define the affective 'deceleration of existential "grasping" (or self-referential agglutination)' (106). As such, these '"decelerated" speeds' are synonymous with an intensification of consistency. When they fall to a quasi-null speed [−∞], the sequences of opening back up can become of a quasi-infinite length' (106): *full consistency, zero speed* [→ **Deleuze 65**].

In opposition, the plane of immanence is defined by 'an infinite speed of transformation [+∞], transgressing the sacrosanct principle of contemporary physics based on the speed of light, which consists in fixing a threshold limiting the size of the ensemble of possible speeds' (105). As this infinite speed never occurs by itself within the fourfold as the plane of consistency, it can only be conceptualized in relation to finite speeds. However, although the only plane that is defined by an infinite speed and thus infinite determinability is the plane of immanence, infinite speed is not lost in the fourfold. In fact, complexity develops within that relation, for instance in the way that the two parameters of infinite speed and infinite change as well as finite speed and finite change are linked to the notions of continuity '$d^{+\infty}$' and discontinuity '$(d^{-\infty})$' (123) respectively.

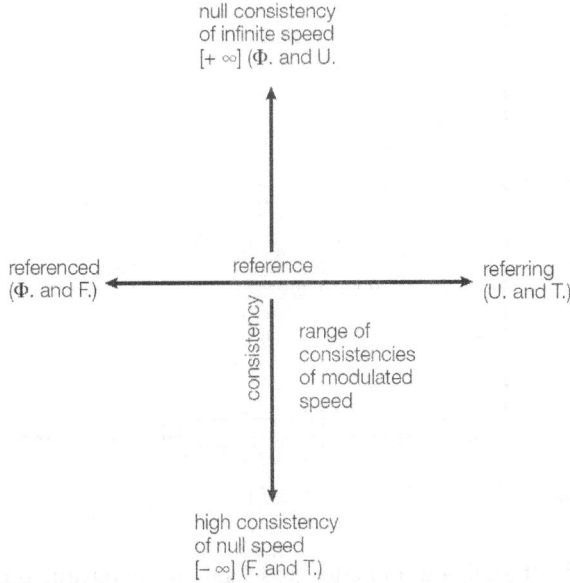

FIGURE 4.2 Intersecting dimensions of reference and consistency

How, on this background, are the abstract speeds that define the fourfold's non-entitarian side of Flows and Phyla related to the concrete speeds of the entitarian side of Territories and Universes? Territorial modules are caught between the real time of Flows, which is defined by the non-relation between infinite speed and slowness, and the possible time of Phyla, in which the time of Flows has been integrated. A general logic of consistencing scans finite and infinite speeds vertically. As Guattari's

Figure 4.2 shows, 'null consistency of infinite speed [+∞] (Φ. and U)' and 'high consistency of null speed [−∞] (F. and T.)' (107). On one vector, 'the series $d^{-\infty}$, on the side of existential Territories', and 'the series $d^{+\infty}$, on the side of possibilistic Phyla' (129). On the other vector, one might add, the infinite speed of Universes and the null speed of Territories. Forces of deterritorialization in Phyla and Universes, forces of territorialization in Flows and Territories. Again, however, let me caution the champions of deterritorialization: territorialization, especially as intensification, is not, in itself, a bad process.

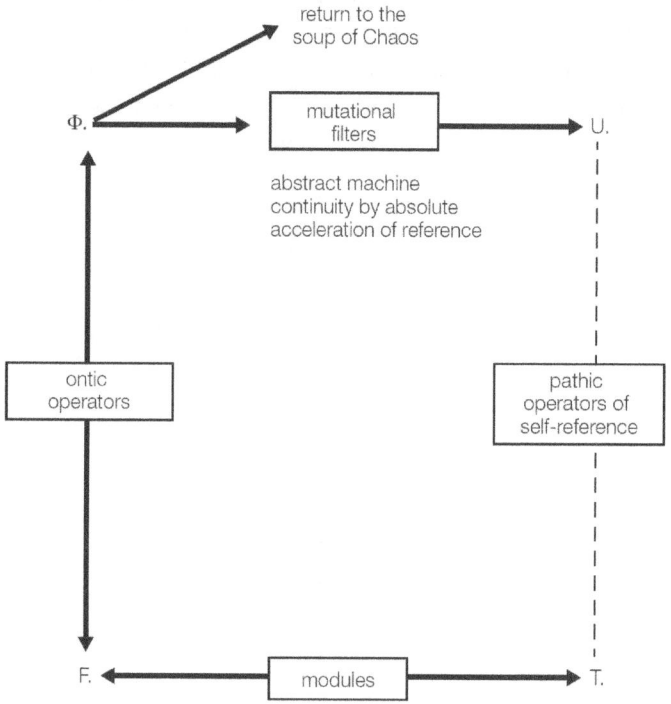

FIGURE 5.1 Ontic and pathic operators

The extremes of total determination and total non-determination, or infinite slowness and infinite speed, create different modes of chronological vertigo. 'The discontinuous, on the side of territorialized references on the axis FT ... must be conceived as the vertigo of an absolute slowing down of determinability ($d^{-\infty}$)' (117). This ultraslow vertigo of absolute deceleration defines a purely territorial position: *the takeover of affective time*. The other, ultrafast vertigo concerns the vector between Phyla and Universes. It refers to the bifurcation in deterritorialized Universes to either create fecund moments or to lose time in a return to what might be seen as a temporal body without organs. The alternative is 'either latching on to new

Constellations of Universes of reference or returning to the soup of chaotic redundancies (Figure 5.1)' (117). This ultrafast vertigo concerns 'the continuous and its absolutely accelerated speeds of reference of determinability ($d^{+\infty}$)' (117): *the takeover of conceptual time.*

Both of these extremes relate a quasi-infinite speed to a quasi-null speed. Along the actual vector, the time of continuous Flows is defined by the paradoxical simultaneity of infinite speed and absolute deceleration, and thus determination, as two fundamentally unrelated registers. By way of the process of fractalization, which cuts up the continuity of flows into a discontinuous, integrated time, these two speeds are related. In *A Thousand Plateaus*, the terms of continuity and discontinuity describe the most abstract levels of the world's machinism and schizoanalysis as the analysis of the cuts and flows that pertain to any given situation. The complex dynamics between Flows and Phyla, then, can be read as the introduction of discontinuity into continuity by way of fractalization; of what I have called earlier the creation of a discontinuous network from a continuous Flow. In fact, Guattari describes these dynamics as 'symmetrical' (172) processes of integration. In Phyla, the paradox of infinite speed and total determination that defines Flows is integrated into a finite, or, perhaps more precisely, an infinitesimal speed. Here, the decrease in continuity is offset by a gain in terms of possible determination. On the side of Phyla, 'there is a taking on of consistency, a deterritorialized circumscribing of traits that were and that remain diffuse, powdery and unlocalizable ... Such a taking on of fractal-molecular consistency defines the Phyla as the integration of negative determinability ($d^{+\infty} \int d^{-\infty}$)' (173). It 'recaptures $d^{-\infty}$ negativity, or rather negativities' (173).

Along the virtual vector, the analogous movement is from Territories to Universes. Modules are drawn towards 'pathic operators (the domain T)' that work according to a fractalization that is 'a continuist one at a speed $d^{-\infty}$' (173). On the side of the giving, the slowing-down (the speed $d^{-\infty}$) 'introduc[ed] a discontinuity that will be proper to sensible and signaletic registers. One can say that here negative determinability integrates positive determinability ($d^{-\infty} \int d^{+\infty}$). At this stage of the ontology of modules, there is a territorialized circumscription of positive determinations without any explicit recapturing of this circumscription as such. There is simply a negative power of freezing and of the selection of positive traits' (173). Territories are operators of deceleration. At the same time, they are drawn towards ultrafast Universes by way of a 'discontinuous fractalization, ... working at a speed $d^{+\infty}$' (172): *Proust at null speed, Proust at infinite speed.*

Ultimately, the issue is one of 'trying to construct *ordinary* consistencies and temporalities from infinitely slow speeds of separability and infinitely rapid speeds of continuity' (129, emphasis added). In Guattari's Figure 5.1 the 'abstract machine' creates 'continuity by absolute acceleration of reference' (118); quasi-continuity, perhaps: '$d^{+\infty}$ = continuity' (123): *the ecological overlap of the given and the giving*. At the same time, there is the complementary formula '$d^{-\infty}$ = discontinuity' (123), which means that there are two modes of fractalization. As I argued in 'Expressionism in Ecology 4: Squaring Media Studies', this paradox is owed to the passage from the given to the giving. While the given is defined by 'a discontinuous fractalization, marked by phase spaces φ working at a speed $d^{+\infty}$ (the domain Φ)' (172), the giving is defined by 'another fractalization, but a continuist one at a speed $d^{-\infty}$ towards pathic operators (the domain T)' (173): *ecological overlap of the giving and the given*.

While Phyla integrate the infinite speed of zero determinability of Flows and thus increase the speed of determinability, in existential Territories, that speed of determinability is decreased in order to create a virtual consistency and a durational time that develops between Flows and Territories and thus between the actual time of discursivity and the virtual time of enunciation. This is why Guattari notes that we are slow beings. As Guattari and Deleuze had noted in *A Thousand Plateaus*, the refrain, as 'a crystal of space-time' (TP: 348), in actual fact 'fabricates time' (349) in the sense of providing memorial traits of specific modular states of existence. This deceleration goes hand in hand with the creation of the virtual Aion and of endo-determinability. The giving reduces the infinite speed of the given in Phyla, while the given accelerates the giving. Entities are defined by the tension between these 'series $d^{+\infty}$ and $d^{-\infty}$' which exist in modules 'in a state of layering, within molar-modular concretions in the domains F and T' (SC: 130) while they exist in monads 'in a state of incorporeal molecular dispersion, in the domains Φ and U' (130). There is speed and aerosolic dispersion in the upper half of the fourfold, slowness and consistency in the lower.

As Guattari notes, there are 'certain topographical constraints' (SC: 58) in the fourfold, such as 'a principle of exclusion that forbids direct tensorial relations between, on the one hand, the consistencies F and U and, on the other hand, the consistencies T and Φ' (58). In other words, direct relations in the fourfold go along its periphery. To conclude this section, let me comment on two diagonal, and thus indirect relations. In Guattari's Figure 7.9 the two dotted lines, although they designate the border between the different sides of the tetrahedron, might be said to align diagonal functors. One relates Flows to Universes. While infinite speed of determination and zero speed of determination are separated in a state of Flows: $d^{+\infty}/d^{-\infty}$, in Universes, infinite speed and infinite stasis oscillate, creating a speed that is both infinitely fast and infinitely slow: $d^{\pm\infty}$. The second diagonal vector pertains between Phyla and Territories. In both of these fields, the relation is integrational. The level of Phyla is defined by an integration of Flows into networks, 'a taking on of consistency' and 'the integration of negative determinability' (173), $d^{+\infty} \int d^{-\infty}$. Phyla integrate an impossible state that is defined by an infinitely fast speed of determinability and a full consistency, into a positive, possible state that is discontinuous and inconsistent. Territories are defined by a similar integration. This time, however, integration goes the other way. 'Negative determinability integrates positive determinability' (173): $d^{-\infty} \int d^{+\infty}$. In the first case, real and actual duration is integrated into real and possible rhizomes, in the second, these rhizomes are integrated into existential dates and durations. If the integration in Phyla leads to a deterritorialized and discontinuous time, in Territories, the determinability of this possible time is integrated negatively into the consistent – literally the territorialized – time of affect: *acceleration and deceleration.*

While the diagonal between Phyla and Territories operates according to a logic of abstract and concrete integration respectively, that between Flows and Universes brings together two originary oppositional terms. Along this diagonal, the intensive, virtual speed of Universes is opposed to the extensive, actual speed of Flows: 'By virtue of the passages from extensity ($d^{+\infty}$ separated by $d^{-\infty}$) to intensity ($d^{\pm\infty}$), the "original" stochasticity finding itself as if hollowed and loaded with new transversalist virtues: it establishes and reinforces symmetries and gestaltist relations between apparently heteroclite situations. In short, it constructs new modalities of circumstance' (156). While finite and infinite speeds are unrelated in Flows, in Universes an infinite fast determinability and an infinitely slow determinability, and thus infinite and null speed, are, deeply paradoxically, complementary. Universes are defined by 'a speed that is at the same time both infinitely rapid and infinitely slow and which will be notated: $d^{\pm\infty}$' (152): *the paradoxical time of Universes.*

In Universes 'determinability $d^{\pm\infty}$ no longer has either positioning or separational function, properly speaking' (155). The time of Universes, that is, brings together the chaotic and the chaosmotic aspects of time, and thus the two temporal aspects of the plane of immanence and the plane of consistency. It is in relation to this point that Guattari had noted that determinability $d^{\pm\infty}$ stays, like an aerosol, in a state of suspension at the heart of the chaosmic Plane of Consistency. This plane of consistencies 'constitutes primitive redundancies (the ensemble of neg-entropic virtualities that haunt the entropic tensions inherent to chaos) as a sort of paradoxical other side of chaos. Entirely separated and yet pairing up unceasingly, these two chaotic and chaosmotic poles of determinability promote new modalities of proximity: 1) of a spatial order, which can be infinitely distanced at the heart of the same infinitesimal circumscription; 2) of a temporal order, by the smoothing of infinitely remote future and past times' (155). The time of Universes, then, brings together two modes of infinity: An actual, abstract infinity of determinability in chronic Phyla and a virtual, concrete infinity of determinability in aionic Universes: *actual rhizomes, virtual rhizomes. Extensive speed and intensive speed.*

Synaptic Time

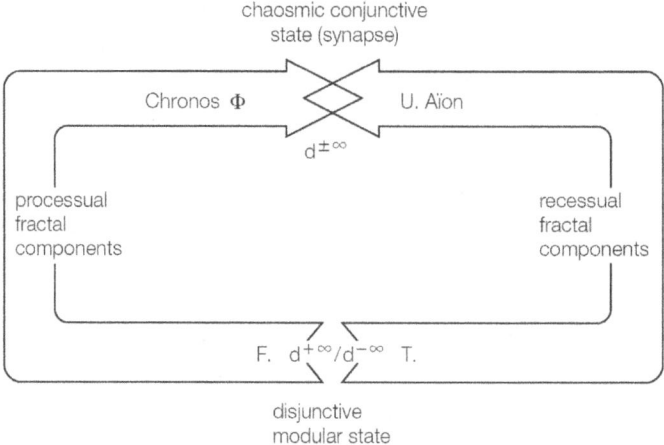

FIGURE 8.5 Chronos and Aïon (repetition of Figure 8.3)

Guattari's Figure 8.5 shows that the two temporal extremes of infinite speed and infinite slowness are disjunct in the space between Flows and Territories. This disjunctive state marks the beginning of two vectors – one actual, the other virtual – that crystallize at the synaptic moment between Phyla and Universes. At this point, the two oppositional vectors create the paradoxical time that is 'at the same time both infinitely rapid and infinitely slow'. It marks 'the coexistence of infinitely fast and infinitely slow speeds!' (140): *full speed, full stasis.*

If Flows had kept infinite speed and null speed unrelated, at the synaptic moment, time is both stable and chaotic, both continuous and discrete, making the analog and the digital coincide by way of a double fractalization. 'It is this irreducible ambivalence $d^{\pm\infty}$ that we are seeking to determine in the cartographic canton called the Constellation of Universes (SU)' (172). This is why, as I noted at the end of the last passage, the time of Universes is paradoxical: $d^{+\infty}$ = *continuity,* $d^{-\infty}$ = *discontinuity.*

These two modes of fractalization are once actual and abstract, and once virtual and concrete. 'Chronic fractalization concerns the systemic articulations and lines of possibility relative to the discursivity of Flows on the basis of attractors that in some way constitute pseudo-territories or deterritorialized Phyla. With Aïonic fractalization, it is no longer a question of territorialized or deterritorialized circumscription at all. It is as if, going against the grain, Aïonic fractalization pushed back down the splinters of time, preventing it from being marked in any way. One crosses a tangent, that of "infinitesimalizing" reduction, with it' (177). For Guattari, the synapse, which, as I noted in 'Expressionism in Ecology 2: Squaring the Unconscious', functions within a logic of the superposition of the actual and the virtual, is both a real figure and a figure of thought. It forms the link between these two fractalizations as the figure of the smallest embodiment of the meeting of an actual and a virtual cut, or *skhiz*, which is, in terms of its structure, the smallest element of schizoanalysis. From within this conceptual positioning, the synapse becomes the most reduced model of the ecological relation between the world and its creatures.

In Guattari's model, the synapse is not only the smallest element of the machine to think with. Although it brings all temporal processes within the fourfold into play, its ultimate function is to be an agent of deterritorialization. In Universes, the existentializing time of Territories is opened up to a time of pure deterritorialization, to the infinite speed of determinability and the virtual freedom of thought: 'a-signifying synapses, which are simultaneously irreversibilizing, singularizing, heterogenesizing and necessitating, push us from the world of memories of redundancies embedded in extrinsic coordinates, into Universes of pure intensive iteration, which have no discursive memory since their very existence acts as such. Synapses can thus be considered operators of "active forgetting"' as well as 'operators for the crossing over of Chronic and Aïonic temporal drives functioning in contrary directions' (178). As such, they constitute bridges, 'generating components of passage between the molar registers of discursive sets and molecular registers of non-discursive intensity' (178): *once more, Proust.*

The meeting of chronic and aionic time at the synaptic moment is, temporally if not generally, the perhaps most fascinating moment in the fourfold. Symptomatically, the neuro-sciences consider the synapse as a cognitive node whose operation aligns digital and analog operations, and as such the discontinuous and the continuous. Although it fires on a digital, on-off basis, it is deeply implicated in analog currents that trigger this firing and that do not stop interfering in the overall process of digital firing. As such, the synapse brings together the discrete and the continuous, the finite and the infinite as well as actual Chronos and virtual Aion. It is also one of the smallest nodes to align the material, actual operations of electric currents and charges with the immaterial, virtual operations of mental currents and charges. It negotiates and ecologically administers the formal difference between the materiality of the medium and the immateriality of the message. On this level of abstraction, every entity that has a system that operates like a synapse partakes of this logic of ecological conjoinment.

The synapse's relation to time and temporality concerns both of these contexts. Guattari's Figure 8.5 shows how the synaptic moment conjoins the actual rhizome in Phyla with the virtual rhizome in Universes. Situated between these, synapses have 'the double function of delimiting fields of the possible whilst reinforcing their virtual scope' (165). In our anthropocentric default position this translates into: the actual world is conjoined with its virtual minds, or more abstractly, the deterritorialized abstract machine is conjoined with the field of similarly deterritorialized concrete machines: *ecological adequation between the world and its entities.*

From within the world of entities, one can also negotiate this moment as conjoining the actual, material brain and the virtual, immaterial mind that Guattari and Deleuze deal with in *What is Philosophy?* As long as the brain is seen 'according to phenomenology' as an organ of pattern production and of pattern 'recognition' (WP: 209), it is impossible to think the brain as a multiplicity. The brain must cease to be seen as an object for thought. Instead, it must be a seen as a subject of thought: 'It is the brain that thinks and not man – the latter being only a cerebral crystallization' (210). In noting that 'the brain is the *mind* itself' (211), Guattari and Deleuze stress the complementarity of the brain-mind complex. 'It is therefore up to science to make evident the chaos into which the brain itself, as subject of knowledge, plunges' (215–16).

Synaptic Ecology

Guattari's notion of the synaptic field defines the relation between Phyla and Universes in their aspect of actuality and virtuality: 'extensity ($d^{+\infty}$ separated by $d^{-\infty}$)' (SC: 156) and 'intensity ($d^{\pm\infty}$)' (156). From a systemic point-of-view, Phyla and Universes are analogous in that both the material landscape and the mental landscape form infinitely complex networks: planes of consistencies and composition in which dynamic, both conscious and unconscious, operations take place. Again, the most important, and initially counter-intuitive concept is that like these planes, synapses have a deterritorializing function as well as a territorializing one. Synaptic firings are 'deterritorialized releases of enunciation and, as such, constitute the incorporeal integrals of sensible refrains' (189). They are double agents. 'The synapse stamps its "seal" of the taking on of consistency' (189) on an enunciative, affective scene. The infinitely connected, rhizomatic network of synapses are networks of flows and pure cuts or breaks. They are virtual figures, in the subject, of the actual abstract machine as a field of bifurcation, change and facilitation between nodes. The synapsis 'initiates a self-enunciative procedure through its character as a caesura, as a-signifying catalysis' (189).

In their relation to the faculty of the imagination, which integrates material stimuli – whether these concern optics, acoustics, touch, smell or taste – into immaterial images and thus forms an arc from the materiality of the senses and affects to the immaterial relationality of mental images and image-architectures, synapses are the hinge between the formally but not ontologically separated fields of the actual and the virtual. The double function of synapses as switches in both the material and the immaterial field resonates with this double coding: Neurologically, it is the synaptic plane of composition that creates both retinal and mental images; their identity as well as their difference [→ **Deleuze 6**]: *the synapsis as electric and imaginative lightning*.

In terms of time, the synaptic moment marks the crystallization of Chronos and Aion. 'The chaosmic-synaptic state occurs when an Aïonic temporal tension is constituted, that is to say, when a field of virtuality invades a state of things in a hegemonic fashion, without any concern for the three stratas of before, during and after' (176). In the crystallization of an abstract and actual with a concrete and virtual rhizome, the functioning of synapses creates a true adequation of subject and world; of actual extensity and virtual intensity.

While in *A Thousand Plateaus* Chronos was the time of cuts and Aion that of durations, in *Schizoanalytic Cartographies*, both Chronos and Aion have, in their alignment along the horizontal axis, a *staccato* and a *legato* aspect. While Flows and Territories are *legato* and durational, Phyla and Universes are *staccato* and momentous. If a *staccato* is speeded up enough, however, one hears it as one tone, which is a characteristic we know much better from the logic of film, in which a seemingly continuous movement is created from separate stills.

Once the fields of the given and the giving are fully installed on the fourfold, one can formally distinguish the field of quantity, which belongs to the given, and the field of quality, which belongs to the giving. Accordingly, one might speak of a quantitative, extensive time in the given and of a qualitative, intensive time in the giving. From this point of view, the synaptic moment describes the meeting of quantity and quality by way of, in ecological terms, the meeting of the quantitative time of the world and the qualitative time of its creatures. A fundamental given of Guattari's thought is that these two parameters are, once more, formally distinct but ontologically complementary. There is no simple choice, such as qualitative time is positive while quantitative time is negative, or vice versa. There is always an analog and a digital level, in the same way that in Deleuze the time-image is not better than the movement-image. In fact, each cannot be thought of without the other.

Although temporal quality can only develop within and from the durational, memorial time of affective existentialization, for Guattari, the synapse escapes the durational time that pertains to the horizontal vector between Flows and Territories. It has to do with the process of cutting into continuities, and as such it is an agent of instantaneity: *the freedom of horizontal schizotime*. The main function of the synapse is to not stop deterritorializing thought. Out of this deterritorialization: *synaptic ecology*.

Ecosophic Spaces

If there is an ecological time in which to administer a situation, is there an ecological space to do so, both practically – as in, where to intervene ecologically in a situation? – but also conceptually – as in, how can I be adequate to the spaces of the world and its creatures or consistencies? How to conceptualize, that is, an inherently ecosophic space? Is there an equivalent to ecosophic time in Guattari's construction of space?

It is safe to assume that Guattari's conceptualization of space is inspired by the mathematics of space, from which he singles out three aspects. Ecosophic space is topological, it is fractal and it is one-sided, or, in mathematical terms, unilateral. In other words, it is pervaded by forces and intensities, it consists of an infinity of surfaces, and it fundamentally complicates the distinction between inside and outside. It shows the utter consistency of Guattari and Deleuze's adequation of intensive and extensive space that these are exactly the characteristics they ascribe to the brain as a surface of thought: It is 'an absolute consistent form that *surveys itself independently of any supplementary dimension*, which does not appeal therefore to any transcendence, *which has only a single side whatever the number of its dimensions*' (WP: 210, emphasis added).

The first aspect distinguishes Guattari's notion of space from Cartesian space, which is empty, abstract, everywhere identical and thus can be surveyed from a dimension outside of it, while topological space, which is filled with forces that make it everywhere site- and time-specific and that is everywhere concrete and local, can only be surveyed from within the infinity of its fractal dimensions. While this characteristic relates it to Guattari's notions of spatial transversality and of fractal time, its unilaterality, which conflates the distinction between outside and inside, makes it adequate to the paradoxical logic of complementarity.

Topological Space

Much of the conceptual strength of Guattari's ecosophy comes from its inherently ecosophic notion of space that he sets against Cartesian space, which is the most common model of how we visualize and measure space. An empty, abstract receptacle for a variety of measurable objects whose properties are described by way of the laws of solid geometry. As Steven M. Rosen notes, classical geometry describes 'transformations in space, but never the transformation of space, for space is classically pictured as an immutable, inert, three-dimensional container for *lower*-order dynamics' (1994: 55). Things happen in Euclidean space. In contrast, topological space describes space itself as a dynamic force-field that is defined by intensive, physical, non-metric relations and energetic tensions. As the German mathematician Riemann noted, in a once more eminently ecological conceit, 'the metric field is not given rigidly once and for all, but is causally connected with matter and thus changes with the latter' (quoted in Weyl 1949: 86–7). In topological space, space happens. Space is no longer understood as empty, but as traversed and literally constructed by forces. It is complex, sensitive and dynamic. As Serres notes, in topological space two points that are a specific distance away from each other can be brought together not through moving them in space, but through a movement of space itself, which means that space is site- and time-specific. 'If you take a handkerchief and spread it out in order to iron it, you can see in it certain fixed distances and proximities. ... Then take the same handkerchief and crumple it, by putting it in your pocket. Two distant points suddenly are close, even superimposed. If, further, you tear it in certain places, two points that were close can become very distant.' The two spaces show 'the difference between topology (the handkerchief is folded, crumpled, shredded) and geometry (the same fabric is ironed out flat)' (Serres and Latour 1995: 60). Symptomatically, Serres notes that this differentiation also applies to time. 'As we experience time – as much in our inner sense as externally in nature, as much as *le temps* of history as *le temps* of weather – it resembles this crumpled version much more than the flat, overly simplified one' (59–60).

In topological space, objects are no longer defined by metrical, extensive measurements within a Cartesian grid, but by immanent, intensive relations between objects and forces within the spatio-energetic field that they themselves create anew at every moment. In other words, topological space is inherently constructivist. 'Space and that which occupies space tend to become identified, to have the same power' (TP: 488). In such a spatial milieu, the invariance of objects lies less in their specific form as in their spatial structure and the effects that space has on them and vice versa. 'A smooth, amorphous space of this kind is constituted by an accumulation of proximities, and each accumulation defines a *zone of indiscernibility* proper to "becoming" (more than a line and less than a surface; less than a volume and more than a surface)' (488). In topological space, that is, the essence of an invariably time- and site-specific object no longer resides in itself, but rather in its relative position within an inherently complex, dynamic spatial milieu, whether that milieu is political, artistic or chemical. In other words, it is ecological rather than essentialist.

As topological space defines the parameters within which an object can be modelled, it is in fact an integral part of that object. As Bernard Cache notes, in such a quasi-ecological topology 'the primary image is no longer the image of the object but the image of the set of constraints at the intersection of which the object is created' (1995: 97). In fact, topological space is inherently ecological in that it defines objects by suspending them into a dynamic force-field with locally differing and changing characteristics and defining them along the intensive tensions between each other.

From an ecological perspective, any abstract, axiomatic geometry needs to be suspended into its adherent milieu, so that space is no longer 'opposed to things . . . like an empty vessel into which they are placed' (Weyl 1949: 172). In such a suspension, the two registers come to mutually influence each other: 'matter excites the field, [and] the field acts upon matter' (173). As Merrill notes, 'in a discrete universe the norm for evaluating experience is inert matter. Things are regarded as constant and autonomous, sufficiently so that they are perceived as "substance" that possesses classifiable "qualities". In a continuous universe, however, time, as a fourth dimension, forces us to perceive things no longer as inert "substances", but as "events" – "All things flow"' (1982: 58). While Weyl notes that 'Euclidean space may be compared to a crystal, built up of uniform unchangeable atoms in the regular and rigid unchangeable arrangement of a lattice' (1949: 88), topological space is 'a liquid, consisting of the same indiscernible unchangeable atoms, whose arrangement and orientation, however, are mobile and yielding to forces acting upon them' (88): *liquid crystal topology*.

Guattari's schizoecology is conceptualized from within the multiplicity of topological spaces that form an 'abstract multiplicity [*variété abstraite*]' and that are 'locally euclidean' but globally non-euclidean' (Serres 1994: 89) and thus simultaneously 'apriori and sensoric [*sensoriels*]' (88). In Guattari's terminology, they are both of the given and of the giving. On this background, 'topology, prepared by Leibniz, seen by Euler, founded by Riemann and others, establishes itself, by and by, as a rigorous aesthetics' (93). In the shift from Euclid to Riemann, which recapitulates the one from global to local space, history is no longer only what happens in space. Rather, space itself becomes historical: 'The old space is . . . restored to the local and finally tumbles into the historical and into the cultural' (93).

If one can no longer talk of a unified global space, there are no longer unproblematic passages from the local to the global: 'a clear and distinct possibility of the practical usage of the global is never given. The ideologies, the philosophies of history, the theories of the state, the universal theories of morals are invariably written in that representational space in which the effects and the conclusions from the local to the global are all rational and can be governed. But that is never really the case. . . . Nobody has ever succeeded in integrating the local into the global' (96). In 'The Smooth and the Striated', in which they once more reference Serres' recourse to the *clinamen* in *The Birth of Physics*, Guattari and Deleuze develop a very similar notion of a multiplicitous space. Space is a fractal, Riemannian manifold assembled from heterogeneous spaces that forms, quite literally, a spatial ecology, in which the difference between the extremes of the local and the global are fractalized into an overall 'patchwork' that defines space as 'an amorphous collection of juxtaposed pieces that can be joined together in an infinite number of ways: we see that patchwork is literally a Riemannian space, or vice versa' (TP: 476).

In Guattari and Deleuze, a space that is dynamic, topological and continuous is smooth, while a space that is static, geometrical and discrete is striated. In smooth space, 'points are subordinated to ... trajectory' (478) – 'in the case of the striated, the line is between two points, while in the case of the smooth, the point is between two lines' (480) – and factualities are subordinated to intensities. 'Smooth space is filled by events or haecceities, far more than by formed or perceived things. It is a space of affects, more than one of properties' (479). Ultimately, smooth space denotes a field of pure intensities and as such is related to what Guattari and Deleuze call the body without organs as a field 'occupied by intensities, wind and noise, forces, and sonorous and tactile qualities' (479).

Space, then, is never empty and it never has been empty except as the phantasm of an idealist topology. Rather, it is a dynamic, energetic field in which a multiplicity of forces are operative. In this space, everything, from biological routines to thoughts, are site- and time-specific. If thought is always and fundamentally thought in space as well as in time, embodied thought is not about thinking other topologies, but about thinking in other topologies. From this perspective, Guattari and Deleuze literally think from within the complex alignments of topological and classical space, which form a new space of thought. As they note, 'it was a decisive event when the mathematician Riemann uprooted the multiple from its predicate state and made it a noun, "multiplicity". It marked the end of dialectics and the beginning of a typology and topology of multiplicities' (482–3). While Cartesian thought is everywhere organized around sets of logical relations and formal distinctions, topological thought is arranged around local sets of signifying distinctions that are defined, in terms of global space, as indistinct complementarities: *Cartesian space is logical, topological space is ecological.*

Fractal Space: Guattari's Leibniz

Much of Guattari and Deleuze's notion of space is developed in *A Thousand Plateaus*. Once again, however, *Schizoanalytic Cartographies* gives that space an ecological spin that concerns in particular fractalization as the perhaps most important and pervasive dynamics in Guattari's ecosophy. It is only from within the notion of fractal space that urgent ecological questions can be posed: How to live in this world? How to inhabit its various spaces? How to create spaces that are adequate to the world? To answer whether fractal space is an adequate space of thought to conceptualize the space of the world, I will trace Guattari's development of fractalization from Leibniz's notion of integration which – although he relied, for instance in his talk on Balthus, on contemporary mathematical notions of fractal space – is perhaps his most fundamental backdrop, and which allowed him to fold mathematics onto philosophy and vice versa.

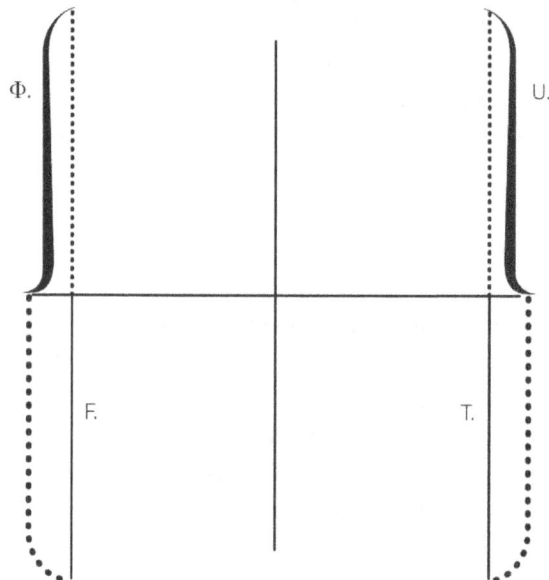

FIGURE 1.3 The integration of the four categories

There is a long Leibnizian shadow that falls onto Guattari's work, in which the Leibnizian term integration is used to conceptualize the speeds of determinability – $d^{+\infty\pm} \int d^{-\infty}$ and $d^{-\infty\pm} \int d^{+\infty}$ – as well as the passages from Flows to Phyla and from Territories to Universes respectively. As shown in Guattari's Figure 1.3, in spatial terms 'Phyla . . . constitute the "integrals" of Flows, as it were, and . . . Universes, the "integrals" of Territories' (SC: 28). Similarly, Leibniz's term monad is used to describe how, in the passage from Territories to Universes 'sensible ex-modules . . . find themselves *monadized*' (182, emphasis added). To understand why these terms are important for Guattari, it is necessary to remember that integration is a mathematical routine that concerns two related topics that are seminal in the conceptualization of schizoecology. It allows one to mathematically measure the continuous, and to conceptualize infinity.

Mathematically, integration consists of two interlocking processes: the treatment and computation of curves by way of mathematical differentiation, and the subsequent summation of the curve's gradient at each of its differential points. If one follows David Forster Wallace in treating a continuous 'straight line' as 'the very simplest kind of curve' (2003: 131), both can be defined mathematically as an infinitely dense set of points that follow each other without intervals. Integration consists in cutting this continuity up into a finite number of discontinuous, discrete segments that Leibniz calls infinitesimals. Integration rests on the mathematical conceit of treating the space in-between the single measurements of the single segments or gradients of a continuous curve as infinitely and therefore neglectably small. While a line embodies the notion of continuity, the process of mathematical integration introduces a conceptually infinite but pragmatically finite number of cuts, or, more generally, of differential discontinuities, into this line in order to be able to to metricize it and thus to make it measurable. In other words, it introduces digital cuts into an analog line. The second process consists of combining the segments thus created into one coherent quantitative form: to sum the single measurements up into one general measurement. As in Lucretius' theory of information, in which the loss of the state of maximum information is the price to be paid for communicability, the loss of an infinite density of points on the curve in favour of a finite number of infinitesimals and integrations, as well as the loss of an infinite precision in the passage from the one to the other, is the price to be paid for mathematical computability and calculability: for metricization. In terms of *Schizoanalytic Cartographies*, the gain is the creation of Phyla as a field of possibility from the fully contingent and thus uncomputable, real field of Flows. In mathematical terms: *the creation of metrical from non-metrical numbers.*

If Leibniz's mathematical genius lies in his development of infinitesimal calculus, his overall genius lies in his superposition of the logic of that calculus onto the operation of perception: Mathematical integration introduces cuts into a continuous line, perception introduces cuts into a world of continuous intensities. By way of differentiations that break up the both structural and temporal continuity of the energetic gradients of scales of stimuli, organisms integrate different modes of intensity, such as electrical, chemical or biological intensity. As Bateson notes, these processes go from the conscious level to 'the "unconscious", down to the hormones as part of the network of pathways along which transformations of difference can be transmitted' (2002: 165). The senses pick up stimuli which they filter, and then transport by way of the nervous system, into the discontinuous network of digital neurons, which either fire or not, and synapses that operate analogically. As Anthony Wilden notes, 'the neurons may be said to operate digitally, but the synapse and axon which connect them appear to be complex analog devices' (1972: 157). Both mathematics and perception, then, can be said to rely equally on a logic of integration.

Philosophically, the notion that a perceptual apparatus works by way of creating discontinuities has had an either very good or a very bad press. While it allows for what Guattari calls deterritorialization, it precludes the possibility of the immediate perception of continuous movement, and as such it can be read as a violence done to, or as the downright loss of, the analog. Bergson, for instance, considered the reduction inherent in digitalization to be tragic, and it took him a long time to accept that the perceptual apparatus itself operates cinematographically, in that it creates the inherently false impression of a continuous movement from discrete perceptual stills. Perhaps a useful definition of both the logic of cinema and of the mathematical spaces constructed by Leibniz's infinitesimal calculus would be that both are quasi-smooth.

According to Leibniz, perceptual and cognitive machines are difference engines that transform, by way of integration, continuous intensities into discontinuous differences. In other words, they turn intensive forces into signaletic materials. They are sampling devices that take analog, quantitative changes in intensities and transform them into digital, qualitative differences. Into data. This explains the straight line from Leibniz to the computer, the difference engine that is based on his prophetic notation of numbers as strings of 1s and 0s. In the context of the difference between digital and analog media, media technologies that rely on programs based on Leibniz's numerical distinction are digital and metric, while those based on changes in unnumbered intensity are analog and non-metric. The analog field is that of quantity, the digital field that of quality. From an integrational perspective, the analog is an ideal field, while the digital is an empirical field, in the same way that Flows are ideal while Phyla, as fields of possibility, are empirical.

If the senses function as analog-to-digital converters, the analog makes up the surplus to any form of perception. It is the name for the level of reality that, although it is lived at every moment, is not perceived. As it is a given machinic function, however, Guattari does not judge or evaluate integration. The evaluation that integration is positive because it leads to conceptual clarity is idealistic, while the evaluation that it is negative because it leads to alienation and a separation from what is imagined as a continuous nature is romantic. All Guattari maintains is that from a machinic point-of-view, deterritorialized rhizomes are created through integrations of the real world. While Territories and Universes are different aspects of entities, in terms of their heterogenesis, existential territories are created from sensible territories through differential codings. Through more processes of integration, these territorial entities then develop deterritorialized Universes. Despite its conceptual neutrality, integration shows both the potentialities and the dangers of organization and of processes of power in relation to the assemblage of actual and virtual consistencies, both of which Leibniz and Guattari consider to be, down to their most molecular levels, heterogeneous aggregates.

While this might explain why integration is an important term for Guattari, what about monads? In philosophy's default setting of monad, this heterogeneous aggregation is often forgotten in that, against its original meaning of indivisible unit, elementary particle or, in terms of biology, single-cell organism, the term monad is by default taken to denote a human being. In opposition to this default setting, Guattari's definition of monad as any assemblage of enunciation '"exceed[s]" the problematic of the individuated subject, the thinking monad delimited by consciousness, the faculties of the soul (the understanding, the will . . .) in their classically accepted sense' (SC: 18). In this context, Guattari is true to Leibniz, whose figure of the world is of a multitude of monads that range in their modes of existence from the atomic to the human. An ecological reading of Leibniz would stress his belief that the world is 'composed of an infinite envelopment of organic creatures' (Rutherford 1995: 226) and that all monads are compositions of an infinite number of smaller monads. On each level of the monadic world, heterogeneous elements assemble themselves into complex aggregates. In terms of media studies, on each level, media of life assemble themselves into forms of life.

Leibniz's fascination with Antonie van Leeuwenhoek, who was the first person to observe single-cell organisms with the help of self-built microscopes – Leibniz visited Leeuwenhoek in 1676 and kept up a correspondence with him until his death in 1716 – lies precisely in that the microscope allowed optical zooms into this infinitely scaled world, at least down to the plateau of cellular life. As Leibniz notes in a famous passage of the *Monadology*, 'each portion of matter may be conceived as like a garden full of plants and like a pond full of fishes. But each branch of every plant, each member of every animal, each drop of its liquid parts is also some such garden or pond' (1925: 256). As Rutherford explains, 'according to Leibniz's doctrine of panorganicism, every organic body is composed of an infinity of lesser organisms, each of whose bodies is in turn composed of an infinity of lesser organisms, *ad infinitum*. Thus, the "functional components" of any organic body will include an infinity of subordinate organisms' (1995: 235, my italics). In terms of perception, recursive assemblages of entities operate on an infinity of levels of integration.

Although integrations take place on each of life's plateaus, Leibniz conceptually integrates the quasi-continuum of these plateaus into three levels by way of a separation that evokes the integration of fractal space into the three natural dimensions. Lines, planes, volumes; perception, memory, consciousness. Naked monads, animal monads, human monads. Although this differentiation can be mapped onto the fourfold, Guattari replaces Leibniz's tripartition by an overall fractal field that allows for transversal passages between these levels. In this, he is more Leibnizian than Leibniz. Naked monads are defined by perception and appetition (*appetitus*) or *conatus*, which is a force that brings about the 'continuous' passage 'from one perception to the next' (Schneider 2001: 61). When Schneider notes that 'appetitus is associated with what Leibniz calls "petites inclinations", which are the instantaneous, or infinitesimal changes from sub-monad to sub-monad' (64), that opens up the eminently Lucretian question 'is there one "first petite inclination" for the whole monadic field?' (72). In other words, is there a monadic *clinamen*?

Naked monads are Leibniz's version of a quasi-anonymous life considered as a heterological arrangement of pure, atomic elements. In another famous passage of the *Monadology*, in which Leibniz describes the crystallization of appetition and perception into a simple substance, naked monads in fact share all characteristics of aperiodic, living crystals. As this crystallization takes place on an infinitely small level, Leibniz describes it through another of his conceptual zooms. 'And supposing there were a machine, so constructed as to think, feel, and have perception, it might be conceived as increased in size, while keeping the same proportions, so that one might go into it as into a mill. That being so, we should, on examining its interior, find only parts which work one upon another, and never anything by which to explain a perception. Thus it is in a simple substance, and not in a compound or in a machine, that perception must be sought for. Further, nothing but this (namely, perceptions and their changes) can be found in a simple substance' (1925: 228). The meeting of perception and life as appetition or *conatus* should be looked for in Lucretian realms that are imperceptible (as in: finer than perception) and unthinkable (as in: faster than thought). As Guattari would say, it lies in the infinitesimally slowed-down plane of immanence as the only fully unintegrated or disintegrated plane: in the first informal diagram embodied by the plane of consistencies.

While naked monads are defined by perception and appetition, animal monads are defined by perception, appetition and memory. Human monads, finally, are defined by perception, appetition, memory and consciousness. In a move that is again more Leibnizian than Leibniz, Guattari and Deleuze do not stress these categorical differences between species, but the fractal spaces in-between them: *animal studies going fractal*. In a field defined by fractal dimensions between animal and human, the question is about becoming-animal or a becoming-human rather than about differentiating species. In fact, fractalization allows quasi-continuous, transversal shifts from plateau to plateau. It also allows conceptual shifts between plateaus. While the default plateau of understanding the passage from Territories to Universes is that of a human being, for instance, one might also insert the story of evolution into that vector, or the beginning of seeing something meaningful or thoughtful in a refrain. In the phase space of the fourfold, moreover, this vector is reversible. Every entity can re-insert itself into a specific position by way of non-regressive atavisms.

This said, let me relate the three Leibnizian levels to Sensible Territories, Existential Territories and Universes as they define a human being. As Serres notes, 'perception, perception-memory, perception-memory-reason' (1968 II: 609) each integrate a specific set of continuities. Perception integrates the continuous flow of 'the infinite multitude of fluent and transient small perceptions'; apperception and memory integrate the continuous flow of events as 'the continuum of adjacent or distant states'; and the reflexive act integrates these two integrations into the concept. 'The reflexive act integrates into the self the infinite (perceptive and mnemonic) series of its complete notion' (609).

On each of the three levels, quantitative irritations are treated, both perceptually and cognitively, by processes of integration. On the second level, the results of the purely perceptual integrations (Sensible Territories) are integrated into a set of dynamic relations between perceptions, which implies the birth of time as duration and history (Existential Territories). On the third level, these reflexive operations are submitted to a level of self-reflection or observation, which provides a conceptual simulation of the initial field (Universes): naked monads have a life (*bios*), animal monads have a history, human monads have universes and historiographies (*zoe*). Systemically, the trajectory goes from unconscious reflex to conscious reflection. 'The hierarchical order is a series of integrations in the mathematical sense: the result is the sum, then the sum of the sum etc.' (609). From very basic to highly complex samplings and pick-ups, monads turn analog, continuous changes in intensity into digital, discontinuous data.

As Rutherford notes, in Leibniz 'the "functional components" of any organic body will include an infinity of subordinate organisms' (1995: 235). In all of his work, Guattari conceptualizes and attempts to imagine worlds in which such a scaled, fractal subordination is thought of from the perspective of a communal pragmatics rather than from the perspective of molar, stable hierarchies. The relations of subordination, which cannot be evaded except in a state of total anarchy, need to be made dynamic, flexible and open to change. In stable organizations and bad ecologies, managers dream of submission while workers and students dream of revolution. Why do we desire our domination? What makes us content to be subjected so thoroughly and so systematically? What keeps us from being and wanting to be experimental and elastic? Why are we not more graceful in our movements through the milieu that we co-create by walking through it? Symptomatically, the motto for *The Three Ecologies*, which is taken from Bateson, notes that 'there is an ecology of bad ideas, just as there is an ecology of weeds' (TE: 27).

In both mathematics and perception, that lack of grace results from the fact that the entity's operational unity is controlled by the most inclusive and integrated element. Mathematically, this concerns the final sum. Biologically, it concerns the organism. In terms of the monad's operation, the sub-monads function as organs, although there are always smaller, sub-sub-monads that are organs of organs, and so on, recursively, *ad infinitum*. Both bodies and subjects must be understood, therefore, as organized aggregates of nested monads that are defined by a complex hierarchical dynamics whose base is formed by a plane of monadic multiplicity. In Guattarian terms, this heterological plane of naked monads is the body without organs, the most disintegrated plane of consistency: *the plane of consistency as the plane of immanence.*

The entity's conviction that it has a body is the result of the installation of a dominant monad that is in a state of surveillance and thus forms the head of a corporeal society of control. As Deleuze notes in *The Fold: Leibniz and the Baroque*, 'all clusters of dominated monads ... exist only in the pure individuality of their dominant as a primary force of surveillance' (2001: 114–15). This is the more sinister connotation of organization. According to the three modes of relation that a human monad has to its body, the first one is that of the observer. The dominant monad has what it thinks is a coherent image of its body and its organization. Guattari ecologizes this function by replacing it with the notion of partial observers. The second relation is perceptual in that by default, the subject experiences itself as a coherent operational unity. The third relation, which traverses the other two, is intensive and thus indifferent. At each moment, an indifferent, unintegrated, anonymous and aerosolic body permeates the other two bodies. Through this third body, the entity is invariably part and parcel of the allover milieu. This is the real, true body, while the other two are virtual and false. As Rutherford notes, 'beings through aggregation thus occupy a curious middle ground in Leibniz's ontology between what is truly real ... and what is merely ideal or imaginary' (1995: 222). What Guattari criticizes in Lacan is that he is only interested in the first two bodies. As Lacan famously argues, the false body-image comes before the true, real body.

Leibniz's body, then, is a dynamic and permeable aggregate whose multiplicity and constant, for the most part unconscious modulations are enveloped by a dominant monad that perceives the inherently dynamic aggregate that it in actual fact is, as a continuous and consistent pattern through time and space that has stabilized itself by way of physically and psychically integrating the heterological assemblage of monads into its larger operative unit. The characteristics of this aggregate, such as extension, mass, duration, stability and movement, concern only that part of its monadic multiplicity that the dominant monad, as well as other monads, has integrated into what it calls a coherent whole. 'A body *is* a plurality of monads, which happens to give the appearance of being an extended object when apprehended by other finite monads' (Rutherford 1995: 218).

As Guattari considers operations of integration to be an ontological given, he maintains, as I noted earlier, that to critique them is either idealistic or romantic. A true critique can only address the measure of the exclusion of the true body without organs from the entity's false, affective and conceptual axiomatics, as well as the measure of its adequation of the false to the true and vice versa. These, in fact, are the main critiques performed in both *Anti-Oedipus* and *A Thousand Plateaus*. As the body is a complex machine that operates on an infinity of levels, there are invariably levels of integration that are too fine to be perceived by the dominant monad. These tiny perceptions make up the entity's machinic unconscious. Smaller monads perceive and operate without the system memory-reason being aware of these secret integrations. Another point of critique is that the dominant monad considers the monads that integrate other monads on levels below its perceptual radar, such as the naked monads of which it is in actual fact an assemblage, as allopoietic machines rather than as its unconscious. If it reduces its unconscious to inert, dead materiality, it is this deadening that must be critiqued – the colonialization of naked monads under a specific monadic regime and their treatment as dead, when in actual fact they are infinitely and insistently alive. This deadening is the ultimate nemesis of Guattari's ecology.

'The very simple sub-monads, which are, according to the theory of dominance, positioned on the lowest level of any organic body can be considered as the purely material aspect of an organic body, i.e. they are assembled into hierarchies and structures, i.e. bodies. As such, bodies are merely naked monads that are closed off from the environment and networked into complex, intelligent architectures. This also shows the relation between matter and obscure [*verworrene*] perceptions: for dominating sub-monads, dominated sub-monads are matter. However, there are aggregates of monads that are not subordinated to a maximal element. These aggregates form merely the fundamentum in re for the well-founded phenomenon of "purely" physical bodies' (Schneider 2001: 44). The difference between the singular and the communal is decisive here. 'Each distinct simple substance or monad . . . is surrounded by a *mass* composed of an infinity of other monads, which constitute the *body belonging to* this central monad, through whose properties the monad represents the things outside it' (Leibniz 1978 VI: 598–9). In this series, 'there is no soul or entelechy which is not dominant with respect to an infinity of others which enter into its organs, and the soul is never without an organic body suitable to its present state' (564). From this position 'the organic body of a higher living being [*höheres Lebewesen*], if it is thought of as consisting of monads, is not an arbitrary [*beliebiges*] aggregate, but a hierarchically organized aggregate' (Schneider 2001: 41).

Are there, then, more gentle hierarchies? If Phyla are rhizomatic, what is the difference between hierarchization and complexification? Rutherford stresses in particular the entrainment of heterogeneous elements into a complexly organized, hierarchical unity: 'The paradigm of this sort of relationship for Leibniz is the relationship that exists between the living body and its separate organs, cells, and subcellular components. In this case, the latter are conceived not simply as spatial parts of the body but as parts whose activities are adapted to the activity of the body as a whole' (1995: 224). Simple monads are integrated into organs, organs are integrated into organisms,

organisms are integrated into societies and so on *ad infinitum*. The world is fully integrated and expressed by its creatures: *fractal ecology*.

Although the dominant monad experiences its body as a coherent unity, it is, in actual fact, an aggregate of a multitude of heterogeneous elements: 'Any mass contains innumerable monads, for although any one organic body in nature has its corresponding [dominant] monad, it nevertheless contains in its parts other monads endowed in the same way with organic bodies subservient to the primary one; and the whole of nature is nothing else, for it is necessary that every aggregate result from simple substances as if from true elements' (Leibniz 1978 VII: 502). Accordingly, there is no part of the world that is not somehow alive. 'Matter is everywhere composed of organic creatures enveloped within organic creatures, each of which is composed of a soul and a suitable organic body' (Rutherford 1995: 231). Even more, 'according to the panorganicist picture, there is no part of matter that is not endowed with life: Either it is itself the body of an animated creature or it is a collection of such creatures, each of whose bodies is in turn composed of smaller organic creatures' (229). As Rutherford notes, '[b]ecause of its division *in infinitum*, matter is essentially an aggregate or multitude of things' (12).

In this complex setup, an aggregate is 'a type of entity whose identity is determined partly by its individual constituents and partly by the relations among its constituents' (221). In other words, it is both actual and virtual. There must be actual atoms in order for there to be atomic aggregates and relations between atoms. Rutherford calls this Leibniz's 'reduction of matter to monads' (219). As with perception, if matter consists of recursive multitudes of living beings, there must be smallest elements or unities that make up the multitudes because 'whatever is a *multitude* must be constituted from true *unities*, for a multitude can only come to be through unity: "for where there is no true unity, there is no true multitude"' (Leibniz 1978 II: 267). As Leibniz notes, 'in real things, unities are prior to a multitude, and there cannot exist multitudes except through unities' (279). Heterogeneous elements before assemblages: 'We can therefore conclude that a mass of matter is not truly a substance, that its unity is only ideal and that (leaving the understanding aside) it is only an aggregate, a collection, a multitude of an infinity of true substances, a well-founded phenomenon' (Leibniz 1978 VII: 564).

For Leibniz, it is not enough to maintain that every material aggregate consists of monads, as each of these monads is in turn an aggregate that consists of even smaller monads. 'I even believe that matter is essentially an *aggregate*, and consequently that there are always actual parts. Thus, it is by reason, and not only by sense, that we judge that it is divided, or rather that it is from the start nothing but a multitude. I believe that it is true that matter (and even each part of matter) is divided into a greater number of parts than can be imagined' (Leibniz 1978 IV: 502).

According to this infinite regress, matter is 'essentially an *infinite* plurality of monads' (Rutherford 1995: 220, my italics). As Leibniz notes, '[m]y fundamental meditations turn on two things, namely *unity* and *infinity*. Souls are *unities* and bodies are multitudes, albeit *infinite* ones' (1978 VII: 542). While each actual monad consists of a material multiplicity and remains a multiplicity *ad infinitum*, the virtual monad unifies that multiplicity in a fundamentally false manner. As an immaterial body-image, the body is a unity; as the material body, it is a multitude: 'in itself', it is 'some aggregate of monads' (Rutherford 1995: 224). Leibniz's conceptual sleight-of-mind, then, consists of reducing the body to an aggregation of atoms. 'In truth, I do not do away with body but reduce [*revoco*] it to that which it is, for I show that corporeal mass ... is not a substance, but a phenomenon resulting from simple substances, which alone have a unity and absolute reality' (1978 II: 275). If what we experience as an undifferentiated mass is in actual fact an assemblage of heterogeneous atomic elements, the body is an aerosolic *phenomenon* rather than a *noumenon*: *philosophy as aerosolic atomism*.

Leibniz animates that heterogeneous body by considering virtual monads to be the hearts and dynamos of material aggregates. As virtual monads have an appetite for change, matter longs for change not by itself, but because each actual element is suffused by a virtual element. In the same way that the plane of immanence suffuses the plane of consistency, an ultrafine, aerosolic *prima materia*, according to Leibniz, suffuses the much denser and much more solid *secunda materia* of the actual body.

If until now I have dealt with the question of how the giving integrates the given, how are Flows and Phyla integrated into assemblages? In other words, how does Leibniz conceptualize, from within the logic of integration, the relation of matter and mind, of the actual and the virtual? Like Guattari's, Leibniz's notion of monads relies on a complicated theory of incorporation that is based on two parallel assemblage theories. One of these is mathematical and virtual, the other physical and actual. One concerns the monad as a virtual, mathematical point without extension; the other the monad as an extended, actual and physical element. Once as an intensive, once as an extensive point. Once as immaterial, once as material. Only the two separate series in conjunction form monads. In terms of the fourfold, the process of incorporation concerns the folding of the field of the material, actual giving onto that of the immaterial, virtual given and vice versa. The two distinct series are taken up in Leibniz's definition of monads as immaterial beings embodied in their specific material extensions. Leibniz treats the complementarity of these two separated series as the difference between mathematics and physics, the conceptual shorthand for the virtuality and the actuality of monads being mathematical and physical points respectively. One might wonder how Leibniz would have conceptualized the relation between the mathematical and the physical point had he had recourse to the modern scientific notion of complementarity. Leibniz's concept of the photonic nature of the monad suggests that he would have embraced the notion quite enthusiastically.

While Leibniz's parallel assemblage theories resonate in many ways with Guattari's, the fourfold further complicates Leibniz in that Guattari differentiates, as Figure 6.6 shows, between modules and monads as two superposed realms or, better, vectors. Another characteristic that relates Guattari's to Leibniz's monads is that they seem to be, famously, without windows. As Guattari notes, because they 'escape from the categories of relation and interaction, . . . they have nothing to do with one another, and are thus absolutely distinct' (SC: 180). At the same time, however, 'they are nevertheless absolutely indistinct, in such a way that one gains access to them by immediate transferential apprehension, or *knowing by affect*' (180, emphasis added): *aisthesis*. While singularization is based on continuous affective Flows, it is instantiated by processes of cognitive integration. 'It isn't just the contingency of being-there, the certified localization of its redundant figures, that gets taken into account but, in addition, the integral of its dis-positions, transpositions, catastrophes and possible accidents, before, after, to the side of, beyond its actual manifestations' (127).

While Leibniz thinks from within a heterological space of naked monads, Guattari's doubly-coded space of given actuality and giving virtuality puts modules and monads on the side of Territories and Universes as concrete existentialities and heteropoietic entities. They remain tied, however, to the given, purely objective, actual side of Flows and Phyla. This is, ultimately, Guattari's figure of ecological adequation. Modular integrations have to do with perception and the concomitant creation of continuous time by way of the instigation of refrains in a passage from open field to territory. Heterogenesis: the petri-dish of individuation. As Guattari noted in relation to the video-scene, 'we will examine heterogenesis as: the scenic apparatus of the intensities it puts to work; a specific fractal process; existential dating; knowledge by transference; a partial nucleus of self-reference; and a proto-energetic basin' (184). From this position, existential envelopes bind free-floating, actual determinations: 'Whilst in a fractal mode, the determinability $d^{-\infty}$ was free to flee into deterritorialized Phyla, it now finds itself prisoner of an eternitarian duration' and of 'the birth-death finitude proper to every non-trivial machine' (183).

The question of integration is particularly pertinent in terms of the difference between psychoanalysis and schizoanalysis. Here, the difference is not that the signifier operates in an always already integrated field. That is simply a given. Rather, while psychoanalysis is deeply interested in the integrations performed by language, it represses, or at least neglects, those of the signaletic and of the field of immanence, which it can treat only as a cognitive vacuum, while schizoanalysis treats it as an analog, meaningless noise that runs through every meaningful digital system; as a white, real noise that is actualized, in the field of consistency, as a pink, ecological noise. At the same time that every integrational level adds to the perceptual and cognitive complexity of the entity, it implies an increasing loss or distance, because perception as integration operates by way of processes of reduction and of framing. If complexity is a measure of integrational processes, it would seem that complex entities perceive less of the intensive multiplicity of the world than less complicated entities. They are at a greater distance from the world, one might say. This, however, is not in itself to be deplored. In fact, they contain a larger amount of molecular levels and entities that make up their unconscious than less complicated entities. An increase in striation, one might say, implies a richer unconscious. Although in the best of perceptual worlds it would be possible to perceive and integrate even the smallest and fastest of irritations – the field of the most minute vibrations and perturbations – every perceptual machine is itself a system of filters and thus defined by specific perceptual thresholds that it cannot cross without ceasing to be a perceptual machine. In fact, the situation is even more complicated. Every complex perceptual entity consists of less complicated systems that gather the material for its more complex perceptions from levels that are unconscious to that complex entity's most comprehensive and conscious perceptual threshold. At the end of this recursive chain infinitely simple – as in: non-integrational – monads would ideally perceive everything. Each complex entity taps into these levels of imperceptible perturbations; into microperceptions that are, although they inherently belong to it, unconscious for its overall perceptual apparatus. As Konrad Cramer notes from within the register of a Freudian unconscious, 'perceptions can take place unconsciously and they do take place to a large, if not to the largest part unconsciously, in that at the moment of their taking place there is no knowledge [*Kenntnis*] of their taking place. Phenomenologically, that is ... a completely correct description. In this context, Freud could refer to Leibniz' (1994: 33–4). One of the most important aspects is that Guattari invariably develops ecology from this level of an automatic, unconscious regime of machinic operations.

At the point-at-infinity of such a scaled logic one would find infinitely minute perceptions that are defined by infinitely small differences or the smallest possible differences. 'The tiny, imperceptible pains, the tiny aids and reliefs, the tiny movements of heat and light, the subliminal solicitations, organic forces [*ressorts*] and changes, the minute motes of dust, the imperceptible prevalences, the small waves [*vagues*] ... are differentials' (Serres 1968 I: 206). When Serres notes that 'the global theory of tiny perceptions is an infinitesimal calculus' (206), this implies that one can reach the infinitely fine and fast level of the pure multiplicity of perturbations only asymptotically, as always already faintly decelerated. From the point-of-view of complex monads, all one can do is open up one's overall perception as far as possible to one's smallest perceptual units. Such a becoming imperceptible – which of course does not mean that one becomes in any way optically or culturally invisible, but rather that one opens oneself up to one's own or also one's milieu's imperceptible plateaus – opens the monad to the most unorganized, heterological life within it; to the naked monads that make up the infinitely fine medium that carries its organization. This is why, when Leibniz scales perception and integration down to the cellular plateau, he considers 'the monads that are only equipped with perception and appetitus in a very broad sense as alive' (Schneider 2001: 39). Down to its most anonymous, aerosolic levels and infinitely small elements, the world, and everything in it, might be considered as being anonymously alive.

From the position of perception, the level of pure Flow is unthinkable, not because it is in any way monstrous, but because thinking is by definition an integrational process. It is not only humans, however, who partake of cognition. We entrain monads that, on their respective levels, also operate cognitively. Similarly, from the position of an intensive, anonymous life, the possible, affective and cognitive level is unliveable for singular entities. Human life is spanned out between these two impossibilities. In Leibniz, some monads are operationally nearer to the intensive and unformed register, while others are nearer to the cognitive register. None of them, however, reach the point-at-infinity at which the extremes become one. All monads are formally suspended between the virtual empire of signification and concepts and the actual empire of forces and intensities. Both Leibniz's and Guattari's monads are part of an infinitely scaled life, and they follow two complementary series of assemblage. Layers of obscure, unconscious microperceptions are integrated and contracted into clear, conscious perceptions. Layers of naked monads are integrated and contracted into organisms. In this context, Leibniz's notion of infinite recursion addresses a debate that is still virulent in today's media studies, when they maintain that in strictly operational terms, media work best when they are completely subservient to the forms they carry. This is part of why Hegel preferred alphabetical script, as the most arbitrary, unobtrusive and invisible mode of notation, over symbolic and pictorial scripts. The computer's digital code is the epitome of this abstraction.

One might conclude that the crucial difference between Guattari and Leibniz does not lie in the internal structure of their respective systems, but rather in that Leibniz relies on a divine harmony, which means that monads are not only structurally coupled to a specific milieu, but also to a divine order of milieus. As Serres notes, 'just as our body integrates the *noise* of minute perceptions into sensible signals, so does God integrate in absolute knowledge, *in white light*, the relative *noise* of our right, flighty thinking' (G: 20, emphasis added). The question is whether the world moves according to a divine, pre-established harmony or whether there is only the world, luminous energy, and the logics of diffraction and integration. If one were to replace the agency of a divine order by the agency of the natural order, if one were to replace God by Sun, that is, monads would be consistencies, and Leibniz would be an ecologist.

Another difference between Guattari and Leibniz is tendential and, perhaps temperamental. While Leibniz tends to stress the vector towards clear, conscious perceptions, Guattari tends to stake the loss of infinity that is inherent in the integration's infinitesimals against the possibility of infinitely small lines of flight and of tiny perceptions. Ecologically, this translates into the idea that the plane of the continuity of life is always finer than the networks created by its perceptual integrations. Although they express it, something of the world forever escapes itself in its monads. There are always levels of the infinitely complex networks of life that escape individual, concrete networks of perception and cognition. There are always abstract levels that are finer than the finest concrete perception. If the digital is understood as a subset of the analog, the symbolic level can no longer be operationally separated from the subsymbolic. As Bateson notes, all data are digital representations of analog processes. As symbols are fundamentally both false and clear – in fact, they are clear because they are obscure – they cannot be taken, as Varela notes in *The Embodied Mind*, 'at face value; they are seen as approximate macrolevel descriptions of operations whose governing principles reside at a subsymbolic level' (1991: 102). This is why 'any symbolic level becomes highly dependent on the underlying network's properties and peculiarities as well as bound to its history' (102). The territory is always larger and more comprehensive than the map. No digital network is able to capture the realm of the analog: philosophy's escape from the logic of the calculus. At the same time, the analog is not an ideal. Rather: *maximum analogicity, maximum digitality*.

'Everything plays out around the springing up of the rupture ..., the point of emergence of expressive fractalization, from which the conversion of certain material Flows into signaletic Flows will make itself felt' (SC: 133), Guattari notes. Why is the process of fractalization so important and why is fractal space the adequate space to model the world? As Guattari maintains, any social or architectural field is not so much defined by its conflicts and contradictions as by the lines of flight that are running through it. 'An assemblage has neither base nor superstructure, neither deep structure nor surface structure; it flattens all of its dimensions onto a single plane of consistency upon which reciprocal presuppositions and mutual insertions play themselves out' (TP: 90). Despite this flattening, why should one speak of a fractal ontology rather than of a flat ontology and of a fractal ecology rather than a flat ecology?

The scientific line from integration to fractalization goes from Leibniz to Benoît Mandelbrot, whose notion of fractality denotes the breaking up of the three natural dimensions into an infinity of fractal dimensions, or, better, surfaces. In fractal space, one can construct dimensions not only with whole or natural numbers, but with an infinity of fractional numbers; with rational, real and imaginary numbers such as

1.236 or 2.789. In other words, fractalization implies the introduction of a potentially infinite number of layers, or plateaus, into the lost spaces in-between the three dimensions we call natural. It introduces, quite literally, an infinity of scaled plateaus into the formerly non-scaled spaces between the 1st, 2nd and 3rd dimensions. Although Guattari and Deleuze take the notion of plateaus from Bateson, the numbering of a thousand plateaus evokes this infinity, somewhat as it does in Scheherazade's 1001 nights.

In classical geometry, the three dimensions are represented by lines, surfaces and volumes respectively, with breaks between points at which a line is a line, a surface is a surface and a volume is a volume. In the same way that fractional numbers are inserted into the gaps between natural numbers, spatial fractalization introduces a quasi-continuum of an infinity of dimensions into the geometry of natural dimensions. As Guattari and Deleuze describe it in *A Thousand Plateaus*, 'fractals are aggregates whose number of dimensions is fractional rather than whole, or else whole but with continuous variation in direction. An example would be a line segment whose central third is replaced by the angle of an equilateral triangle; the operation is repeated for the four resulting segments, and so on ad infinitum, following a relation of similarity – such a segment would constitute an infinite line or curve with a dimension greater than one, but less than a surface' (486).

Two things follow from fractalization: First, a two-dimensional surface is never a true surface that would be different in kind from a one-dimensional line, because there is an infinite number of plateaus that one can insert into the space that was lost in jumping from the 1st to the 2nd dimension. To call something a line or a plane, therefore, is in some ways an idealization, because a line and a plane are simply specific, singled-out moments within a non-metric spatial continuum or a fractalized, metric quasi-continuum. The same holds true for the other dimensions. A zoom into a volume will show it fractalize into planes. A zoom into these planes will show them fractalize into points. Second, despite the fact that the numbering of the natural dimensions is an idealization that isolates a specific plateau from a continuum, pragmatically, a line with the dimension of 1.9 still behaves almost like a surface, while a surface with 2.1 also behaves almost like a surface. A surface with the dimension 2.9, however, behaves almost like a volume. Fractalization, then, allows Guattari and Deleuze to conceptualize a space in which a multiplicity of lines becomes a true surface only at infinity, as a point at which infinitely many lines together create a surface, similar to the way that only an infinity of points create a line or an infinite number of surfaces create a volume. When fractalized, metric space becomes a quasi-continuum of fractal dimensions between points, lines, surfaces and volumes.

I have used the term quasi-continuum because the expression 'a continuum of fractal dimensions' – Guattari's 'infinitesimal deterritorialized continuum' – is deeply paradoxical and problematic. After all, the process of fractalization implies precisely the break-up of a continuum. The paradox of a quasi-continuum can be understood by way of the logic that the German mathematician Richard Dedekind applied, in 1858, to the line of numbers [→ **Deleuze 120**]. The mathematical routine of what has come to be known as the Dedekind cut (*Dedekind'scher Schnitt*), which Guattari and Deleuze reference a number of times, is related to integration in that it solves, like Leibniz's integration, the logical problem of how to make a continuum, in this case the continuum of numbers, countable. The procedure consists of replacing the given continuum of the line of numbers by an infinity of cuts into that line. It rests on the conceit that a continuous, non-metric line between two points can be made measurable and thus metric by partitioning it into infinitely many (rational, irrational, real) numbers. One only needs to part the length of the line and repeat this routine infinitely often. In that every number functions as a cut into the original continuum of the line, one might maintain that it makes it more discontinuous. At the same time, however, it converges towards a renewed, but now measurable continuum – that is, the quasi-continuum of infinitely many, infinitely near-to-each-other cuts – made up of an infinite discontinuity: *more discontinuity, more continuity!*

In *A Thousand Plateaus*, one of Guattari and Deleuze's most important, and in the light of the theory of fractal geometry perhaps overly imaginative definitions of fractalization has to do with the relation between the non-metric and the metric as analogous to smooth and striated space. It can explain why Guattari maintains that smoothing has to do with the space in-between consistencies. 'Any aggregate with a whole number of dimensions' is 'striated or metric' (TP: 488), Guattari and Deleuze note. As such, striated space is equivalent to a measured, metric space, while smooth space is equivalent to a non-metric, unmeasured space. Against this background, an aggregate that thinks of itself, or is being thought of, as existing in a space with fixed, natural dimensions and as itself having separate dimensions, such as the aggregate of classical geometry, the aggregate of the subject of psychoanalysis or also the aggregate of classical architecture, each repress 'nonmetric smooth space', which 'is constituted by the construction of a line with a fractional number of dimensions greater than one, or of a surface with a fractional number of dimensions greater than two' (488). Guattari and Deleuze's rhetorics set a metric geometry against a non-metric topology. Smooth spaces are related to fractional dimensions and to states of disorder, such as 'Brownian motion, turbulence, and the sky' (487). Although this is somewhat misleading as fractal space is not implicitly disordered, at this moment, the notion of fractality is not yet, as it will be in *Schizoanalytic Cartographies*, a given characteristic of space, but part of the binary system of classification between smooth and striated space.

As the reference to turbulence and Brownian motion as two examples of smooth space suggests, and as I have shown earlier, in *A Thousand Plateaus* Guattari and Deleuze develop smooth space from Lucretius. 'Let us try to understand in the simplest terms how space escapes the limits of its striation. At one pole, it escapes them by *declination*, in other words, by the smallest deviation, by the infinitely small deviation between a gravitational vertical and the arc of a circle to which the vertical is tangent. At the other pole, it escapes them by the *spiral or vortex*, in other words, a figure in which all the points of space are simultaneously occupied according to laws of frequency or of accumulation, distribution; these laws are distinct from the so-called laminar distribution corresponding to the striation of parallels. From the smallest deviation to the vortex there is a valid and necessary relation of consequence: what stretches between them is precisely a smooth space whose element is declination and which is peopled by a spiral. Smooth space is constituted by the minimum angle, which deviates from the vertical, and by the vortex, which overspills striation' (489).

Even though striated and smooth space seem to be attached to the specific sides of a spatial binarism, Guattari and Deleuze note that they are always, much like minor and major science, in a state of transformation and as such complementary rather than oppositional. Still, only a smooth space can be the model of the space of immanence as a space which 'does not have a dimension higher than that which moves through it or is inscribed in it; in this sense it is a flat multiplicity, for example, a line that fills a plane without ceasing to be a line' (488). Although there are striated, metric spaces within smooth space, in the same way that there are arborescent structures within a rhizome, smooth space should always envelop striated space. Never the other way around. Venus should always envelop Mars, non-metrical space should always envelop metrical space: *non-metrical Venus, metrical Mars*.

While this slogan remains true, in *Schizoanalytic Cartographies*, Guattari develops the general logic of the fundamental scaling of space more ecologically. Guattari's figures of fractal space are no longer turbulence and chaos but rather the spaces of Phyla and of Universes. Fractal space is important not so much as a promise of smoothness, but because transversal movements are only possible in a space whose fractal dimensions allow for quasi-smooth movement through and transitions between different plateaus. At this point, smooth and striated spaces are both aligned from within the given of transversality. 'In part, it is this requirement of transversality that calls for the recourse to infinite speeds of reference, a sweeping of all spaces and a recursive smoothing of all possible temporalities, but this processual character also imposes the striation of relative speeds of reference' (SC: 107).

In *A Thousand Plateaus*, the argument is that metric aggregates can be disturbed or subverted by various strategies of fractalization. In *Schizoanalytic Cartographies*,

Guattari argues, more abstractly, that fractalization has to do with the bringing-into-being of metric space in Phyla from the given, non-metric space of Flows, and, in analogy, with the bringing-into-being of metric space in Universes from the non-metric space of Territories. As such, it concerns less a socio-political fight between smooth Phyla and Universes on the one hand and the oppressive machines of striated Flows and Territories on the other, as it does the creation of the in itself differential fields of Phyla and Universes from fields of the given and giving indifference of Flows and Territories.

In a fractal space, transversal movements can cut through the infinity of scaled dimensions as smoothly as if it were through a continuous volume. In the same way that Dedekind treats the line of unmeasured numbers as an infinity of measured points, fractalization introduces an infinity of measured cuts into a non-measured spatial continuum. The resulting infinity of cuts creates a numbered universe that is quasi-continuous, or quasi-smooth, in the same way that in Leibniz, an integrated curve is quasi-continuous. As such, infinite fractality is the measured aspect of continuity, in the same way that Phyla are the measured aspect of Flows. Fractalization is the mode of translation between all of these registers. A fractal space, then, is a quasi-volume in the same way that mathematically, in the Dedekind procedure, the reconstruction of the continuum of a non-metric line by way of an infinite number of metric cuts into that line creates a quasi-line. In this way, fractalization opens up the field of the possible and allows the administration of actual Flows. Phyla are quasi-real in the same way that transversal movements are quasi-smooth and quasi-continuous: *quasi-ecology*.

Media studies have developed a similarly quasi-smooth, fractal space in relation to the difference between entities and their milieu, which they address as the difference between forms and media. It is along this structural analogy that Guattari's fractal ecosophy might help to ecologize media studies. As I noted earlier, in most versions of media studies, the media from which forms are assembled, such as photons, stone or air, should be, in the best case, completely unspecific, as in uneigen, and thus completely unconscious. When media are in themselves formed, they become both troublesome and conscious, as when air is formed into a storm, or water into a perfect wave. Fog disturbs an electronic signal transmitted via a laser beam. Such formations interfere in the formations that the respective medium is supposed to passively carry. Information theory usually registers such disturbances as noise, resistance or irritation. The informational ideal is completely unformed media. This idealization of the operational silence and invisibility of media, however, has important conceptual drawbacks. As it is conceptualized from the point-of-view of formation, and as such rests on a strict separation or uncoupling of medium and form, it disregards the fact that each form is at the same time a medium and vice versa. What it also disregards is that true unspecificity defines only the point-at-infinity of media as the overall ground of formation: *the plane of immanence as white noise.*

For Guattari, the art of art, as well as the art of life, lie precisely in finding modes by which the inevitable specificity of a medium can be used for and be integrated into specific forms and formations. The plane of immanence slowed down into the pink plane of consistency. From this position, the ecosophic resides in finding adequate modes to attribute forms and media, whether it is the hardness of a block of marble, the grain of a piece of charcoal, or the grain of a voice, the site of a city or a house, the architecture of a corporation: *media ecology.*

In terms of sound, Roland Barthes has shown in what way the surface of the vocal chords is one element in the sonorous media ecology. The grain of the voice lies precisely in the fact that this surface is always to some degree striated. Its dynamic landscape of rough and smooth parts interferes directly in what would be called, from a position of the optimization of information, the ideal of a perfectly clear and smooth, distinct sound. It is that frictional element of noise in the sound that makes up a voice's specific eigensound and defines the singularity of specific voices. If the grain of the voice can be heard, the grain of wood can be seen. What, however, about the graininess of media on levels that are imperceptible? Another way to say that each respective media plateau is imperceptible for the formal plateau above it is to say that each medium is unconscious for the higher plateau of formation. On this conceptual background the unconscious is, quite literally and simply, the unperceived, which is why Guattari maintains that both the art of art and the art of life – poetics and ecosophy – lie in aligning the unconscious and conscious levels, and that as many imperceptible levels as possible should be made perceptible. As he notes, 'the forms that traverse the fractal symmetries of the striation of Phyla lose their character of spatio-temporal identity so as to undergo infinite topological deformations and a deterritorialization that makes them topple over into an infinitesimal molecular register. The possibilistic smoothing brought about by this fractal deconstruction allows an extrinsic contiguity to be established between the "visible" molar levels and the "invisible" molecular levels. What a paradox this infinite contiguity is, constantly feeding on an equally infinite separability beyond contingency, at the heart of a milieu of infinitesimal implosion!' (SC: 158). In a very real way, this is the perfect description of what happens in a Balthus painting.

In the Saussurean notion of the arbitrariness of the medium, the 'reciprocal independence' (Luhmann 2000: 201) of medium and form guarantees the variety of forms and formations. Ask any architect, however, whether the relation between medium and form is defined by the arbitrariness of the stones, which are not themselves meaningful in the sense that the grammar and the syntax of their consistency is not linked directly to the grammar and syntax of their combination into a meaningful house. Does one need to consider the level of the media of the stones, such as sand and water, as the stones' unconscious? Ask any writer whether the mode of construction of a word is merely related to the fact that it is not a meaningful aspect of the semantic construction of a sentence for which the words function merely as carriers. While such a belief has led to an aesthetics of mimesis and representation – as well as to what Guattari bundles under the term postmodernism – Guattari's poetics lead to an expressionism that rests on the specificity of any specific medium, whether that is sand, pigment, a string of letters, or a string of ones and zeros. Both Phyla and Universes, in fact, consist of an infinite number of media-form plateaus that are recursively stacked into each other. This recursive, fractal entanglement allows for the transversal interactions of plateaus that range from micromedia and microforms such as photons, atoms and molecules, to macromedia and macroforms such as cars and houses. The basic idea is that, somewhat like the relation between the analog and the digital, any set of organized, formed elements becomes, from the position of a plateau on which these organizations and formations are no longer perceptible, or are considered operationally unimportant, the loosely coupled medium for a higher, coarser form. According to this logic, imperceptible, molecular dynamics function as what Deleuze calls the dark precursors that bring about perceptible, molar changes. These dark precursors are 'the fractal faults that, in the last analysis, pilot the molar order' (SC: 141).

Bearing in mind their reciprocal presupposition, both actual and virtual media are any-sets-whatever of loosely coupled elements that can be formed into larger aggregates by way of processes of distinction and combination. What Guattari and Deleuze call, in *What is Philosophy?*, taking up Deleuze's *Difference and Repetition*, actual 'contracting' (WP: 212) and virtual 'contemplation' (213). Extensive and intensive. Actual and virtual. In fact, the sets form themselves into larger aggregates like actual atoms and virtual letters did in Lucretius. In terms of language, sounds, letters and words are loosely coupled elements that can be formed into any number of sentences by way of the *ars combinatoria* of alphabetical script. It is another echo of Leibniz that, according to the infinite recursion of scaling and zooming that defines both material and immaterial media platforms, every molar object consists of molecular objects, and every molar thought consists of more molecular thoughts. As this recursion is infinite, with media-form plateaus reaching from the infinitely fine to the infinitely coarse, there can be no most molecular element, even though nuclear physics finds – or better, constructs – more and more elementary particles.

If Leibniz took the cellular level, Guattari and Deleuze take, by default, the photonic, the atomic and the molecular levels as convenient conceptual reference points. To choose a specific level as the finest medium, however, is a purely pragmatic move that isolates one level as the level of observation from a potentially infinite number of coarser but also finer levels. As if he were rehearsing the story of *The Incredible Shrinking Man* from Guattari and Deleuze's *A Thousand Plateaus*, Guattari notes that 'one will never encounter a basic building block, the ultimate quantum. Today, the element of the living machine is the organ, the cell, the chains of organic chemistry, the building blocks of atoms. Tomorrow it will be particles, quarks ... without it being possible to fix an endpoint to this recursion' (SC: 181). As with the temporal logic, one must, in the spatial logic, invariably differentiate between the level of perceptual entry and the level of operational relevance. The ideally infinite recursion allows one to relate the level of microscopic differences, such as those that happen on the levels of photonic or chemical microscales during the photographic process, to levels of human perception and observation. Although certain media-form aggregates cannot be perceived because they occupy, from the relative position of a specific observer, a plateau that is imperceptible, this does not imply that these media are irrelevant to the overall operation on the specific formal plateau on which they are positioned, and thus to the system at large. In fact, while the perceptual level can be defined according to whether the elements are conscious or unconscious to a given observer, their operational importance goes beyond this distinction. In other words, the anonymous abstract machine lies completely open to itself. *It has no unconscious.*

If, as I have shown in 'Expressionism in Ecology 2: Squaring the Unconscious', the unconscious emerges on the side of the giving, the question is how, from within the infinite scaling of levels of integration, to conceptualize a fractal unconscious whose ground is fully deterritorialized and which is, simultaneously, everywhere constructed? How would an unconscious look that is adequate to the countless machinic, automatic and imperceptible, both formational and informational operations that take place within an entity on all of its a-signifying and signifying levels? In other words, how to conceptualize, spatially, a truly ecological, fractal unconscious? Where in the fourfold would such an unconscious be positioned? Famously, the Freudian unconscious is the unconscious of the observer. As that observer is considered as a function of language, its level of entry into the multiplicity of unconscious planes is the linguistic level, which is why the unconscious of the observer is linguistic. In Guattari, the entity is a recursive aggregate made up of nested and meshed sub-aggregates, each of which has its own thresholds of what is it is conscious of and what not. While these levels include those of the observer, they are by no means restricted to them. They are the levels of partial observers that define assemblages of enunciation. As something can be said to be unconscious only in relation to the specific perceptual machines and levels of perceptual entry, each level of the unconscious is relative. Also, each unconscious is to a similar degree virtual and actual because it is made up of imperceptible physical and psychic irritations. As Guattari notes, there are always moments of automatic living. How often, Guattari notes, does one drive a car for a frighteningly long time without consciously watching the road? As Lazzarato notes, 'Guattari always uses the same example of driving a car in order to describe how subjectivity and consciousness function in machinic assemblages. When we drive, we activate subjectivity and a multiplicity of partial consciousnesses connected to the car's technological mechanisms' (2014: 89). Automatic responses are part of the molar unconscious of the observer, although they might well be conscious for partial observers.

Such an ecological unconscious differs radically from the Freudian or the Lacanian one. While the latter is an unconscious specifically designed by and reserved for the level of the observer – it is structured like a language, it concerns only the imperceptible levels of the uses and the forms of language and follows a fixed oedipal logic – Guattari and Deleuze's 'unconscious does not speak, it engineers. It is not expressive or representative, but productive' (AO: 180). To 'schizophrenize the domain of the unconscious' means to create an unconscious that is 'machinic'. An unconscious that is neither Imaginary nor Symbolic but 'the Real in itself, the "impossible real" and its production' (53). Only such an ecological unconscious allows one to register 'the thousand break-flows of the unconscious' (61) and to address a world that has, everywhere, its own qualities and quantities. A Saussurean linguistics in the service of psychoanalysis covers up the fact that each operation that is imperceptible to other levels of perception within the system is to some degree and in some context unconscious. As Guattari states in *Molecular Revolution*, 'the illusion of the double articulation consists of flattening out this multiplicity of intensities on the signifying machine by using the fiction of a level of representation. Intensities have thus been doubly refused: first to fit the signifiers' contents and then to fit the signifier, whose despotic ambition is to put everything that could represent it through a process of repetition that always brings it back to itself' (92). This exclusion of intensity is not only an error in terms of the conceptualization of the unconscious, it also has immediate political reverberations. 'The intensities can now only be noted, connoted as having to remain outside the semiotic sphere, which means, in the last resort, outside the political sphere' (92).

Serres provides a very concise spatial image of an unconscious that consists of a recursive stacking of black boxes, each of which contains not-yet integrated unconscious operations. Today, many of these levels are made conscious by data-tracking devices that bring to consciousness what used to be, for instance, the medical unconscious [→ **Deleuze 140**]. This unconscious 'gives way from below [recedes into the depths]; there are as many unconsciousnesses in the system as there are integration levels. It is merely a question, in general, of that for which we initially possess no information. . . . Each level of information functions as an unconscious for the global level bordering it ... What remains unknown and unconscious is, at the chain's furthermost limit, the din of energy transformations: this must be so, for the din is by definition stripped of all meaning, like a set of pure signals or aleatory movements. These packages of chance are filtered, level after level, by the subtle transformer constituted by the organism ... In this sense the traditional view of the unconscious would seem to be the final black box, the clearest box for us since it has its own language in the full sense' (1983: 80). (On recursion and science see Atlan 1987.) At the bottom of this unconscious, Serres finds pure transformations of energy. A world of movement entirely without codes and codings. An a-historical world of pure latitudes and longitudes. 'The plane consists abstractly, but really, in relations of speed and slowness between unformed elements, and in compositions of corresponding intensive affects (the "longitude" and "latitude" of the plane). In another sense, consistency concretely ties together heterogeneous, disparate elements as such: it assures the consolidation of fuzzy aggregates, in other words, multiplicities of the rhizome type' (TP: 507, emphasis added).

The Lacanian unconscious is an inherently old, historical unconscious that is conceptualized according to the solidity of geometrical space, while the aerosolic unconscious is conceptualized in topological space. According to Serres, in relation to the subject, it denotes youth. 'The more the human body is young and the more it is possible, the more it is capable of multiplicity ... The more undetermined it is ... The entire volume of the old body is occupied by archives, museums, traces, narratives, as if it had filled up with circumstances' (G: 32–3). Leibniz's calculus informs the fractal, infinitely scaled space of Guattari's ecosophy in terms of mathematics and perception, as well as in terms of fractal organisms. On this background, let me return for a moment to 'Cracks in the Street', in which Guattari refers to Mandelbrot's notion of fractality as an update of Leibniz's notion of integration. Integration 2.0.

In Balthus' painting *Le passage du Commerce Saint-André*, Guattari not only detects immediate references to fractalization, he also considers the painting as itself a carrier of fractalization. In fact, in his talk, Guattari moves transversally and with incredible conceptual speed from *Le passage du Commerce Saint-André*, with its de Chirico-like cracks in perspective and the cracked lines of its gazes, to a fundamentally fractured space as the figure of a new mode of being in and thinking about the world. In Guattari's reading, the painting's specifically pictorial logic destabilizes and thus puts into question the registers of representation, of structure, and of geometry. Taking up the actual and virtual sides of the fourfold, Guattari states that 'referring to the research of Mandelbrot on "fractal objects", ... I would like to say that a double, objective and subjective, process of "fractalization" is operating here' (SC: 259). 'It will be recalled', he goes on to note from the depths of his investment in nonlinear dynamics, 'that a fractal set is indefinitely extensible through internal homothety [*sic*] and that its representation tends to lose any fixed identitarian contour – at least when it is generated in a stochastic fashion' (260).

At this point, Guattari shifts from Balthus' fractal pictorial topology to a critique of the ordered conceptual geometry of psychoanalysis, which, he proposes, should be dissolved into the fractal topology of what, in the fourfold, are Phyla and Universes respectively. From the triangular, three-dimensional logic of psychoanalysis, Guattari proposes to shift to the fractal logic of schizoanalysis, which implies the spatial shift from a logic of three dimensions to one of an infinity of fractal dimensions. 'In my view it would be worth broadening fractal analysis beyond the frames of geometry and physics in which it was born and applying it to the description of certain limit states of the psyche and the socius. Thus the dream could be considered a fractal state of representation, and I don't doubt that going down this route, certain questions like those of the dualism of drives, the "splitting" of the Ego, the symbolic break and the castration complex might be freed from the impasse in which Freudianism and its structuralist relays left them' (260). If the main topics of schizoanalysis – which are also, according to Guattari, the ultimate topics addressed by Balthus' painting – are transition, process, and transversality, then 'Winnicott's notion of the transitional object would also particularly merit being rethought' (260). Instead of charting a transition from a state of all-me to a state of me and not-me, why not make transition itself the overarching model and define space as inherently transitional or, in Guattari's notation, as transversal and fractal?

In his description of that space, Guattari already uses, five years before the publication of *Schizoanalytic Cartographies*, the terminology of the fourfold. 'What is an operator for the transition of reference? How do the subjectivity converters that make us pass from one Constellation of Universes to another function? With *Le passage du Commerce Saint-André* we can see that in certain circumstances a pictorial representation can trigger a fractal impulse that indicates and vectorizes a transformation that echoes "in a cascade" (according to Mandelbrot's fine expression) not just from one spatial dimension to another but equally across other temporal and incorporeal dimensions' (260). Through its alignment of Content and Expression, as well as by way of its complexification of references, which in Balthus' pictorial case concern the weird topology of gazes, movements and colours, a painting can bring about an impulse of fractalization that runs through the phase space of thought in a cascade of positive feedback loops.

If a painting can lead to an impulse to fractalize coarse oppositions, the same can be done by a piece of music, an architectural object, a philosophical concept or a theory of economics. These oppositions can be that of, say, the Imaginary and the Symbolic, of the body and the mind, or, in ecological terms, that of the human subject and the world. All of these distinctions can be fractalized into infinitely fine conceptual spaces that are defined by an infinity of plateaus; into an infinitely dense network of similarities and differences. This spatial and conceptual shift into infinity is the ultimate conceptual concern of Guattari's ecosophy. 'In the era of artificial intelligence, is it not finally time to rid oneself of the massive oppositions between mind and body once and for all, and to study the interface operators between these two modalities of existence?' (260). Again, the slogan must be: *more smoothing, more striation.*

Projective Space

Fractalization concerns the internal characteristics of the space of the plane of consistency. It accounts for the fact that even a flat plane has, because of its fractal number of dimensions, a certain depth to it. As Guattari and Deleuze note, it surveys itself from within its own dimension and it allows, although it is a plane, for transversal movements within the plane [→ **Deleuze 103**]. Unilaterality, which is the third characteristic of Guattari's ecological space, concerns both the plane of consistency as well as the spatial relation of the plane of consistency and the plane of immanence.

It is safe to assume that Guattari's interest in unilateral space was initially sparked by Lacan, who relied on its topology throughout his career, from the extended reference to the Borromean knot to his late forays into knot theory [→ **Deleuze 156**]. (On Lacan's influence on Guattari's diagrams, see also Watson 2011: 4.) Guattari's Figure 2.4 in *Schizoanalytic Cartographies* (60), for instance, looks like a variation of Lacan's diagram of the eye and the gaze in *The Four Fundamental Concepts of Psychoanalysis*. For Lacan, the most important and basic topological figure is the real projective plane, a mathematical figure of thought that allows him to think the unilaterality of psychic reality. As he notes quite programmatically in a footnote added in 1966 to 'Seminar on "The Purloined Letter"' in *Écrits*, 'concepts related to subjectivization progressed hand-in-hand with a reference to the *analysis situs* [topology], in which I claim to materialize the subjective process' (1977: 48, my brackets). The notion of the real projective plane originates at the intersection of the visual theory of the central perspective, which brings together classical geometry, which is objective and abstract, and projective geometry, which is subjective and concrete, in that it describes the way human subjects perceive the world. Unlike Euclidean space, it concerns a topological space that always has its own optical and visual weather.

In 1874, the German mathematician Felix Klein proposed that 'the projective plane has only one side' (1928: 158). This new plane models a space in which the differentiation between inside and outside holds only on a local level. It is 'locally like a sphere, but has a different global topology' (Weeks 1985: 61). It is locally two-sided, but globally one-sided. If one conceptualizes this plane as a logical surface, conceptual opposites are chiastically crossed on a global scale, while locally, a two-sided logic remains in operation, which is a characteristic to which I will return. On the plane, space is folded back upon itself at what are called points-at-infinity. Two diametrically opposed points are no longer defined as infinitely far away from each other and thus as both spatial and logical opposites. Rather, they are conceptualized as identical. Because of the plane's curvature, opposites meet at infinity: opposites are reconciled; once more, *contraria sunt complementa*. All unilateral spaces fundamentally undecide the notions of inside and outside as well as the topological distribution of extremes, which are all laid out on the same plane and folded onto each other at infinity. Thought from within a unilateral topology of thought, opposites, such as the actual and the virtual, remain operative locally, but are identified at infinity: *epistemological distinction, ontological complementarity; local distinction, global complementarity*.

Why would Guattari criticize Lacan when his use of topology inspired Guattari to take up the concept of unilaterality in the first place? Guattari's critique is not directed at Lacan's use of topology as such, however, but rather at the way in which he uses it. For Lacan, topology materializes and instantiates psychoanalytic givens, while Guattari constructs schizoanalysis from within the givens of topology. Lacan 'makes a lateral use of science, the statements of which retain a character of exteriority in relation to the discipline under consideration, or are only used metaphorically' (SC: 34). When Lacan twists the semiotic plane into a real projective plane, he situates the Symbolic realm of the signifier on the one side of the plane, and the Imaginary realm of the signified on its other side, although the two sides are in actual fact part of a unilateral topology that is globally one-sided. On Lacan's projective plane the Real realm is excluded in analogy to the way that the referent is excluded from language. It is crucial in the functioning of the plane, however, in that it materializes the 180 degree twist that brings about the plane's unilateral topology in the first place. As such, it insists in Lacan's plane as both its origin and as its fundamentally excluded term. It embodies, quite literally, its constitutive lack. When Guattari takes over Lacan's topology of the real projective plane, he uses its logic to position various modes of complementarity, such as the actual, extensive given on the one side, and the virtual, intensive giving on the other. In this alignment, the twist is provided by the logic of the reciprocal presupposition or complementarity of the two series.

The difference between Guattari and Lacan is that while Lacan derives theorems from within the axiomatics of psychoanalysis, Guattari derives schizoanalytic axiomatics from within topology. For Lacan, topology materializes psychoanalysis, for Guattari, schizoanalysis materializes topology. For Lacan, topology materializes the subjective process, for Guattari, topology constructs the subjective process. This difference is one of the reasons why Guattari and Deleuze argue so vehemently against Lacan's logic of metaphors. 'The desiring-machine is not a metaphor' (AO: 41) they stress. Similarly, the 'body without organs and its intensities are not metaphors, but matter itself' (283).

Unlike machines, metaphors comment on scientific givens from a position outside of that science. Topology provides images such as the real projective plane, which can then be used to illustrate how psychoanalysis relates the signifier, the signified and the referent. In terms of the notion of topological space, therefore, the question concerns the level on which that space is taken seriously. If one takes topological space to be the space that is adequate to both the given and the giving, its logic must include not only the levels of language and of psychic reality but all levels of reality. In other words, if one reduces the logic of topological space to the realm of psychic reality, one is no longer in adequation with the given. This reduction of the power and the implication of topology is why 'when the apostles of the Signifier plunder structural linguistics or get started on a mathematical topology' this is 'of no help at all!' (SC: 34).

Guattari's ecology aims to be in every aspect adequate to topological space. In other words, he takes topology seriously. 'Rather than returning constantly to the same, supposedly foundational, structures, the same archetypes, the same "mathemes", schizoanalytic meta-modelling will choose to map compositions of the unconscious, contingent topographies, evolving with social formations, technologies, arts, sciences, etc.' (22). Only meta-modelization can address the machinic dynamics that allow for a pragmatic, site- and time-specific approach to the world. While Lacan uses topology to trace the stable contours of psychoanalysis, meta-modelling maps an inherently dynamic, and thus topological space. 'The map is open and connectable, in all of its dimensions; it is detachable, reversible, susceptible to constant modification. It can be torn, reversed, adapted to any kind of mounting' (TP: 12). In this context, one might say that Guattari reverses the Lacanian approach to topology. While the conceptual ground of Lacanian psychoanalysis is the logic of psychoanalysis, onto which he then grafts topology, the conceptual ground of Guattari's schizoanalysis is the logic of topology itself: *projective ecology*.

4 SCHIZOANALYTIC ECOLOGY

Everything Is Right Here Now.
> Peter Matthiessen, *The Snow Leopard* (56)

Nothing is given in itself.
> Félix Guattari, *Schizoanalytic Cartographies* (211)

Problems live in the same way as do other, living beings, with the difference that they do not move about in the same coordinates.
> Félix Guattari, *Schizoanalytic Cartographies* (74)

The architecture of tomorrow will be a means of modifying present conceptions of time and space. It will be a means of knowledge and a means of action.
> Gilles Ivain (Ivan Chtcheglov), 'Formulary for a New Urbanism' (3)

Solaris: Photonic Ecology

'LET'S GO FROM happy nihilism to dark nihilism', Timothy Morton writes in *Dark Ecology* (2016: 116–17). Already in *Ecology without Nature*, which 'plays with, reinforces, or deconstructs the idea of nature' (2009: 5) on the background of Jacques Derrida's 'profound thinking on the "without", the *sans*' (21) – in *Dark Ecology* it is 'animism' (2016: 137), therefore, rather than immanence – Morton had developed the 'melancholic ethics' (2009: 186) of an ecology that is based on the proposition that 'we can't escape our minds' (201). After it has been charged by object-oriented-ontology in *Dark Ecology*, this attitude is intensified even more, as are the rhetorics. While Guattari cherishes the powers of the false [→ **Deleuze 39**], Morton resents them. 'There is a fundamental, irreducible gap between the raindrop phenomenon and the raindrop thing' (2016: 93) he notes, echoing both Schrödinger and Graham Harman. While Schrödinger considered this to be an epistemological problem and Harman considers it an ontological one, Morton charges the retreat of objects into the depths with dark romanticism. 'Flowering is thus indeed a type of "evil", a necessary evil that comes with existing, since existing means having a gap between what you are and how you appear, even to yourself. Flowers of evil' (104). As 'ecological awareness is dark, insofar as its essence is unspeakable' (110), Morton can go on to argue that *'ecognosis is abjection'* (123).

The programme of 'agrilogistics' (45), Morton argues, has created the Anthropocene, which is Nature in its most gothic version. 'The Anthropocene is Nature in its toxic nightmare form. Nature is the latent form of the Anthropocene waiting to emerge as catastrophe' (59). The extreme political version of the Anthropocene is 'accelerationism: capitalism should be sped up in the name of anticapitalism to bring out its contradictions, with the hope (underline hope) that it might then collapse' (139). Although, as for Guattari, the main nemesis of what might be called dark theory is capitalism, the aim of accelerationism is the destruction of the capitalist field. 'That is what accelerationism is hoping for. The name of this hope is despair' (140). Similarly, if there is an allover network of life and the living that includes the strife I talked about in the context of Venus and Mars, this 'interdependence, which is ecology, is sad and contingent' (150). Even while this strife is also a given in Guattari, how different is this theoretical sadness from the pragmatics and the constructivism that Guattari's schizoecology develops in the light of this given strife.

Since Guattari considers the false, as Friedrich Nietzsche did in his 1873 essay 'On Truth and Lies in a Nonmoral Sense', as a potentiality rather than as a cause for melancholia, schizoecology is both rhetorically and conceptually opposed to the notion and to the sentiment of ecological bleakness, although Morton ends his text with an image of ecognosis as 'the Ganzfeld effect of The Joy' (158). Against the postapocalyptic darkness, but without hoping to escape it, Morton proposes a 'pathway toward The Joy' (153) that seems to be a kind of 'ecosexual' (129) *jouissance*. 'This plasma field is a Ganzfeld effect of affect' (157) is how Morton describes it. This field is 'haptic, elemental: so close that you lose track of something to be seen', and it allows one to shift from 'simply thinking ecologically' to 'thought as susceptibility, thinking as such as ecology' (158). Even while this hallucinatory, curiously solipsistic experience of an ecological, 'nonhuman' (158) thought might in some aspects resonate with Guattari, it remains a weak weapon against bad ecologies. The world meta-modelled in the transversal space of the fourfold is not a Ganzfeld. Perhaps the plane of immanence is, but to look into the plane of immanence would be like looking directly into the sun.

While Morton stakes the affect of an a-signifying Ganzfeld *jouissance* against the ecological darkness of an unspeakable world, when Guattari grounds language in the a-signifying operations of the world, this does not highlight the gap between language and world. Rather, it charges language with the world in order to turn language into an immensely important and rich power of the false that humans use not to get to any sort of objective truth, but to regulate their living together. As Margulis notes, 'as Charles Peirce and William James recognized, there may be no better measure of "truth" than that which works – that which helps us survive' (Margulis and Sagan 1995: 32). In fact, not only language, but all qualitative images are inherently false in that they differ from quantities, which are neither true nor false but simply what they are.

Both the imagination and cognition are powers of the false, which makes sense in its relation to and as an attribute of the inherently meaningless, quantitative powers of the true. 'Language is not in the brain or in the nervous system, but rather in the domain of mutual coherence between organisms', Maturana notes (1987: 81). In this function, language, as a system of signifying and a-signifying components, is never arbitrary and is always ecological. The minor, non-metric literatures Guattari and Deleuze describe in *Kafka: Toward a Minor Literature*, for instance, 'oppose a purely intensive use of language to all symbolic or even significant or simply signifying usage of it' (1986: 19). Samuel Beckett 'proceeds by dryness and sobriety, a willed poverty, pushing deterritorialization to such an extreme that nothing remains but intensities' (19). Minor literatures describe milieus in which it is impossible to separate the entity from the communal and from the surroundings.

One might look for the difference between the sentiment of schizoecology and that of today's dark ecologies in the potentialities of the false that were instantiated, for instance, in the superposition of the four greens that I described in 'Expressionism in Ecology 1: Squaring the Concept – Chlorophyll'. The difference, however, goes deeper and is, ultimately, of an economic nature. If Morton as well as Negri and Lazzarato, with whom I will deal in more detail in 'Ecosophy: In the Cracks of Capitalism' (pp. 209–14), consider mainly human economies and late-capitalist theories of consumption, Guattari's machinic ecosophy ultimately asks what the resource is that sustains the plane of immanence as a plane of surplus intensity and potentiality. As such, as in George Bataille's notion of a general economy, one needs to study 'the system of human production and consumption within a much larger framework' (1988: 20). Like Guattari, Bataille considers that framework to be of cosmic proportions: *cosmic ecology*.

'Solar energy is the source of life's exuberant development. The origin and essence of our wealth are given in the radiation of the sun, which dispenses energy – wealth – without any return. The sun gives without ever receiving' (28), Bataille writes. Both a general economy and a general ecology have to take this photonic excess into account. As 'solar radiation results in a superabundance of energy on the surface of the globe' (29), a general economy is less about poverty, as in Negri's repudiation of consumption, or about what Morton might have meant to be a dark gesture of repudiating Negri's repudiation when he proclaims that 'consumerism is the specter of ecology. When thought fully, ecological awareness includes the essence of consumerism, rather than shunning it. Ecological awareness must embrace its specter' (2016: 125).

Against these two versions of repudiating capitalist economy – economic ascesis and accelerated consumption respectively – schizoecology is developed from within a given, excessive wealth. In Guattarian terms, from within the plane of immanence. 'Everything that is commensurate with the universe' is 'rich' (Bataille 1988: 13). The world is 'a play of energy that no particular end limits: the play of *living matter in general*, involved in the movement of light of which it is the result. On the surface of the globe, for *living matter in general*, energy is always in excess' (23). There is 'no growth but only a luxurious squandering of energy in every form' (33) in the world. 'The history of life on earth is mainly the effect of a wild exuberance' (33). Economy turns into ecology when it is adequate to this wild exuberance. When it trails this wild exuberance behind. The ecological question, in fact, is how to integrate this uneconomical excess, which is not part of a logic of work and growth, into economy. 'Beyond our immediate ends, man's activity in fact pursues the useless and infinite fulfillment of the universe' (21). This solar, photonic surplus-energy 'must be spent, willingly or not, gloriously or catastrophically' (21).

Already in *The Machinic Unconscious*, in which Guattari compares abstract machines to 'the particles of contemporary physics' (47), the photonic is a conceptual reference. These particles 'do not have any "real" existential consistency; they do not have any "mass", their own "energy", or memory. They are only infinitesimal indications hyper-deterritorialized from crystallizations of a possible between states of affairs and states of signs' (47). In 'Expressionism in Ecology 4: Squaring Media Studies', I noted Guattari's mention of the 'series of paradoxes from contemporary physics – when the same quantum of energy is incarnated in forms that are simultaneously wave and particle, discontinuous and continuous, separable and inseparable' (110).

Ultimately, the photonic concerns the cosmic luminosity that like, or perhaps even better as, the plane of immanence traverses the world, and that quite literally carries and sustains life as its most deterritorialized medium. In this context, the term cosmic luminosity is not a metaphorical or poetic flourish, but rather an energetic fact. If the earth were a closed system, chances are that it would already have consumed all of its inherent energy. Both in terms of philosophical figure and scientific energy source, solar energy is the luminous, ungrounded ground of life on our planet. For all forms of individuation, the sun functions as the self-consuming provider of surplus-energy. This is why schizoecology finds its point-of-perspective in the notion of the electromagnetic field as the true plane of immanence. Again, however, although this electromagnetic field is the source of life, it is not a friend, even though solar energy is charged with affective intensity in the shift from electromagnetism to light. Perhaps one might think of the plane of immanence as electromagnetic and of the plane of consistencies as luminous and as such enchanted. Perhaps this is why many ecologists celebrate the shades and intensities of the play of light that bathes the planet in waves, but also in storms of energy. Of course this does not mean that the only ecologically adequate way to produce energy is solar energy. As always, such administrations are complicated and invariably site- and time-specific. It seems, however, to be a good measure of adequation to fold the need for energy into the milieus of renewable energies, as embodiments of the energetic excess that defines the natural world.

The difference between electromagnetism and light also plays itself out on the plane of consistencies. On the side of the giving, light is an existential term that carries singular lives both biologically and in terms of affect and emotion. While light is of the giving, electromagnetism is of the given, where light and darkness are just forms of the distribution of radiation, and as such purely radiological. It is only for entities with eyes that this radiation is experienced as the play and the ecology of light. In the living world, the light of the plane of immanence invariably operates within the specific economies of the giving. Both light and dark milieus form habitats for life-forms, from the dark, pressured depths of the ocean to the most subtle currents of air. Even if entities experience only small spectra of light, however, what always remains is the photonic field as a carrier medium of life and heterogenesis: *solar economy, photonic, luminous ecology*.

Squaring the Abstract Machine

Throughout this text, I have stressed the site-specificity of schizoecology. If the two aspects of an actual site are territorialized, real Flows and deterritorialized, possible Phyla, it is only Phyla, or abstract machines, that allow for an intervention in and administration of the world. It is as such a site of intervention that the abstract machine is seminal in Guattari's schizoecology, as well as in the work of Guattari and Deleuze. As the conceptual contours of the term differ in Guattari's and Deleuze's singular and communal works, and as its philological and conceptual history runs through a number of phases, let me disentangle some of its main conceptual strands before I deal with its function within an ecosophic architecture.

In Guattari and Deleuze as well as in Deleuze, the position of the abstract machine its not always clearly contoured. In his 1986 book *Foucault*, Deleuze notes the 'mutual [reciprocal] presupposition between ... abstract machine and concrete assemblage' (2006: 32, my brackets). It is 'the cause of the concrete assemblages that execute its relations; and these relations between forces take place "not above" but within the very tissue of the assemblages they produce' (32). This description comes close to its position in the fourfold, in that it stresses both its expressionist aspect and the difference between the abstract world and its concrete modes. It is the allover plane of consistency considered as the abstract, anonymous aspect of the concrete plane of consistencies. When Guattari and Deleuze note in *A Thousand Plateaus* that it creates a 'continuous region . . . of intensity . . . a piece of immanence' (158), however, it designates the plane of immanence as the world's allover ground. At still other moments, it seems to be positioned between these two complementary planes. It would be too easy to read these different positionings as symptoms of a conceptual weakness. At the same time, how to explain them?

At various points, the abstract machine designates: 1. the aspect of the plane of consistency as completely deterritorialized, which makes it identical to the aspect of the world as the plane of immanence; 2. the infinitely complex, anonymous movements of the world's territorializing and deterritorializing operations on the plane of consistency; and 3. specific abstract machines that are constructed on and that populate the plane of consistency as the plane of consistencies. The common denominator of all of these aspects is that the abstract machine replaces generalizations such as genus and species with the logic of a constructivist machinics. As Guattari notes in *The Machinic Unconscious*, there are 'no biological, economic, social, linguistic, psychoanalytical universals . . . but abstract machines that differentiate themselves, on the basis of the plane of consistency of all possibles, and which hook up to the singular crossroads points of the machinic phylum' (29).

When the abstract machine designates the world as a both actual and virtual multiplicity, it tends to come in the singular, as an agent that deterritorializes the plane of consistency. It 'cuts across all stratifications, develops alone and in its own right on the plane of consistency whose diagram it constitutes, the same machine at work in astrophysics and in microphysics, in the natural and in the artificial, *piloting flows of absolute deterritorialization*' (TP: 56, emphasis added). When it is related to concrete assemblages, such as the Kafka machine or the Berlioz machine, it comes in the plural. Singular abstract machines retain the function of being 'the cutting edges of decoding and deterritorialization' (510) and they retain the potentiality for potentiality, in that they relate an entity to the plane of immanence that pervades the overall milieu. They 'make the territorial assemblage open onto something else, assemblages of another type, the molecular, *the cosmic*; they constitute becomings. Thus they are always singular and immanent' (510, emphasis added).

However, while the abstract machine as an agent of an overall deterritorialization denotes the fully virtual plane of immanence, singularized abstract machines are invariably embodied and thus actualized in and enveloped by territorialized entities, regardless of whether these are energetic, conceptual or human. In this aspect, although they remain agents of deterritorialization, abstract machines are 'prisoner to stratifications, are enveloped in a certain specific stratum whose program or unity of composition they define (the abstract Animal, the abstract chemical Body, Energy in itself) and whose movements of relative deterritorialization they regulate' (56). Although they pilot individual lines of flight, abstract machines in the plural do not only disassemble, they also assemble 'plane[s] *of consistency*' (11). In the singular, the abstract machine cuts across all consistencies irrespective of their concrete status; abstract machines in the plural are embodied and thus actualized in the territorialized entities that they have helped to produce and in which their function is that of being tensors of deterritorialization. In both of these modes, however, abstract machines are productive and expressive rather than representational. This characteristic connects them to the informal diagram, which has real effects in the milieu it surveys. Like that diagram, they imply 'the abolition of all metaphor; all that consists is Real. These are electrons in person, veritable black holes, actual organites, authentic sign sequences. It's just that they have been uprooted from their strata, destratified, decoded, deterritorialized, and that is what makes their proximity and interpenetration in the plane of consistency possible. A silent dance. *The plane of consistency knows nothing of differences in level, orders of magnitude, or distances. It knows nothing of the difference between the artificial and the natural. It knows nothing of the distinction between contents and expressions, or that between forms and formed substances*; these things exist only by means of and in relation to the strata' (69–70).

In many aspects, the abstract machine enters *A Thousand Plateaus* by way of the texts gathered together in Guattari's *The Machinic Unconscious*. As Deleuze notes in *Dialogues II*, the term came 'from Félix's side' (19). Already at this early stage, Guattari introduces a characteristic of the abstract machine that will become increasingly important in his later ecosophy. Abstract machines are inherently dynamic. They are themselves processes rather than objects. Verbs rather than nouns. 'Abstract *deterritorialized interactions* or, more briefly, . . . *abstract machines*' (MU: 11, my emphasis). As Guattari notes, the abstract machine '*itself is produced by its production*' (31). In *The Machinic Unconscious*, the abstract machine in the singular is, as it will be in *Schizoanalytic Cartographies*, on the side of a processual and '*transformational matter*' (16). This living matter allows for the 'polyvocality' (118) of the world and its 'optional subjects', who are, in actual fact, 'composed of the crystals of the possible' (16). This processual abstract machine will make its way into *Schizoanalytic Cartographies* as the world's aspect as actual and possible Phyla. In that position, it designates the operations of a specific milieu's surplus potentialities from which germinal entities draw matters of energy and matters of code in order to come into being. While the abstract machine in the singular sometimes denotes the pure, virtual chaos of the plane of immanence, the abstract machine as Phyla, which is its position in the fourfold, denotes the infinite complexity of the plane of consistency in its aspect of an actual and abstract, deterministically chaotic machine.

Somewhat counter-intuitively, in fact, the deeper one reaches into the world's Phyla, the more multiplicitous their dynamics become. Both physical and psychic assemblages emerge from molecular levels that are more destratified than the molar structures into which they are arraigned by processes of '*a capture of consistency*' (189). Programmatically, Guattari notes that what seems to be the level of the deadest of materiality is in fact the level of purest potentiality. 'The most complex combinations are capable of emerging at the level which is believed to be that of "brute matters" or "primary matters"' (158). The conceptualization of the actual world as a deterritorializing abstract machine calls for 'preserving the multiplicity and heterogeneity of all possible entries, all catastrophes, and all emergences of new points of "metabolic crystallization"' (151): *living ecosophy*.

If the most general abstract machine is the fully deterritorialized plane of an actual life and of nature, already the emergence of a first crystal counts as a reduction from this ideal multiplicity, in that a crystal is at least minimally formed and thus stabilized and territorialized. 'A three-dimensional crystal, or a solution in the process of becoming crystallized, only "de-codes" the organization of another crystal from outside; it can only model or adapt itself to it . . . a crystal remains too territorialized to be able to reach the level of abstract machines that govern the process of physico-chemical de-territorialization' (131), Guattari notes. Although brute matter is violently alive, already in *The Machinic Unconscious* the subtle dynamics of nature as transformational matter go in two directions simultaneously. They 'traverse various levels of reality and *establish* and *demolish* stratifications' (11, emphases added). It is by way of its actualization and crystallization that the abstract machine in the singular aspects – to turn another noun into a verb – into the field of abstract machines. It 'crystallize[s itself] from heteroclitic compositions' (162, my brackets) and as such it has always already 'begun to take on consistency and crystallize multiple and heterogeneous potentialities' (251). In this aspect, abstract machines are, somewhat paradoxically, 'crystal[s] of potentiality' (254). Already at that early stage, the abstract machine follows the logic of complementary that will define it in *A Thousand Plateaus* and in *Schizoanalytic Cartographies*. 'At most, we may distinguish in the abstract machine two states of the diagram, one in which variables of content and expression are distributed according to their heterogeneous forms in reciprocal presupposition on a plane of consistency, and another in which it is no longer even possible to distinguish between variables of content and expression because the variability of that same plane has prevailed over the duality of forms, rendering them "indiscernible"' (TP: 91).

Both logically and topologically, then, the conceptual space of the abstract machine is fundamentally paradoxical. 'We must try to conceive of this world in which a single fixed plane – which we shall call *a plane of absolute immobility or absolute movement* – is traversed by nonformal elements of relative speed that enter this or that individuated assemblage depending on their degrees of speed and slowness. A plane of consistency peopled by anonymous matter, by infinite bits of impalpable matter entering into varying connections' (255, emphasis added). The imperceptible molecular movements of the abstract machine, which are more deterritorialized and more abstract than their individuated molar arrangements, can never be repressed and they are always repressed. This, in fact, is the given state of natural, individual and cultural ecologies alike.

It is in its fundamentally paradoxical, complementary state that the notion of the abstract machine is adequate to the world. It is always both actual and virtual. Both singular and plural. Nature itself is an 'immense Abstract Machine, *abstract yet real and individual*' (254, emphasis added). When it becomes part of the fourfold, this complementarity is central, although the virtual aspect of the abstract machine now has its own position in and as the field of Universes. This topological separation is the result of its ecologization, according to which the virtual realm is invariably that of concrete entities. In other words, in the fourfold, the difference between singular and plural abstract machines is marked by the difference between Phyla and Universes as two aspects of the world. Once without, and once as its creatures. As if it were laid out on a real projective plane, the abstract machine as abstract machines and vice versa – Phyla as Universes and vice versa, that is – aligns, on the unilateral conceptual surface of the fourfold, virtuality and actuality along its horizontal vector, as well as realness and possibility along its vertical vector. From these complementary points-of-perspective, the abstract machine defines the superposition of the multiplicity of the given, actual world to which every concrete entity is immanent and the diversity of that given world as and within its giving, virtual and concrete entities: *abstract ecology, concrete ecology*.

Another spin Guattari gives to the abstract machine in 1979 is owed to his background in psychoanalysis. The abstract machine is the most subtle medium of an anonymous, free-floating surplus desire: 'abstract machines are *not an affair of psychological instances*; before depending on sciences of culture, ideologies, or teachings, they arise from a *politics of desire* "before" objects and subjects have been specified' (MU: 167). In this aspect, the abstract machine denotes the movements of an anonymous life and of a living world. It is the figure of a 'negentropic passion at every stage of the cosmos' (159). Its diffraction into abstract machines is why the abstract machine is neither universal nor global. As its spatial separation in *Schizoanalytic Cartographies* shows, it is a concrete universal, or universal concrete.

Although the abstract machine in the singular is the infinitely complex global medium in and from which concrete abstract machines emerge, in the concrete plural, abstract machines are invariably site- and time-specific, providing the potentialities and possibilities singular entities have of entering into and of leaving specific molecular milieus and ecologies. When Guattari talks about an abstraction involved on the level of abstract machines, this never implies universalization. It merely marks that on this level, states and entities are defined in purely abstract terms of levels of speed and slowness, organization and disorganization, longitude and latitude; of flows and rates of change. Already in *A Thousand Plateaus*, the separation into abstract Phyla and concrete Universes is implied in that on the level of abstract machines, movements can only be defined in purely abstract terms: as elements 'that no longer have either form or function, that are abstract in this sense even though they are perfectly real. They are distinguished solely by movement and rest, slowness and speed. They are not atoms, in other words, finite elements still endowed with form. Nor are they indefinitely divisible. They are infinitely small, ultimate parts of an actual infinity, laid out on the same plane of consistency or composition' (TP: 253–4). At the same time, in *A Thousand Plateaus*, Guattarian and Deleuzian registers tend to be superposed: 'on the plane of consistency, *a body is defined only by a longitude and a latitude*: in other words the sum total of the material elements belonging to it under given relations of movement and rest, speed and slowness (longitude); the sum total of the intensive affects it is capable of at a given power or degree of potential (latitude). Nothing but affects and local movements, differential speeds. The credit goes to Spinoza for calling attention to these two dimensions of the Body, and for having defined the plane of Nature as pure longitude and latitude' (260).

In its twofold conceptualization, the abstract machine 'makes no distinction within itself between content and expression, even though outside itself, it presides over that distinction and distributes it in strata, domains, and territories. An abstract machine in itself is not physical or corporeal, any more than it is semiotic; it is *diagrammatic* (it knows nothing of the distinction between the artificial and the natural either). It operates by *matter*, not by substance; by *function*, not by form. Substances and forms are of expression "or" of content. But functions are not yet "semiotically" formed, and matters are not yet "physically" formed. The abstract machine is pure Matter-Function – a diagram independent of the forms and substances, expressions and contents it will distribute' (141). In the 'morphogenesis' (MU: 116) of an individual assemblage, the abstract machine is on the side of actual constructivism. 'The assemblage itself [is] conceived as the manifestation of the more functional side, abstract machinisms being the more constructivist side' (199).

Within the various aspects and modes of the abstract machine, Guattari spans out a general catalytic field. 'What counts in these "crystallizations" of behaviors seems to be less the intrinsic nature of each one of their components – hormonal, perceptive, ecological, social ... –than the spatial and rhythmic devices that they generate and from which diagrammatic strategies and tactics of stratification make it possible to create "interchanges" launching semiotic bridges between parallel universes which seemed to never have to communicate together' (116). It is only the ensemble of all of these relations that creates 'the diagrammatic potentialities, the creative lines of flight through which evolution selects its adaptive paths' (117). The function of these imperceptible and anonymous molecular machines is to connect and to disconnect, within an overall fractal space, diverse strata according to a subtle system of attractions and repulsions. It is as such that they are measures of an entity's potentialities and possibilities.

In chemistry, such potentialities are called 'valences' (128), which is a term that traverses fields as diverse as physics and linguistics, in that it denotes the inclinations and possibilities of an entity to connect to one or many other entities and thus this entity's measure of possible potentiality. The measure of what it can do. These subtle systems of valences work hand in hand with complicated sets of resonances, which is why a 'veil, a fuzzy resonance is woven over all the machinic singularities' (212). As these valences operate on all levels of the plane of consistency, Guattari can note that 'a certain kind of freedom and even grace exists on the level of the nervous or digestive system' (127). The freedom of an assemblage lies in the leeway it has within the medium of such valences and resonances: 'the form of quanta of freedom in a sort of valence system' (166). As the finest machinic medium, the abstract machine has a quasi-infinite factor of valences, which allows moving transversally in all of the fractal spaces between distinct strata. 'Some "transversals" connect the "most social" with the "most biological" or the "most ecological"' (144), for instance. As such conductors, abstract machines are 'pragmatic operators' (156) that are equally able to capture consistency and to capture change; to compose consistencies as well as to decompose them. They 'traverse various levels of reality and establish and demolish stratifications' (11). As 'pure quanta of potential deterritorialization, abstract machines are everywhere and nowhere, *before* and *after* the crystallization of the opposition between machine and structure, representation and referent, object and subject' (166): *ecological valences.*

Squaring Architecture

A temperamental difference between Deleuze and Guattari might be said to be that while Deleuze is interested in philosophy and art, Guattari is interested in architecture. Although Guattari has, like Deleuze, a deep interest in literature, music and the visual arts, architecture is the perhaps most consistent interest in his work. (On

Guattari and film, see 'Minor Cinema' in Genosko 2009.) In Guattari's work, the architectural references range from the conceptual architecture of psychoanalysis to the experience of contemporary urban space. From 'Cracks in the Text', that is, to 'Cracks in the Street'. Guattari's continued interest in architecture is inherently ecological in that, more immediately than literature, painting, music or philosophy, architecture partakes, like design in general, of the insertion of human registers into the allover milieu. It is an embodied figure of concrete entities' direct creation of and intervention in the world. From birds' nests to badgers' caves, from coral reefs to chemical vortices, concrete entities design and construct Territories and Universes from the world's allover Flows and Phyla. On all levels, they design and thus administer the world. In this sense, engineered sites, artistic *disegnos* and computer simulations are all equally architectural. As an important element in the construction of existential Territories, architectures are deeply related to the realms of affects, habits and habitats. As built concepts, however, they are equally deeply related to the field of Universes. Architectures are concrete, more or less formal or informal diagrams of how the giving expresses and creates the given. As spatio-temporal compositions, they construct spaces of potentiality, offering possibilities of movement and rest, modes of expression, and fields of kinetic process. In creating membranes between entities and their milieu, architecture in the expanded field is one of the most important modes of the design of life and of modes of living.

I have spent so much time with the abstract machine not only because it is a very contested notion in Deleuze Studies, but also, and more importantly so, because it lies at the conceptual centre of Guattari's ecosophic architecture. Architecture, Guattari maintains, should be adequate to the abstract machine which, in architectural terms, pertains equally and paradoxically to both movement and stability as two complementary modes of relating to and inhabiting the spaces of the world. Symptomatically, in *A Thousand Plateaus*, Guattari and Deleuze talk of '*an intermediate state between the two states of the abstract Machine* . . . – the state in which it remains enveloped in a corresponding stratum (ecumenon), and the state in which it develops in its own right on the destratified plane of consistency (planomenon)' (63).

From within a logic of complementarity, Guattari and Deleuze argue that the abstract machine is not spanned out between two irreconcilable states. Rather, two irreconcilable states are inherent to the overall topology of the abstract machine. 'There is a single *abstract machine* that is enveloped by the stratum, and constitutes its unity. This is the Ecumenon' (50), which is 'defined by the identity of molecular materials, substantial elements, and formal relations' (52). The Planomenon, on the other hand, is 'the Earth, the absolutely deterritorialized' (56). This complementary relation between the Ecumenon and the Planomenon is seminal in Guattari's notion of an architectural ecosophy. Here as well, the ecosophic logic must not be less Ecumenon, more Planomenon, but rather: *more Ecumenon, more Planomenon.*

The term Ecumenon derives from the Greek *oikoumene* and denotes the whole inhabited world. In a religious context, it refers to the largest possible Christian unity; in cartography to a specific type of world map. In both contexts, it models 'the *unity of composition of a stratum*' (55, emphasis added), which is frequently read as designating a bad state of striation. A first indication that such a reading might be too simple is that Guattari and Deleuze do not consider this space to be an ideal unity. Rather, its univocity expresses itself in polyvocity. The unified Ecumenon 'exists only as shattered, fragmented into epistrata and parastrata that imply concrete machines and their respective indexes, and constitute different molecules, specific substances, and irreducible forms' (52).

The term Planomenon derives from the Greek word *plános*, which means to wander, roam or drift and is related to the term *planomania*, which in psychiatry designates the morbid impulse to leave home and to discard social restraints. As denoting all free-living organisms that are not rooted or attached to a substratum, the term is frequently read as designating a good, in the sense of smooth, space. These readings stress that Guattari and Deleuze relate the Ecumenon to settlers, territorialization and striation, while they relate the Planomenon to the deterritorialized, smooth space of nomads.

On a more general scale, the Ecumenon refers to formed matter, the different, subjectivation, territorialization and what Simondon calls the associated milieu, while the Planomenon refers to unformed matter, the diverse, singularization, deterritorialization and the allover milieu. Once more, however, *contraria sunt complementa*. In that they are both Ecumenon and Planomenon, abstract machines incorporate a true *coincidentia oppositorum*. '*We may even say that the abstract machines that emit and combine particles have two very different modes of existence: the Ecumenon and the Planomenon*' (56). This duplicity implies, against many romanticizing readings of Guattari and Deleuze, that the abstract machine is not a friend: Never believe that the abstract machine will suffice to save us. Crucially, in Guattari's ecology this warning also applies to the notion of Nature. Never believe that Nature will suffice to save us. At the same time, neither the abstract machine nor Nature are enemies. The deeply ecological twist lies in considering the relation between us and nature as expressive rather than as representational and as such oppositional. As Guattari notes 'is it enough to say that the ancient surfaces of Yin and Yang, raw and cooked, analogical iconicity and "digital" discursivity, still manage to merge opposites?' (quoted in Genosko 2002: 142).

Topologically, Guattari and Deleuze's description of the abstract machine as complementary translates into its unilaterality. In *A Thousand Plateaus* Guattari and

Deleuze in fact maintain that 'along its diagrammatic or destratified vector' the abstract machine '*no longer has two sides*; all it retains are traits of expression and content from which it extracts degrees of deterritorialization that add together and cutting edges that conjugate' (145, emphasis added). And earlier: 'the plane of consistency is always immanent to the strata; the two states of the abstract machine always coexist as two different states of intensities' (57). In terms of Hjelmslev's semiotics, it gathers both content and expression onto one plane. 'A true abstract machine has no way of making a distinction within itself between a plane of expression and a plane of content because it draws a single plane of consistency' (156). It is according to this double coding that the abstract machine is both generative and disruptive. 'The abstract machine exists enveloped in each stratum, whose Ecumenon or unity of composition it defines, and developed on the plane of consistency, whose destratification it performs (the Planomenon)' (73). As Guattari and Deleuze note about architecture in *What is Philosophy?*: 'House and Universe, *Heimlich* and *Unheimlich*, territory and deterritorialization' (186). There are, thus, 'two complementary movements, one by which abstract machines work the strata and are constantly setting things loose, another by which they are effectively stratified, effectively captured by the strata' (144).

A third plane, 'that of organization or formation' (TP: 368), intervenes in the twofold dynamics of the plane of immanence as the plane of consistency or composition. It is on that third plane that questions of the relative openness of assemblages to the milieu play themselves out. 'The plane of organization is constantly working away at the plane of consistency, always trying to plug the lines of flight, stop or interrupt the movements of deterritorialization, weigh them down, restratify them, reconstitute forms and subjects in a dimension of depth. Conversely, the plane of consistency is constantly extricating itself from the plane of organization, causing particles to spin off the strata, scrambling forms by dint of speed or slowness, breaking down functions by means of assemblages or microassemblages. But once again, so much caution is needed to prevent the plane of consistency from becoming a pure plane of abolition or death, to prevent the involution from turning into a regression to the undifferentiated. Is it not necessary to retain a minimum of strata, a minimum of forms and functions, a minimal subject from which to extract materials, affects, and assemblages?' (270, see also 190).

The ecological problematics lie in how to always be tendentially on the side that opens up the dynamics of formation to the milieu. Ecology is a constant endeavour 'to tip the most favorable assemblage from its side facing the strata to its side facing the plane of consistency or the body without organs' (134). Not to be either ecological or not, but rather to be more or less ecological. To stay with the architectural reference: to keep as many operations of smoothing operative within an architectural form. To keep the complex striation of architecture linked to the changes in and of the milieu. In their 1991, post-*Schizoanalytic Cartographies* book *What is Philosophy?*, Guattari and Deleuze note, in a passage that is conceptually pervaded by Guattari's fourfold, that 'the town does not come after the house, nor the cosmos after the territory. The universe does not come after the figure, and the figure is an aptitude of a *universe*. We have gone from the composite sensation to the plane of composition, but only so as to recognize their strict *coexistence or complementarity*, neither of them advancing except through the other. . . . the composite sensation is reterritorialized on the plane of composition, because it erects its houses there' (196, emphases added).

How do architectures relate to the abstract machine? If the abstract machine tends to be considered in its ontological aspect in *A Thousand Plateaus*, this aspect is downplayed in the fourfold, where it has shifted into a relational position as one of four functors within which its function is distributed. The abstract machine is an actual given that is complementary to virtual, giving Universes. It is from within this shift that Guattari develops his unilateral ecology, whose programme is to create concrete architectonic consistencies that are adequate to the world. In this context, the abstract machine is elemental in the superposition of the contested sites of the given and the giving.

In *A Thousand Plateaus*, Guattari and Deleuze note that the 'diagrammatic' or abstract machine 'does not stand outside history but is instead always "prior" to history', and that it is from this position that it 'plays a piloting role' (142). In the same way that the pre-philosophical plane of immanence has '*diagrammatic features*' (WP: 39), and that the sweeps of anonymous pigment form the non-pictorial diagram of Bacon's figures, the pre-architectural site forms the ground for the informal, non-architectural diagram of architecture. It provides the complex field of potentiality and possibility with and within which architectural compositions take and assemble place and time. In *Schizoanalytic Cartographies*, the position of the abstract machine as an architectural site is that of an actual rhizome: the abstract site as a deterritorialized field of the possible. In relation to the virtual giving, it denotes the field on which and with which the giving operates. The pre-architectural site does not function as a field of pure, immediate and as-yet-indifferent intensities and resonances, however, in and with which architectures, as local expressions and creations of that milieu, emerge. It is not the quantitative, to-be-qualified and thus to-be-falsified construction site.

This for two reasons. The first is that the actual site is already pervaded by codes and codings. The second is that although it is purely quantitative in terms of its formal distinction from the realm of virtual quality, it is, in the ecological superposition of these two fields, populated by an infinity of non-human actors that bring to it their virtual Territories and Universes. Guattari's ecosophy is keenly aware that there are any number of non-human actors at work in the ceaseless folding of the given site onto the field of the giving and vice versa. As Guattari and Deleuze had noted, every landscape has its own haecceity. Rotterdam in the rain. Clouds over Paris. Drops in temperature. Changes in luminosity. No site is ever only actual and anonymous. It is invariably and at the same time a virtual, infinitely individuated and singularized, territorial and universal milieu. It is simultaneously Flow, Phylum, Territory and Universe. Accordingly, an architectonic project should not be thought of as spiritualizing an actual milieu in the way that, say, Werner Herzog's Fitzcarraldo aims to spiritualize a purely actual jungle by bringing to it the übervirtuality of the opera. Rather, architecture should aim to find an adequate way to oikonomize a specific site for human habitation.

It is always within a superposition of the given and the giving that human architecture comes into being. The architectural challenge is to find an adequate way to insert a human habitat into the heterogeneous ecology of the bodies and the spirits of the site; into what the Romans called its *genius loci*. To insert architecture into the spaces, or perhaps cracks between that milieu's given and giving elements. For this project, both the ensemble of ordered multiplicities as well as the unformed pure multiplicity that forms the ground and the immanent site of formation must be taken into architectural consideration. The multiplicity of light and sound as the site of vision and language, the multiplicity of pigment as the site of the painting, the multiplicity of the geographical and meteorological milieu as the site of architecture: *local colour, local light, local architecture.*

There are echoes of the photonic nature of ecosophy in Guattari's description of an architectural site's luminosity in his essay 'The Architectural Machines of Shin Takamatsu'. Takamatsu's buildings are defined by 'an almost obsessive repetition of vertical lines' (2015a: 82). These, however, as in the interior of his Dance Hall in Nagoya from 1985, 'are often crossed by diverse transversal elements, for example, by rays of luminous white light' (82). These rays of light link the building to the adjacent milieu of Kyoto, 'in which light, air, wind, and thought are different and which he apprehends as a fractal organism pulsating on every level in an extraordinarily slow movement, must therefore be secretly rejoined, recreated, reinvented through each component of its architectural machines . . . In each element of the architectural ensemble, whether interior or exterior and whatever the size, every ray of light, every possible point of view or angle will therefore contribute to the overall effect' (80–1). In terms of how to achieve an architectural adequation between site and architecture, the architectural object needs to be developed from within the superposition of the actual and the virtual; as the superposition of the given and the giving. It is only in such a superposition that a truly ecosophic architecture can be conceptualized. If it does not undergo this ecologization, the architectural object will operate as what one might call the colonization of a given site by a formal, Cartesian diagram. Only its ecologization allows for an insertion of concrete buildings into a given topological site and this site's ecological modulations: *projective architecture*.

Again, however, let me hold my breath. Before analysing specific architectures with Guattari, let me take some more time to analyse the architectural machine in and of Guattari's work. As I have noted, in the scholarship on Guattari and Deleuze, the figure of good architecture is by default the architecture of the planometric nomad. While there is some truth to this, I think this notion needs qualification. First, as with all other distinctions, it is too easy to set one's belief and hope in any one side of a binarism. Second, each problematic needs to be considered as radically singular and thus as situationist. Perhaps it is too easy to consider the nomads that roam today's megacities, the transients, the lost souls and bodies that populate the empty spaces of capitalism, or the kids that roam the sites of architectural crowd-control and surveillance such as mega-malls and train-stations, as subversive elements that put the relentless economization of space into question. In terms of the relentless capitalization of the globe, failure has been theorized as a viable option. In terms of ecology, calls for an anarchic politics are too simple to adequately administer the contested fields of the given and the giving. The distinctions between good movement and bad stasis, positive speed and negative slowness, bad order and good disorder, are entirely too general. All too often, transient architectures are those of refugee camps, favelas and trailer parks. In fact, all architectonic territorialization is inherently related to the creation of an existential slowness.

If the nomadic, with its tents and moveable architectures, implies an openness to the milieu while settlements imply closed-off and permanent sites, the art of architecture cannot consist in staking a fluid, open nomadism against solid, closed-off settlements. Such a rhetorical slant suffuses even otherwise very balanced and convincing accounts of a Guattari and Deleuzian architecture, like that of Andrew Ballantyne in *Deleuze and Guattari for Architects*. While Ballantyne acknowledges that Guattari and Deleuze define architecture as 'the art of the abode and the territory' (TP: 328–9), he immediately, like many Deleuzians, links that territory to regimes of social control. 'What buildings produce most often is a territory – *a space where a particular order prevails or seems implicit*' (2007: 60, my emphasis). At an earlier point, Ballantyne had quoted a longer passage from Guattari and Deleuze in which they develop, on the background of the work of Eugène Dupréel, a theory of territorialization and consolidation in which 'there is no beginning from which a linear sequence would derive, but rather densifications, intensifications, reinforcements, injections, showerings, like so many intercalary events ("there is growth only by intercalation"). Second, and this is not a contradiction, there must be an arrangement of intervals, a distribution of inequalities, such that it is sometimes necessary to make a hole in order to consolidate. Third, there is a superposition of disparate rhythms, an articulation from within of an interrhythmicity, with no imposition of meter or cadence. Consolidation is not content to come after; it is creative. The fact is that the beginning always begins in-between, intermezzo. Consistency is the same as consolidation, it is the act that produces consolidated aggregates, of succession as well as of coexistence, by means of three factors just mentioned: intercalated elements, intervals, and articulations of superposition' (TP: 328–9).

From this description, Guattari and Deleuze modulate to architecture and its materialities, in particular to reinforced concrete, which Jean Baudrillard had, four years earlier, related to second-order simulacra and which would not, perhaps, be considered an ecologist's most preferred building material. In that seemingly unecological concrete, however, Guattari and Deleuze find a promise of both singularity and of improved possibilities of architectural administration. 'Matters like reinforced concrete have made it possible for the architectural ensemble to free itself from arborescent models employing tree-pillars, branch-beams, foliage-vaults. Not only is concrete *a heterogeneous matter whose degree of consistency varies according to the elements in the mix, but iron is intercalated following a rhythm*; moreover, its self-supporting surfaces form a complex rhythmic personage whose "stems" have different sections and variable intervals depending on the intensity and direction of the force to be tapped (armature instead of structure). . . . It is no longer a question of imposing a form upon a matter but of elaborating an increasingly rich and consistent material, the better to tap increasingly intense forces' (329, emphasis added).

Ballantyne reads concrete metaphorically, noting that, similar to the way reinforcing steel is intercalated in concrete, 'architecture is intercalated into life, structuring and framing it' (54). More concretely, however, reinforced concrete is also the objective architectural correlative to the superposition of heterogeneous, deterritorialized Phyla and Territorial rhythms. This everywhere singular mix carries a much more nuanced ecological sentiment than the one Ballantyne implies when he stakes a presumably molar and striated territory against a molecular and smooth politics of architectural deterritorialization. Against monumental order, Ballantyne stakes Guattari and Deleuze's assumed promotion of 'un-monumental aspects of life' (2007: 97) and their assumed preference for fluid process architectures. Like many other readings, Ballantyne notes that Guattari and Deleuze prefer 'fluidity and creativity ("becoming") to establishing any sort of fixity'. As such, 'their thought is a challenge for any architects who choose to engage with it, as its volatility is at odds with the profession's traditional preoccupation with form' (97). If there are formal and territorial elements in architecture, these elements 'are things that Deleuze and Guattari themselves would be trying to go beyond, to mobilize and deterritorialize, so that, having developed to a certain extent, one opens up to chaos, makes oneself receptive to what one finds there, steps outside the structured world of habits and common sense, and sees what happens' (99).

While Ballantyne's text is extremely compelling in how it develops a Deleuze and Guattarian ecology of architecture, at this point I wonder whether the question is not so much whether architecture is ecological enough, but rather whether architecture can in fact be too ecological. To show what I mean by this, let me turn to Ballantyne's reading of Le Corbusier as what he calls a promoter of an architecture of pure form. Le Corbusier, who, in *Towards a New Architecture*, coined the eminently Guattarian phrase 'a house is a machine for living in' (1986: 107), defines architecture as 'the masterly, correct and magnificent play of masses brought together in light' (29). Ballantyne takes issue with this definition, which he considers to be 'delivered from a higher stratum: "magnificent" is clearly above the milieu, and "masterly" and "correct" behaviours conform to a pattern determined from above. And we have learnt to see form (here "masses") as "what the man in command has thought to himself", and has been able to express. So Le Corbusier's definition of architecture belongs entirely to the mindset of the state, and we can enlist him to the service of the fonctionnariat and have him design buildings as limited well-defined object-parcels that tend to separate themselves from their surroundings. The cult of pure form, of beautiful shapes that enchant us with their other-worldly promise of an unencumbered life, is the staple of the glossy architectural magazines' (2007: 88–9). Ballantyne sets architecture's immersion into the milieu against Le Corbusier's obsession with form. 'Architects sometimes like to make the claim that architecture is autonomous, but to make such a claim is merely to deny the legitimacy of some of the multiplicity of planes, which nevertheless remain real even if we do not allow ourselves to talk about them' (97). However, might one not consider, from a more distanced, sober and perhaps more Guattarian position, Le Corbusier's definition to be, in particular in reference to its luminism, quite beautifully ecological? While such a reading would question Ballantyne's architectural judgement, my point is that it is not a solution to position oneself on either side of a debate that sets, categorically, an ecological against a non-ecological architecture. At the same time, the one thing that is perhaps even worse than positioning oneself on one side of the debate is to opt for a compromise between them, as in: *some nomadism, some settlement*.

In 'The Architectural Machines of Shin Takamatsu' Guattari's solution to this dilemma is to opt for an architectural paradox. Guattari, who considers Le Corbusier as more ecological than Ballantyne assumes him to be, notes that in the debate between architects who, 'like Le Corbusier, take the overall context into account' and those who, 'like Mies van der Rohe, detach the work from its surrounding environment', one might propose a third architectural position 'in which the work is both complete as an aesthetic object *and* totally open to its context' (2015a: 80, emphasis added). Genosko calls these positions – which Guattari also relates to 'the position of a Butoh dancer like Min Tanaka, who completely folds in on his body and remains, nevertheless, hypersensitive to every perception emanating from the environment' (2015a: 80) – those of 'detachment' and 'attachment' (2002: 140). Perhaps the default slogan for a Guattarian architecture, more nomadism, less settlements!, should be rewritten as: *more nomadism, more settlement!*

What kind of architectural programme might be deduced from this paradox? Should each generation tear down the houses built by the older generation in order to build its own houses, as Nathaniel Hawthorne famously proposes in *The House of the Seven Gables*? Are energetically sustainable houses invariably ecological? Should territorialized architectures be replaced by deterritorialized ones? Quite exasperatingly, Guattari and Deleuze do not provide a universal programme that addresses and answers these questions. As everything in this world is site- and time-specific, each administration – whether architectural, economic or libidinous – must respond to a specific milieu and to a specific time. Although it sounds dangerously like a truism, there are no easy and no final solutions. To shift a chair in a room might be more deterritorializing in a given situation than building what architects would consider to be a free, communal space. What can be said is that as an expression of the living, the architectural field is not closed. In *Soft Subversions*, Guattari mentions the 'Federation of Study Groups in Institutional Research' (FGERI) as an example. As part of that programme, 'a group of fifteen architects and city planners discussed, for almost two years, not only their projects and their profession, but also many questions concerning their lives, their interpersonal relationships' (35). Never separate the map from the territory. 'Determining this requires the juxtaposition of different kinds of discourses, not only the discourse of general theorization, but also a "minor theorization", a cartography of affects, on the level of daily relationships, the relationship to space, etc. . . . In this view, analysis consists in connecting and making coexist, neither to homogenize nor to unify – but rather to arrange these different levels of discursivity according to a principle of transversality, and make them communicate transversally' (45–6). This implies what Guattari calls 'research into research itself' (34); a meta-research 'that takes into account the fact that the researchers cannot reach their goal unless the organizers also put themselves into question with regard to things that don't appear in any way related to the goals of their research' (34–5).

Such an expansion of research lies at the heart of any ecosophic debate. In his more hopeful moments, Guattari believes that ecosophy will lead to 'the formation of innovative forms of dialogue and collective interactivity and, eventually, a reinvention of democracy' (298). In these processes, 'the emphasis will be put on "contingent choices" circumscribing and giving existential consistency to new pragmatic fields. Investigations must give special attention to the singular virtues of semiotic links that support such choices (ritournelles, facial features, becoming-animals, etc.). In parallel to their semiotic functions of signification and designation, they develop an existential function that catalyzes new universes of reference' (303).

As itself a specific site, every architectural object expresses a matrix of conditionings and constructions of life, as well as specific vectors within these constructions. This is why the question posed to and by architecture must be non- or pre-architectural, in the same way that a question posed to history must be non- or pre-historical. Architecture must address the overall milieu with its specific viabilities and affordances; its specific histories, alliances and constraints. It must design the potentialities of shelter and movement, together with their overall politics. It must concern itself not so much with striated space as a problem, as with the singularization of a space that has its specific temperatures, densities and coagulations. It must be both intensely personal and intensely impersonal. In the latter context, an ecosophic architecture must be a highly abstract architecture, just like ecology must be a highly abstract ecology: *more abstract, more concrete.*

If a new architectural object is introduced into the overall milieu, the challenge is that it should be, like thought, adequate to and in resonance with the operational logic of the abstract machine that is the world. From this, one might develop a both situated and elemental architecture that sees itself as immanent to the fractal space and the quantitative forces of the elements of Air, Water, Earth, Fire and of the luminiferous Æther that animates the four. For Guattari, architectural objects are developed from within a Universe that is, like Proust's writing and Balthus' painting, freed from the constraints of Territories, Flows and Phyla, but that is, at the same time, always already related to the other functors and trails these functors behind. Although thought might suppress these relations, everything, including acts of technical invention and intervention, has emerged from these relations and thus should be considered as always already ecological. The question, therefore, is about how much of that given ecology is repressed in such acts and interventions and thus how adequately they make the blind and mute truth of the world speak in and through them. How much can architecture make the world express itself? How adequate is it to its modes of operation?

This adequation is the topic of Guattari's essay 'Drawing, Cities, Nomads' from 1992, which literally embodies Guattari's ecosophic architectonics in that it is a text about urban planning and architecture that itself consists, like a city, of a layered, fractal space in which different typographical plateaus relate, transversally, heterogeneous conceptual plateaus, such as the individual body's relation to the city, the history of architecture and architectural theory. Guattari's given is that 'interactions between the body and constructed space unfold through a field of virtuality whose complexity verges on chaos' (18G1). If that is so, urban planners need to be adequate to this complexity. For models of such complexifications, Guattari turns once more to nonlinear dynamics: 'perhaps it belongs to architects and urban planners to think both the complexity and the chaos along new lines. The equivalent of the "strange attractors" from the thermodynamics of states far from equilibrium (from the field of nonlinear dynamics) could be sought here' (119G2).

At one point in his folding of the situationist urbanism onto Deleuze's 'baroque city' (2006: 138), O'Sullivan provides an important bridge, via Deleuze, to Guattari's architectural ecosophy. For Deleuze, 'architecture has always been a political activity, and any new architecture depends on revolutionary forces, you can find architecture saying "We need a people", even though the architect isn't himself revolutionary' (1995: 158, quoted in O'Sullivan 2006: 139). In fact, O'Sullivan maintains that 'Deleuze shares with the Situationists this prophetic orientation', which also suffuses 'Chtcheglov's manifesto for a "New Urbanism"', according to which 'architecture is the simplest means of *articulating* time and space, of *modulating* reality, of engendering dreams' (139). O'Sullivan notes that in the context of the 'psychogeography of the Situationists', 'the geopolitical conditions' are 'economic and social, *but also environmental and ecological*'; although 'not "of" the event', they 'provide its ground' (141, emphasis added).

On an urban plateau, Guattari is not concerned so much with details of style and aesthetics as with the creation of an ecological architectural milieu and its coherencies. In *Chaosmosis*, he will ask what would happen if one were to 'view autopoiesis from the perspective of the ontogenesis and phylogenesis proper to any mechanosphere superposed on the biosphere' (40)? The 'notion of autopoiesis – as the auto-reproductive capacity of a structure or ecosystem – could be usefully enlarged to include social machines, economic machines and even the incorporeal machines of language' (93), he notes. What if one were to expand autopoiesis from biological machines to technical, social and, above all, conceptual machines? To envision a 'machinic autopoiesis' (37)? Guattari had always considered the structural uncoupling of these two levels of machinism – the uncoupling of 'incorporeal Universes of reference' (TE: 38) and 'value' from 'existential Territories' and their 'idiosyncratic territorialized couplings' (C: 4) – as a mistake that recapitulates the fateful uncoupling of nature and culture he and Deleuze had critiqued in *Anti-Oedipus*, in which they had treated it from within the relation of the production of production and the production of recording, arguing that 'the production of recording itself is produced by the production of production' (16).

If the city is itself an 'autopoietic system' (Guattari 1992: 119G2), this calls for 'broadening the concept of the machine beyond its technical aspects and taking into account its economic, ecological, and abstract dimensions, and even the "desiring machines" that populate our unconscious pulses. It's the ensemble of urbanistic and architectural wheelings, all the way down to their smallest sub-ensembles that have to be treated as machinic components' (119G2). To be adequate to 'the urban mentalities of the future' (123G6), therefore, one needs a 'transdisciplinarity between the urbanists, architects and other fields' (125G8). Once more, this project is without nostalgia. If there are no more native lands, that should not be lamented. Instead, there must be 'a particular rapport to the cosmos and to life' (123G6). If that sounds naïvely holistic, one should recognize that this holism is the result of or, perhaps even better, the other side of, a deep ecological pragmatism. It is a strictly machinic and thus anything but a naïve holism. In fact, against the dreaminess of the situationists, Guattari stakes a sober, dead-pan empiricism. If we go on like we do, this will simply but inexorably lead to a world defined by the 'incompatibility with human life, more generally with animal and vegetal life' (125G8).

As architectures are themselves 'abstract machines' that 'carry incorporeal universes that are not universals' (118G1), the specific *'ambiance'* (120G3) is important, as well as a 'return to an animist conception of the world' and to what Viktor von Weizäcker calls 'pathic knowledge' (120G3) or 'pathosophy'. In their interventions, architects should work on 'the heterogenesis of the components and of the processes of resingularization'. Although architecture works from within the tableau of pragmatic constraints, architects do have a 'margin of maneuver' (121G4) to build 'foyers of resingularization'. To do so, they need to 'take the greatest account of situations in their singularity' (120G3; see also Antonioli 2018): *situationist architecture.*

In *What is Philosophy?* Guattari and Deleuze refer to Bernard Cache in terms of defining architecture as the art of spatial framing and deframing. Deframing measures architecture's insertion into the milieu; the presence of the abstract machine in the interior of the architechnical machine. 'However extendable this system [of framing] may be, it still needs a vast plane of composition that carries out a kind of *deframing* following lines of flight that pass through the territory only in order to open it onto the universe, that go from house-territory to town-cosmos, and that now dissolve the identity of the place through variation of the earth . . . on this plane of composition, as on "an abstract vectorial space", geometrical figures are laid out . . . which are no more than cosmic forces capable of merging, being transformed, confronting each other, and alternating; world before man yet produced by man. The planes must now be taken apart in order to relate them to their intervals rather than to one another and in order to create new affects' (187). Architecture, then, should intervene adequately in the fractal spaces of the given site. In *A Thousand Plateaus*, Guattari and Deleuze had called this site of intervention the mechanosphere, as 'the set of all abstract machines and machinic assemblages outside the strata, on the strata, or between strata' (71).

If the pre- and non-architectural site is described as the architectural unconscious, can one envision a schizoanalytic architecture? If psychoanalytic architecture is decidedly familial, how would a schizoanalytic architecture – a schizoarchitecture – be more open and communal? Although it would often share its underlying ethos, such an architecture would not exhaust itself in what we tend to think of as a green architecture – self-sustained, with a low carbon and silicone footprint and energetically up to date – but in the sense of an architecture that is in touch with its ecological unconscious. Along these lines, architectural theory should become a schizoanalysis. In such a project, Guattari and Deleuze stress specifically that architecture as a machinic assemblage concerns questions of adequation. 'Machinic assemblages *effectuate* the abstract machine insofar as it is developed on the plane of consistency or enveloped in a stratum. The most important question of all: given a certain machinic assemblage, what is its relation of effectuation with the abstract machine? How does it effectuate it, with what *adequation*? Classify assemblages' (71, emphasis added): *architectural schizotheory.*

The Architectural Unconscious: Building Schizoanalysis

The architectural milieu is an overall mechanosphere that includes 'social machines, economic machines and even the incorporeal machines of language' (C: 93) in that 'the abstract machine connects a language to the semantic and pragmatic contents of statements, to collective assemblages of enunciation, to a whole micropolitics of the social field' (TP: 7). In this context, Guattari and Deleuze introduce another form of abstract machine. 'There are different types of abstract machines that overlap in their operations and qualify the assemblages: *abstract machines of consistency,* singular and mutant, with multiplied connections; *abstract machines of stratification* that surround the plane of consistency with another plane; and *axiomatic or overcoding* and *abstract machines* that perform totalizations, homogenizations, conjunctions of closure. Every abstract machine is linked to other abstract machines, not only because they are inseparably political, economic, scientific, artistic, ecological, cosmic – perceptive, affective, active, thinking, physical, and semiotic – but because their various types are as intertwined as their operations are convergent. Mechanosphere' (514).

Already in *Kafka: Toward a Minor Literature* from 1975, Guattari and Deleuze note that abstract machines can be co-opted. In fact, Kafka's infernal machines, such as the law in *The Castle,* the sadistic architectures of the penal colony and the name of the father as the despotic signifier are all co-opted abstract machines that are detrimental 'to concrete machinic assemblages' (1986: 86). In these cases, the abstract machines are of an ecumenical order that has gone completely territorial and transcendental. As Guattari and Deleuze note, 'the more it is an abstract machine in the first sense of the word, the more it is despotic' (87). The reference to despotism is telling in that Guattari often describes the regime of the signifier as despotic. One of the most detrimental abstract machines for Guattari, in fact, is that of the signifier and the way it overcodes an inherently productive desire.

On the battleground of abstract machines, psychoanalysis tends to favour the vector of territorialization, while schizoanalysis favours that of deterritorialization. Either 'an abstract machine (abstract in the primary, transcendental sense) ... is realized only in the assemblage' as an agency of overcoding and territorialization, or 'the assemblage ... moves toward the abstract machine (in a secondary and immanent sense)' (88) that implies processes of decoding and deterritorializing. The first form of abstract machine is despotic and transcendental, the second ecological and immanent. 'In another sense of abstract (a sense that is nonfigurative, nonsignifying, nonsegmental), it is the abstract machine that operates in the field of unlimited immanence and that now mixes with it in the process or movement of desire' (86). As I noted earlier, the displacement of a chair or a table can be a micropolitical architectural operation that creates new lines of flight, as can the construction of a new building in a megacity. Similarly, of course, both of these operations can also close off such lines of flight.

In this context, the architecture of the La Borde site is not in itself a schizoarchitecture. In fact, the site takes a given architecture, the Chateau La Borde, within which it constructs a social field that allows for a schizoecology to live in. Its schizoecology does not concern its architecture, that is, but the social architecture of the lives and the situations that are made possible within it, and of which it in fact consists. Its schizoarchitecture is social rather than architectural. As I have mentioned, the most direct of these was *la grille*, the 'evolving organigram' (Guattari 1998: 3) that allowed for the rolling allocation of duties that were shared by patients and staff, without a strict border between medical and household tasks. This conceptual schizoarchitecture – La Borde's abstract machine – operates according to a logic of immanence that encompasses the transcendental signifier of psychoanalysis and that, like all abstract machines, operates, as a regulator of deregulation, in-between processes of ordering and disordering. In all of these frames, the decisive question is invariably ecological and thus time- and site-specific: Does a specific abstract machine remain in touch with the plane of immanence and the potentialities of deterritorialization, or does it attempt to close itself off from that potentiality?: *in the cracks of psychoanalysis.*

When Guattari and Deleuze propose the term schizoanalysis as an alternative to psychoanalysis in *Anti-Oedipus*, this is both politically provocative and conceptually inevitable. The provocation consists in setting up a figure that psychoanalysis considers to be beyond therapeutic reach as the hero who presides over the dismantling of psychoanalysis and its adherent politics: 'schizophrenization ... must cure us of the cure' (AO: 68). Schizoanalysis is a both conceptual and practical attempt to rescue the subject from the oedipal ecology of the family triangle, and to release it into the much more general ecology of the living. To create, quite literally, an 'orphan unconscious' (82). An unconscious without family. In very abstract terms, if psychoanalysis is based on the three conceptual cuts of father, mother and child, schizoanalysis, which refers directly to the act of splitting or cutting – schizo, from the Greek *skhizein* – is the analysis of the multiplicity of machinic cuts that define an entity as something cut out from a milieu to which it is nevertheless immanent: *schizoecosophic cut-outs*.

Guattari and Deleuze develop schizoanalysis in both *Anti-Oedipus* and *A Thousand Plateaus*. As 'desiring-production is pure multiplicity, that is to say, an affirmation that is irreducible to any sort of unity' (AO: 42), all entitarian assemblages are nothing but systems of 'interruptions or break[s]' (40). A machine 'cuts into' a 'continual material flow (*hylè*)' (38). It cuts up a phylum 'into distinct, differentiated lineages, at the same time as the machinic phylum cuts across them all' (TP: 406). As each flow is cut by machines and, at the same time, each of these cuts produces new flows, the diagram of the world consists of 'the thousand breaks-flows of desiring-machines' (AO: 81). As both actual|abstract and virtual|concrete assemblages are infinitely machined, Guattari and Deleuze can talk even of molecular biology as 'schizophrenic' (289), which implies that schizoanalysis concerns the logic of the assembly of both human and non-human life in general. It concerns a much larger field than that of the human or, even more restrictedly, of the psychic. Equally, in that they designate any form of deterritorialized state, regardless of whether that state is actual or virtual, the reach of the terms schizophrenic and schizophrenia goes well beyond a psychoanalytically defined pathology. On the most general level, schizoanalysis concerns the analysis of the assemblage of all forms of entities as 'chronogeneous machines engaged in their own assembly (*montage*)' (286) within their milieus as well as within the allover milieu.

Schizoanalysis, then, is any analysis of the ensembles and the dynamics of machinic cuts and of the arrangements these cuts produce. In analogy, schizoecology is the practice of unfreezing molar organizations and relations of power with the aim of making them more plastic and more open to the milieu. When schizoanalysis addresses the human unconscious, it is not as something that is structured like a language, but as a machinic system whose 'true activities' are 'causing to flow and breaking flows' (325). Schizoanalyses are conceptually organised around a multiplicity of machines that assemble heterogeneous elements into fragile assemblages that are not pre-formed or organised into sets of psychoanalytically overcoded structures, and that at the same time disassemble pathologically molar consistencies: *what Guattari often calls petrified systems.*

As the book's subtitle announces, *Anti-Oedipus* sets up schizoanalysis as a parallel critique of psychoanalysis and capitalism. This twofold critique fell on very fertile ground with countercultural currents in the 1960s and '70s. Today, some of the more extreme readers of Guattari and Deleuze take it once more as a rallying cry to instigate anarchy considered as complete freedom from cultural and political constraints. At the same time, it was violently criticized by the psychoanalytic and philosophical establishment as an endorsement of madness as philosophy's new muse. The book's main argument is that capitalism functions like psychoanalysis and vice versa in that both are based on states of pure flow – the flow of desire and the flow of money respectively – which they organize from within the axiomatics of a strictly economic retrieval. In the case of psychoanalysis, these axiomatics are those of the oedipal family, in the case of capitalism, those of the modern state and its entanglement in capitalist economy. If Guattari and Deleuze call this state an 'apparatus of regulation' (AO: 252), the institution of psychoanalysis is a similar state apparatus installed to order the subjects' state of mind.

In both critiques, the schizo is a figure of the absolute limit of these axiomatics, and as such it heralds each system's deterritorialization. As 'social production is purely and simply desiring-production itself under determinate conditions' (29), the schizo aims at opening up the psychoanalytic and capitalist determinations of the social field to the world's multiplicity. In terms of *Schizoanalytic Cartographies*, the schizo is a figure of the force of the plane of immanence as the reservoir of infinite determinability, and of its presence in the plane of consistency, of which the social, political and economic fields are important parts. The schizo 'plunges further and further into the realm of deterritorialization, reaching the furthest limits of the decomposition of the socius on the surface of his own body without organs' (35). In other words, the schizo injects a positive and productive, Lucretian desire into the social field. As Guattari and Deleuze note, 'schizophrenia is desiring-production as the limit of social production' (35). At infinity, it would disorganize the social until only the body without organs is left as 'the ultimate residuum of a deterritorialized socius' (33). The a-signifying multiplicities of social life and its architectures.

Ecosophy: In the Cracks of Capitalism

In my introduction, I mentioned the modern, globally integrated architectures of a worldwide capitalism that shows itself preferably in the architectures of corporate milieus, high-end hotels and resorts, luxurious signature showrooms as well as museums and other prestige architecture such as concert halls. Of course the ultra-smooth architectures of cell phones and computers also belong to these architectures of affluence, which might be read, at first sight, as symptoms of the complete pervasion of social life by the spirit and the reality of capital, attesting to what Maurizio Lazzarato calls 'the relationship between asignifying semiotics and semiologies of signification in the exercise of capitalist power' (2014: 122). Lazzarato sees the great merit of Guattari's work 'in its problematizing the relationship between the discursive and the non-discursive, exploring the modalities of articulation of the existential with economic, social, and political flows' (220).

For Lazzarato, the 'urgent underlying question' is 'what is to be done?' (22) at a time when the capitalist-controlled enslavement of subjectivities 'works with decoded flows (abstract work flows, monetary flows, sign flows, etc.) which are not centred on the individual and human subjectivity but on enormous social machinisms (corporations, the collective infrastructures of the welfare state, communications systems, etc.)' (28). In fact, for Lazzarato, the political effectiveness of capitalism lies to a large degree in how it 'activates pre-personal, pre-cognitive, and preverbal forces (perception, sense, affects, desire) as well as suprapersonal forces (machinic, linguistic, social, media, economic systems, etc.)' (31). It is thus the 'preindividual subjectivity [that] is brought to bear by capitalist machinic enslavements to exploit affects, rhythms, movements, durations, intensities, and asignifying semiotics' (102). In fact, capitalism now exploits 'machines and semiotic systems that conjoin functions of expression and functions of content of every kind, human and non-human, microphysical and cosmic, material and incorporeal' (88).

At this point, at which the capitalist machine overcodes and controls both the world's allover signifying and a-signifying semiotics, it opens itself up to an ecosophic critique that extends the more narrow political and cultural critique of capitalism and that might allow for a more site- and time-specific conceptualization of capitalism. From an ecosophic perspective, capitalism should never be considered as homogeneous. Why should it be, and how could it be, when everything else is heterogeneous? In order to illustrate the a-signifying – as in unconscious and machinic – modes of capitalist control and operation, Lazzarato quotes a passage from *Schizoanalytic Cartographies* in which Guattari comments on the actual, a-signifying operations that pertain between Flows and Phyla. It is a quote that I have used earlier in reference to Guattari's Figure 6.8: 'The inversion of deterritorialization': 'The expressive function meshes directly with material flows, and becomes capable of catalyzing machinic "choices", such as feedback, and bringing about changes of state ... the diagrammatic formula inscribed on my parking permit sets off the mechanism of the entrance barrier: it allows me to go from an "outside" to an "inside" state' (SC: 86).

In Guattari, this passage is about the excretion of code in the transformation of Flows into Phyla, and about how far this code is a 'correlative to energetic conversions' (168). On an ontological level, the passage is about 'the existence, at the most elementary levels of encoding and signaletic expression, of energetically minimal quantum thresholds marking the passage to a register of *machinic-pragmatic Effects*' (169). For Lazzarato, Guattari's parking permit illustrates how a-signifying semiotics define communications between technological machines, such as those that pertain to 'stock listings, currencies, corporate accounting, national budgets, computer languages, mathematics, scientific functions and equations as well as the asignifying semiotics of music, art, etc.' (Lazzarato 2014: 80). The real, energetic and computational effects of these a-signifying semiotics are brought about by levels below that of signification. 'Asignifying semiotics are not beholden to significations and the individuated subjects who convey them. They slip past rather than produce significations or representations' (80). And further, 'instead of referring to other signs, asignifying signs act directly on the real, for example, in the way that the signs of computer language make a technical machine like the computer function, that monetary signs activate the economic machine, that the signs of a mathematical equation enter into the construction of a bridge or an apartment building, and so on' (40–1).

These effects, one might argue, form the operational unconscious of the world. 'Asignifying semiotics act on things' regardless of 'whether they signify something for someone or not' (40). While Guattari considers this level as an ontological given, Lazzarato is interested in how much capitalism 'depends on asignifying machines' (40) in its implementation of agendas of enslavement; an enslavement that takes place on levels that are fully overcoded by and subject to capitalist manipulation. 'The simplest example of direct intervention is that of the microchip, where sign flows act directly on the material components. The polarities of iron oxide particles are converted into binary numbers when a magnetic strip is passed through a reader equipped with the appropriate computer program. The signs function as the input and output of the machine, bypassing denotation, representation, and signification. Sign flows engage real flows, *giving orders* and producing *a change in conditions*' (85, emphases added): *darkly capitalist a-signifying permits.*

Lazzarato's political proposition is to subversively counter-actualize the a-signifying realm. We must first 'analyze the way in which asignifying semiotics are increasingly used' (117) to install hierarchies, and then 'discover, deploy, and give consistency to collective logics, to the people who are in us and who make us speak and thanks to whom we produce utterances. This is what Guattari and Deleuze have in mind when they set "a whole field of experimentation, of personal and group experimentation" against both psychoanalysis and traditional political organizations' (168; the quotation is from Deleuze 2004: 276). It is on this micropolitical level, Lazzarato notes, that real and possible revolts can emerge. A 'revolt occurs first of all as an asignifying existential crystallization, as the emergence of focal points of subjectivation that take on consistency through a multiplicity of materials of expression' (186). What would it mean for directly political work such as Lazzarato's to become aware of the ecologics that inform and underlie Guattari's politics? In that context, my project aims to do both less and more than Lazzarato. Less in terms of addressing urgent political problematics, more in terms of bringing ontological and ecological pressure to bear on the political: *ecology before politics*.

In *Schizoanalytic Cartographies*, Guattari makes a point of carefully separating technologies from their cultural uses, which is the field on which political battles are fought. If a-signifying semiotics, whether these are technical, chemical or biological, are ontological facts, one needs to differentiate between a microchip as an actual node within the field of connectivity through which programs are run in the same way that computations run through a calculator, or politics run through technology, and the level of giving orders that are related to the overcoding of specific technological routines by strategies of economic and political power. While it is important to trace such economic and political overcodings, such as the algorithms that run stock-market decisions, it is equally important to note that for Guattari, algorithms are first economically neutral fields of potentially, and that capitalism is, at all times, open to forces of deterritorialization. It is in relation to this auto-deterritorialization that Lazzarato's analysis falls short of the ecosophic. What he calls 'capitalist deterritorialization' (2014: 68) is not the same as the deterritorialization of capitalism. Like the market economy and everything else, a-signifying semiotics can work for the better or for the worse: *luminous a-signifying potentialities*.

It is exactly here that Guattari's general ecosophy, which expands the field of deterritorialization from capitalist machines to the world's allover machinics, is situated. This ecological level enters Lazzarato's text only fleetingly by way of a quote from Pier Paolo Pasolini. 'Things express themselves by themselves, constitute focal points of subjectivation; they have a power of expression, a "luminosity", a capacity for proto-enunciation and action specific to them and that in no way depends on man' (126–7). If for Lazzarato and Negri capitalism remains ultimately a monolithic force, for Guattari and Deleuze, the good thing about capitalism is that, unlike earlier despotic or feudal forms of economy, its own operation duplicates the ontological force of deterritorialization that functions as the ontological ground of that very operation. '*At the same time as capitalism is effectuated in the denumerable sets serving as its models, it necessarily constitutes nondenumerable sets that cut across and disrupt those models*' (TP: 472). Even while it constantly opens itself up to its own a-signifying semiotics, however, it immediately – at the same time, one might say – represses them, and, in that gesture, it represses its own a-signifying ground. It is in itself schizophrenic, that is, although it forecloses its schizophrenia in the same way that psychoanalysis forecloses its schizo. In other words, capitalism cannot enjoy itself. 'Capitalism is indeed the limit of all societies, insofar as it brings about the decoding of the flows ... But it is a *relative* limit of every society ... because it substitutes for the codes an extremely rigorous axiomatic that maintains the energy of the flows in a bound state on the body of capital as a socius that is deterritorialized. Schizophrenia, on the contrary, is indeed the *absolute* limit that causes the flows to travel in a free state on a desocialized body without organs. Hence one can say that schizophrenia is the *exterior* limit of capitalism itself or the conclusion of its deepest tendency, but that capitalism only functions on condition that it inhibits this tendency ... by substituting for it its own *immanent* relative limits' (AO: 246).

Once the capitalist use of a-signifying semiotics is understood as a repression of its own built-in force of deterritorialization, capitalism should be treated, in each of its invariably site-and time-specific actualizations, as a patient rather than as an allover evil institution. In fact, to generalize capitalism does not allow for a truly ecosophic administration of capitalism. To see capitalism as a totalizing force, as Antonio Negri does – O'Sullivan notes Negri's belief in the 'total subsumption of life by Capital. A colonization of all space, but also of time itself' (2012: 118) – is to disregard the multiplicity of capitalisms and the modes of the auto-repression of its own schizophrenia. Today's Integrated World Capitalism is an inherently pathological, cramped-up abstract machine. As Guattari notes, 'today a new ecological power formation is appearing under our noses and, consecutively, a new ecological industry is in the process of making a place for itself within other capitalist markets. The systems of heterogenetic valorisation – which counterbalance capitalist homogenesis rather than passively contesting the ravages of the world market – have to put in place their own power formations which will affirm themselves within new relations of forces' (C: 123–4): *schizocapitalism*.

If, as O'Sullivan notes, 'a politics of singularity' must 'invariably be one of continuous experimentation and testing; it cannot be given in advance as a general, or transcendent rule' (2012: 96), then this must also go the other way [→ **Deleuze 92**]. One cannot generalize or transcendentalize capitalism. Rather, one needs to schizo-ecologize it. In each capitalist situation, one should help capitalism find ways to escape its cramped-up, obsessive frame of mind; to relax and take a walk. It should be treated, that is, in the same way patients were treated at La Borde: *capitalism in schizotherapy*. One has to produce its deterritorialized unconscious, and bring capitalism into the ecological, machinic fields around it, not so much for our sake, even, as for its own sake. One needs to find modes of intervention that allow it to become more graceful, more open and more anticapitalist. If capitalism is indeed an 'apparatus of regulation', it needs to be grilled, in the sense that *la grille* was 'a sort of instrument to regulate the necessary institutional deregulation'. As Guattari notes in 'Entering the Post-Media Era', 'even capital can be reconverted into a dependable instrument of economic writing. All it takes is reinventing its usage, not in a dogmatic and programmatic manner, but through the creation of other "existential chemistries", open to all the recompositions and transmutations of these "singularity salts" whose secret arts and analysis can deliver up' (SS: 306): *the soft, ecological subversion of capital.*

When Guattari and Deleuze note in *A Thousand Plateaus* that 'it is by leaving the plan(e) of capital, and never ceasing to leave it, that a mass becomes increasingly revolutionary' (472) this image perfectly describes the movement of leaving and never stopping to leave capitalism. Of continually leaving it, while forever remaining within its bounds. As Guattari notes in *Soft Subversions*, there might be hope for capitalism. 'I am in favor of a market economy, but not one geared only on profit and its valorization of status, hierarchy and power. I am in favor of an institutional market economy, one founded on another mode of valorization. Instead of being more capitalistic, we want to make an anticapitalism within capitalism' (116). Similarly, there might be hope for psychoanalysis. Again, the quote comes from *Soft Subversions*. 'Maybe it would be worth saving an analytic practice by reinventing it. So I started again from scratch, to arrive at my current position, much more relaxed, with greater freedom, a kind of grace' (67). Both times, the hope lies in the process of ecologization: capitalism against itself, psychoanalysis against itself: *schizocapitalism, schizoanalysis.*

Schizosexual Ecologies

Both capitalism and psychoanalysis might profit from their ecologization. It would be easy, in fact, to replace anticapitalism within capitalism by schizoanalysis within psychoanalysis. In the same way that capitalism represses its built-in deterritorialization, 'schizophrenia is the *exterior* limit of psychoanalysis itself or the conclusion of its deepest tendency', but 'psychoanalysis only functions on condition that it inhibits this tendency ... by substituting for it its own *immanent* relative limits'. In a very Spinozist passage, Guattari and Deleuze note that 'the goal of schizoanalysis' is 'to analyze the specific nature of the libidinal investments in the economic and political spheres, and thereby to show how, in the subject who desires, desire can be made to desire its own repression' (105).

The schizo, then, is the figure of a state of what psychoanalysis terms the unrepressed. 'We knew the schizo was not oedipalizable, because he is beyond territoriality, because he has carried his flows right into the desert' (67). In the topology of the fourfold, he is the figure of the plane of immanence, although, as the fourfold also shows, 'the movement of deterritorialization can never be grasped in itself, one can only grasp its indices in relation to the territorial representations' (316). When Guattari and Deleuze, in the passages about Lenz's schizo stroll, set the schizo up as someone who is in touch with the reality of the milieu, this is a direct response to Lacan's notion of the schizophrenic as a limit to psychic reality. In these eminently ecological passages, in fact, the schizo becomes the hero of an idealized ecology, 'the self and the non-self, outside and inside, no longer have any meaning whatsoever' (2). He is 'amid falling snowflakes' and 'with nature' (2). Guattari and Deleuze stake this idealized schizo against the 'artificial schizophrenic found in mental institutions' (3). In fact, 'our society produces schizos the same way it produces Prell shampoo or Ford cars' (245). The artificial schizophrenic is a human patient and thus a victim of the cure, while the idealized schizo is a conceptual position: 'schizophrenia is the universe of production and re-productive desiring-machines, universal primary production as "the essential reality of man and nature"' (5). For Guattari and Deleuze, the schizo is invariably more of a field or an attitude than a concrete subject. In fact, in *Schizoanalytic Cartographies*, the space of the chaotic plane of immanence, as a state of infinite potential and infinite determinability, is the ultimate schizo state.

'A schizophrenic out for a walk is a better model than a neurotic lying on the analyst's couch' (2), Guattari and Deleuze note in reference to the figures of the curable neurotic and the incurable psychotic. The cure captures the patient in the closed-off space of psychic reality. More ecologically, schizoanalysis is conducted in the social field itself rather than in the transferential scene of analyst, couch and patient. In the terminology of the fourfold, it makes use of 'everything that allows the a-signifying facets of the refrains that it encounters to be stimulated, in such a way that it is better able to set off their catalytic functions of crystallizing new Universes of reference (the fractalizing function)' (SC: 214).

Again, although *Anti-Oedipus* is the cradle of much of what Guattari develops in *Schizoanalytic Cartographies*, it should be read from within a different conceptual milieu. As programmatically anti-oedipal, the former stakes the actuality of the body against that of the signifier, the schizophrenic against the neurotic, and production against the theatre. After a short discussion of psychoanalysis in relation to the fourfold, *Schizoanalytic Cartographies* shifts from these rhetorics to an analytics; from production to construction. The open, fractal situations described in *Schizoanalytic Cartographies* allow for a move beyond the logics of psychoanalytic hermeneutics and transference as an axiomatics of one-way affects: 'analysis no longer rests on the interpretation of fantasms and the displacement of affects but endeavours to render both operative, to score them with a new range (in the musical sense)' (214). Once analysis is freed from its both conceptual and practical frames, it can open itself up to experimentation, can begin to detect 'encysted singularities – what turns around on itself, what insists in the void, what obstinately refuses the dominant [self] evidence, what puts itself in a position contrary to the sense of manifest interests . . . –and to explore their pragmatic virtualities' (214).

As I noted, the schizo could only become a hero as a conceptual figure of infinite potentiality and determinability. Nobody ever asked a concrete entity to be the plane of immanence. As Guattari observes in an interview, 'schizophrenics are poor, unfortunate people who are imprisoned in psychiatric hospitals. What we did say is that there exists a *schizo* process' (2015b: 35). The schizo is the hero of inconsistency in that consistencings need a violently schizoid and inconsistent plane of immanence as their field of potentiality. In fact, the plane of immanence might well be renamed the plane of inconsistency or the plane of indifference. The difference between the human body and the body without organs of the plane of immanence is that the former is already a specific, topologically and temporally bounded, consistent entity, whereas the latter consists of the infinite set of the relations of all bodies, things and materials, making up the set of infinitely fast movements and affects that traverse every consistent body and architecture.

In the light of this genetic schizoid space, to position an excluded Real in its place is inadequate to the world. As Guattari and Deleuze note, 'the three errors concerning desire are called lack, law and signifier' (AO: 111). In mathematical terms, the difference between a Lacanian and a Deleuzian ontology is that Lacan, as well as Lacanians such as Alain Badiou, start with a zero state, while Guattari starts with a state of infinity. As Guattari notes in *Schizoanalytic Cartographies*, the unconscious is 'generative', constituting 'an ensemble of lines of alterity, virtual possibilities, unprecedented new becomings' (30). As local changes in the field have repercussions throughout global space, 'the entities arising from these four domains will not have any fixed identity. They will only be able to sustain their own configurations through the relations that they entertain with each other; they will be required to change state and status as a function of their overall Assemblage. In other words, they will not arise from a structural topography, and it is to their systems of transformation that the task of "administering" their modelling is allotted' (27).

Consider that, 'from a quantitative point of view, the energy charges associated with molecular chips of negentropic hypercomplexity are incommensurably smaller than the molar charges whose Assemblages they pilot' (101). The notion that a-signifying levels pilot signifying levels pertains directly to the difference between an ecosophic unconscious that thinks a signaletics before linguistics, and a linguistic unconscious that thinks a linguistics before a signaletics and that finds the privileged way to administer the unconscious in a hermeneutics based on the 'celebrated Lacanian formula according to which a signifier was supposed to represent the subject for another signifier' (204), which Guattari calls 'an old adage of Lacan's ... [that] could be the epigraph for ... [a] new ethic of disengagement' (40, see also 162).

For Guattari and Deleuze, this formula is symptomatic of the 'imperialism' (TP: 65) of the signifier and its relentless 'overcoding' (428) of all other signaletic materials and processes, and thus of the exclusion of the infinity of signaletic plateaus by the inherently 'reductionist' (SC: 17) logic of psychoanalysis: 'what psychoanalysis missed, in the course of its historical development, is the heterogenesis of the semiotic components of its enunciation. . . . with its structuralization, psychoanalysis pretended to reduce everything to the signifier, even to the "matheme". Everything leads me to think that, on the contrary, it would be preferable for psychoanalysis to multiply and to differentiate the expressive components that it puts into play, as much as possible' (213). If psychoanalysis reduces 'subjectivity to only being the result of signifying operations, as the structuralists wished', schizoanalysis sets out 'to map the diverse components of subjectivity in their fundamental heterogeneity' (204). In other words, schizoanalysis, as 'the analysis of the impact of Assemblages of enunciation on semiotic and subjective productions in a given problematic context' (18), opens up the unconscious to the milieu of which it is also a part: *it literally ecologizes the unconscious.*

Like the Real – which is excluded even while it causes the twisted topology of Lacanian psychoanalysis (remember that its real projective plane positions the Symbolic and the Imaginary on its two sides, excluding the Real as the topology's fundamental twist) – schizophrenia is itself famously excluded from the psychoanalytical field. Symptomatically, the uneconomical, excessive violence of *jouissance*, which can only be reached *in extremis* (orgasm, violence, madness), 'must be refused in order to be attained on the inverse scale of the Law of desire' (Lacan 2007: 700). In Guattari and Deleuze's terms this implies the refusal of a constructive desire. 'I reach desire when I arrive at castration' (AO: 268). When Guattari and Deleuze state that, according to Lacan, '*jouissance* is impossible, but impossible *jouissance* is inscribed in desire. For that, in its very impossibility, it is the Ideal, the "*manque-à-jouir* that is life"' (TP: 154), they provide a concise commentary on the topological distribution of the Symbolic, the Imaginary and the Real on Lacan's real projective plane. According to the distribution of realms within this topology, *jouissance* can be in psychoanalysis only in relation to its fundamental unrepresentability and its inherently uneconomical violence. If Guattari and Deleuze note that 'all sexuality is a matter of economy' (AO: 11), this includes *jouissance* in that it embodies the force that is the plane of immanence.

The overcoding of sexuality by the psychoanalytic economy of desire and the signifier's semiotic overcoding of any number of 'nonsignifying signs' (73) and sign-systems go hand in hand. Rather than making a choice between the two levels, Guattari and Deleuze conceptualize an a-signifying, molecular sexuality and a signifying, molar sexuality, both of which originate in the schizophrenic plane of immanence as actualized in and as the plane of consistency. This ecologization of sexuality fundamentally realigns the notions of desire, which is no longer a compensation of lack but a productive machinics, and of the field of sexuality, which is no longer conceptually contained in the family but in a much larger ecology of sexual milieus. In fact, every fractal milieu is pervaded by a host of sexual forces and thus inherently sexual. Although it disavows it, Lacan's signifying unconscious is piloted by molecular, communal choreographies and masses. As Guattari and Deleuze maintain, 'we each go through so many bodies in each other' (TP: 36) and 'everyone is a little group (*un groupuscule*)' (AO: 362). In fact, 'there are no individual statements, only statement-producing machinic assemblages' (TP: 36) that link the subject – considered as a desiring machine in the sense that it is, like any machine, a machine that desires – to a given, a-signifying schizosexuality: to 'the faceless figure of the libido' (36), to 'collective assemblages' (80) and to a 'nonsubjective living love' (189).

In operational terms, the molecular sexualities of both the abstract sexual machine and of the concrete sexual machines relate and distribute, at every moment, heterogeneous elements into machinic arrangements and, in doing so, dissolve other arrangements: 'Sexuality is no longer regarded as a specific energy that unites persons derived from the large aggregates, but as the molecular energy that places molecules-partial objects (libido) in connection, that organizes inclusive disjunctions on the giant molecule of the body without organs . . . and that distributes states of being and becoming according to domains of presence or zones of intensity . . . For desiring-machines are precisely that: the microphysics of the unconscious' (AO: 183). Even generation is only supplemental to this experimental molecular sexuality at play with itself. 'Sexuality is not a means in the service of generation; rather, the generation of bodies is in the service of sexuality as an autoproduction of the unconscious' (108). From this point of view, oedipalized individuals organize the ecological distribution and construction of sexuality, freezing up the molecular conduits that animate the movements of desire. 'The only subject is desire itself on the body without organs, inasmuch as it machines partial objects and flows, selecting and cutting the one with the other, passing from one body to another, following connections and appropriations that each time destroy the factitious unity of a possessive or proprietary ego (anoedipal sexuality)' (72). Subjectification under the oedipal law of castration slows the speed of determination down and reduces the potentialities and possibilities operative within specific ecologies. It closes entities off from the allover milieu, whereas molecular sexuality, as 'an anoedipal sexuality, an anoedipal heterosexuality and homosexuality, an anoedipal castration' (74), speeds up determinability and opens subjects up to the milieu: *ecosexuality*.

Against the axiomatic familial triangularization of desire and the psychic realm, schizoanalysis sets site- and time-specific analyses of the relation of assemblages to themselves, to adjacent assemblages and to the world at large. In doing so, the questions it asks are implicitly ecosophic. 'How does one Assemblage relay another

Assemblage so as to "administer" a given situation? ... How do several Assemblages enter into relation and what is the result? How are the potentialities for the constitution of new Assemblages ...? How are the relations of production, of proliferation and the micropolitics of these new Assemblages to be "aided" in such a case?' (SC: 20). The anti-oedipal question is thus about the viability of an ecosophic entity suspended in the fourfold. More importantly, an entity that moves within the fourfold and thus changes its allover milieu, creating new Universes that are shot through with the infinite determinability given and secured by the schizo state. Universes that allow for lines of flight that never lead out of the milieu but that allow the entity to move more freely through its internal striations and external smoothings. The definition of such an operational space calls for a pragmatics rather than for a hermeneutics that assumes it can operate without interfering with and changing the allover space. While hermeneutics might be adequate to geometrical space, the adequate practice for topological space is, as Guattari never stops stressing, experimentation: *ecological pragmatics.*

Another ecologization lies in the fact that schizoanalytic operations never take place in a dimension outside of the milieu, as fractality allows only for internal dimensions and transversal movements between these. As I noted earlier, schizoanalytic subjectivity is established at the intersection of Flows of signs and machinic Flows, 'at the junction of the facts of sense, of material and social facts, and, above all, in the wake of transformations resulting from their different modalities of Assemblage' (20). Even while *Anti-Oedipus* is driven by a strong rhetorical pull towards the creation of a new society, rather than ask whether Guattari and Deleuze's schizoanalytic endeavour is utopian, one should ask whether it is adequate to the operation of the allover world.

Psychoanalysis has very accurately described the cultural attractors operative during a specific period of time. What schizoanalysis argues is that the oedipal organization is neither ontologically given nor timeless. Like everything else, it is constructed, and as such it can be dismantled. In fact, on the basis of a given schizo-ground, everything can be dismantled. New arrangements can always be implemented. Again, however, the schizo-ground is not a friend. It does not favour specific implementations. It is nothing more and nothing less than a field of sheer potentiality. The rest is up to the entities as expressions of the world.

Still, Guattari's meta-modelling project does not aim at simply denying the Lacanian unconscious. As O'Sullivan notes, 'Guattari does not dismiss the Lacanian theorisation *tout court* (as we have seen, signifying economies of narrative might well be crucial in cohering a subject), but places it along side other modelisations in a more expanded analytic – and aesthetic – framework' (2012: 274–5). Here, the crucial word is expanded, which, importantly, O'Sullivan relates to art practices such as sculpture in the expanded field. In other words, its project is to fractalize the subject, to open it up to the world and thus to ecologize it. Why would one go on maintaining, for instance, that the libido is male? In a schizoanalytic milieu, the libido will 'find itself "denaturalized", deterritorialized: it will become a sort of abstract matter of possibility' (SC: 30): *schizoecology as queer ecology*.

Ecosophic Administrations of Life

To sum up: in the fourfold, the birth of a fractal and ecological, although still anonymous unconscious happens already with the excretion of codes on the vector between Flows to Phyla. It is concretized and develops further in the shift from Phyla to the creation of refrains in Territories: 'One can now see that the ontological status of concrete machines implies not only the entry of abstract machinic functions but equally existential operators allowing them to be aggregated with the incorporeal Universes and existential Territories that confer on them a self-consistency, a necessary character which in fact requires a complete looping and inversion of the cycle of Assemblages' (SC: 97). Programmatically, Guattari relates the creation of virtual Territories and Universes, and thus the emergence of human consciousness, to the function of a-signifying operators. 'Although no longer falling under the signaletics of quantification, self-reference is only produced as quantities of intensity through the intermediary of non-oppositional, non-discursive traits (which is what separates them from the signifying traits dear to structuralists, which they substituted for libidinal energy)' (100). The genesis of Territories as fields of affect begins in the space of virtual Flows and it results, along the vertical axis, in the fractalization and thus the striation of virtual space that creates the existential space from which, after an intermediate process of smoothing, Universes come into being.

A fundamental move towards a schizoecology, then, lies in replacing the notion of the linguistic unconscious with the notion of an ecological unconscious considered as the plurality of black-boxed levels of not-yet-integrated irritations and piloting processes. In that it asks us to consider non-human operations in the human, it binds together the logics of schizoanalysis, schizoecology and a schizoevolution that Henry Adams described in *The Autobiography of Henry Adams*: 'Evolution was becoming change of form, broken by freaks of force, and warped at times by attractions affecting intelligence, twisted and tortured at other times by sheer violence, cosmic, chemical, solar, supersensual, electrolytic' (1961: 401). Adams's description is echoed in Maturana and Varela's pachinko evolution when they describe evolutionary operations as 'a *natural drift*, a product of the conversation of autopoiesis and adaptation' (1998: 117). In Guattarian terms, the entity finds the appropriate or adequate way through processes that are directly coupled to the given and the affordances and constraints of the milieu in which they find themselves. It glides, more or less gracefully, down its irregular, site-specific slope of life, without a transcendental knowledge intervening from the outside or a pre-formed blueprint intervening from the inside. Rather, it finds its way 'very simply – by itself. It slides – like one wedels when skiing ... I call this dance-like slalom through life "drifting"' (Maturana, 1994: 66). As von Foerster notes, with his trademark laconics, in rolling down a hill, 'the best possible way for the ball is the one that it takes' (2014: 7). As DeLanda argues, entities 'grow and *evolve by drift*' (2002: 63, my emphasis) and 'endogeneously generate their own *stable states* (called "attractors" or "eigenstates")' (63).

As they are immanent to both the chaotic schizospace and the drifts of the chaosmotic state of the plane of consistency, their agency and survival lies in their ability to avail themselves of potential (given) and of possible (administrable) energies, such as the ability of birds to use currents in the air, or the ability of surfers to fold themselves into the energy contained in a wave. 'At any one moment in the system's history it is the *degree of intensity* of these parameters (the degree of temperature, pressure, volume, speed, density, and so on) that defines the attractors available to the system and, hence, the type of forms it may give rise to' (263). If all consistencies, which DeLanda differentiates into 'energetic, genetic, [and] linguistic' (21), follow such an operational logic, 'human culture and society (considered as dynamical systems) are no different from the self-organized processes that inhabit the atmosphere or hydrosphere (wind circuits, hurricanes), or, for that matter, no different from lavas or magmas, which as self-assembled conveyor belts drive plate tectonics' (55). DeLanda calls the operator in such a non-human computation 'a blind probe head capable of exploring a space of possible forms' (264): *the dark precursor as probe head.*

A general schizoanalytics, therefore, attempts to administer situations along the lines of specific molecular forms of organizations with the objective of 'disengaging the nature of the crystallizations of power which function around a dominant transformational component' (MU: 178). In other words, the ecological project is to singularize analysis and to make it time- and site-specific. As Guattari notes in *Schizoanalytic Cartographies*, 'how does one Assemblage relay another Assemblage so as to "administer" a given situation? How does an analytic Assemblage, or one that is alleged such, mask another? How do several Assemblages enter into relation and what is the result? How are the potentialities for the constitution of new Assemblages to be explored in a context that appears totally blocked? How are the relations of production, of proliferation and the micropolitics of these new Assemblages to be "aided" in such a case? This is the kind of question that schizoanalysis will be led to pose. This work of subjectivity – in the sense that one works iron – or on musical scales on or fecund moments in the weft of existence – is identified here with the production of [a] referent, or more precisely, a *meta-modelling of trans-Assemblage relations'* (19–20). To fold this back onto La Borde: take a walk, as in lay down a path, or rotate within the deterritorializations produced by the grid (*la grille*).

In *The Molecular Unconscious*, Guattari argues that an entity made up of heterogeneous elements is defined by how the single elements are entrained into a coherent set of resonances – 'the generalized coupling of . . . a *population of molecular oscillators*' (146) – and suspended into a milieu defined by a multitude of rhythms and resonances. As Guattari notes, 'content does not crystallize a universal world but a worldliness marked by contingent fields of force centralized around very precise systems of *subjective resonance*' (46, my emphasis). This also concerns frequencies and resonances in the context of what Varela calls, in *The Embodied Mind*, embodied or enacted cognition, which is based on 'the emergence of a global state among "adaptive resonant neuronal networks"' (1991: 96). Such systems, 'instead of *representing* an independent world . . . *enact* a world as a domain of distinctions that is inseparable from the structure embodied by the cognitive system' (140). As Varela describes it, 'it is not a mirroring of the world, but the *laying down* of it' (1987: 62). Ultimately, *Schizoanalytic Cartographies* is Guattari laying down the plane of the fourfold.

In this resonant and rhythmic world, far-from-equilibrium systems are more sensitive to minute perturbations within the allover medium of frequencies. It might be read as a political allegory that frequency catastrophes are often the result of too much regularity, as when large groups of people, such as marching soldiers, cross a bridge in step – a fact that might be read as a natural commentary on the physics of fascism – or when the minor aperiodic variations in the rhythm of the heart, and thus heart rate variability, stops and the heart begins to beat in a completely repetitive, periodic manner. In fact, whenever living systems become fully periodic, something tends to be seriously wrong, be it in the body, on bridges, in politics or in architecture.

'Start at the End': Guattari's Ecosophic Writings

Finally! Many readers will sigh. After 222 pages of preliminaries and readers' guides, I have reached the two books in which Guattari develops his ecosophy: *The Three Ecologies* and *Chaosmosis*. Both works trace the shift from Guattari's earlier theory of molecular revolution to what might be called a theory of molecular evolution. In the introduction I noted that one of the reasons for this delay is that it is virtually impossible to make sense of these two books without the conceptual backdrop provided by *Schizoanalytic Cartographies* and by Guattari's work in general. In fact, the two books make explicit the implicit schizoecology of *Schizoanalytic Cartographies*, which pervades them both in different ways. Although not itself explicitly ecological, *Schizoanalytic Cartographies* is perhaps in actual fact more ecosophic than the two other books, which provide specific ecosophic instantiations that are based on the conceptual ground laid down by the former. Dealing with these two, therefore, will involve a recapitulation – a retrospective conceptual collation, one might say – of what I have argued up until now.

Guattari's ecosophy is strongest when it is most abstract. This is why *Chaosmosis* will be a more lasting book than *The Three Ecologies* which is, for today's readers, curiously dated because the specific political circumstances and urgencies it addresses have changed. *The Three Ecologies* works best as the document of a timely ecological and political intervention. *Chaosmosis* is less time-specific and it relies on the reader's thorough knowledge of Guattari's other work, in particular of *Schizoanalytic Cartographies*, which provides the ecosophic meta-model that allows for changing circumstances to be negotiated at any specific time without falling into the trap of a timeless structuralism. Both books might also be considered in the context of the misunderstandings between Guattari and the Green movement in France. As Berardi remembers in *Félix Guattari: Thought, Friendship, and Visionary Cartography*, what the French Greens desired from Guattari was less his ecosophy than his direct political involvement, for instance as a potential political candidate. They desired his name rather than his thought, while Guattari, as he states in *Chaosmosis*, was looking for 'an expanded ecological consciousness going far beyond the electoral influence of the "Greens"' (122). Rather than concentrate on 'how to keep themselves at an equal distance from the left and the right', the Greens should be concerned with 'how to contribute to the reinvention of progressivist polarity, how to rebuild politics on different bases, how to rearticulate transversally the public and the private, the social, the environmental and the mental' (128).

Another aspect of the failed attempt to start a meaningful conversation with ecological groupings was that although the books' rhetorics share the ethical urgency of much of mainstream ecology, their arcane scientific references and take-no-prisoners terminologies make them eminently unfit for the more activist and political projects of the Greens. In particular, *Chaosmosis* is a literally unreadable book not only for the Greens, but for the default ecologist and the uninitiated layperson in general. Then there is Guattari's explicit critique of the Greens as an ecosystem. 'The technical and associative aspects of ecology will be recuperated by the traditional parties, State power and eco-business', Guattari predicts, adding that 'the ecological movement should concern itself, as a matter of priority, with its own social and mental ecology' (129). Not a good beginning for a meaningful dialogue.

What are the conceptual givens of Guattari's ecosophy? If processes of life are immanent to the global situation and implicated in the circumstances within which that global situation unfolds, the challenge is how to superpose the field of natural machines, the 'pre-personal traits' that operate on the levels of what Varela calls the sub-personal, the personal, and 'social systems or their machinic components' (TE: 61). How to implement a 'mental, a natural and a cultural ecology' that combines 'the environment, the socius and the psyche'? (C: 20). To consider ecology as a given process that cuts transversally across Flows, Phyla, Territories and Universes. To conceptualize a transversal space that links chemical to societal milieus; a machinic ground from which entities emerge and to which they remain immanent. In *The Three Ecologies* and *Chaosmosis*, Guattari links this general machinism to ecological registers and to a world that is everywhere alive and whose 'machinic segments are autopoietic' (C: 30). When Guattari notes that an 'ecology of the virtual is thus just as pressing as ecologies of the visible world' (91), this refers to the plane of consistency that is laid out in the fourfold, both in its aspect of the given actuality in the guise of the extensity of the visible world, and in the aspect of the virtual fields of the giving. In the terminology of chaos theory mixed into that of *Schizoanalytic Cartographies*, the virtual is a 'deterministic chaos animated by infinite velocities' (59) that is defined by both an 'ontological heterogeneity' (61) and an 'ontological intensity' (29). In fact, if by default ecology deals with actual ecologies, Guattari stresses the importance of the ecologies of affect and of thought. The aim is an ecology not only of Flows and Phyla, but also one of Territories and Universes; an ecology that crosses over the distinction between the given and the giving: *ecological heterogenesis*.

As Guattari maintains about the shifting ground defined by the interactions of disparate and heterogeneous machines, 'beneath the diversity of beings, no univocal ontological plinth is given, rather there is a plane of machinic interfaces' (58). Every living entity, Guattari argues, from a single cell to a city, emerges from this machinic multiplicity, which provides both perceptible and imperceptible fields of possibility. Even thought entities are operationally and informationally closed, every slowed-down entity remains immanent to this field. 'It is out of this chaos that complex compositions, which are capable of being slowed down in energetico-spatio-temporal coordinates or category systems, constitute themselves' (59). Every form is born from within the foam, or aerosol, of this machinic chaos. In its inclusion of both given and giving ecologies, and of the often invisible levels of the physical, chemical and biological mechanospheres, Guattari's ecosophy goes beyond the more visible and mainstream versions of ecology and their mostly anthropocentric agendas of saving the environment, cutting back on the use of natural resources, maintaining biodiversity by saving trash species, or fighting climate change. At the same time, in its inclusion of the larger socio-cultural and cosmic levels, it also goes beyond the more science-oriented versions of ecology, which do address many of the more technical levels of ecosophy but which often refrain from relating their conclusions to cultural and political regimes and agendas. This twofold inclusion allows Guattari to combine the theoretical and scientific aspects of ecology with its practical and political aspects into what William Irwin Thompson calls 'a new ecology of consciousness' (1987: 12). Ultimately, it proposes to superpose a given and a giving machinism rather than a natural and a cultural one.

Although such a 'generalized ecology – or ecosophy – will work as a science of ecosystems' (C: 91) and address the overall politics of the ecological project, it is not limited to the operational and informational field and to general political and cultural agendas. Ultimately, the aim of ecosophy is to bring about practical and communal ad-hoc interventions into specific situations in order to adequately administer them. For this, it needs to be in direct resonance with the specific situation within which it intervenes. In particular, it needs to be in touch with this situation's inherent potentialities and with the possibilities of bypassing its often imperceptible constraints that work against the health of the overall ecosystem of which this situation is a part. As such, ecosophy might be defined as an ecological seismography of the living. The 'primary purpose of ecosophic cartography is not to signify and communicate but to produce assemblages of enunciation capable of capturing the points of singularity of a situation' (128; see also Radman 2018): *ecology meets multiplicity.*

The second given of ecosophy concerns the genesis of entities and their relation to the milieu. In this context, Guattari's terminological complexity and obscurity make themselves felt. 'Auto-referential existential assemblages engaging in irreversible duration' (TE: 44), for instance, is Guattari's translation of autopoietic entities. These entities (auto-referential assemblages) are the subjects of ecosophy. Even while they are, as 'living organisms', what von Foerster calls 'entropy retarders' (2003: 193), they slide down an evolutionary slope (engaging in irreversible duration).

Within an inherently processual milieu (the machinic field of existential territories), which is 'never given as object but always as intensive repetition, as piercing existential affirmation' (C: 28), individual systems emerge through processes of polarization and habit formation: 'process, which I oppose here to system or to structure, strives to capture existence in the very act of its constitution, definition and deterritorialization. This process of fixing-into-being relates only to expressive subsets that have broken out of their totalising frame and have begun to work on their own account, overcoming their referential sets and manifesting themselves as their own existential indices, processual lines of flight' (TE: 44). On the background of this processualization, 'the [ecological] event . . . becomes a nucleus of processual relay' (C: 105–6). Consistencing, therefore, always involves a deceleration of the speed of determination. This is why in *What is Philosophy?* Guattari and Deleuze talk of '"the slow beings" that we are' (36).

Guattari conceptualizes the gradual contraction of intensities into consistencies (complex compositions) as local decelerations of the infinitely fast and chaotic movements that at infinity and thus ideally define the plane of immanence as the plane of a fully virtual chaos. Stressing the process of consistencing that accompanies every deceleration of virtual intensities into actual entities, Guattari describes the formation and consolidation into temporally and spatially stable systems as a 'crystallization of intensity' (C: 30). Intensive waves become consistent when they are embodied in extensive particles. Crystals with their own 'autopoietic consistency' (78). From the very first moment of such a crystallization, the resulting consistencies are defined by the complementarity of actual and virtual components. Although they are informationally and operationally self-referential, they are, simultaneously, immanent to the energetics of 'intensive and processual becomings' (117). Like von Foerster, Guattari stresses that in consistencies, as actualizations of a virtual field of potentiality, an open, infinite chaos is reduced to a finite, complex system. 'Every species of machine is always at the junction of the finite and the infinite, at this point of negotiation between complexity and chaos' (111).

As a constant process of carefully calibrated territorialization and deterritorialization, existence is never original, but everywhere and always singular. Caught within a multiplicity of forces and vectors, its structural stability is always precarious. As René Thom (1989) shows in *Structural Stability and Morphogenesis*, it can fold, at any moment, into any number of other morphogeneses and mutations (see also C: 125). Guattari expresses the paradox of a precarious coherence that does not truly cohere in terms of music. What carries and holds the entity as a coherent system within a constantly changing landscape is neither an immaterial soul nor a material body but rather an existential motiv: 'a leitmotiv or refrain that installs itself, like an "attractor", within the sensible and significational chaos' (C: 17): *subsistence rather than substance*. Both actually and virtually, the entity is defined as a 'plural and polyphonic' (1) assemblage that has organized itself around a number of more or less stable attractors. It is a heterogeneous assemblage that moves within and thus creates a habitual field or territory. As such, is is not only open to mutation, it must constantly mutate, without, however, losing its stability. As Guattari notes, 'the different components conserve their heterogeneity, but are nevertheless captured by a refrain which couples them to the existential Territory of my self' (17). While an attractor exerts a continuous centripetal force, a refrain couples heterogeneous components – musically: the series of stanzas – paratactically and chronologically. Sub-personal, personal, cultural and cosmic habits and routines are all existential refrains that hold the subject within a spatio-temporal envelope inside an allover dynamics. At the same time, as Guattari had noted in *The Machinic Unconscious*, a refrain always needs 'ungluing' (354) from the 'general networks of signs' (111) and from unduly molarized social conditions.

Every entity, then, is a metastable formation suspended within an inherently multiplicitous chaos and, simultaneously, an arrangement of heterogeneous elements enveloped within a larger, equally heterogeneous field of attractors. The site of the entity's living is this recursive, multidimensional and fractal attractor space from within which it emerges and within which it moves: 'this object-subject of desire, like strange attractors in chaos theory, serves as an anchorage point within a phase space ... without ever being self-identical to itself, in permanent flight on a fractal line' (C: 95). Finite entities move within this space along an 'infinite twisting line of flight whose circumvolutions, like those of strange attractors, give chaos a consistency at the intersection of the actualization of finite configurations and an always possible processual recharge' (116). From within this description, which evokes quite directly von Foerster's definition of strange attractors, Guattari conceptualizes the 'complexification' of a 'deterritorialised' (19) subject that is suspended between complete chaos and total control. From within these extremes, Guattari opts for a 'controlled complexity' (115). The entity must be adequate to the state of deterministic chaos in which it is defined as a consistency within a dynamic process. The milieu, which forms a both actual and virtual envelope to this consistency is, in turn, involved in an endless becoming: 'a processual, polyphonic Being singularizable by infinitely complexifiable textures, according to the infinite speeds which animate its virtual compositions' (51).

The third given concerns Maturana and Varela's third-order structural couplings, which pertain to the relation of entities to each other and to their cultural milieu. Ultimately, Guattari aims at nothing less than a 'generalised ecology – or ecosophy ... as a science of ecosystems, as a bid for political regeneration, and as an ethical, aesthetic and analytic engagement' (91–2). This project, which will 'tend to create new systems of valorisation, a new taste for life, a new gentleness between the sexes, generations, ethnic groups, races' (92), calls for an allover ecosophic contract.

The conceptual power of Guattari's ecosophy lies in that it considers 'the machinic production of subjectivity' to be in itself neither good nor bad. It can 'work for the better or for the worse' (5). For Guattari, the aim of ecosophy can only be to keep the possibility of choice and the coefficient of change as high as possible without leaving the system's overall frame of sustainability. To ensure this, the bonds between the single elements of an assemblage must remain as elastic as possible. Too much order or too much disorder are equally detrimental. Complete order leads to fascism, while the break-up of all bonds leads to anarchy and clinical schizophrenia.

Given the overall cultural situation, ecosophy should instigate, tendentially, a controlled dismantling of too-molar structures and redefine the individual as an emergent machine. This calls for a re-complexification of a culture that has become too hard and too periodic; a controlled chaosmotic deterritorialization like the one I described in 'Expressionism in Ecology 3: Squaring Aesthetics'. One might also imagine, however, given different circumstances, ecosophy instigating a controlled assembly of molar structures. A state of complete deterritorialization is not a promise. It is as toxic as a state of complete territorialization.

Guattari's general ecology engages all levels of the entity, from the physical, the chemical and the microbiological to the artistic, the political and, ultimately, the planetary. The autopoietic reference provides a systematics for this project, especially when it is related to the field of nonlinear dynamics, which also underlies Maturana and Varela's conceptualization of evolution. To bring about a controlled chaosmotic deterritorialization implies energizing entities in order to let them escape their too-routinized attractors and to bring them into new states of metastability and disequilibrium. As Guattari's interpretation of Balthus had shown, one field that can bring about such a destabilization is art. Encounters with art can 'generate fields of the possible "far from the equilibria" of everyday life' (131). Only a controlled chaotization allows the entity to escape the artificial equilibrium ensured by all-too-attractive habits and routines. Only a softening of its coherence can lead to a re-creation and a re-invention of the individual that goes, beyond a merely cultural re-invention, towards a true becoming that involves an overall heterogenization into a 'fractal alterity' (45): 'Not only is I an other, but it is a multitude of modalities of alterity' (96).

On the last page of *Chaosmosis*, Guattari defines his overall ecosophic project of the re-singularization of consistencies by way of decomposing consistencies enough for their components to realign themselves in a predominantly aperiodic rather than a predominantly periodic manner; to make them more alive. Subjectivity 'is not a natural given any more than air or water. How do we produce it, capture it, enrich it, and permanently reinvent it in a way that renders it compatible with Universes of mutant value? How do we work for its liberation, that is, for its resingularization? Psychoanalysis, institutional analysis, film, literature, poetry, innovative pedagogies, town planning and architecture – all the disciplines will have to combine their creativity to ward off the ordeals of barbarism, the mental implosion and chaosmic spasms looming on the horizon, and transform them into riches and unforeseen pleasures, the promises of which, for all that, are all too tangible' (135). While Guattari's machinic pragmatics preclude any resolution of the world's inherent strife and thus any idealist or classical humanist teleology, the singularization and deterritorialization of contingenced, sensible modules creates entities that are truly human: *entities squared within the ecosophic fourfold*.

This is why 'it would be to misjudge Deleuze and Foucault to suspect them of taking anti-humanist positions!' (C: 9). In fact, their emphasis on the non-human part of subjectivity makes them only the more humanist. Although the proposition that any number of technological machines, amongst them 'machines of information and communication operate at the heart of human subjectivity' (4), might at first not sound like it, Guattari's project is eminent humanistic and sober: 'how can I maintain a relative sense of unicity, despite the diversity of components of subjectivation that pass through me?' (16). If a consistency is decelerated to almost zero, the results are 'normopaths – following Jean Oury's felicitous expression' (72). When certain forces become too oppressive to allow for graceful movement, the results are 'petrified systems' (68). The centripetal forces of oedipalization, for instance, sit like a 'deterministic lead cape, like a deathly fate, on the possible bifurcations of incorporeal Universes. The eternisation of desire, mentioned by Lacan, is a petrification' (74). Not only psychoanalysis, however, but any master discourse that has 'the job of overcoding all the other Universes of value' (105) functions as such a deadening attractor.

These are the stakes schizoanalysis sets against psychoanalysis and its logic of reduction and lack. 'Rather than moving in the direction of reductionist modelisations which simplify the complex, [schizoanalysis] will work towards its complexification, its processual enrichment, towards the consistency of its virtual lines of bifurcation and differentiation, in short towards its ontological heterogeneity' (61). Schizoanalysis aims at creating individuals that are once more 'capable of connecting with the singularities and mutations of our era' (106). The project is not to shield the subject from such mutations, but to open up their potentialities: 'a singularity, a rupture of sense, a cut, a fragmentation, the detachment of a semiotic content ... can originate mutant nuclei of subjectivation' (18). The aim of schizoanalysis is a 'deterritorialising complexification' (19) – a smoothing-striation complex, one might say – that brings about an emergent individual with a stress on 'processuality, irreversibility and resingularisation' (29), as well as on 'unlimited combinatories and creativity' (45): *more smooth ecology, more striated ecology*!

At a point in *Chaosmosis* at which Guattari sets the logic of 'heterogeneous machines, as envisaged from our schizonanalytical perspective' against 'the structuralist signifier [which] is always synonymous with linear discursivity' (C: 48), he brings up the notion of hypertext to illustrate one actualization of a nonlinear, rhizomatic network. As hypertexts were often theorized in reference back to the concept of the rhizome, Guattari's recourse to hypertext creates a strange feedback loop, a refolding of the notion of the rhizome onto Guattari's thought: if the rhizome functioned as a diagram of hypertextual space, that hypertext now provides a model for the inventor of the originary metaphor. Guattari, one might say, is inspired by himself.

The rhizosphere can adequately describe the discursive topology of hypertext and vice versa in that both realize a deterritorialization of time as well as space. As the hypertext is in a constant movement of reorganization and becoming, only the middle remains from the tryptich of beginning, middle and end. In other words, the hypertext no longer constitutes a stable, linear narrative structure that carries a similarly stable, linear and pre-given meaning. Rather, it is a field of kinetic energies and dynamic lines of force that are created, ad hoc, by the decisions of the readers to actualize singular paths from a set of possibilities. It is in reference to these choices that reading becomes ergodic, and, in its actualizations, inherently time- and site-specific. Singular. Within the given, coded set of possibilities, islands of narrative order emerge in an ocean of possibilities and overall potentiality. Like the rhizome, the hypertext consists, then, of a continuous re- and de-teritorialization. Like felt, or steel wool, the hypertext, like the rhizome, no longer has a clearly fixed dimension. Instead, it is a fractal surface. As Guattari describes it, 'the informational lines of hypertexts can recover a certain dynamic polymorphism and work in direct contact with referent Universes which are in no way linear and, what is more, tend to escape a logic of spatialized sets' (49). In fact, the topology of a hypertext evokes the ideal of a book that consists of one, endlessly folded, unfolding and refolding page. The computer screen, one might argue, is the instantiation of this book, and its topology forms the background to Guattari's statement that 'the time has come for hypertexts in every genre, and even for a new cognitive and sensory writing that Pierre Levy describes as "dynamic ideography." Machinic mutations understood in the largest sense, which deterritorialise subjectivity, should no longer trigger in us defensive reflexes, backward-looking nervous twitches' (96–7).

In such a new media environment, Guattari notes, thought itself will be fundamentally changed: 'the junction of informatics, telematics, and the audiovisual will perhaps allow a decisive step to be made in the direction of interactivity, towards a post-media era and, correlatively, an acceleration of the machinic return of orality. The era of the digital keyboard will soon be over; it is through speech that dialogue with machines will be initiated – not just with technical machines, but with machines of thought, sensation, and consultation . . . All of this, I repeat, provided that society changes, provided that new social, political, aesthetic and analytical practices allow us to escape from the shackles of empty speech which crush us, from the erosion of meaning which is occurring everywhere' (97). Hypertexts, as instantiations of rhizomes and vice versa, demand a continuous administration of the scene, or the situation of reading, a reading practice beyond the consumption of ready-made texts.

To not acknowledge the need and responsibility to enter and administer each and every situation leads to an alienation that is not the gentle alienation defining those within a unilateral distinction, but rather a painful rift between thought and life. In a system of unilateral distinction, conceptual and operational closure is always part of a larger participation with and in the world. At the end of his ecological 'cartography' (11) Guattari formulates a question about the possibility of a machinic humanism and about a general ecology that allows entities to move in such as way as to be able to develop, within the given stresses and tensors, their own consistencings. The question is not about complete freedom, but about creating a milieu that allows for elastic, graceful subjects: 'How do we produce [the subject], capture it, enrich it, and permanently reinvent it in a way that renders it compatible with

Universes of mutant value? How do we work for its liberation, that is, for its resingularization?' (135). How to suspend the globalized, oedipalized, ordered, decelerated, binarized and rationalized subject from the cultural balcony, like Duchamp, in his *Unhappy Readymade*, suspended a copy of Euclid's *Elements* from the balcony to make the mathematical elements once again part of the natural elements? How can one once again make the wind blow through the individual and through science? How can the individual be singularized, processualized and suspended into a ceaseless movement of complexification and becoming?

When Guattari asks for the creation of elastic and mobile ecosophic entities, he is thinking of entities that acknowledge the whole spectrum from the photonic to the psychological as part of the immanent space of the world. To set nature against culture is never helpful. Each being is woven from an infinity of heterogeneous elements. Each sentient being is a partial ecology suspended into a larger ecology. Between the two, there is a constantly changing field of resonance and reciprocal expression. Similarly, language should be suspended from the balcony in order to let it interact with the a-signifying intensities of the milieu that is the world: 'While the logic of discursive sets endeavours to completely delimit its objects, the logic of intensities, or eco-logic, is concerned only with the movement and intensity of evolutive processes' (TE: 44). In its most basic definition and its most general logic, therefore, Guattari's ecology is radically intensive and virtual. Virtual, communal waves never stop pervading the actual, singular particle. They do not stop blowing through it. The entity's living takes place within the complementarity of these two registers.

Guattari's perhaps most radical ecological move has to do with the definition of thought within the fully machinic fields of Flows, Phyla, Territories and Universes. Going even further than radical constructivism, which sees thought as formed, albeit in a 'distributed' (Varela et al. 1991: 85) and decentralized way, inside the entity, Guattari stresses that thought is itself multiplicitous and that a thought is in actual fact an ensemble of pure thoughts whose alliances form a mental plane of consistency. In fact, the perhaps most important concept of schizoecology is that there is not only a material assemblage theory, but also a virtual one. As it operates between world and entity, thought is 'a thought with "n" dimensions where everything starts to think at the same time, individuals as well as groups, the "chemical" as well as the "chromosomal" or the biosphere' (MU: 126). To be adequate to such a distributed thought is the ultimate challenge. A thought has crossed my mind, one says.

Conclusion: Right Here, Right Now

This is how the instant fuses with the world. It's in this register that the category of poetic performance, the music of John Cage, the ruptures of Zen – it doesn't matter what you call it – are found.

Félix Guattari, *Soft Subversions* (70)

GUATTARI'S FOURFOLD PROVIDES a conceptual frame within which it is possible to develop an attitude towards the world that can also be found in other places and at other times. As a conceptual crystal, it is suspended into a landscape of many other, comparable conceptual crystals. Into an ecology of other ecologies. Into a landscape of other concepts and philosophies. Other political practices. From within different circumstances, all of these conceptual crystals, many of which are ecological in nature, attempt, like Guattari, to answer the question of how to be adequate to the world. Guattari's references to and borrowings from other theoretical and practical fields enact this conceptual openness. Although schizoecology is an eigentheory, it is everywhere open to its allover conceptual and cultural milieu. Even more, it is meant to be itself part of the world's pachinko evolution. As Guattari notes in *Chaosmosis* 'who knows what will be taken up by others, for other uses, or what bifurcations they will lead to!' (126).

To return to an earlier question. If ecology aims at an adequation of the world and its creatures, how to be ecological? In order to administer the world, Guattari asks us to develop, within a multiplicity of actors and agendas, an overall ecological attitude that not only reaches from chemical research to political activism and from artistic practice to economic and political theory, but that reaches into and touches literally every moment of our lives. Although Guattari has very specific ideas about all of the above fields, his lesson does not lie in following these ideas to the letter, but rather according to their spirit. As the world's circumstances are constantly changing, modes of thought as well as modes of life should aim to be adequate to the present moment and to the present world, as well as to the specific position of wherever one is at any given moment.

It would be utopian, however, to believe that assuming an ecological stance and attitude would solve the many problems addressed by ecology. If these problems could be easily solved, chances are they would have been already. Also, if the most viable attitude is the one that is most adequate to the system of the world, what does adequate mean in this context, especially if one cannot really know how the world in and of itself operates? This attitude should factor in, therefore, one's distance to, but at the same time, one's fundamental and given immanence in the world. One's separation from, but simultaneous suspension within the constantly changing weather of the world.

Does this ecological asymmetry allow us to develop an adequate ethics? Often, the difference between science and ecology is either understood as science before ethics, or ethics before science. In fact, from the first point-of-view, the main weakness of ecological thought is often thought to be that it refuses to keep up this very distinction. This is often what is meant when science notes that ecology is holistic. Not only does it refuse to maintain discursive and conceptual borders, it is also said to give up scientific objectivity for a naïve, and thus implicitly unscientific belief in the possibility of an unproblematic and unreflected identity with an anthropomorphized world that is taken to be a friend with which one could live in peace and harmony if only the given political, cultural and scientific circumstances would allow that. At the same time, from an ecological perspective, science is often taken to be the equally naïve belief in the possibility of mastery over an inherently passive nature that exists only in order to be manipulated and administered. The danger of these misreadings is that science and ecology drift further and further apart, with people either following a scientific hard line or sentimentally reaching back to a time when life was closer to and more intimate with a living and ultimately benevolent nature. All of Guattari's work attests to the fact that such a separation is counter-productive. In fact, a marriage of science and ecology has been, from its very beginning, at the centre of the ecological project.

Consider, for instance, Jan Smuts' definition of nature as 'holistic without being a real whole' in *Holism and Evolution* (1926: 349). Holism, from this position, does not imply that the world is some kind of unity, but rather the natural tendency to form assemblages through processes of creative evolution. By way of that reference to Bergson, Smuts' holism can be aligned with Michel Serres' notion of nature as a multiplicity of ordered multiplicities and chaotic multiplicities, as well as with Deleuze's Lucretian idea of a diverse nature that is an 'infinite sum' that 'does not totalize its own elements' (1990a: 267) and with Guattari's notion of ontological complementarity and epistemological difference. As Guattari and Deleuze note in a passage from *A Thousand Plateaus* that is as much a comment on the paradoxical logic of complementarity as it is on a schizoarchitectural ecosophy, the aim is to 'arrive at the magic formula we all seek – PLURALISM = MONISM – via all the dualisms that are the enemy, an entirely necessary enemy, *the furniture we are forever rearranging*' (TP: 20–1, emphasis added). If Alistair Welchman notes that Guattari and Deleuze 'strenuously resist any concept of holism' (2008: 124), that refers only to readings that either equate holism with romanticism, or that have themselves a romantic image of holism. Rather than promote such a romanticism, Smuts refers specifically to 'the new science of Ecology', which is 'a recognition of the fact that all organisms feel the force and moulding effect of their environment as a whole' (1926: 394). This 'sensitivity to appropriate fields is not confined to humans, but is shared by animals and plants throughout organic Nature' (349). As I noted in reference to Lovelock at the beginning of my text, holism does not imply that entities have an unproblematic relation to nature, that nature is inherently friendly to its creatures, or even that nature is a whole: *polyvocal univocity; univocal polyvocity*.

Smuts insists that nature is an in itself heterogeneous assemblage that has no teleology other than to continually produce newness and variety: 'Everywhere we meet the new, which is irreducible to the old elements from which it seems to have sprung; the qualities and characters on which new stable varieties or species are founded cannot be explained on the basis of known pre-existing qualities or characters' (137). The only way in which we, as nature's nervous system or as its expressive modes, are directly connected to this world is that we are quite literally of it. The challenge is thus not to translate supposedly worldly qualities such as love and caring into human qualities, but to translate worldly quantities that impinge upon human beings and on human culture in general into adequate qualities and to develop, by way of these qualities, viable ways of a human life within the quantities. At the same time, the fear of holism should not lead to a dark romanticism that considers the world and nature only as something that we are apart from and that we can only access negatively as a fundamental lack. Neither the bright light of a holism considered as the delirium of a phantasmatic correlationism, nor the darkness of an object-oriented-ontology allow for an adequate attitude towards the *chiaroscuro* of the world: *neither nostalgic past, nor post-ecosophic future*.

Guattari's schizoecology, in its programmatic chiasm of abstract concreteness x concrete abstraction, as well as in the mutual expressionism that pertains between the world and its creatures, replaces the one-sided conceptual aesthetics of either lightness or darkness with the more complex logic of complementary: *more lightness, more darkness*. Somewhat counter-intuitively, only such a conceptual paradox allows for a nuanced, site-and time-specific, future-oriented ecosophy. As Guattari remarks in *Soft Subversions*, 'I don't know. I'm hyperoptimistic and hyperpessimistic at the same time!' (28). The aerosol of immanence forms a plane that is at the same time a plane of consistency and of composition that is defined by the interactions of in themselves disparate and heterogeneous machines. This notion of multiplicity leads directly to the notion of the infinite connectivity that underlies ecological thought. That everything is connected to everything else implies the world's fundamental site- and time-specificity. Given the singularity of every situation, a situation needs to be negotiated and administered by bringing into play all, or as many as possible, of the agents that are immanent to that specific situation. It is never enough to look at and analyse a given situation from the outside. While the notions of signification and communication are related to a transcendental semiotic practice, the project of any ecosophic cartography is to capture the given complexity and underlying multiplicity of any-situation-whatever, and to administer it from within, according to a schizoanalytic model and attitude: *squaring the situation; schizoecology*.

As any given situation is at the same time scientific, political, philosophical, biological and chemical, these registers can no longer be treated in isolation. Each situation is a complex composition. To look at a situation ecosophically is to trace the relations between the various actors and fields of reference, with the practical aim of creating a viable environment; a multiplicitous, open and elastic milieu that is conducive to processes of singularization. The ethics for such an environment are that it should be adequate to keeping the world a multiplicity of ordered and disordered multiplicities. As I noted in 'The Joy of Ecosophy', a schizoecologic ethics must be the guardian of potentiality and of the possibility of choice. The guardian of diversity and pure plurality. In this context, I tend to refer to Heinz von Foerster's 'ethical imperative' to 'act in such a way that the number of possibilities of choice increases!' (1993: 234).

In large areas of contemporary discourse the notions of animism or vitalism have become a marker of conceptual naïveté. It is, perhaps, a sign of our increasingly dark ecologies that the notion of a living world has come to be regarded as unscientific, and is often attacked as vitalist, essentialist or romantic; often, as if these three were the same. Maybe Guattari's ecosophy can give the notion of life back some of its conceptual power in that it quite openly relies on a given energy, force or *conatus*. How could it be otherwise? How could a living entity claim that its operation has nothing to do with life? Why would one maintain and defend such a weird position? How convoluted would one's argument need to be in order to circumvent the literally luminous evidence provided by an anonymous life actualized in concrete entities?

The question, it seems to me, is not whether the world is alive, but what exactly that life consists of and how it can be defined. Of how thoroughly it permeates the world and what our attitude to a living world should be in order to be adequate to its living, which is, simultaneously, our living.

An anonymous life that we express by our living. Laying out an expressive schizoecology can take many forms. It can be political, social or artistic. Take John Cage's notion that art should be an 'imitation of nature'. While this seems to reach back to the notion of mimesis, the sentence continues 'in her manner of operation' (1961: 100). It is by way of this addition that Cage's poetics become truly ecosophic. As schizoecology is 'at once applied and theoretical, ethico-political and aesthetic' (TE: 44), Guattari invites us not only to conceptualize, but also to explore and to live, at every moment of our lives, a transversal, site- and time-specific schizoecology in the extended field. Ecology, as schizoecology, is neither in the past nor in the future. For the better or for the worse, it is always *right here, right now*.

Bibliography

Adams, Henry (1961), *The Education of Henry Adams. An Autobiography*, Boston: Houghton Mifflin.

Antonioli, Manola (2018), 'What is Ecosophy?', in *Schizoanalysis and Ecosophy: Reading Deleuze and Guattari*, ed. Constantin V. Boundas, London: Bloomsbury, pp. 74–86.

Atlan, Henry (1987), 'Uncommon Finalities', in *Gaia, a Way of Knowing: Political Implications of the New Biology*, ed. William I. Thompson, Hudson: Lindisfarne Press, pp. 110–30.

Ballantyne, Andrew (2007), *Deleuze and Guattari for Architects*, New York: Routledge.

Bataille, George (1988), *The Accursed Share: An Essay on General Economy, Volume 1: Consumption*, New York: Zone Books.

Bateson, Gregory (1991), *A Sacred Unity: Further Steps to an Ecology of Mind*, ed. Rodney E. Donaldson, New York: Harper Collins.

Bateson, Gregory (2002), *Mind and Nature: A Necessary Unity*, Creskill: Hampton Press.

Bellour, Raymond (2011), 'Going to the Cinema with Félix Guattari and Daniel Stern', in *The Guattari Effect*, ed. Eric Alliez and Andrew Goffey, London: Continuum, pp. 220–34.

Berardi, Franco (2008), *Félix Guattari: Thought, Friendship, and Visionary Cartography*, trans. and ed. Giuseppina Mecchia and Charles J. Stivale, Basingstoke: Palgrave Macmillan.

Berressem, Hanjo (2014), 'Motel Architectures', in *Display | Dispositiv. Ästhetische Ordnungen*, ed. Ursula Frohne, Lilian Haberer and Annette Urban, Paderborn: Wilhelm Fink Verlag, pp. 305–20.

Berressem, Hanjo (2015), 'Vibes: Tape-Recording the Acoustic Unconscious', in *America and the Musical Unconscious*, ed. Julius Greve and Sascha Pöhlmann. New York/Dresden: Atropos Press, pp. 152–200.

Böhme, Hartmut, (1997), 'Die vier Elemente: Feuer Wasser Erde Luft', in *Vom Menschen. Handbuch der Historischen Anthropolgie*, ed. Christoph Wulf, Weinheim/Basel: Beltz, pp. 17–46.

Borges, Jorge Luis (1962), 'The Library of Babel', in *Ficciones*, New York: Grove Press, pp. 79–88.

Butler, Edward P. (2008), 'Hercules of the Surface: Deleuzian Humanism and Deep Ecology', in *An [Un]Likely Alliance: Thinking Environment[s] with Deleuze/Guattari*, ed. Bernd Herzogenrath, Newcastle upon Tyne: Cambridge Scholars Publishing, pp. 139–58.

Cache, Bernard (1995), *Earth Moves: The Furnishing of Territories*, ed. Michael Speaks, John Wheeler and W. H. Zurek, trans. Anne Boyman, Cambridge, MA: MIT Press.

Cage, John (1961), *Silence: Lectures and Writings*, Middletown: Wesleyan University Press.

Castoriadis, Cornelius (2000), 'Entretien Cornelius Castoriadis et Francisco Varela', in Cornelius Castoriadis, *Post-scriptum sur l'insignifiance: Entretiens avec Daniel Mermet, suivi de dialogue*, Paris: Éditions de l'Aube, pp. 97–120.

Conley, Verena Andermatt (1997), *Ecopolitics: The Environment in Poststructuralist Thought*, London: Routledge.

Conley, Verena Andermatt (2009), 'Artists or "Little Soldiers?" Félix Guattari's Ecological Paradigms', in *Deleuze/Guattari & Ecology*, ed. Bernd Herzogenrath, Basingstoke: Palgrave Macmillan, pp. 116–28.

Cooper, Gregory J. (2003), *The Science of the Struggle for Existence: On the Foundations of Ecology*, Cambridge: Cambridge University Press.

Cramer, Konrad (1994), 'Einfachheit, Perzeption und Apperzeption', in *Leibniz und die Frage nach der Subjektivität*, Renato Cristin, Stuttgart: Franz Steiner Verlag, pp. 19–46.

Dedekind, Richard (1984), *Essays on the Theory of Numbers*, La Salle: The Open Court Publishing Company.

DeLanda, Manuel (2002), *Intensive Science and Virtual Philosophy*, London: Bloomsbury.

Deleuze, Gilles (1988), *Spinoza: Practical Philosophy*, trans. Robert Hurley, San Francisco: City Lights.

Deleuze, Gilles (1989), *Cinema 2: The Time-Image*, trans. Hugh Tomlinson and Robert Galeta, Minneapolis: University of Minnesota Press.

Deleuze, Gilles (1990a), *The Logic of Sense*, trans. Mark Lester and Charles Stivale, New York: Columbia University Press.

Deleuze, Gilles (1990b), 'Lucretius and the Clinamen', in *The Logic of Sense*, trans. Mark Lester and Charles Stivale, New York: Columbia University Press, pp. 266–79.
Deleuze, Gilles (1994), *Difference and Repetition*, trans. Paul R. Patton, New York: Columbia University Press.
Deleuze, Gilles (1995), *Negotiations: 1972–1990*, trans. Martin Joughin, New York: Columbia University Press.
Deleuze, Gilles (2001), *The Fold: Leibniz and the Baroque*, trans. Tom Conley, Minneapolis: University of Minnesota Press.
Deleuze, Gilles (2004 [1973]), 'Five Propositions on Psychoanalysis', in *Desert Islands and Other Texts*, ed. David Lapoujade, trans. Mike Taormina, New York: Semiotext(e), pp. 274–80.
Deleuze, Gilles (2006), *Foucault*, trans. Séan Hand, London: Continuum.
Deleuze, Gilles (2007), 'For Félix', in *Two Regimes of Madness*, ed. David Lapoujade, trans. Ames Hodges and Mike Taormina, New York: Semiotext(e), pp. 382–3.
Deleuze, Gilles and Claire Parnet (2002), *Dialogues II*, trans. Barbara Habberjam, Eliot Ross Albert and Hugh Tomlinson, New York: Columbia University Press.
Dillard, Annie (1976), *Pilgrim at Tinker Creek*, London: Picador.
Elliott, Paul (2012), *Guattari Reframed: Interpreting Key Thinkers for the Arts*, New York: I. B. Tauris.
Foerster, Heinz von (1993), *Wissen und Gewissen: Versuch einer Brücke*, ed. Siegfried J. Schmidt, Frankfurt a.M.: Suhrkamp.
Foerster, Heinz von (2003), *Understanding Understanding: Essays on Cybernetics and Cognition*. New York: Springer.
Foerster, Heinz von (2014), *The Beginning of Heaven and Earth Has No Name. Seven Days with Second-Order Cybernetics*, ed. Albert Müller and Karl. H. Müller, trans. Elinor Rooks and Michael Kasenbacher, New York: Fordham University Press.
Freud, Sigmund (1954 [1917]), 'Project for a Scientific Psychology', in Sigmund Freud, *The Origins of Psycho-analysis: Letters to Wilhelm Fliess, Drafts and Notes, 1887–1902*, ed. Marie Bonaparte, Anna Freud and Ernst Kris, trans. Eric Mosbacher and James Strachey, London: Imago, pp. 347–445.
Genosko, Gary (2002), *Félix Guattari: An Aberrant Introduction*, New York: Continuum.
Genosko, Gary (2009), Félix Guattari: A Critical Introduction, New York: Pluto.
Genosko, Gary (2015), 'Happy Depression: Franco Berardi and the Unpaid Bills of Desire', in *Contemporary Italian Political Philosophy*, ed. Antonio Calcagno, Albany: SUNY Press, pp. 199–216.
Glasersfeld, Ernst von (2011), 'Eine Einführung', in *Schlüsselwerke des Konstruktivismus*, ed. Bernhard Pörksen, Wiesbaden: VS Verlag.
Gleick, James (1987), *Chaos: Making a New Science*, New York: Viking.

Goddard, Michael (2013), 'Félix and Alice in Wonderland: The Encounter Between Guattari and Berardi and the Post-Media Era', in *Provocative Alloys*, ed. Clemens Apprich, Josephine Berry Slater, Anthony Iles and Oliver Lerone Schultz, Lüneburg: Post-Media Lab & Mute Books & PML Books, pp. 44–61.

Grafton, Anthony, Glenn W. Most and Salvatore Settis (eds) (2010), *The Classical Tradition*, Cambridge, MA: Harvard University Press.

Guattari, Félix (1984a), *Molecular Revolution: Psychiatry and Politics*, trans. Rosemary Sheet, Harmondsworth: Penguin.

Guattari, Félix (1984b), 'Transversality', in *Molecular Revolution: Psychiatry and Politics*, trans. Rosemary Sheet, Harmondsworth: Penguin, pp. 12–23.

Guattari, Félix (1989), *The Three Ecologies*, trans. Ian Pindar and Paul Sutton, London: Athlone Press.

Guattari, Félix (1992), 'Drawing, Cities, Nomads', in *Semiotext(e) Architecture*, ed. Hraztan Zeitlian, Cambridge, MA: MIT Press, distr. for Semiotext(e), pp. 118G1–125G8.

Guattari, Félix (1995), *Chaosmosis: An Ethico-Aesthetic Paradigm*, trans. Paul Bains and Julian Pefanis, Bloomington and Indianapolis: Indiana University Press.

Guattari, Félix (1996), 'Microphysics of Power/Micropolitics of Desire', in *The Guattari Reader*, ed. Gary Genosko, Oxford: Blackwell, pp. 172–81.

Guattari, Félix (1998), 'La "Grille"', *Chimères* 34, Autumn, pp. 1–14.

Guattari, Félix (2006), *The Anti-Oedipus Papers*, ed. Stéphane Nadaud, trans. Kélina Gotman, New York: Semiotext(e).

Guattari, Félix (2007), 'Semiotic Energetics', in *Molecular Revolution in Brazil*, ed. Suely Rolnik, Los Angeles: Semiotext(e), pp. 392–402.

Guattari, Félix (2009a), 'Entering the Post-Media Era', in *Soft Subversions: Texts and Interviews 1977–1975*, ed. Sylvère Lotringer, trans. Chet Wiener and Emily Wittman, Los Angeles: Semiotext(e), pp. 301–6.

Guattari, Félix (2009b), 'Postmodern Deadlock and Post-Media Transition', in *Soft Subversions: Texts and Interviews 1977–1975*, ed. Sylvère Lotringer, trans. Chet Wiener and Emily Wittman, Los Angeles: Semiotext(e), pp. 291–300.

Guattari, Félix (2009c), *Soft Subversions: Texts and Interviews 1977–1985*, ed. Sylvère Lotringer, trans. Chet Wiener and Emily Wittman, Los Angeles: Semiotext(e).

Guattari, Félix (2011), *The Machinic Unconscious: Essays in Schizoanalysis*, trans. Taylor Adkins, Los Angeles: Semiotext(e).

Guattari, Félix (2013a), *Schizoanalytic Cartographies*, trans. Andrew Goffey, London: Bloomsbury.

Guattari, Félix (2013b), 'Cracks in the Street', in *Schizoanalytic Cartographies*, trans. Andrew Goffey, London: Bloomsbury, pp. 253–62.

Guattari, Félix (2013c), 'Refrains and Existential Affects', in *Schizoanalytic Cartographies*, trans. Andrew Goffey. London: Bloomsbury, pp. 203–14.

Guattari, Félix (2013d), 'Towards a Post-Media Era', trans. Alya Sebti and Clemens Apprich, in *Provocative Alloys*, ed. Clemens Apprich, Josephine Berry Slater, Anthony Iles and Oliver Lerone Schultz, Lüneburg: Post-Media Lab & Mute Books & PML Books, pp. 26–7.

Guattari, Félix (2015a), 'The Architectural Machines of Shin Takamatsu', in *Machinic Eros: Writings on Japan*, ed. Gary Genosko and Jay Hetrick, Minneapolis: Univocal, pp. 77–86.

Guattari, Félix (2015b), 'Translocal: Tetsuo Kogawa Interviews Félix Guattari', in *Machinic Eros: Writings on Japan*, ed. Gary Genosko and Jay Hetrick, Minneapolis: Univocal, pp. 17–42.

Guattari, Félix and Gilles Deleuze (1977), *Anti-Oedipus. Capitalism and Schizophrenia 1*, trans. Robert Hurley, Mark Seem and Helen R. Lane, New York: Viking.

Guattari, Félix and Gilles Deleuze (1986), *Kafka: Toward a Minor Literature*, trans. Dana Polan, Minneapolis: University of Minnesota Press.

Guattari, Félix and Gilles Deleuze (1994), *What is Philosophy?*, trans. Hugh Tomlinson and Graham Burchell, New York: Columbia University Press.

Guattari, Félix and Gilles Deleuze (2005), *A Thousand Plateaus: Capitalism and Schizophrenia 2*, trans. Brian Massumi, Minneapolis: University of Minnesota Press.

Guattari, Félix and Suely Rolnik (2007), *Molecular Revolution in Brazil*, Los Angeles: Semiotext(e).

Haeckel, Ernst (1866), *Generelle Morphologie der Organismen. Allgemeine Grundzüge der organischen Formen-Wissenschaft, mechanische Begründet durch die von Charles Darwin reformirte Descendenz-Theorie. Volume II: Allgemeine Entwick-elungsgeschichte der Organismen*, Berlin: Georg Reimer.

Haeckel, Ernst (1917), *Kristallseelen: Studien über das Anorganische Leben*, Leipzig: Alfred Kröner.

Hansen, Mark B. N. (2009), 'System-Environment Hybrids', in *Emergence and Embodiment: New Essays on Second-Order Systems Theory*, ed. Bruce Clarke and Mark B. N. Hansen, Durham, NC: Duke University Press, pp. 113–42.

Ivain, Gilles (Ivan Chtcheglov) (2006a [1953]), 'Formulary for a New Urbanism', ed. and trans. Ken Knabb, Berkeley: Bureau of Public Secrets, pp. 1–8.

Ivain, Gilles (Ivan Chtcheglov) (2006b [1958]), 'Preliminary Problems in Constructing a Situation', ed. and trans. Ken Knabb, Berkeley: Bureau of Public Secrets, pp. 49–52.

James, Henry (1984), 'The Art of Fiction', in *Partial Portraits*, New York: Macmillan, pp. 386–404.

James, William (1890), *The Principles of Psychology*, 2 Vols, New York: Henry Holt.

James, William (1976), *The Works of William James, Vol. 3: Essays in Radical Empiricism*, ed. Frederick H. Burkhardt, Fredson Bowers and Ignas K. Skrupskelis, Cambridge, MA: Harvard University Press.

Jonas, Hans (1984), *The Imperative of Responsibility: In Search of an Ethics for the Technological Age*, Chicago: University of Chicago Press.
Kauffman, Stuart (1993), *The Origins of Order: Self-Organization and Selection in Evolution*, Oxford: Oxford University Press.
Kauffman, Stuart (2000), *Investigations*, Oxford: Oxford University Press.
Klein, Felix (1928), *Vorlesungen über Nicht-Euklidische Geometrie*, Berlin: Springer Verlag.
Lacan, Jacques (1977), 'Seminar on "The Purloined Letter"', in *Écrits: A Selection*, trans. Bruce Fink, New York: W. W. Norton & Co., pp. 11–48.
Lacan, Jacques (1988), *Radiophonie Television*, Berlin: Weinheim Quadriga.
Lacan, Jacques (2007), *Écrits*, trans. Bruce Fink in collaboration with H. Fink and R. Grigg, New York: W. W. Norton & Co.
Lazzarato, Maurizio (2014), *Signs and Machines: Capitalism and the Production of Subjectivity*, Los Angeles: Semiotext(e).
Le Corbusier (1986), *Towards a New Architecture*, New York: Dover Publications.
Leibniz, Gottfried Wilhelm (1925), *The Monadology and Other Philosophical Writings*, ed. and trans. Robert Latta, Oxford: Oxford University Press.
Leibniz, Gottfried Wilhelm (1978 [1875–90]), *Die philosophischen Schriften von Gottfried Wilhelm Leibniz*, ed. C. I. Gerhardt, 7 vols, Berlin: Weidmann, repr. Hildesheim: Georg Olms.
Lorenz, Edward N. (1993), *The Essence of Chaos*, Seattle: University of Washington Press.
Lovelock, James (1975), 'The Quest for Gaia', *New Scientist* 65: 935, 6 February, pp. 304–6.
Lovelock, James (2000), *Gaia: A New Look on Earth*, Oxford: Oxford University Press.
Lucretius (1973), *About Reality (De Rerum Natura)*, trans. Philip F. Wooby, New York: Philosophical Library.
Luhmann, Niklas (2000), *Art as a Social System*, trans. Eva M. Knodt, Stanford: Stanford University Press.
Mach, Ernst (1914), *The Analysis of Sensations and the Relation of the Physical to the Psychic*, trans. C. M. Williams, Chicago and London: The Open Court Publishing Company.
Margulis, Lynn and Dorion Sagan (1995), *What is Life?*, New York: Simon & Schuster.
Matthiessen, Peter (1996), *The Snow Leopard*, London: Penguin.
Maturana, Humberto (1987), 'Everything is Said By an Observer', in *Gaia, a Way of Knowing: Political Implications of the New Biology*, ed. William I. Thompson, Hudson: Lindisfarne Press, pp. 65–82.
Maturana, Humberto (1988), 'Reality: The Search for Objectivity or the Quest for a Compelling Argument', *The Irish Journal of Psychology* 9:1, pp. 25–82.

Maturana, Humberto (1994), *Was ist Erkennen?* Munich: Piper.

Maturana, Humberto and Francisco Varela (1998), *The Tree of Knowledge: The Biological Roots of Human Understanding*, trans. Robert Paolucci, Boston: Shambhala Publications.

Merrill, Thomas F. (1982), *The Poetry of Charles Olson: A Primer*, London: University of Delaware Press.

Möbius, August Ferdinand (1886), *Gesammelte Werke*, ed. F. Klein and S. Hirzel Leipzig, Vol. 2, Cambridge, MA: Harvard University Press.

Morton, Timothy (2009), *Ecology without Nature: Rethinking Environmental Aesthetics*, Cambridge, MA: Harvard University Press.

Morton, Timothy (2016), *Dark Ecology: For a Logic of Future Coexistence*, New York: Columbia University Press.

Muir, John (1911), *My First Summer in the Sierra*, Boston: Houghton Mifflin Harcourt.

Nail, Thomas (2018), *Lucretius I: An Ontology of Motion*, Edinburgh: Edinburgh University Press.

Negri, Antonio (2003), 'Kairòs', in *Time for Revolution*, trans. M. Mandarini, London: Continuum, pp. 151–82.

Nietzsche (1873), 'Über Wahrheit und Lüge im aussermoralischen Sinne', in *Friedrich Nietzsche: Sämtliche Werke. Kritische Studienausgabe, Band 1*, ed. Giorgio Colli and Mazzino Montinari, Berlin and New York: De Gruyter, pp. 875–90.

O'Sullivan, Simon (2006), *Art Encounters Deleuze and Guattari: Thought Beyond Representation*, New York: Palgrave Macmillan.

O'Sullivan, Simon (2012), *On the Production of Subjectivity: Five Diagrams of the Finite–Infinite Relation*, New York: Palgrave Macmillan.

Pelbart, Peter Pál (2011), 'The Deterritorialized Unconscious', in *The Guattari Effect*, ed. Eric Alliez and Andrew Goffey, London: Continuum, pp. 68–83.

Plotnitsky, Arkady (2006), 'Chaosmologies: Quantum Field Theory, Chaos and Thought in Deleuze and Guattari's *What is Philosophy?*', *Paragraph* 29:2, pp. 40–56.

Querrien, Anne (2011), 'Maps and Refrains of a Rainbow Panther', in *The Guattari Effect*, ed. Eric Alliez and Andrew Goffey, London: Continuum, pp. 84–98.

Radman, Andrej (2018), 'Double Bind: On Material Ethics', in *Schizoanalysis and Ecosophy: Reading Deleuze and Guattari*, ed. Constantin V. Boundas, London: Bloomsbury, pp. 241–56.

Rosen, Steven M. (1994), *Science, Paradox, and the Moebius Principle: The Evolution of a 'Transcultural' Approach to Wholeness*, Albany: SUNY Press.

Rovelli, Carlo (2018), *The Order of Time*, New York: Riverhead Books.

Rutherford, Donald (1995), *Leibniz and the Rational Order of Nature*, Cambridge: Cambridge University Press.

Ruyer, Raymond (1952), *Neo-Finalisme*, Paris: Presses Universitaires de France.

Sauvagnargues, Anne (2011), 'A Schizoanalytic Knight on the Chessboard of Politics', in *The Guattari Effect*, ed. Eric Alliez and Andrew Goffey, London: Continuum, pp. 172–85.

Schneider, Christina (2001), *Leibniz' Metaphysik: Ein Formaler Zugang*, München: Philosophia Verlag.

Schrödinger, Erwin (1935), 'The Present Situation in Quantum Mechanics', in *Quantum Theory and Measurement*, ed. John Wheeler and W. H. Zurek, Princeton: Princeton University Press, pp. 152–67.

Schrödinger, Erwin (1976), 'Mind and Matter', in *What Is Life?*, Cambridge: Cambridge University Press, pp. 93–164.

Serres, Michel (1968), *Le système de Leibniz et ses modèles mathématiques System of Leibniz, Tome I: Étoiles, Tome II: Schémas – Point*, Paris: Presses Universitaires de Paris.

Serres, Michel (1983), *Hermes: Literature, Science, Philosophy*, ed. Josué V. Harari and David F. Bell, Baltimore: Johns Hopkins University Press.

Serres, Michel (1994), *Hermes V: Die Nord-West Passage*, trans. Michael Bischoff, Berlin: Merve Verlag.

Serres, Michel (1995), *Genesis*, trans. G. James and J. Nielson, Ann Arbor: University of Michigan Press.

Serres, Michel (2000), *The Birth of Physics*, ed. David Webb, trans. Jack Hawkes, Manchester: Clinamen Press.

Serres, Michel and Bruno Latour (1995), *Conversations on Science, Culture, and Time*, trans. Roxanne Lapidus, Ann Arbor: University of Michigan Press.

Simondon, Gilbert (1980), *On the Mode of Existence of Technical Objects*, trans. Ninian Mellamphy, Ontario: University of Western Ontario Press.

Smuts, J. C. (1926), *Holism and Evolution*, London: Macmillan & Co.

Stauffer, Robert C. (1957), 'Haeckel, Darwin, and Ecology', *The Quarterly Review of Biology* 32:2, pp. 138–44.

Thom, René (1989), *Structural Stability and Morphogenesis: An Outline of a General theory of Models*, trans. David H. Fowler and Addison-Wesley, Reading: Westview Press.

Thompson, William I. (ed.) (1987), *Gaia, a Way of Knowing: Political Implications of the New Biology*, Hudson: Lindisfarne Press.

Thoreau, Henry David (1995), *Walden; or, Life in the Woods*, New York: Dover Publications.

Tinnell, John (2012), 'Transversalising the Ecological Turn: Four Components of Félix Guattari's Ecosophical Perspective', *Deleuze Studies* 6:3, pp. 357–88.

Tödliche Doris, Die (2019), quoted in *Mutant Sounds*, at http://mutant-sounds.blogspot.com/2007/02/die-toedliche-doris-same1982sechs1986lp.html.

Varela, Francisco (1987), 'Laying Down a Path in Walking', in *Gaia, a Way of Knowing: Political Implications of the New Biology*, ed. William I. Thompson, Hudson: Lindisfarne Press, pp. 48–64.

Varela, Francisco, Eleanor Rosch and Evan Thompson (1991), *The Embodied Mind: Cognitive Science and Human Experience*, Cambridge, MA: MIT Press.

Wallace, David Foster (2003), *Everything and More: A Compact History of Infinity*, New York: W. W. Norton & Company.

Watson, Janell (2011), *Guattari's Diagrammatic Thought: Writing Between Lacan and Deleuze*, London: Continuum.

Watson, Janell (2012), 'Culture as Existential Territory: Ecosophic Homelands for the Twenty-first Century', *Deleuze Studies* 6:2, pp. 306–27.

Weeks, Jeffrey R. (1985), *The Shape of Space: How to Visualize Surfaces and Three-Dimensional Manifolds*, New York: Marcel Dekker.

Welchman, Alistair (2008), 'Deleuze and Deep Ecology', in *An [Un]Likely Alliance: Thinking Environment[s] with Deleuze/Guattari*, ed. Bernd Herzogenrath, Newcastle upon Tyne: Cambridge Scholars Publishing, pp. 116–38.

Weyl, Herman (1949), *Philosophy of Mathematics and Natural Science*, Princeton: Princeton University Press.

Whitehead, Alfred North (1978), *Process and Reality: An Essay in Cosmology*, ed. David R. Griffin, and Donald W. Sherburne, New York: The Free Press.

Wilden, Anthony (1972), *System and Structure: Essays in Communication and Exchange*, London: The Tavistock Institute.

Žižek, Slavoj (2004), *Organs Without Bodies: Deleuze and Consequences*, New York: Routledge Classics.

Index

accelerationism
    dark ecology, capitalism, 184
    ecology, 128
    rhetoric of, 141
activism
    Guattari, 2, 9
    ecology, 233
adaptation
    Maturana and Varela, 220
    structural coupling, 98
adequation
    actual and virtual, 166
    architectural, 198, 203, 206
    creatures and world, 3, 150, 233
    ecology, 31
    extensity and intensity, 151–2
    false and true, 162
    fourfold, 122
    non-metric and metric, 6
    solar energy, 187
    the given, 182
aerosol, aerosolic
    Balthus, 114
    chaos, 224
    digital, 121
    ecosophy, 56
    fourfold, 45–50, 55
    Leibniz, 162, 165, 168
    phyla, 58, 75–6, 78, 123
    plane of immanence, 42, 63, 68–9, 124, 147, 235
    time, 131, 146
    unconscious, 178
    Venus, 34–5
aesthetics
    architectural, 204
    Balthus, 112, 114–18
    fourfold, 109
    Guattari's, 53,
    La Borde, 20
    light, 235
    mimesis, 175
    molecular, 141
    Proust, 91
    topology, 154
æther
    aerosol, 45
    elements, the, 203
    plane of immanence, 124
affect, affective
    abstract machine, 206
    Aion, 132–3
    aisthesis, 166
    architecture, 194
    art, 50
    Bacon, 56
    Balthus, 115–17
    body and mind, 108
    cartography of, 202
    colour, 102
    ecology, 224
    fourfold, aerosolic, 56
    integration, 162
    intensity, 178, 192
    Lacan's imaginary, 112
    language, 79
    Lazzarato, 210
    life, 168
    light, 187
    maps, 13
    media, 123
    Morton, 184
    new, 205
    plane of consistency, 196
    plane of immanence, 216
    Proust, 139–40

psychoanalysis, 215
refrain, 90, 137
singularization and transversalization, 139
space, 155
speed of, 142, 144, 147
synapse, 150–1
Territories, 60, 80–3, 88, 114–15, 220
affiliation, speed of determination, 67
Aion, aionic
   actual and virtual, 148–9
   clinamen, 37
   fourfold, 129–33
   given and giving, fractalization, 146–7
   synapse, 151
aisthesis
   affect, 166
   Baumgarten, 115
allopoietic, machines, 163
Althusser, Louis, interpellation, 116
analog
   clinamen, 41
   cut and line, 157
   digital, 158, 169
   Flow, 48, 77
   fractalization, 148
   iconicity, 195
   indifference, 42
   intensity, 18
   media ecology, media studies, 120–4, 175
   minor science, 38
   monad, 161
   neurons, 157
   quantity and quality, 151
   schizoanalysis, 166
   synapse, 149
   time, 37
   see also digital
années d'hiver, les années divers, 2
antecedence
   Flows and Phyla, 73
   fluid over solid, 48
anthropocene
   ecology, 16
   dark ecology, 184
anticapitalism
   dark ecology, 184
   Guattari, 214
   see also capitalism
any-situation-whatever, fourfold, 52, 104
a-signifying semiotics
   capitalism, 210–13
   Freud, 106
   signaletic material, 17
   signifier, 25–6
   structural coupling, 99
Aquinas, Thomas, 3
ars combinatorial, language, 175
Arte Povera, Negri, 134
assemblages of enunciation
   abstract machine, 206

complementarity, 122
ecology, 54
ecosophy, 225
monad, 159
partial observers, 176
processualization, 18
Proust, 138–9
schizoanalysis, 19, 217
subject, 53
Universes, 93
atom / atomic / atomism
   abstract machine, 192
   aerosol, 46–7, 49, 76, 78
   assemblage, 15
   closed systems, 27
   Lucretius, 30–6, 38–9, 142
   media, 21, 175–6
   monad, 159–60, 164–5
   networks, 60
   Phyla, 58
   space, 154
attractor
   cultural, 219
   fourfold, 43, 88, 94–5, 101, 103, 135, 137, 148
   Lacan, 112
   refrain, 226
   stable states, 221, 228–9
   strange, 118, 204, 227
attribute
   actual and virtual, 24
   language, 100
   media and forms, 174
   the false and truth, 185
   thought and extension, 55, 73
autopoiesis
   ecosophy, 19
   evolution, 220
   Maturana and Varela, 14
   mechanosphere, 204

Bacon, Francis, informal diagram, 55–6, 197
Ballantyne, Andrew, Deleuze and Guattarian architecture, 199–201
Balthus (Balthasar Klossowski de Rola)
   architecture, 203
   chaosmotic deterritorialization, 228
   fourfold, 109–18, 123
   fractal space, 156, 174, 178–9
   Proust, 139–40
Balzac, Honoré de, 'The Unknown Masterpiece', 31
Barthes, Roland, grain of the voice, 174
Bataille, George
   The Accursed Share: An Essay on General Economy, 133–4
   cosmic ecology, 185–6
Bateson, Gregory
   analog and digital, 169
   ecology, 7, 161
   integration, 157

Mind and Nature: A Necessary Unity, 14, 43
  plateaus, 170
  second-order cybernetics, 11
Baumgarten, Alexander Gottlieb, *aisthesis*, 115
Beckett, Samuel, deterritorialization, 185
Bergson, Henri
  analog and digital, 158
  Creative Evolution, 234
  temps and durée, 130
bifurcation
  abstract machine, 150
  Guattari's thought, 233
  molecular, 91
  multiplicity, 136
  oedipalization, 229
  plane of consistencies, plane of immanence, 67
  potentiality, 64
  schizoanalytic objects, 27
  singularization, 79
  Universes, 144
black box
  Schrödinger's cat, 71
  Serres, the unconscious, 177–8, 220
body without organs
  ecology, 196
  Flows, 46
  intensity, 155, 182
  naked monads, 162
  plane of immanence, 216
  schizo, 209, 213
  sexuality, 218
  time, 144
Borde, La
  architecture of, 207
  capitalism, 213
  grid (*la grille*), 222
  Guattari's career, 2
  Guattari's death, 1
  ecosophy at, 20–1
  implicit ecology of, 10
  *path*ologies, 97
  transversality, 74
  video technology, 120
Borges, Jorge Luis, 'On Exactitude in Science', 53–4
breaching (*Bahnung*), Freud's 'Project for a Scientific Psychology', 106
Brownian motion
  Serres and Guattari, 64
  smooth space, 171–2
Büchner, Karl Georg, 'Lenz', 110

Cache, Bernard
  architecture, 205
  topology, 153
Cage, John, poetics, 233, 236–7
capitalism
  accelerationism, 184
  anticapitalism, 214
  Capitalism and Schizophrenia, 96
  cramp, 19
  ecosophy, 185
  fractalization, 135
  Integrated World Capitalism, 8, 28, 134, 213
  Lazzarato, 210–13
  psychoanalysis, 26
  Negri, 134
  nomadism, 199
  schizoanalysis, 208–9
  see also anticapitalism; Integrated World Capitalism
Cartesian
  Chronos, 130
  diagram, 198
  diver, 115
  grid, 153
  space, 34, 152
  subject, 18
  thought, 155
Castoriadis, Cornelius, 101, 109
catalyst, Balthus, 116–17
chaos theory
  deterministic chaos, 224
  nonlinear dynamics, 29
  order and disorder, 34
  strange attractors, 227
chaosophy, ecosophy, 4
chiaroscuro
  light and dark, 235
  particles and waves, 130
Chronos
  Aion, 149
  clinamen, 37
  fourfold, 129–33
  synapse, 151
clinamen
  Deleuze, 30
  fourfold, 52
  Leibniz, 160
  Lucretius, 32–43
  space, 154
  speed of determination, 142
computer-aided subjectivity, 128
conatus
  ecosophy, 236
  Lucretius, 160
  monads, 159
concrete universal
  abstract machine, 191
  code, 39
  Universes, 93
constructivism
  abstract machine, 192
  crystals, 24, 27
  Guattari, 11–18
  La Borde, 20
  linguistic, 109
  measurement, 71
  plane of immanence and consistencies, 65–6
  radical, 231

schizoecology, 10, 184
space and time, 126
unconscious, 109
contingencing, point of
    actual and virtual, 14
    territorialization and deterritorialization, 86
contingency
    being-there, 166
    constructivism, 11
    modules, 104
    plane of consistency, 77
    separability, 174
    zone of, 103
Cramer, Konrad, 167
Cronenberg, David, *The Fly*, 101
crossroads, *carrefours d'agencements*
    abstract machine, 188
    fourfold, 1, 2, 74
crystal, crystallization
    abstract machine, 140, 190, 192–3
    actual and virtual, 69
    amorphous, 142
    brain and mind, 150
    clinamen, 42–3
    existential, 81, 139, 211
    expressionism, 86
    fourfold, 233
    intensity, 226
    language, 120
    Leibniz, 160
    Lucretius, 30–1, 34
    of the possible, 189
    ontology of, 23–8, 93
    photonics, 186
    processes of, 21
    Proustian Event, 139
    refrain, 146, 215
    resonance, 222
    schizoanalytics, 221
    space, 154
    synaptic moment, 148, 151
    Venus, 48
cut-out
    abstract machine, 115
    milieu, 208
    perception and cognition, 13, 89
    Territories, 95
cybernetics
    causal complexity, 86
    Foerster, von, 11
    observer, 16

dark precursor
    Deleuze, 175
    ecology, 98
    probe head, 221
    structural couplings, 99
Darwin, Charles, nature's polity, 7
De Chirico, Giorgio, Balthus, 115, 178
Dedekind, Richard, Dedekind cut, 171, 173

Deleuze, Gilles, 1–2, 4–5, 10, 14, 17, 23, 29–30, 45–7, 54–6, 58, 62, 64, 67, 75–6, 80, 91, 96, 101–3, 109–10, 131–2, 141, 151, 162, 175, 187, 189, 193, 204, 228
Deleuze Studies
    abstract machine, 194
    smooth and striated space, 96
Derrida, Jacques
    dark ecology, 183
    psychoanalysis, 54
    signifier, 109
design, designed
    architecture, 194, 201, 203
    computer-aided, 128
    unconscious, 177
determinability
    infinite, 77, 94, 104
    minimal, 93
    schizo, 216, 219
    sexuality, 218
    speed of, 67–8, 141–7, 149, 156, 166, 209, 215
deterministic chaos
    chaos and control, 227
    Lucretius, 30
    pink noise, 33
    pure chaos, 66
    sensitivity to initial conditions, 136
    virtual, 224
    see also chaos theory
deterritorialization
    abstract machines, 76, 188–9, 193, 196
    architecture, 200
    Beckett, 185
    capitalism, 210, 212–13
    chaosmotic, 118, 227–8
    existential registers, 90
    La Borde, 222
    media, 119
    perceptual apparatus, 157
    plane of immanence, 63, 74, 94
    Planomenon, 195
    process, 225–6
    Proust, 140
    rhizome, 79
    schizo, 209
    schizoanalysis, 207, 214
    synapse, 151
    territorialization, 66, 85, 107
    time, 125, 13
    topology, 174
    transversality, 77
    Universes and Phyla, 93, 144, 149
diagram
    abstract machine, 101, 189
    architecture, 194, 197
    deceleration, 142
    fourfold, 53–6
    plane of immanence, 64, 160
digital
    analog, 169, 175

252 | INDEX

data, 18, 161
difference and indifference, 42
discursivity, 195
distinctions, 77
either-or operations, 61
Flows, 48
hypertext, 230
iconic, 112
integration, 157–8
media, 120–4
noise, 166
royal science, 38
synapse, 149, 151
thought and life, 41
time, *clinamen*, 37–8, 130, 148
see also analog
Dillard, Annie, 13
dispersion
  aerosol, 45–6
  Brownian, 64
  monads, 146
  Phyla, 131
  Proustian refrain, 140
  subjectivity, 116
diversity
  diagram, 52
  difference, 58
  ethics, 41, 236
  les années divers, 2
  nature, 18, 94, 191, 224
  plane of, 11
  plane of immanence, 45, 63, 65
  subjectivation, 228
Duchamp, Marcel
  Great Glass, 106
  Unhappy Readymade, 231
duration
  capitalism, 210
  Chronos and Aion, 151
  continuity, 85
  embodied time, 36–7, 39, 44
  entropy, 225
  existential, 130
  Flows and Territories, 132–3, 136, 138, 140, 146, 161, 166
  Leibniz' body, 162
  real and actual, 147
  refrain, 135, 137
dureé, actual and virtual time, 37, 130; *see also* temps

ecogenesis
  consolidation, 43
  fourfold, 58
  heterogenesis, 17, 27
  multiplicity, 23
  A Thousand Plateaus, 28
eco-ontology, eco-epistemology, 14, 53
ecosemiotics, pink noise, 26
Ecumenon, Planomenon, 194–6

eigenbehaviour, objects, 99
eigenecology, schizoecology, 23
eigensound, Barthes, 174
eigenstate
  Schrödinger's cat, 71–2
  attractors, 221
eigensurface, existential modules, 87
eigentheory
  eigenecology, 23
  Foerster, von, 12
  schizoecology, 233
eigenvalue, intrinsic value
  Naess, 5
  plane of immanence, 63
  schizoecology, 23
  superposition, 72
eigenvector, orientation, 34
elective affinity, Guattari and Deleuze, 4–5
Elements, the
  architecture, 203
  Euclid, 231
  fourfold, 48, 123–4
  media ecology, 20
Empedocles, 123
enrichment
  architecture, 103
  complexity, 79
  Guattari and Deleuze, 4
  ontological heterogeneity, 229
  possible and virtual, 97
  potentiality, 89
entrainment
  Leibniz, 163
  time, 126
entropy
  entities, 225
  irreversibility, 136
  reduction of, 79
ethics
  aesthetics, 20, 227
  Chaosmosis, 223
  closure and openness, 27
  ecosophic, 41, 58, 236–7
  elasticity, grace, 19
  fractalization, 117
  Lacan, 216
  melancholic, 183
  Naess and Deleuze, 5
  science and ecology, 234
event
  Aion, 130
  crystal, 26, 139
  Deleuze, 45, 68–9, 103
  ecological, 225
  existential stamps, 139
  memory, 161
  multiplicity, aerosol, 46
  situationism, 104, 204
  smooth space, 155
  territorialization, 199

things, 154
virtual, 132
evolution
    Adams, Henry, 220
    Bergson, *Creative Evolution*, 234
    crystals, 28, 86, 193
    entity and medium, 101
    James, William, 47
    molecular, 220
    pachinko, 82, 225, 228, 233
    Phyla and Universes, 160
    structural coupling, 98
    Universes, 58, 141
exo and endo-consistency, fourfold, 84–5
exo- and endo-reference, fourfold, 84–5, 95, 121
expressionism, expressionist
    abstract machine, 188
    aesthetics, 109
    Balthus, 114
    ecology, 8, 100
    fractalization, 78, 86
    Guattari's poetics, 175
    Hjelmslev, 81
    logic of, 56
    media studies, 118
    ontological and ecological, 68
    painting, 24
    planes of chaos and consistency, 61, 77
    schizoecology, 235
    unconscious, 105

figure of thought
    fourfold, 104
    psychoanalysis and art, 117
    real projective plane, 180
    synapse, 149
foam
    aerosol, 48, 224
    fluidity, 47
    Venus, 31, 34
Foerster, Heinz von
    eigentheory, 12
    entropy, 225
    ethics, 236
    evolution, 221
    Infinite and finite complexity, 226
    intensity, 99
    object, 13
    quantity and quality, 98
    second-order cybernetics, 11
    strange attractor, 227
Freud, Freudian
    breaching, 106
    dream, 179
    ecological, 177
    hermeneutics, 117
    Lacan, 108
    libido, 85
    observer, 176
    psychoanalysis, 105–6

superego, 116
topological model, 107
unconscious, 59, 167

genius loci, 198
given as given
    ecology, 131
    the given, 76, 101–2
    the giving, 58
glissando, analog and digital, 122
grace
    biological, 193
    capitalism, 213
    ecology, 161
    elasticity, 19–20
    Guattari's thought, 214
    Kleist, 98
    milieu, 221
    oedipalization, 229
    subject, 230
grasping, graspings
    existential, 85, 87, 110, 142
    ontological appropriation, 121
grid, *la grille*
    abstract machine, 207
    capitalism, 213
    deterritorialization, 222
    La Borde, 74
groupuscule
    desiring machine, 218
    group-being, 19

habit
    architecture, 200
    chaotization, 228
    habitat, 194
    individuation, 225
    iteration, 43–4, 89
    lines of flight, 100
    refrain, nomos, 60, 226
    see also habitat
habitat
    architecture, 194, 198
    Haeckel, 7
    light, 187
    refrain, 60
    Territories, 89
    see also habit
haecceity, haecceitas
    kairos, 134
    milieu, 198
Haeckel, Ernst
    crystals, liquid crystals, 24
    ecology, 7
Harman, Graham, phenomenon and thing, 184
Heidegger, Martin, fourfold, 8
Herzog, Werner, *Fitzcarraldo*, 198
heterogenesis
    abstract and concrete machines, 114
    architecture, 205

autopoiesis, 14
constructivism, 91
crystals, 24
ecology, 224
existential territories, 158
fourfold, 52, 88, 92–3
individuation, 166
infinite and finite relations, 90
machinic, 136
photonic field, 187
process of, 135
Proust, 139
psychoanalysis, 217
The Three Ecologies, 8
video at La Borde, Varela, 17, 166
Hjelmsjev, Louis
   content and expression, 60, 67, 83, 112, 196
   expressionism, 80–1
   semiotics, 26
holism
   Guattari, 205
   Guattari and Deleuze, 235
   Holism and Evolution, 234
hypertext, rhizome, 229–30

Incredible Shrinking Man, The, 176
indifference
   analog and digital, 42
   Flows and Territories, 173
   plane of, 216
   plane of immanence|consistency, 11
   world, 74
infinitesimal
   aerosol, 45
   calculus, 37
   determinability, 147
   deterritorialization, 131, 170, 186
   fractalization, 148
   Leibniz, 157–8, 160, 167, 169
   molecular, 174
   ontology and epistemology, 44
   speed, 145
   squaring of green, 102
informal
   architecture, 194, 197
   diagram, 31, 53–6, 64, 101, 142, 160, 189,
   emergence of form from, 24, 28
   plane of immanence, 67
   uneigen, 63
   world, 94
informational closure
   energetic openness, 14
   linguistics, 108
   striation, 98
   truth, 15
   see also operational closure
integral
   Phyla, 86, 107
   Phyla and Universes, 59, 76, 156
   singularization, 166
   synapse, 150
Integrated World Capitalism
   cramp, 213
   Negri, 134
   The Three Ecologies, 8
   see also capitalism
invariance
   computation, 43
   formal, 98
   ideal, 44
   process, 42
   topological space, 153
irreversibility
   fourfold, 136
   individuation, 229
   kairos, 134
irritation
   actual and virtual, 176
   constructivism, 18
   intensity, 99
   noise, 173
   quantity and quality, 90, 98, 161
   speed of, 167,
   surface of sensation, 13
   unconscious, 220
Ivain, Gilles, (Ivan Vladimirovitch Chtcheglov), 183

James, Henry, aerosol, 46–7
James, William
   aerosol, 47, 49
   Janet, 46
   the false, 185
Jonas, Hans, *The Imperative of Responsibility*, 41
Jouissance
   Ganzfeld, 184
   violence, 217

Kafka, Franz
   abstract machine, 188
   The Castle, 206
kairos
   Negri, 134–5
   synapse, 132
   synaptic time, 133
Klein, Felix, real projective plane, 180
Kleist, Heinrich von, 'On the Marionette Theatre', 98

Lacan, Jacques, Lacanian
   body-image, 162
   Borromean knot, 112
   fourfold, 94
   Freud, 177, 178
   Guattari and, 52
   object *a*, 27–8
   oedipalization, 229
   ontology, 216–19
   Saussurian semiotics, 17, 26, 81, 83

schizophrenia, 215
semiotic energetics, 106
signifier, 105
subject, 18
symbolic order, 20
topology, 180–2
unconscious, 108–9
Le Corbusier (Charles-Édouard Jeanneret), architecture and form, 201
legato
  staccato, 151
  style, 10
Leeuwenhoek, Antonie van, microscope, 159
libido
  actual, 59
  Flows, 60
  fourfold, 105–8
  Freud, 85
  sexuality, 218, 220
light
  aerosol, 45
  architecture, 198, 201
  Bataille, 186
  chiaroscuro, 130
  climate, 7
  darkness, 235
  Leibniz, 167
  lines of, 63, 135
  planes of immanence and consistency, 187
  polarization, 13
  Schrödinger, 100–2
  speed of, 62, 143
  storms of, 55
  virtual, 123
  white, 168
  see also lightning; luminosity
lightning, synapse, 151; *see also* light; luminosity
logic-at-infinity, *clinamen*, 35–6
Lovelock, James E.
  holism, 235
  influence on Guattari, 7
  'The Quest for Gaia', 6
luminosity
  architecture, 198
  cosmic, 186
  Pasolini, 212
  see also light; lightning

Mach, Ernst, aerosol, 49–50
Mandelbrot, Benoît
  fractalism, 178–9
  integration, 169
Margulis, Lynn
  bacteria, 40
  Lovelock, 6
  membranes, 13
  pragmatism, 185
  Vernadsky, 130
matters-of-fact, fourfold, 103

Maturana, Humberto and Francisco Varela
  autopoiesis, 14
  influence on Guattari, 7
  pachinko evolution, 220, 228
  structural coupling, 12, 227
  see also Maturana; Varela
Maturana, Humberto
  evolutionary drift, 221
  language, 99, 185
  milieu, 98
  see also Maturana and Varela; Varela
McLuhan, Marshall, cool and hot media, 119
mechanosphere
  abstract machines, 205
  architecture, 206
  biosphere, 204
  ecosophy, 224
media ecology
  extended, 21
  fourfold, 123
  language, 17
  natural media, 6
  planes of immanence and consistency, 174
  production of subjectivity, 119
  superposition, 120
  videoanalysis, 20
media studies
  constructivism, 18
  fractalization, 173
  Leibniz, 168
  media and forms of life, 159
  squaring of, 53, 118, 120, 123
Melville, Herman, *Moby Dick*, optics, 101
minor geometry, royal geometry, 96
minor science, nomad science
  Chronos and Aion, 131
  definition of, 30
  purity and contamination, 41
  unconscious of royal science, 97
modulation
  analog, 122
  architecture, 199
  chronological, 126, 130
  continuity, 79
  energy, 15
  modes of sensation, 13
  smoothing, 90
  unconscious, 162
  virtual, 11
Muir, John, ecology, 8

$n-1$, informal diagram, 54
$n+1$, transcendental plateau, 54
Naess, Arne
  deep ecology, 4
  Guattari, 5–6
Negri, Antonio
  capitalism, 185–6, 212
  kairos, 134

256 | INDEX

Newton, Isaac, fluxions, 37
Nietzsche, Friedrich, 'On Truth and Lies in a Nonmoral Sense', 184
noise, pink
   deterministic chaos, 33
   ecology, 26, 166
   plane of consistency, 174
noise, white
   information theory, 26
   pure chaos, 33, 65
   plane of immanence, 174

object *a*
   architecture, 179
   Lacan, 27–8
observer, partial
   automatisms, 177
   monad, 162
   unconscious, 176
Olson, Charles, the real, 32
operational closure
   truth, 15
   unilateral distinction, 230
   see also informational closure
orientation
   crystallization, 34
   refrain, 60
   topological space, 154
   vector space, 42

particle-signs
   actual discursivity, 80
   aerosol, 76
   energetic semiotics, 108
   see also signaletic material
Pasolini, Pier Paolo, luminosity, 212
periodic, aperiodic
   crystals, 160
   ecology, 228
   order and disorder, 34, 39, 222, 227
phase space
   Balthus, 179
   definition, 61
   discursive, 91
   fourfold, 81, 94, 160
   Phyla, 86
   plane of immanence, 77
   strange attractor, 227
   the given, 146
   see also state space
photon, photonic
   Bataille, 185–6
   ecology, 183, 187, 198, 231
   media studies, 173, 175–6
   monad, 166
   politics of, 41
point-at-infinity
   analog and digital, 123
   chronological, 35

Leibniz, 167–8
media and forms, 174
speed of light, 62
positivity, of nature, 6, 40
post-media era
   capitalism, 213
   ecology, 119–20
   interactivity, 118, 230
power of the false
   language, 185
   Universes, 94
Prigogine, Ilya
   influence on Guattari, 7
   negentropy, 136
process philosophy
   Flows, 76
   Guattari, 47
   Guattari and Deleuze, 45
   speed, 33
processual -ization, -ize, -izing, -ity
   ecosophy, 225
   fourfold, 130
   human subject, 18, 231
   schizoanalysis, 118, 229
   terminology, 104, 135
   world, 42, 45
Proust, Marcel
   architecture, 203
   Guattari on, 138–41
   involuntary memory, 129
   poetics, 91
   speed of determination, 145
   synapse, 149

quantity
   analog and digital, 122
   energy, 79
   facilitation (*Bahnung*), 106
   irritation, 98
   metric and non-metric, 158
   quality, 91
   the given, 85, 151
   ultrafast, 69
quantum, physics, field theory, theory
   analog and digital, 122
   complementarity, 67, 71
   ecology, 75
   energy, 49, 186, 211
   Lucretius, 47
   particle and wave, 73
   recursivity, 176
   superposition, 66

real projective plane
   abstract machine, 191
   Lacan and Guattari, 181–2, 217
   mathematical figure, 180
reciprocal presupposition
      abstract machine and concrete assemblage, 187

actual and virtual, 175
assemblage, 169
beings and milieu, 14–15, 44
Chronos and Aion, 132
complementarity, 67, 72, 81, 181
diagram, 190
fourfold, 58
refrain
  conceptual, 27
  crystal, 146
  evolution, 160
  existential, 8, 82, 87–92, 135, 137
  leitmotif, attractor, 226
  Proust, 138–41
  schizoanalysis, 215
  synapse, 150
  Territory, 60, 166, 220
resonance
  architecture, 203
  consistency, 222, 231
  ecology, 19
  ecosophy, 225
  Guattari and Deleuze, 5
  intensity, 197
  medium and entity, 101
  milieu, 98
  temporal, 129
  valence, 193
rhizome
  abstract machine, 58
  architecture, 197
  axiomatics, 78–9
  hypertext, 229–30
  integration, 158
  multiplicity, 178
  network, 60
  Phyla, 88–90, 95
  plant-nutrition, 102
  smooth and striated space, 172
  speed of determinability, 147
  synapse, 149, 151
  Universes, 92, 135
Rovelli, Carlo, 126
royal science, major science, definition, 30, 37–8;
    see also minor science; nomad science
Ruyer, Raymond, *survol*, 54

Saussure, Ferdinand de
  arbitrariness of code, 174
  Balthus, 112
  double articulation, 87
  Lacan, 17, 26
  psychoanalysis, 177
  referent, 27
  representational semiotics, 80
  signifier, signified and referent, 81, 83
schizo, the
  psychoanalysis, 209, 214–16
  state, 219
schizoaesthetics, Balthus, 117–18

Schrödinger, Erwin
  crystal, 28
  fourfold, 74
  light, 100–2
  ontology and epistemology, 184
  Schrödinger's cat, 71–2
Serres, Michel
  analog and digital, 37
  Brownian motion, 64–5
  Leibniz, 167–8
  Lucretius, 7, 30–1, 33, 35–42, 45, 47
  monads, 160
  multiplicities, 35, 62, 234
  time, 126
  topology, 153–4
  unconscious, 177–8
signaletic material
  a-signifying semiotics, 17, 25–6, 80
  intensity, 158
  signifier, 216
Simondon, Gilbert
  actual and virtual, 68, 89
  crystal, 27
  heteropoiesis, 66
  milieu, 195
  molar and molecular, 30
situationism
  architecture, 199, 204–5
  ecosophy, 104, 118
  La Borde, 120
Smuts, Jan
  holism, 234–5
speed of determination
  consistencing, 225
  fourfold, 146
  grace and elasticity, 5
  molar and molecular, 89
  subjectification, 218
Spinoza, Baruch de
  actual and virtual, 55
  expressionism, 80
  plane of Nature, 192
  Universes, 93
staccato
  style, 10
  time, 151
state space, definition, 61; *see also* phase space
Stengers, Isabelle
  influence on Guattari, 7
  negentropy, 126
structural coupling
  language, 99–100, 227
  radical constructivism, 12
  striation, smoothing, dark precursors, 98
  unconscious, 21
surfaces of sensation
  invariance, 44
  membranes, 13
  sensible Territories, 87

synapse, synaptic
   analog and digital, 157
   brain-mind complex, 129
   ecology, 8
   kairos, 133
   synaptic moment, 132, 134–5, 148–51
   time, 49, 106

temps
   Chronos and Aion, 37
   Bergson, 130
   time and weather, 153
   see also *durée*
Thom, René, 226
Thoreau, Henry David
   non-human agents, 17
   Walden, 16
   'Walking', 50
transversality
   abstract machines, 78
   aerosol, 64
   Balthus, 117–18, 179
   definition of, 59
   discursivity, 202
   fourfold, 60, 74
   fractality, 91
   Guattari and Deleuze, 5
   horizontality, 100
   La Borde, 97
   Proust, 140
   psychophysics, 106
   space, 152, 172
turbulence
   Brownian motion, 171–2
   chaos, 65
   clinamen, 33
   fluid and aerosolic, 42, 45
   Lucretius, 28, 31, 34, 38, 40–1
   plane of immanence, 63
   semiotic, 39

ultrafast, überfast
   Bacon, 55
   intensities, 142
   plane of immanence, 49, 69
   time, 127
   Universes, 145
   vertigo, 144–5
ultrafine
   aerosol, Leibniz' *prima materia*, 165
   chronometrics, 127

ultralight
   aerosol, 63
   plane of immanence, 49
ultraslow, vertigo, 144
ultrasmooth, capitalist architecture, 209
ultrathin, aerosol, 69
uneigen
   media studies, 173
   plane of immanence, 63

valence
   conceptual, 5
   ecology, 193
   fractalization, 89
Varela, Francisco
   autopoiesis, 61
   embodied cognition, 222–3
   Lindisfarne Conference, 7
   'Laying down a Path in Walking', 50
   light, 101
   organism and medium, *karma*, 44
   perception, 169
   sentience, 17
   see also Maturana, Maturana and Varela
Venus
   aerosol, 34, 48
   ecosophy, 29
   Lucretius, 3, 31–2, 40
   Mars, 123, 172, 184
   Nail, 47–8
viability
   fourfold, 219
   mathematic elegance, 96
   truth, 44
Victor, Renaud, 110
video
   analysis, 24
   La Borde, 17, 20, 91, 120, 166
   medium, 21
   television, 119

Wallace, David Foster, 156
war machine
   Lucretius, 31
   plane of immanence, 65
wave function, Schrödinger's cat, 71–2
Weizäcker, Viktor von, pathic knowledge, 205
Weyl, Herman, 154
Whitehead, Alfred North, aerosol, prehension, 49
Wilson, Robert, Balthus, 115

EU representative:
Easy Access System Europe
Mustamäe tee 50, 10621 Tallinn, Estonia
Gpsr.requests@easproject.com

www.ingramcontent.com/pod-product-compliance
Lightning Source LLC
Chambersburg PA
CBHW060231240426
43671CB00016B/2913